Women in Asia

RESTORING WOMEN TO HISTORY
Series Editors: Cheryl Johnson-Odim and Margaret Strobel

Women in Asia
Barbara N. Ramusack and Sharon Sievers

Women in Latin America and the Caribbean
Marysa Navarro and Virginia Sánchez Korrol, with Kecia Ali

Women in the Middle East and North Africa
Guity Nashat and Judith E. Tucker

Women in Sub-Saharan Africa
Iris Berger and E. Frances White

Women in Asia

RESTORING WOMEN
TO HISTORY

by Barbara N. Ramusack and
Sharon Sievers

Indiana
University
Press
BLOOMINGTON AND INDIANAPOLIS

Maps on pages 10 and 11 are from Anthony Reid, *Southeast Asia in the Age of Commerce, 1450–1680*, Yale University Press, 1988. Reprinted by permission.
Map on page 153 is from Wontack Hong, *Paekche of Korea and the Origin of Yamato Japan*, Kudar International, 1994. Reprinted by permission.

This book is a publication of
Indiana University Press
601 North Morton Street
Bloomington, IN 47404-3797 USA

http://www.indiana.edu/~iupress

Telephone orders 800-842-6796
Fax orders 812-855-7931
Orders by e-mail iuporder@indiana.edu

Library of Congress Cataloging-in-Publication Data

Ramusack, Barbara N.
Women in Asia : restoring women to history / by Barbara N. Ramusack and Sharon Sievers.
p. cm. — (Restoring women to history)
Includes bibliographical references and index.
ISBN 0-253-33481-0 (cloth : alk. paper). — ISBN 0-253-21267-7 (pbk. : alk. paper)
1. Women—Asia—History. 2. Women—Asia—Social conditions. 3. Feminism—Asia. I. Sievers, Sharon L. II. Title. III. Series.
HQ1726.R36 1999
305.4'095—dc21   99-21719

*For Joel and Martine, who encouraged
me in the beginning,
For Gerry and Antoinette, who sustain
me in the middle.*

BARBARA N. RAMUSACK

*For students of women's history (that flash-
in-the-pan, faddish undertaking that
continues to energize and amaze us).*

SHARON SIEVERS

Joel,
    I offer this work to you
with great gratitude for
encouraging me to go to
graduate school and for opening
my intellectual horizons to Asia.
It has been an exciting journey.
        With affection and love,
        Barbara   1 July 1999

CONTENTS

SERIES EDITORS' PREFACE

This book is part of a four-volume series entitled "Restoring Women to History": *Women in Sub-Saharan Africa; Women in Asia; Women in Latin America and the Caribbean;* and *Women in the Middle East and North Africa.* The project began in 1984, bringing together scholars to synthesize historical information and interpretation on women outside of Europe and the United States of America. Earlier versions of the volumes were produced and distributed by the Organization of American Historians (OAH) as *Restoring Women to History: Teaching Packets for Integrating Women's History into Courses on Africa, Asia, Latin America, the Caribbean, and the Middle East* (1988; revised, 1990).

These volumes are intended to help teachers who wish to incorporate women into their courses, researchers who wish to identify gaps in the scholarship and/or pursue comparative analysis, and students who wish to have available a broad synthesis of historical materials on women. Although the primary audience is historians, scholars in related fields will find the materials useful as well. Each volume includes a bibliography, in which readings suitable for students are identified with an asterisk. Each volume is preceded by a broad, topical introduction written by Cheryl Johnson-Odim and Margaret Strobel that draws examples from all four volumes.

This project is the culmination of many years' work by many people. Cheryl Johnson-Odim and Margaret Strobel conceived of the original single volume, extending OAH projects published in the 1970s and 1980s on U.S. and European women's history. Joan Hoff (then Joan Hoff-Wilson, Executive Director of the Organization of American Historians), Cheryl Johnson-Odim, and Margaret Strobel wrote proposals that received funding from the National Endowment for the Humanities for a planning meeting of eight other authors, and from the Fund for the Improvement of Postsecondary Education (FIPSE) for the preparation, distribution, and dissemination of the manuscript. Under the leadership of Executive Director Arnita Jones, the OAH took on the responsibility of printing and distributing the single volume. The FIPSE grant enabled us to introduce the project through panels at conferences of the African Studies Association, the Association of Asian Studies, the Latin American Studies Association, the Middle Eastern Studies Association, and the World History Association.

Because of the strong positive response to the single volume, Joan Catapano, Senior Sponsoring Editor at Indiana University Press, encouraged the ten of us to revise and expand the material in four separate volumes. In the decade or so since the inception of this project, the historical literature on women from these regions has grown dramatically. Iris Berger and E. Frances White added important new information to their original contributions. White was assisted by Cathy Skidmore-Hess, who helped revise some of the material on West and Central Africa. Barbara Ramusack and Sharon Sievers found new material for Asia, with certain regions and periods still very unstudied. Marysa Navarro and Virginia Sánchez Korrol, with help from Kecia Ali, reworked their previous essays on Latin America and the Caribbean. Guity Nashat and Judith Tucker developed further their material on the Middle East and North Africa from the earlier volume.

This project is a blend of individual and collective work. In the 1980s, we met twice to discuss ways to divide the material into sections and to obtain consistency and comparability across the units. Each author read widely in order to prepare her section, reworking the piece substantially in response to comments from various readers and published reviews.

Scholars familiar with each region read and commented on various drafts. For this crucial assistance, we wish to thank Edward A. Alpers, Shimwaayi Muntemba, and Kathleen Sheldon for Africa; Marjorie Bingham, Emily Honig, Veena Talwar Oldenberg, Mrinalini Sinha, and Ann Waltner for Asia; Lauren (Robin) Derby, Asunción Lavrin, Susan Schroeder, and Mary Kay Vaughan for Latin America and the Caribbean; and Janet Afary, Margot Badran, Julia Clancy-Smith, Fred Donner, Nancy Gallagher, and Jo Ann Scurlock for the Middle East and North Africa. In revising the introduction, we received useful comments from Janet Afary, Antoinette Burton, Nupur Chaudhuri, Susan Geiger, and Claire Robertson. Anne Mendelson ably copyedited the OAH publication; LuAnne Holladay and Jane Lyle copyedited the Indiana University Press volumes. At various times over the years, undergraduate and graduate students and staff helped with nailing down bibliographic citations and/or preparing the manuscript. These include Mary Lynn Dietsche, Geri Franco, Jill Lessner, Lisa Oppenheim, and Marynel Ryan from the University of Illinois at Chicago, and Carole Emberton, Maryann Spiller, and Esaa Zakee from Loyola University Chicago.

This project owes much both to the Organization of American Historians and to Indiana University Press. We thank the following OAH staff members, past and present, who contributed to the project in various ways: Mary Belding, Jeanette Chafin, Ginger Foutz, Brian Fox, Kara Hamm, Joan Hoff, Arnita A. Jones, Nancy Larsen, Barbara Lewis, Michelle McNamara, and Michael Regoli. Our editor at IUP, Joan Catapano, waited months on end for the completion of our work. Without her prompting, we would probably not have taken the initiative to attempt this revision and publication of separate volumes. We appreciate her patience.

From reviews, citations, and comments at conferences, we know that scholars, teachers, and students have found our efforts valuable. That knowledge has helped sustain us in those moments when each of us, having moved on to other scholarly projects or having assumed demanding administrative positions, questioned the wisdom of having committed ourselves to revising and expanding the original materials. This kind of scholarship, what Ernest Boyer calls the "scholarship of integration," is typically not rewarded in academe as much as is traditional research, what Boyer terms the "scholarship of discovery."* For this reason we are particularly thankful to the authors for their willingness to commit their minds and energies to revising their work. Although our effort to get ten authors simultaneously to complete all four volumes sometimes made us feel like we were herding cats, we appreciate the intellectual exchange and the friendships that have developed over the years of our work together.

Cheryl Johnson-Odim
Chicago, Illinois

Margaret Strobel
Chicago, Illinois

*Ernest L. Boyer, *Scholarship Reconsidered: Priorities of the Professoriate* (Princeton, N.J.: Carnegie Foundation for the Advancement of Teaching, 1990), 16–21.

AUTHORS' PREFACE

When Margaret Strobel first invited me to participate in the project known as Restoring Women to History in early 1984, little did I realize that thus would begin a fifteen-year collaboration. During this period I feel privileged to have been both a participant in and synthesizer of the exciting development of women's history and gender studies with all my multi-talented co-authors and editors. My intellectual world and my circle of friends have greatly expanded. Because of logistical constraints, Peg asked me, a specialist on South Asia, to write the section on Southeast Asia since these world regions seemed to be closely related because of a shared prominence of Hinduism, Buddhism, and Islam, the apparent transfer of some social and political forms, and the extensive trade relations, especially in textiles, between them. Ignorance rather than impudence led me to agree. Now, fifteen years later, I realize how different are the experiences and historiographies of women in South and Southeast Asia. Hence my decision to treat these two regions separately rather than to integrate them, as Sharon Sievers did for East Asia. Coincidentally, the depth of research available on women in South Asia had made it difficult for me, even in my own field, to present adequately its complexity. After writing the initial survey from 1985 to 1987 and having undertaken no less than five subsequent revisions, I am extremely sympathetic to anyone who attempts syntheses. I am painfully aware of how difficult it is to achieve a balanced, perceptive, and equitable survey and apologize for any errors of fact and misinterpretations that remain.

Although much of this essay is based on secondary sources, it has been significantly enriched by my own archival and field research in

India. Consequently I wish to express my deep appreciation for grants to support that research from the American Institute of Indian Studies, the Fulbright-Hays Faculty Research Abroad Program, the National Endowment for the Humanities, the Smithsonian Institution, and the Charles Phelps Taft Memorial Fund at the University of Cincinnati. Although this project was not the main focus of my memorable year at the National Humanities Center in 1986–1987, I am most grateful that I had the time to work on this essay and to place it in a broader perspective as a result of both formal seminars and informal conversations with other fellows there.

During this project, many colleagues have been unusually helpful, both professionally and personally. Although space considerations limit those who can be mentioned, I must acknowledge some. Geraldine Forbes initiated me into the field of South Asian women's history when I began my research on the interaction among British and South Asian women on women's rights issues in 1976. Her incomparable command of empirical data, her work to recover women's voices, her extensive contacts among scholars in South Asia, and her unstinting friendship have been invaluable. In India, Neera Desai, Maithreyi Krishna Raj, and Aparna Basu were pioneers in women's studies who magnanimously facilitated my research and produced scholarship which introduced me, as well as many others, to major issues and people in women's history. Veena Talwar Oldenburg carefully reviewed the first version of this essay and offered significant insights. Mrinalini Sinha thoughtfully critiqued the penultimate version of this essay and unselfishly shared sources which I found difficult to obtain. The scholarship of Antoinette Burton and Tanika Sarkar stimulated me to new ways of understanding women's history and their friendship greatly enriches my life.

Since I have not done primary research in Southeast Asia, I have benefitted greatly from Hanna Papanek's early willingness to share her insights and library on this area with me. For this revision, Frances Gouda and Barbara Watson Andaya were extraordinarily collegial in critiquing the section promptly and perceptively and in answering numerous e-mail enquiries. Professor Andaya graciously allowed me to participate in the conference she organized in March 1998, "Engendering Early Modern Southeast Asian History," and Mimi and Jagdish Sharma provided princely hospitality. Here I learned of the most current research and was able to meet several outstanding scholars whose works I had utilized, as well as emerging scholars who were completing their doctoral dissertations. Finally, I wish to acknowledge the extraordinary thoughtfulness, generosity, and support from Peg Strobel and Cheryl Johnson-Odim, who are scrupulous editors, dedicated feminists, and supportive friends.

Barbara N. Ramusack
Cincinnati, Ohio

This project, begun in a Chicago winter fifteen years ago, has taken all of us on an interesting, challenging, and sometimes unexpected journey. Walking the city's icy streets after our first intense sessions, braced by Lake Michigan's *very* fresh air, I remember wondering whether the project could ever work. We were embarking on a global, "big history" project at a time the field was moving in the opposite direction. All of us were being asked to sort out and bring together major issues raised in the work of a very large number of historians, most of whom would probably not appreciate having their work "synthesized" by someone else. And how would we walk the tightrope stretched between the presentation of a "global" picture of women's history to a North American audience on the one hand, and avoid "universalizing" the history of women on the other?

In spite of the fact that some of those questions still exist for me, I am absolutely certain this entire project has been worth the risk and the effort we have all put into it. There was never any question that some kind of survey of women outside of Europe and North America, supported by accessible (meaning English-language) sources, was critically needed; and as I look now at the development of undergraduate students and returning teachers who must master the elements of world history in order to teach in California, I am very much aware of just how important our work could be.

My work on East Asia has been made possible by the impressive output of women historians working in the area over the last decade; that much of that important work has been translated from Chinese, Japanese, and Korean into English is extremely significant. For the first time in my memory, it is becoming routine for North American women to read the research of East Asian women in translation, a development I expect will transform our knowledge of the field in significant ways. I am especially grateful for the recent work being published on Korean women, something that enabled me to 1) learn a great deal more about them, and 2) include more of their history in this volume. It is true that, compared to this volume's coverage of Chinese and Japanese women, Korean women do not fare as well, but it should be clear from what I *have* been able to say just how important their stories are to the history of women in East Asia. The election of a reformist Korean president in 1992, coupled with the very good work being done in this country, means that we are likely to see much more research on Korean women published in the next few years, a welcome prospect for all of us.

First and most importantly, I would like to thank Peg Strobel and Cheryl Johnson-Odim for challenging us to undertake this work, guiding us through all of the twists and turns of the project, and being such good friends. All of us can testify to the truth of the suggestion that, for them, getting us through this was often like herding cats. I am grateful to Emily Honig, Ann Waltner, and Marjorie Bingham for reading drafts of my section and offering helpful suggestions and criticisms, as well as to Kathryn McMahon, whose work I admire and who is always willing to discuss difficult projects. Xiaolan Bao offered her own infectious energy and encouragement, and a number of my students offered helpful comments as the work progressed.

Sharon Sievers
Long Beach, California

SERIES EDITORS' INTRODUCTION

Conceptualizing the History of Women in Africa, Asia, Latin America and the Caribbean, and the Middle East and North Africa

CHERYL JOHNSON-ODIM AND MARGARET STROBEL

In this thematic overview* we hope to do, with beneficial results, what historians are loath to do: dispense with chronology and introduce several themes common to the histories of women in the "non-Western" world. A thematic focus will accomplish several purposes. First, we can discuss the significance of phenomena—for example, the existence of female networks and subcultures—so that the authors' references to such phenomena are given a broader context than the sometimes-scant evidence allows. Second, we can introduce and synthesize approaches and ideas found in feminist scholarship. Third, because regions often develop distinctive sets of research questions and ignore others, our overview may suggest new areas of exploration. Finally, we can suggest possibilities for comparative investigation.

We cannot here do justice to the specificity of the historical tradition in each region; readers may use the indexes of relevant volumes to locate elaborations on the examples cited below. Our themes highlight the similarities in women's experience across these very diverse regions, but the differences, not dealt with here, are equally crucial.

*An earlier version of this essay appeared in the *Journal of Women's History* 1, no. 1 (Spring 1989): 31–62.

The intellectual justification for addressing these four regions together rests on the assertion that most of these areas have experienced broadly comparable relationships with Western Europe and the United States in the past five hundred years. Although these volumes examine the long eras in each regional area before the last five hundred years, it is because of their histories of the last five hundred years that they are broadly viewed in the United States as "Third World," or "non-Western." We understand the need to problematize viewing *most* of the world's people, in all their diversity, in such "catch-all" categories and do not mean to claim the commonality of their relationship(s) with the West as the only reason for their appearance here.

It was difficult to decide on a common terminology that allowed us to keep from constantly listing the regions under consideration. "Third World" (despite some controversy) was often appropriate as a geopolitical designation, but it left out places such as Japan that are not generally regarded as Third World due to a high degree of industrialization. "Non-Western" also seemed appropriate, except that after many centuries of contact, Latin American societies cannot legitimately be regarded as entirely non-Western. Although we prefer not to refer to people by a negative term such as "non-Western" and are aware that terms such as "Third World" are problematic, we ended up employing both terms despite sometimes imperfect usage, in addition to the cumbersome listing of all four geographic regions.

A final word about terminology: we distinguish between "sex" as a set of biological (physiological) differences and "gender" as socially constructed roles that may build upon or ignore biological sex. Hence, in place of the common term "sex roles," in this text, we will instead use "gender roles."

THE CHALLENGE OF THIRD WORLD WOMEN'S HISTORY

It is important to avoid three common pitfalls: interpreting women as the exotic, women as victims, and women as anomalies. Stereotypes regarding the non-Western world (particularly those labeling it as "primitive," "backward," or "barbaric") are very prevalent in our society and frequently provide the only knowledge many North Americans have about other cultures. The roles, positions, and statuses of women in non-Western societies are often as central to those stereotypes today as they were when European colonizers first pointed to women's "oppression" in Africa, Asia, Latin America and the Caribbean, and the Middle East and North Africa as partial justification for their own imperialist designs. "Brideprice," women as "beasts of burden" and female genital mutilation (FGM) in Africa, *sati* and footbinding in Asia, *machismo* in Latin America, female hypersexuality in the Caribbean, and the harem and seclusion of women in the Middle East frequently represent the extent of the Western public's exposure to the lives of women in these regions. It is in fact such images of women that help fuel our pictures of these societies as exotic. Feminist historians challenge this notion of the female exotic by placing cultural practices in an appropriate sociocultural framework and by looking at a multitude of women's activities over the broad scope of their lives.

Women, just because they are women, have undeniably been disadvantaged in their access to political and economic power. Where the fact of being a woman intersected with belonging to a racial, ethnic, religious, or other minority, or with poverty or lower-class status, women could be doubly or triply disadvantaged. But women have never been a monolithic group even within the same society; class, race, and/or ethnicity could have consequences as significant for women's opportunity and status as did (does) gender. Women's history, however, is not primarily a history of disadvantage and degradation. Such a "victim analysis" fails to present a picture of the variety of women's multiple statuses and relationships (including those with other women), the dynamism and creativity of their activities, and their importance in various cultures.

Women's agency and initiative, as well as their subordination, must therefore be explored. Integrating the histories of women in Africa, Asia, Latin America and the Caribbean, and the Middle East and North Africa in part poses the same challenge as that of European and U.S. women's history: the expansion and transformation of conceptual categories that, in explaining male, rather than integrated, human experience, have treated women as anomalies. For example, political history has tended to focus on activity in the public sphere and on office holders, both of which highlight male experience. The evidence demonstrates that women also have exercised power. Historically, however, it was most often within gender-segregated settings that ordinary women were able to exercise their greatest degree of power and decision-making. And, when they acted collectively, women could exercise considerable power even within male-dominated societies. Individual women—for example, Eva Perón—were often important political actors and exerted influence, both inside and outside of formal political structures. Because women's political participation did not always appear in obvious places or ways, it has been regarded as peripheral or absent, a view that ignores the complex processes through which power is exerted in societies. An investigation of gender relationships can add a critical element of analysis to our scrutiny of history and to definitions and explanations of the operation of political power and the conceptual category of political activity.

In addition to challenging definitions of what constitutes political history, the study of women can reveal important insights into the study of an entire region. For example, if one looks at the actual impact of Confucianism on women's lives in East Asia, the system of teachings becomes a much less monolithic historical force than it has hitherto been considered.

Similarly, looking at gender clarifies our understanding of Latin American society. Scholars have long studied the development of racial division there, yet gender and class were central to that development in several ways. Sex both opened and closed racial barriers: sexual activity across racial lines was legitimized through the practice of concubinage and was sanctioned because of the unequal sex ratios among the colonizers. But concubinage, while protecting status differences between the colonizers and the colonized, also resulted in a mestizo and mulatto population whose existence undermined racial barriers. Thus the control of (female) sexuality was linked to the control of racial purity.

In the Middle East, aspects of women's position that are at the core of historical and contemporary Islamic society (e.g., seclusion and veiling) have their roots in pre-Islamic practices. Hence, Islam can be seen not only to have introduced important changes in the Middle East, but also to have built upon existing practices; the introduction of Islam does not mark as sharp a break as some scholars have claimed.

In the study of Africa, the recent emphasis on examining gender has transformed our understanding of the Atlantic slave trade, a topic of longstanding importance in African historiography. Scholars had noted that African males outnumbered females on the Middle Passage, but why this was the case received little attention. As scholars began to problematize gender roles within Africa—and noted the extraordinary role women played in agriculture—some came to view the Atlantic slave trade as being partially shaped by the desire of African slave-owning societies to accumulate female labor.

The act of including women in the histories of these regions represents a more profound challenge than the "add women and stir" approach, as it has often been identified. The mere insertion of famous women, like the insertion of only "exotic" and hurtful practices, gives a distorted and inadequate history of the bulk of women's experience in a given society.

Just as adding information about women challenges the existing histories of Africa, Asia, Latin America and the Caribbean, and the Middle East and North Africa, so too does adding information about women from these regions challenge the writing of women's history. Because the oppression of Third World women is the result of both internal sexism and externally induced dynamics (e.g., mercantile capitalism, colonialism, neo-colonialism), being citizens of the Third World is as crucial as gender. Therefore, studying women in the Third World means studying not only a less powerful category within society, but also a category within societies that have often been dominated in the international arena. Thus, some things that oppress(ed) women also oppress men (slavery, indentured labor, alienation of land from indigenous owners or conversion of land to cash crop production, export of raw natural resources and import of finished products made from those resources and even of food), though often in different ways. And many issues that are not obviously gender-related, such as lack of self-sufficiency in producing staple foods and provision of water, bear their heaviest impact on women who are disproportionately charged with providing food and water.

Finding women in the histories of the non-Western, just as in the Western, world requires persistence due to the silence or obliqueness of "traditional" historical sources such as documents written by historical actors themselves. The roles of women in agriculture, health, crafts, religion, politics, the arts, and other arenas have often been regarded as negligible, exceptional and infrequent, or irretrievable for other than the very recent period. However, far more is available than one may think; much of it lies hidden in non-obvious sources: oral testimony, mythology, life histories, genealogies, religious records, missionary and explorer accounts, archaeological excavations, language, legal codes, land tenure arrangements, oral and written literature, or cultural lore and fable. For women's histories, case studies often come after the general treatise, which frequently concentrates as much on exposing the lacunae and generating hypotheses as on synthesis. The historical literature on women in Africa, Asia, Latin America and the Caribbean, and the Middle East and North Africa

has greatly increased in the years since these essays were first published, and that has led to their revision. Still, a great deal remains to
be done. These general overviews are meant to acquaint scholars with
the possibilities as much as to show what has been done.

THEORIES THAT EXPLAIN THE
SUBORDINATE STATUS OF WOMEN

Trained to look to the specifics of place and time more than to the
creation of theory, historians have often left to anthropologists the
task of theorizing about the origins of women's oppression or the
factors that account for women's subordinate status. One basic division runs between biologically oriented and socioculturally oriented
theories. The former finds significance in a relative universality of
physical characteristics among humans and of a gender division of
labor that assigns men to certain tasks and women to others, a division that sometimes characterizes the public sphere as a male domain
and the private sphere as a female domain. This commonality is attributed to genetic or physical differences.

Environmentalists stress the equally apparent diversity of humans,
physically and culturally, and claim that biology alone cannot cause
this diversity. Moreover, they view "natural" features of society as
fundamentally culturally and ideologically determined. Even childbirth and lactation, they argue, do not predestine women to stay at
home; rather, societies can devise a division of labor that enables such
women to be mobile.

Embedded in these positions are views about the appropriateness
of men's and women's roles. Biologically oriented theories tend to
assume that gender differences are best not tampered with. Sociocultural theories tend to see the pattern of women's subordination as
subject to change; thus, the search for the causes of women's oppression becomes linked to the possibility of creating gender-equal societies. If the universality of women's subordinate status can be proved
untrue, then the possibilities of creating gender-equal societies are
strengthened; hence, some scholarship focuses on the search for ma-
triarchies, or for gender-equal societies, past or present. While most
scholars find evidence lacking, the discussions of matriarchy and gen-
der-neutral societies have raised important questions about the relationship between the actual power of living women in a particular
society and (a) kinship and residence patterns (e.g., matrilineality and
matrilocality), (b) social structure and mode of production (e.g., patriarchy, pre-industrial), or (c) the ideological representations of wom-
en in art, ritual, or belief systems.

Another approach to the issue of the causes of women's oppression links women's power or lack of it to economic forces. Research in this area has generated questions about the link between gender inequality and levels of production or technology, class formation, women's and men's control of the products of their labor, etc. Furthermore, these theorists dispute the universality of the notions of public and private, arguing that these categories follow historically from the development of industrial(izing) societies. In the modern period discussion of women's oppression in postcolonial Third World countries must take into account the effects of colonialism and neo-colonialism on the construction of gender. In several places colonialism and neo-colonialism marginalized women in the economy, displaced them politically, cooperated with indigenous males to keep women socially subordinated, or increased the social subordination of women themselves.

Feminism challenges both European colonial and indigenous patriarchal ideologies regarding women. The relationship between Western and non-Western feminist thought has often, however, been adversarial. In part the tension between the two groups results from the explanation given for the oppression of women. Many non-Western women (even those who identify themselves as feminists) object to Western feminist theories that posit men as the primary source of oppression. Recently this debate has generated theories that focus on the interrelationship of multiple forms of oppression, such as race, class, imperialism, and gender.

THE INADEQUACIES OF THE CONCEPTS OF TRADITIONAL AND MODERN

The concepts of "traditional" and "modern" are often both ahistorical and value-laden. It may be legitimate to talk about ways people have done/do things "traditionally" (evolving at some unspecified time in the past) or in the "modern" way (coming into use relatively recently). However, for Africa, Asia, Latin America and the Caribbean, and the Middle East and North Africa, often the term "traditional" describes everything in the long eras before European intervention, and the term "modern" describes those phenomena following European intervention. This establishes a false dichotomy, with all things indigenous being "traditional" and all things Western being "modern." This usage often implies that the traditional is static and the modern, dynamic; it fails to portray and analyze each regional history within the context of its own internal dynamics, in which encounters with the West prove to be only one element among many. Such a view also obscures the fact that most societies were not isolated and had contact with other peoples before Western contact, that they are not homogeneous, and that several traditions often co-exist (to more or less peaceful degrees) within the same society or nation-state.

Sometimes this ahistoricity results from equating "modernization" with higher levels of technology; sometimes it is cultural arrogance and implicitly defines "modern/Western" as somehow better. Since colonialist ideology in Africa, Asia, and the Middle East often used indigenous "oppression" of women as a justification for intervention in these societies, colonizers promoted the belief that the arrival of Western civilization would improve women's lives. For example, in India in the early nineteenth century, one of the central arguments British officials employed to legitimate political control based on the use of military force was that British policies would "improve" the status of Indian women. Thus the colonizers made women central to the politics of colonialism.

The study of the lives of Third World women, in fact, challenges the legitimacy of the notion of a strict dichotomy between traditional and modern. Women's lives, especially, show that traditional cultures in these regions are not static, monolithic, or more misogynist than Western culture, and that there is no automatic linear progress made in the quality of women's lives by following a Western pattern of development. Regional studies provide evidence that the "traditional" ways of doing things, especially in the political and economic arenas, were often less inimical to women's collective interests than the "modernization" that colonialism purported to export.

The concept of tradition has also sometimes been used as a rallying point in anti-colonial liberation struggles. That is, by conceptualizing their struggle against European domination in "anti-Western culture" terms, various peoples have politicized the return to tradition as a liberating strategy. Because this "return to tradition" was often formulated during eras of high colonialism, when the promotion of Western culture was inseparable from the colonial presence, women were as central to the vision of tradition that emerged as they were to justifications for colonialism. Even after the colonial presence was gone, Western culture still symbolized continuing economic dominance. Gandhi claimed that women's superior ability at self-sacrifice made them better practitioners of *satyagraha* or non-violent resistance. In response to French cultural imperialism, wearing the veil became a political act of resistance in Algeria. Similarly, veiling became identified with opposition to Western influence and to the

Shah in Iran. In the 1970s, Mobutu Sese Seko of Zaire (now the Democratic Republic of the Congo) constructed his policy of *authenticité*, a major tenet of which was a return to the "traditional" value of women as mothers and housekeepers who obeyed male relatives. These are but a few examples that show women have often been on the losing end of a return to tradition—a "tradition" misused by ideologies of both colonialism and liberation. A view of culture as dynamic, as well as a better understanding of women's roles in the pre-European-contact periods, can help demythologize the concept of tradition.

RELIGION

Religion has been a source of power for women, or a source of subordination, or both.

Religious authorities have often functioned as politically powerful figures. In Inka society, women played important roles in the religious structure, even though male priests held religious and political power. As virgins, or *aqlla*, they were dedicated as "wives of the Sun" to prepare an alcoholic beverage for religious rituals and officiate at the same. Even in less-stratified societies of a much smaller scale, indeed perhaps more often in these societies, women acted as religious/political leaders. Charwe, a medium of the spirit Nehanda, led resistance to British colonialism in late-nineteenth-century southern Rhodesia. In the eighteenth century, the legendary Nanny drew upon her mediating relationship with ancestral spirits in leading her maroon community in Jamaica. Even where they did not hold religious office, women exercised power through religion: in peasant and nomadic regions of the Middle East, women continued, into the twentieth century, to control popular religious activities and thus to exert influence through their intercession with the supernatural.

Religious beliefs may point to the equality of women as sacred beings or the importance of female life force. Female clay figurines suggest the worship of female deities in Egypt around 3000 B.C.E., but we can infer little about the lives of women in general. Full-breasted female figurines, presumed to be fertility goddesses, are associated with the Indus Valley in South Asia around 2000 B.C.E. Aztec religion embodied many goddesses associated with fertility, healing, and agriculture. The presence of such goddesses did not signal a society of gender equality but rather one of gender complementarity, as in the Inka case. One of the largest temples in Ancient Sumer, at Ur, was headed by the priestess Enheduanna, who was also a renowned poet and writer.

On the other hand, religious beliefs may both reflect and reinforce the subordination of women. Women in many religious traditions are seen as polluting, particularly because of those bodily
functions surrounding menstruation or childbirth. In West Africa,
Akan fear of menstruating women limited even elite women's activities: the *asantehemaa*, the highest female office, could be held only by
a post-menopausal woman from the appropriate lineage. Even though
such beliefs may ultimately derive from women's power as procreators, women's status as polluting persons can restrict their activities
and power. Moreover, traditions that stress the importance of male
children to carry out ancestral rituals—for example, those in Confucianism—contribute to the negative valuation of female children and
women. Other customs repressive and/or unhealthy to women—for
example, *sati*, ritual suicide by widows—are sanctioned by religion.
Finally, the traditions of Christianity, Confucianism, Hinduism, Islam,
and Judaism all legitimate male authority, particularly patriarchal familial authority, over women: Christianity through biblical exhorta-
tion to wifely obedience, Confucianism in the three obediences,
Hinduism in the Laws of Manu, Islam in the Qur'an's injunction regarding wifely obedience, and Judaism in the Halakhah Laws.

However much these traditions carry profound gender inequalities in theology and in office, these same traditions spawn groupings
that attract women (and other lower-status people). In India, the
Gupta period, in which the Laws of Manu increased restrictions on
Indian women, also witnessed the rise of Saktism, a cult derived from
pre-Aryan traditions that envision the divine as feminine. In this set
of beliefs, the female divinity appears in three major incarnations:
Devi, the Mother goddess; Durga, the unmarried and potentially dangerous woman; and Kali, the goddess of destruction. Subsequently,
in the Mughal period in South Asia, women in search of help with
fertility or other psychological problems flocked to devotional Hinduism, becoming followers of *bhakti* saints, and to Muslim Sufi holy
men. Women in the Middle East and in Muslim parts of Africa were
also attracted to these mystical Sufi orders, which stressed direct union
with Allah and believed there were no differences between men and
women in their ability to reach God. Among syncretic Christian off-
shoots in Africa, women play much more central, albeit often expres-
sive, roles.

SEXUALITY AND REPRODUCTION

Many theories about the origins of the oppression of women see control of female sexuality and the reproductive process (or female pro-

creative power) as central. For this reason, it is useful to examine basic questions, if not patterns, in societies' construction of female sexuality. Just as gender is socially constructed, so too is sexuality— that is, which sexual practices (and with whom) were considered socially acceptable and which were considered deviant are specific to time and place, and often contested. Scholarship on homosexuality, for instance, is in its infancy in many of these histories, particularly that regarding lesbianism. Some scholars, though, posit the harem or *zenana* as a site of lesbian relationships.

Throughout history, societies have generated ideological systems that link female identity to female sexuality, and female sexuality to women's role in procreation. Thus one reason for controlling women's sexuality was to control their role in procreation. Women were aware of their important role in the procreative process, and sometimes used such sexual symbolism as a power play. African women on several occasions utilized sexual symbolism to protest threats to themselves as women. For example, in the Women's War of 1929, Nigerian women challenged the offending officials to impregnate each of them, drawing upon an indigenous technique to humiliate men: they were protesting men's right to interfere in women's economic power and thus women's obligations as wives and mothers. In 1922, Kenyan women, by exposing their buttocks at a public protest of colonial officials' actions, challenged their male colleagues to behave more "like men," that is, more bravely.

Religions project varied views of female sexuality. Islam acknowledges women's sexual pleasure, as it does men's, while advocating that it be channeled into marriage. In contrast, the Mahayana Buddhist views female sexuality as a threat to culture. In this religious group, women have been associated with bondage, suffering, and desire; female sexuality, then, is to be controlled by transcendence (or by motherhood).

Often the control of female sexuality and reproduction is linked to concerns about purity. The Aryan notion of purity was reflected throughout Hindu ritual and beliefs, but in particular it provided the impetus for early marriage and for *sati*. Colonial constraints upon Spanish women's behavior in the New World derived from the elite's desire to maintain "blood purity."

Expressed through virginity and chastity, in several cultural traditions a woman's purity had implications for her family. A Muslim woman's behavior affected her family's honor, for example, resulting in the ultimate penalty of death for adultery. Infibulation (briefly, the sewing together of the labia and one form of female genital surgery), found in both Muslim and non-Muslim areas, is commonly associated with virginity and the control of female sexuality. Although virginity was of little consequence in Inka society, adultery on the part of noblewomen was punishable by death. In seventeenth-century China, chastity was raised to a symbolic level not found in Japan or Korea. The 1646 Manchu rape law required women to resist rape to the point of death or serious injury; otherwise, they were considered to have participated in illicit intercourse.

The point here is not to list the multitude of ways in which women have been unfairly treated, but to understand the cultural construction of female sexuality. These examples, all drawn from religious traditions or the ideological systems of states, highlight the control of female sexuality. But the earlier African examples remind us that sexuality and sexual symbolism, like all cultural phenomena, are a terrain of struggle, to be manipulated by women as well as used against them. In their critique of Japanese society, the Bluestockings, a group of literary feminists in early twentieth-century Japan, saw sexual freedom as an integral aspect of women's rights.

Societies have sought to control men's sexual access to females through a combination of beliefs, laws, customs, and coercion. At times men enforced these sexual rules; at other times women policed themselves as individuals or curtailed the activities of other women—peers, younger women, daughters-in-law. Male control of sexual access to females has sometimes been a violent assault upon women, such as in enforced prostitution or rapes associated with wars. During the conquest of the Americas, for instance, Amerindian women were raped, branded, and viewed in general as the spoils of war. Also, enslaved women were often the sexual prey of their male owners, valued as both productive and reproductive laborers. Sexual tourism in the twentieth century, particularly in Asian and Pacific regions, exploits young girls primarily for the benefit of expatriate "tourists."

Concubinage, another institutionalized method of controlling female sexuality, existed in all the regions covered in this survey. Concubinage legitimated a man's sexual access to more than one woman outside of marriage. Although it clearly represented a double standard, concubinage as an institution offered certain protections or benefits to women. In the New World some Amerindian women gained substantial wealth and status as concubines; in addition, slave concubines might be manumitted at their owner's death and their children legitimized. Similarly, Islamic slave owners manumitted some concubines, encouraged by the belief that such action was rewarded by God. The protections offered by the institution of concubinage, albeit within a grossly unequal relationship, were lost with its abolition, and compensating institutions did not always replace concubinage. Hence, abolition in parts of Africa left poorer women, former concubines, without the legal rights of wives or concubines but still dependent financially. In contemporary Africa, women who in the past might have become concubines because of their economic or social vulnerability might today have children outside of formal marriage without the previous assurance that their children will be supported financially by the fathers.

Historically, prostitution has occurred under a variety of conditions that reflect different degrees of control of female sexuality. Prostitution may be seen as a strategy for a family's survival: impoverished Chinese families in the nineteenth century sold their daughters as prostitutes in the cities to earn money. Elsewhere in Asia, prostitutes functioned as part of larger institutions, or even imperial expansion. Hindu *devadasi*, or temple dancers, served as prostitutes tied to temples. In the nineteenth century the British, in an attempt to limit military expenditures, provided prostitutes rather than wives for non-commissioned British troops in India. During the period of imperial expansion in the 1930s, Japanese prostitutes were sent to service brothels in outposts of the empire, a process described in the film *Sandakan No. 8* (Brothel Number 9). Under these circumstances, prostitution did not mean increased autonomy for women, whether or not it provided subsistence.

In some places and times, however, prostitution has offered an alternative of increased autonomy. New colonial towns in Africa created spaces for women to escape from abusive or unwanted marriages. There, operating as entrepreneurs rather than under the supervision of pimps or other authorities, they supported themselves and their children by selling sexual and other domestic services to men, who frequently were migrant laborers. In addition, prostitutes were able to keep their children, an option that was not available to women in patrilineal marriages, where offspring belonged to the husband's patrilineage and were lost to a woman who divorced or absconded. Even under circumstances in which prostitutes had more control over their sexuality and their lives, it is important not to romanticize prostitution. It has been, and remains, an option for some women within a context of gender and class oppression.

The production of offspring (especially male offspring in strongly patrilineal societies) is often a measure of a woman's value. In some

African societies, this value is represented by bridewealth, the gifts
that a groom must give to the bride's family in order to obtain rights
to the offspring in a patrilineal society. The production of male offspring is essential for some religious rituals, for example, in Confucianism.

We have little historical information about control of reproduction. But even prior to the recent rise of reproductive technology,
women found ways to limit birth. For example, in Congo in the late
nineteenth century, slave women limited the number of children they
had. In the complex conditions created by the internal African slave
trade, slave women saw few advantages to producing children who
belonged to their owners and who could not be expected to care for
their mothers in old age. Advances in reproductive technology such
as amniocentesis, which project the sex of an embryo or fetus, have
sometimes been used to select male children and abort female children.

Recently, with the advent of population control programs adopted
by nation-states and promoted by international agencies, control of
reproduction has shifted away from individually initiated actions to
highly bureaucratized operations. In that shift, the balance has slipped
from birth control, which empowers women by giving them options,
to population control, which regulates female reproduction in the interests of a nation-state or a donor country. Women may be encouraged or coerced to have babies for the nation, or the revolution, or
conversely they may be manipulated or coerced into limiting childbirth. Stringent population policies were introduced in India, prompting protests by women's groups, and in China, where urban couples
recently have been allowed to have only one child. In Puerto Rico
one-third of the women of childbearing age were sterilized by the
1960s in one of the early attempts at widespread population control
following policies initiated by the U.S. government. The white regime in South Africa promoted "birth control" among blacks as part
of the larger plan of apartheid. In none of these population policies
does birth control unambiguously empower women, since the elements of choice and safety have been compromised.

HOUSEHOLD RELATIONS

Household relationships are at the heart of most societies, since families act as the primary culture-bearing unit. In pre-industrial societies
the family is also an important economic unit. Indeed, the way that
families are organized is linked as much to the relations of production

as to culture. Among other factors, a sedentary, nomadic, or hunting-and-gathering lifestyle, sex ratios, or the availability of land can affect family organization—and all of these factors also help determine the relations of production and culture. With few exceptions (Japan, for instance), the areas under discussion are still in the process of industrializing. Even while allowing for different levels of industrialization and cultural specificity, we can make some general observations.

In the Third World, historically and presently, domestic relationships have involved far more people than a nuclear family. The family most often functionally (not just emotionally) encompassed a wide range of relatives, including grandparents, parents, children, brothers and sisters, cousins, aunts and uncles, etc. Even when these people do not all inhabit the same household or compound, the sense of communal responsibility, obligation, and authority is wide-ranging and strongly felt and encouraged. The importance of the individual, as a general value, has been subordinated to that of the collective. Thus, domestic relationships and decision-making even between a husband and wife and their own children are often influenced by a wide variety of individuals and situations. Issues of polygyny, birth control, sexual conduct, education, allocation of economic resources, and so on are often group decisions, with elders frequently carrying more weight than younger members. The authority of a wide group of people who know about and sanction or approve behavior is accepted. Increasingly, however, factors such as class, personal mobility, and the proliferation of ideas about greater individual freedom are beginning to disrupt this pattern.

Historically, marriage was an important alliance that could not be viewed as a relationship between individuals, but between two kin groups, because the family was a primary unit for economic production and the concentration of wealth, for the allocation and legitimation of political power, and for conflict resolution. Consequently, marriages were often arranged for both women and men by other family members or by marriage brokers. Among the Aztecs, for instance, marriages were arranged by a go-between known as a *cihuatlanque*. Among the Spanish and Portuguese in Latin America, however (until 1776 when the Crown enacted new laws requiring parental consent for marriage), so long as a girl was twelve and a boy fourteen they could marry without such consent. Still, marriage was generally seen as an alliance between families by both the Spanish and the Portuguese, especially by those of the upper classes, where property was at stake and marriage between relatives was common. In the nineteenth-century Middle East, families exercised close control over marriage arrangements, and first-cousin marriage was commonly used as a method for ensuring political alliances and centralizing wealth. Arranged marriages seem to have held less importance for the poor, however, reflecting less wealth to protect and perhaps even the need to decrease the number of dependent kin. In Africa, also, arranged marriages were a prevalent means of ensuring the continuity of the transfer of resources. As men undertook wage labor their ability to pay their own bridewealth and hence arrange their own marriages increased, but rarely would this have been done over family objections to choice of a mate.

Gifts passed between families (and still do in many places) and between the bride and groom at the time of marriage. Dowry was brought by a bride to her marital home, and other transfers, such as bridewealth or brideservice, went from the groom (or his family) to the bride's family. The degree of access to and control over these gifts exercised by a bride varied greatly among the societies discussed here.

The institution of dowry served an important economic as well as social function. The dowry (or *dote*) was not a requirement for marriage among the Spanish and Portuguese in Latin America, but it served as a way of both compensating a husband for assuming the economic burden of a wife as well as providing a woman with some economic independence. Though it was administered by a husband, it remained the property of the wife and could not be alienated without her consent. If the husband mismanaged the dowry, a woman could petition in court to control it herself, and in the case of divorce, the dowry had to be repaid. In the case of the wife's death, however, the dowry was either divided among the children or returned to the wife's parents. In India, dowry encompassed both *stridhan*, which was usually jewelry and clothing belonging to the bride alone, and a broad array of household goods and other valuables that were gifts to the couple and to the groom's family, with whom they lived.

In various societies, wealth moved in the reverse direction, from the groom and his kin to the bride and hers. The system of bridewealth found in Africa was generally a gift from a man to the parents of his bride and signified their compensation for the loss of their daughter as well as his rights to the children of the marriage and, to varying extents, her labor. Among matrilineal peoples in Central Africa, a groom had to perform brideservice, (that is, labor in the bride's family's fields). Forms of bridewealth varied (including cloth, beads, cattle, and, after the introduction of wage labor during the colonial period, cash), and, in the case of divorce, it frequently had to be returned. In some places in Africa, women assumed control over a portion of their bridewealth. Some East Asian and Middle Eastern societies had both dowry and bridewealth. Under Islamic law, women retained rights to the personal ownership of their bridal gift, or *mahr*.

Polygyny, or the taking of more than one wife, was commonly practiced in a number of places. Sometimes, as noted above, it had an important political function in cementing alliances. In Islamic societies in the Middle East, Asia, and Africa, men could legally wed up to four wives. In non-Islamic areas of Africa and among some early Amerindian societies, such as the Inka in Latin America, polygyny also existed, but the number of wives was not limited. Judaism allowed polygyny by c.e. 70 in the Middle East. The economic obligations entailed by taking more than one wife could operate to curtail the degree to which polygyny was actually practiced; however, since women also produced wealth through trade, agricultural activities, and production of crafts, as well as by the exchange of bridewealth, it was often true that polygyny could be economically advantageous to men. Polygyny could sometimes be economically advantageous to women by allowing them to share household duties and obligations and by affording them more freedom to engage in trade and craft production.

Concubinage or the forging of sexual (and sometimes emotional) extramarital alliances was common in all four regions. Though concubines, as discussed above, were generally in a very vulnerable position, sometimes there were indigenous laws governing their treatment, and because these women often came from poor families, concubinage could represent a way of improving their economic position and even status. For example, Khaizuran, concubine of Caliph al-Mahdi during the Abbasid period in Iraq, saw two of her sons succeed their father as caliph, and she herself intervened in state affairs.

Since one of women's primary responsibilities was considered the production of heirs and the next generation, infertility could be a devastating circumstance and was the subject of many religious practices aimed at prevention or cure. Infertility was most often blamed on women until fairly recently. In Sumeria (3000–2000 b.c.e.) men could take another wife if their first did not bear children, historically a fairly common practice worldwide. Among the Aztecs a sterile woman could be rejected and divorced.

Some form of divorce or marital separation has existed for women nearly everywhere. (Among Zoroastrians, only men could divorce.) Although in general divorce was easier for men than women, there were exceptions to this rule. Extreme physical cruelty and neglect of economic duty were fairly common grounds by which women could petition for divorce. Adultery and a wife's inability to produce children, among a much wider range of other less consequential reasons, were common grounds on which men exercised their right to divorce women. In the early Spanish societies of Latin America, marriages could be annulled due to failure to produce children. Legal separation, known as *separación de cuerpos* (or separation of bodies) was also available on grounds of extreme physical cruelty, adultery, prostitution, or paganism, but such a separation forbade remarriage. From the sixteenth century onward, women were often the initiators of divorce in Spanish Latin America. In Southeast Asia women easily exercised their right to divorce, a situation some historians speculate was due to their economic autonomy. Prior to the twentieth century, however, divorce initiated by women was much harder in other parts of Asia, such as China and Japan. The ease with which divorce could be obtained was sometimes related to class. For instance, the divorce rate among the urban poor in nineteenth-century Egypt was higher than among the upper classes, for whom the economic components of marriage were more complicated. In Africa, because divorce often involved the return of bridewealth, women were sometimes discouraged from divorcing their husbands.

The treatment and rights of widows varied widely. During the Mauryan era in India (322–183 B.C.E.), widows could remarry, although they lost their rights to any property inherited from their deceased husbands. During the Gupta era (320–540), however, the Laws of Manu severely limited women's rights in marriage, including the banning of widow remarriage. Though its origins are unknown, the ritual suicide of widows among the Hindu known as *sati* is one of the most controversial treatments of widowhood. A complex practice, it appears to have economic as well as socioreligious foundations. Among the Aztecs widows not only retained the right to remarry but were encouraged to do so, especially if they were of childbearing age. In the colonial period in Spanish America, widows had the rights of single women who, after a certain age, were considered to have attained a legal majority. They could acquire control over their children or remarry. In parts of Africa, Asia, and the Middle East, widows were sometimes "inherited" by male kin of their deceased husbands. This practice, known as the levirate, could entail conjugal rights, but could also mean only the assumption of economic responsibility for a widow and her children. Women sometimes retained the right to refuse such a marriage. Among the Kikuyu of East Africa, for instance, women could opt instead to take a lover.

In many places women's activity in reform and nationalist movements, especially in the twentieth century, has been characterized by their struggle to liberalize laws governing marriage and family relationships. The Egyptian Feminist Union, led by Huda Sha'rawi, agitated for reform of laws governing divorce and polygyny in the 1920s and 1930s. Women (and men) of the May Fourth generation struggled in early twentieth-century China to make the reform of marriage and family law and practice central to their revolutionary effort. Even after the success of the Cuban revolution and the passage of a family code that explicitly gives women the same rights as men in economic and political arenas as well as in the family, women's organizations, with state support, continue to work to implement equality. In Africa women and men activists in liberation movements, such as the PAIGC in Guinea-Bissau in the 1960s and 1970s, clearly articulated the need to transform domestic relations as an important tenet of revolutionary ideology.

Women's roles, statuses, and power within the family have varied both through time within the same society and from one place to another. As reflections of material culture, they tell us more about societies than about women's place in them. For the regional areas under discussion, we can see the common threads, but we can also distinguish the wide variation.

WOMEN'S ECONOMIC ACTIVITY

In virtually all societies, the gender division of labor associates women with family maintenance. Overwhelmingly, gender segregation and domestic subsistence production have characterized the lives of women in the economic sphere, although before industrialization there was little distinction between the private and public economic spheres as most production took place in the family and in and around the home. In Nubian civilization in ancient Africa, for example, there is evidence that women were involved in the production of pottery for household use, while men specialized in producing wheel-turned pottery for trade. At times there were disincentives for women to be economic actors. In medieval Islamic society, elite urban men were cautioned not to marry women who engaged in economic activities in the public arena. But such observations should not be construed as an indication of lack of importance and variety in women's roles in agriculture, craft and textile production, the tending of livestock, trade, and other areas. In fact, many women engaged in economic activity that not only supplied subsistence but generated wealth, especially in agricultural and trade sectors of the economy.

In nearly all of sub-Saharan Africa, women historically played and continue to play important roles in agricultural production. In one of the few areas of sub-Saharan Africa where private property in land pre-dated European arrival, among the Amhara of Northeast Africa (present-day Ethiopia), women could control the entire agricultural production process. They owned, plowed, planted, and harvested their own fields. Amerindian women were important in agricultural production in Latin America before the arrival of the Spanish and Portuguese, who then sought to enlist men as agricultural laborers in cash crops. Although for the early centuries of the Atlantic slave trade the sex ratio was heavily imbalanced toward males, African women performed important agricultural labor, which was essential to the economies of colonial Latin America, the Caribbean, and what would become the United States. Women were cultivators in much of Asia, usually in family-centered production units. Even where women did not cultivate, they often performed other roles associated with agricultural production. For instance, in nineteenth-century Egypt, women did not plow land, but they worked at harvesting and in pest control activities.

Women undertook various kinds of manufacturing activities. In the Chewa-Malawi area of nineteenth-century East Africa, women were involved in producing salt and in other manufacture. In the eleventh-century Pagan Empire in Southeast Asia, women were important in the spinning of yarn and weaving of cloth. In eighteenth- and nineteenth-century Egypt, women were important in the textile crafts, though they were squeezed out by industrialization. In the nineteenth century, partially due to demand created by a European market, women became important to the growth of the silk industry in Lebanon and the carpet industry in Iran. Women were important weavers among the Inka, where they also worked in the mines. In the sixteenth and seventeenth centuries, women among the Shona of southern Africa worked in the gold mines.

Perhaps the most ubiquitous economic activity undertaken by women was that of trading. In Africa, Asia, Latin America and the Caribbean, and the Middle East and North Africa, women traded a number of items, including agricultural products, cooked food, cloth, beads, and handicrafts. Although women's trading activities were sometimes on a small scale, often referred to as "petty trading," that was not always the case. In Southeast Asia, women in twelfth- and thirteenth-century Burma were engaged in trade that included the large-scale buying and selling of rice and other commodities. They were also identified with the production and trade of a particular food-stuff, betel leaf, for which they made elaborate jewelled containers. Sometimes women engaged in long-distance trade that required their absence from home for extended periods of time. Among the nineteenth-century Kikuyu of East Africa, women engaged in long-distance trade and retained control over some of the wealth they accumulated. Even where women engaged in local, small-scale trade, they could be very important to the growth and development of long-distance trade and of port towns and urban centers. Such was the case with women traders along the west coast of Africa in the eighteenth and nineteenth centuries.

Residence in a harem and the practice of seclusion placed restraints on women's ability to engage directly in public-arena economic activity, thus forcing them to use intermediaries to conduct their business operations. This use of intermediaries, and the higher economic status that seclusion usually implied, meant women sometimes held considerable wealth and became significant economic actors. In the nineteenth century in parts of the Middle East (notably Cairo, Istanbul, Aleppo, and Nablus), upper-class women employed agents to conduct their business transactions in the public arena. They also invested capital as "silent partners" in other ventures and loaned money to men. Among the Hausa of northern Nigeria, Islamic women who were secluded used prepubescent girls to trade for them in public.

In some places, however, the strict gender segregation of Islamic societies in fact expanded women's economic alternatives, since only women could perform certain services for other women. In nineteenth-century Egypt women of lower economic status served as entertainers, cosmologists, and midwives to women of higher economic status who were in seclusion. Strict gender segregation opened up the professions (medicine, education, etc.) to women in the late twentieth century, especially in countries where economic resources are plentiful, such as Saudi Arabia.

The absence of male heirs, or the fact of widowhood, could also create economic opportunity for women. Under such circumstances women ran businesses and were important in trades. In sixteenth-century Mexico, Mencia Perez, a *mestiza*, married a rich merchant. When he died, she took over the business and became one of the wealthiest merchants in the province. In Syria, the *gedik*, a license that allowed one to practice a trade, was normally inherited by sons from their fathers. In the absence of a male heir, women could inherit the *gedik,* and although prevented from practicing the trade, they could sell, rent, or bequeath the license. In coastal West Africa creole women traders descended from African mothers and European fathers served as cultural intermediaries and often became very successful and wealthy businesswomen.

Yet women's tremendously varied and important roles in economic activity did not translate into economic, legal, or political equality with men. The more economic autonomy women had, however, the greater their freedoms. Whatever the origins of women's inequality, the complex processes through which it has been perpetuated will not fall in the face of economic parity alone.

POLITICAL POWER

In general histories of the Third World, political access is not normally discussed with gender as a factor of analysis, although frequently class, race, ethnicity, and other factors are considered. And being of a particular class, race, or ethnicity could influence women's power and status as much as gender. Still, the type and degree of women's political participation both as individuals and as a group have been underreported, and the present has frequently been mistaken for the past.

One of the most obvious ways women exercised direct power was by ruling. In the ancient African kingdom of Kush, women assumed power in their own right as well as sometimes co-ruling with their sons. There were women who ruled in early Austronesian societies from Polynesia to Madagascar, including the Philippines and Indonesia. In tenth-century Abyssinia in Northeast Africa, Gudit was a powerful queen of the Agao. Two African queens ruled in the sixteenth century, Queen Aminatu or Amina of Zaria and Queen Njinga of Matamba. The Mende of West Africa also had a tradition of women chiefs. Mwana Mwema and Fatuma ruled in Zanzibar in the late seventeenth and early eighteenth centuries, and Mwana Khadija ruled in Pate on the East African coast in the mid-eighteenth century. In India, several Hindu and Muslim women ruled small kingdoms during the late eighteenth century. In fifteenth- and sixteenth-century Burma and the Malay peninsula women also ruled.

What the existence of women rulers has to say about women's power qua women is a complex question. Most women who ruled were elite by birth, but then so were ruling men. However, Queen

Njinga certainly achieved rather than inherited her power, moving from the position of palace slave to that of a reigning monarch. Although the existence of women rulers indicates that women were not universally absent from the highest seats of power, having a woman ruler did not necessarily reflect the status of other women or empower them, any more than it does today.

Women also exercised direct power within arenas viewed as the female province; these varied based upon material culture. In Africa female networks seem to have arisen from the gender division of labor, and over many centuries women exercised considerable power and autonomy within society as a whole through all-female organizations. Women leaders of women such as the *iyalode* among the Yoruba and the *omu* among the Igbo are examples of such power. The *coya*, known as the "queen of women" among the Inka, is another example; she even had the power to rule in the absence of the male ruler. Women exercised considerable power within the royal harem in both Turkey and Iran.

Women exercised power as members of collectives of their own sex organized for particular purposes. Practices similar to the Nigerian institution of "sitting on a man" are found in various African societies. This phrase describes organized political activities of women who gathered as a group to protest policies or protect another woman by confronting a man and ridiculing him or making demands, sometimes even destroying his property as a punishment for some act against a woman or women as a whole. Women directed this practice against recalcitrant husbands and colonial officials alike. There is also evidence of the existence of this kind of activity in early twentieth-century China, where women forced husbands who had maltreated their wives to march through town wearing dunce caps.

Perhaps the most ubiquitous example of women's indirect and influential power is the existence of the queen mother, normally the progenitor of a male ruler although sometimes a woman appointed as his "mother." These women had power over women and men. Their power resulted not only from their access to the ruler, serving as his "ear," so to speak, but also because they often commanded formidable financial and personnel resources and/or had specific responsibilities over the governed. Queen mothers existed in ancient Kush, India, the Ottoman Empire, and West, East, and Northeast Africa, to name a few places. Some queen mothers, such as Shah Turkan of thirteenth-century Delhi, could be very instrumental in installing their sons on the throne, and consequently exercised considerable state power. Others, like Mihrisah, mother of the Ottoman ruler Selim II, who ruled in the early nineteenth century, exercised considerable power through largesse; she built a mosque and a medical school. Yaa Kyaa, mother of the West African Asante ruler Osei Yaw, also exercised considerable state power, even signing a peace treaty between the Asante and the British in the 1830s, and Yaa Asantewa led a large revolt against British rule. The *magajiya*, the title given to the queen mother in several of the Hausa states of the western Sudan in West Africa, even had the power to depose the ruler, or *sarki*. The queen mother, however, usually owed her power to her relationship to a male ruler and not to her relationship to other women. Even though she might be regarded as "queen of the women," she did not necessarily represent women's interests as a whole. Still, these women were often at the center of power, and many displayed formidable political acumen.

We also cannot discount the power and influence of women who were the wives, sisters, daughters, and consorts of powerful men. Precisely because of the intimate context in which such situations occurred, they are admittedly hard to document, but evidence exists. Women such as Inés Suárez, who accompanied Captain Pedro de Valdivia as his lover in his campaign to conquer Chile, played an important role as a spy and confidante and eventually took part in the conquest. Wives of emperors in the Byzantine empire wielded considerable political influence. Nineteenth-century Confucian reformers in China were influenced by increased contact with literate women at court and in elite families. The nineteenth-century Islamic reform movement led by Uthman dan Fodio in West Africa was certainly influenced in its ideas on greater education for women by the women in Fodio's own family, which produced five generations of women intellectuals who left bodies of written work in Fula, Arabic, and Hausa. In the West African kingdom of Dahomey, by the eighteenth century at least, no man could become king without the support of the powerful palace women. Royal women in nineteenth-century Iran also exercised considerable power and independence, even from inside the harem. There are many other examples which suggest to us that women's influential roles in politics were consequential.

Women's military participation as individuals and as organized corps of women fighters was also widespread. In many places women accompanied male troops, such as in Aksum and early Ethiopian kingdoms, in early Arabia, in Latin America, and elsewhere. But women were also actual combatants. The African Queen Amina of Zaria led troops into battle, as did the renowned Nguni warrior Nyamazana, of early nineteenth-century southern Africa, and Indian women in Delhi and Bhopal in the second half of the eighteenth century. In C.E. 40 two Trung sisters in Southeast Asia (in present-day Vietnam) led an army, including female officers. In eighteenth-century Jamaica, slave women played important roles as combatants in maroon societies composed of runaway slaves. One woman, Nanny, is still revered as a fighter and ruler of one of the most famous maroon communities, Nanny Town. Actual corps of trained women soldiers also existed, such as those in Java and in the West African kingdom of Dahomey, where they formed the king's bodyguard and were an elite unit of "shock troops." In eighteenth-century Egypt, women went into battle against Mamluks and the French. In the nineteenth century women fought in Japan, in the T'ai p'ing Rebellion in China, and in the Mexican Revolution. In early twentieth-century China, corps of women fought as the "Women's Suicide Brigade" and the "Women's National Army." Twentieth-century anti-colonial and liberation struggles are replete with examples of women as combatants, for example, in the 1950s "Mau Mau" rebellion in Kenya, the Frelimo liberation army in Mozambique, and the Cuban and Nicaraguan revolutions.

In addition to serving in military roles, women organized in other capacities with men and in women's groups against colonial policies that they viewed as inimical to their interests. In India at the turn of the twentieth century, women were active in the *swadeshi* movement, which sought to encourage the use of indigenously made products as opposed to European imports. In the 1930s Indian women participated in anti-colonial protest marches in Bombay and elsewhere. In 1929 the "Women's War" of the Igbo and Ibibio of eastern Nigeria was a massive uprising of women against the threat of female taxation by the colonial state. In 1945 the market women in Lagos, Nigeria were very instrumental in a general strike against economic and political policies of the British. Women in Egypt, Iran, and the Ottoman Empire worked with men in organizations promoting independence from European imperialism by participating in street demonstrations, public speaking, and writing. In the Algerian War of Independence against the French (1954–62), women were couriers of weapons, money, and messages, as well as actual combatants.

Women's participation in general strikes, major protest marches, economic boycotts, and armed rebellion was prevalent everywhere there was an anti-colonial struggle. As with any major societal upheaval resulting in challenges to existing authority, colonialism both created opportunities for and oppressed women. In the final analysis, however, the vast majority of women have opted to work for the independence of their societies and to pursue the issue of gender equality in the context of an independent and autonomous state.

Despite all of this, and despite the fact that improving women's status has often been a central point of anti-colonial ideology, women have usually not become the political and economic equals of men in newly evolving independent societies. In fact, the development of nationalist movements, at least in the nineteenth and twentieth centuries, has often operated to subordinate women. In nineteenth-century Japan the growth of nationalism and patriotism tended to subjugate women, requiring that they be good wives and mothers as their first "patriotic" duty. Although initially instituting reforms that served to empower women, within a few years the Kuomintang nationalist movement in early twentieth-century China began to repress a developing feminist movement that had supported its rise to power. The 1922 Egyptian constitution denied women the right to vote and barred them from the opening of Parliament, despite the active role they had played in the nationalist movement. After the success of the Algerian Revolution, women's roles in the war were viewed as validation of their "traditional" roles of wife and mother. After gaining independence, the Indonesian nationalist movement encouraged women to go back into the home to provide "social stability." In Nigeria, although the nationalist movements of the mid-twentieth century had courted women and counted them as strong supporters in the independence struggle, women remained generally excluded from political power after independence and especially under military rule. In many disparate places and cultures, nationalism left women unrewarded after independence was achieved.

There are exceptions, as some national liberation movements have challenged sexist ideologies regarding women. Frelimo in Mozambique criticized both the traditional initiation rites that included notions of female subordination as well as the colonial exploitation of women's labor. This kind of struggle was termed "fighting two colonialisms" by the PAIGC, a comparable liberation movement in Guinea-Bissau. In Cuba the government also sought to address the issue of women's equality in the post-independence period in a written family code that explicitly delineates women's equal status compared to that of men. The revolutionary Nicaraguan government of the 1980s also attempted to officially stipulate women as the equals of men. The positive difference in these countries, however, seems as related to women's continued organization as women (such as the Organization of Mozambican Women and the Cuban Federation of Women) as to state-supported revolutionary ideology.

CENTRALIZATION, BUREAUCRATIZATION, AND STATE FORMATION

Women's role in centralization, bureaucratization, and state formation poses some challenging questions. In the processes of state formation and centralization, women often have tremendous importance and potential for autonomy and power as marriage partners who centralize wealth, cement alliances, merge cultures, and produce heirs. In the Middle East the practice of first-cousin marriage helped establish the family as a base of centralized wealth and political solidarity. In the pre-colonial West African kingdom of Dahomey, the king took wives from wealthy and powerful families to cement political alliances. Among both the Hindus and the Muslims in India, marriages reinforced political bonds with the nobility and among rival states. In Latin America the Spanish sought unions with elite Amerindian women to legitimize and consolidate their control over indigenous societies. However, it appears that when the state begins to bureaucratize, making these relationships less important to state organization, women lose much of their potential for being central to state power. In the Middle East the growth of the state meant that the great family houses that had served as centers of societal organization and power lost much of that role. Similarly, in the West African kingdom of Dahomey, kinship ties became much less important in power relations as the state solidified and shifted to a merit system based more on service to the king than lineage connections.

Nationalist struggles in the nineteenth and twentieth centuries mobilized women nearly everywhere in the Third World. But once the state was established (or gained its independence from external conquerors), women often seemed to lose in the process. Particular and comparative research with gender as a central analytical factor can test this hypothesis and may open new windows on studies of state formation and the development of nationalism.

WOMEN'S CULTURE, NETWORKS, AND AUTONOMOUS SPACE

In male-dominant societies, women's activities, values, and interactions often form a "muted" subculture: their worldview is non-dominant and does not generally claim to represent that of the entire society of men and women. This subculture is reinforced by a strong gender division of labor that results in women and men spending most of their time in same-sex groupings and, occasionally, is augmented by ideological formulations or social rules (e.g., notions of pollution, or purdah).

At times, women demanded the separate space or take advantage of it as a refuge from oppressive features of their society. For example, the sisterhoods of silk workers in southern China, who pledged to resist marriage, provided an alternative to the patriarchal family. Buddhism allowed women to pursue the monastic life, albeit as less than equals to male monks. Still, Indian Buddhist nuns taught religion to other women and composed religious poetry. (Jainism accepted nuns as the equals of monks.) Women who joined Buddhist nunneries in China were criticized for ignoring female responsibilities of motherhood, although these nunneries, we might suspect, provided a space less controlled by male authority than the rest of Chinese society. Convents in colonial Latin America housed single women with various motives: some sought to escape marriage, others searched for religious fulfillment, and a few sought access to education. And not all who resided in a convent lived by vows of poverty and chastity.

Whatever its source or structural manifestation, this social space and the resulting female-controlled institutions offered women rich opportunities. Among the most important of these opportunities was the potential for female solidarity. Various African societies institutionalized female solidarity through activities such as "sitting on a man" (a Nigerian practice noted earlier). In Mende society in West Africa, the women's secret society known as Bundu (parallel to a men's secret society) provided a political base for female chiefs (it also perpetuated, as a central initiation ritual, the practice of clitoridectomy).

In addition to encouraging female solidarity, the separation of women and men had economic consequences at times. Islamic seclusion provided the impetus for the development of occupations serving the women of the harem or *zenana,* such as midwives, educators, entertainers, musicians, or cosmologists; for reasons of honor and modesty, these occupations were filled by women. The same rationale prompted the expansion of professions open to women: medicine, nursing, and teaching.

The physical separation of women contributed to a flowering of artistic, oral, and written culture from the female subculture. The world's first novel, *The Tale of Genji,* is only one example of the fine literary work of Japanese women writers in the eleventh century. Unlike men, who were restricted by gender norms to writing rather arid, but higher-status, poetry in Chinese characters, these women composed prose in *kana*, the language of indigenous expression of sentiment. Even where excluded from education and certain cultural outlets, women's networks produced a fine and rich tradition of oral expression, as in Bedouin communities in North Africa.

Women's networks and women's subculture, because they often derive from the marginalization of women from the centers of power, have been controversial in the scholarship. Even in extreme forms (perhaps more so there), the separating of women can provide a source of psychological support and connectedness and protection. In assessing the actions of women among themselves, the important issues of victimization and agency are played out and we must ask certain questions: On whose initiative are the women grouped? How do women respond to this grouping? How does the clustering of women, apart from men, empower and/or limit women? Is this a condition that encourages women's oppression of other women (since there are now distinctions of power drawn between women) as much as it encourages female solidarity?

WOMEN IN CROSS-CULTURAL CONTACT

Women are important intermediaries for cultural exchange. For several reasons, they are likely to end up marrying outside their community of birth. First, patrilineal societies outnumber matrilineal societies, and in patrilineal societies a woman marries into her husband's patrilineage and generally resides with her husband's kin (patrilocality).

Second, women have often been exchanged, as wives and as concubines, to cement alliances. In eighteenth-century Dahomey in West Africa, lineages were required to send their daughters to the king. During the same period in Java, the male ruler gave various women from his court to noblemen as wives. In sixteenth-century Japan, warrior families cemented alliances by the exchange of wives.

Third, in cases of European expansion into the Third World, the gender division of labor in Europe resulted in most explorers being male, which in turn created particular conditions for indigenous women to link with these men as sexual partners. Perhaps the best-known individual woman in this category was the slave Malinche (or Malintzin), who became the first Mexican mistress of Cortés. She served as translator in Maya, Nahuatl, and Spanish and apprised Cortés of the inland empire of Moctezuma. In the seventeenth century, the *signares* along the West African coast became wealthy traders and intermediaries through their relations with European men. Their mulatto children, familiar with two worlds, served as power brokers.

Similarly, initially in the seventeenth century, the Dutch administration encouraged the marriage of its junior officers to Indonesian women to provide a form of social order through mestizo culture on the frontiers of Dutch colonization. By the nineteenth century, the status of these mixed-race individuals had declined. The same gender division of labor, in which men were the agents of expansion, is also characteristic of societies outside of Europe. Most conquerors were male—for example, in the nineteenth-century Zulu expansion through southern and East-Central Africa, and among the Muslims who infiltrated Nubia from the sixteenth century on.

Women were thus well placed—as socializers of children, farmers, or traders—to transmit new ideas about social practices or mores, technology or techniques, religion, kinship, and so on to their new community. Female African slaves, valued for their horticultural labor and transported far from their natal villages, brought with them ways of planting or cultivating, thus encouraging agricultural innovation. Women, for the same reasons, were well placed to resist the cultural aspects of imperialism by perpetuating indigenous culture and customs. Amerindian women in Latin America, for example, continued indigenous religious practices in the face of Catholic proselytizing, as did African female slaves.

Women may become empowered by their intermediary position: it may give them pivotal control of information or material resources. On the other hand, as intermediaries they are sometimes marginal within their society of origin. They may lose the protections from their natal group accorded by custom without gaining those granted to indigenous women. As in-marrying strangers, they may suffer isolation. It is important to note, too, that the individuals and cultures resulting from these cross-racial liaisons were not valued everywhere: Anglo-Indians were shunned by both the English and the Indian communities during the Raj. The female intermediary risked being polluted by contact with outsiders and subsequently cast out or made a scapegoat when illness or other negative circumstances plagued a community. And some women who served as intermediaries—for example, Malintzin, or Eva in seventeenth-century southern Africa—have been labeled historically as traitors because they were seen as helping to facilitate conquest of their people by outsiders.

GENDER PLUS CONQUEST: COLONIALISM AND IMPERIALISM

Contact resulting from conquest held vast implications for women as a group. Customs were transferred from one society to another. New practices that restricted women's physical mobility might be forced upon the indigenous groups or adopted by them in emulation. For example, although the *jihad* of Uthman dan Fodio improved conditions for Hausa women in numerous ways, such as providing greater access to Qur'anic education, it also led to the increased seclusion of elite women and a loss of their religious and political power.

Recent scholarship on women in European-dominated colonial societies presents evidence that there was no one colonial experience for all women, even within the same national boundaries. However, the position of most women declined under the aegis of colonialism both because of its sexist bias and because women were members of politically dominated and economically exploited territories. In general, women were dislocated economically and politically within a weakened indigenous order, and in those spheres at least, women were rarely compensated in the new order. Nevertheless, though women were often the victims of colonialism, they also took initiative both in resisting policies they viewed as harmful to them and in using new situations to their advantage. And sometimes the social fluidity created by the colonial experience allowed for the creation of alternative roles for women. As one scholar suggests, however, studies of gender need to be located as much in the changing relationships of production as in the political and social policies engendered by colonialism. Another scholar underscores this point in emphasizing that it was the integration of the Middle East into a global economic system which is the real canvas on which we must paint an analysis of women's changing economic roles.

Women were members of colonizing as well as colonized societies, and members of the former group eventually accompanied colonizers to conquered territories. For most of the regions under consideration here, these women were a small minority in colonial territories. In the initial phase of conquest, they were nearly absent; then a trickle came to join husbands; then more came, depending on the degree of expatriate settlement that the colonizers encouraged and the needs and size of the colonial bureaucracy.

In Latin America (and South Africa), however, the era of European conquest was marked by the rise of commercial capitalism rather than the industrial capitalism that would fuel the colonialist thrust of the nineteenth century, and it also pre-dated (by several hundred years) the colonization of other regions. After the initial phase of conquest, during which few women from the Iberian peninsula were in residence in Latin America, much larger numbers began to migrate there. The Amerindian population of Latin America was decimated due to European diseases and attempts at their enslavement (the Khoi Khoi of South Africa suffered a similar fate). Though the population of African slaves grew considerably from the sixteenth to the nineteenth centuries in Latin America, European immigration outstripped it. The region was effectively colonized centuries before widespread colonial penetration into other areas. Thus, by the nineteenth century, Latin American nations were gaining their independence, and the descendants of Europeans in Latin America were the predominant people in the population of the continent. In many regions Latin American culture became an amalgam of African, Amerindian, and European cultures, shaped on the anvil of a centuries-old slave mode of production and forced Amerindian labor. Therefore, the following discussion of women under European colonialism does not apply to Latin America after the early decades of the conquest.

Imperial and colonial expansion had economic, social, and cultural consequences for women. The greater development (or in some places the introduction) of wage labor that accompanied colonialism predominantly involved men, whom it drew away from work on the land, increasing women's subsistence agricultural labor. Among the Tonga of Zambia the absence of male laborers had a particularly deleterious effect on the agricultural labor of older women, who were no longer able to depend upon help from sons and sons-in-law. This situation was also common in West and West-Central Africa. Sometimes, however, women left alone on the land exercised greater power in the economic decision-making process. An example is late-nineteenth- and early twentieth-century western Kenya, where Luo women were able to experiment with new crops and agricultural techniques that improved their economic position.

In some places the existence of widespread wage labor among men eroded the importance of the family economy and women's role in it. In forcing male migration to wage labor in mining and other work among the Aztecs, Inkas, Mayas, and Arawaks, the Spanish eroded the significant role women performed in the pre-Columbian family economy. In Morocco during the French colonial era, women were only seasonal wage laborers but were still dislocated in the family economy.

The development of the cash-crop system created greater interest in establishing private property in areas where it had not previously existed. This change to private property often distorted land tenure arrangements and usufruct (usage) rights and seems to have operated overall against women's interests. In Morocco the French, pursuing a policy of consolidating landholdings, helped destroy a family-based economy in which women played an important agricultural role. The Swynnerton Plan, begun by the British in 1954 in Kenya, was a policy of consolidating and privatizing landholdings that severely disadvantaged women and set the stage for their loss of rights to land after independence. In West and West-Central Africa women also lost out in the privatization of land occasioned by the growth of wage labor and cash crops. In a few instances women were able to resist erosion in their economic viability; from the 1920s through the 1940s, women in the cotton-producing areas of Nyasaland (now Malawi) were able to utilize cash cropping to their advantage. There, remaining collectively organized, women delayed the privatization of land, participated in cotton production, and maintained their precolonial agricultural autonomy.

Competition from European imports often displaced women occupationally and pushed them to the margins of areas in the economy where they were formerly quite important. For instance, in the Middle East and North Africa, European cloth imports in the nineteenth century devastated local textile production in which women had been heavily involved. Among the Baule of the Ivory Coast, French monopolization of local cloth production, and its alienation to factories, displaced women's former predominance in producing cloth and related items, such as thread. Sometimes the colonial economy created jobs for women, and though they were often overworked and underpaid, this independent income still provided women with some autonomy. Often it was the situations fostered by the colonial economy, especially in the urban areas, that created room for women to establish their own occupations. These urban areas often had large populations of single adult men (or men separated from their families) and entrepreneurial women engaged in occupations that provided them with services normally provided by the family. Although sometimes these occupations were marginal (such as beer-brewing, selling cooked food, and doing laundry) or even dangerous and possibly degrading (such as prostitution) women seized whatever opportunity was available to stabilize themselves, and often their children, economically and to gain independence from men and other adult family members.

The colonial need to control the economy also marginalized women who had often exercised control over the production, pricing, and distribution of agricultural, textile, and household goods. In southwestern Nigeria, for instance, the British were constantly in disputes with Yoruba market women over the location of markets, their internal control, and the setting of prices for staple commodities—all areas women had formerly controlled and which the colonial state sought to regulate.

A small number of women in some places were able to benefit economically from an increase in market scale that accompanied European contact and colonial rule, such as Omu Okwei of Nigeria. This benefit came to few individuals and often at the expense of other women, since women's economic power had historically emanated from their operation in collectives.

Political independence in many countries did not eliminate economic dependence on former colonial powers and was often followed in the post–World War II period by the arrival of multinational corporations. Since colonialism situated women overall as an easily exploitable class of labor, this situation has had profound economic implications for women. On the one hand, a number of multinational industries, especially electronics and textiles, have shown a marked preference for female labor. This has meant women have been drawn into the formal wage-labor force and therefore have had independent income. On the other hand, it has also meant the severe exploitation of their labor at depressed wages in unskilled and low-skilled jobs with little stability or possibility of promotion, and under unhealthy conditions.

Yet colonialism was not merely an economic and political relationship; it was a social relationship as well. By the eighteenth and nineteenth centuries, European colonizers hailed from societies that had rejected prominent and public political roles for women and that empowered men to represent women's interests. Alternative colonialist definitions of femaleness reflected a European gender division of labor and sexist bias. Women's education was viewed as a vehicle for making them better wives and mothers, since women's role was to be domestic and dependent. The schools of colonial Latin America shared with those of colonial Africa, the Middle East, and India an emphasis on education for domestic roles. The provision of suitable wives for the male Christian elite and the importance of mothers as socializers of their children dominated the colonial agenda, as articulated by both the colonizers and the indigenous male elite. Colonialism sought to impose not only political dominance and economic control, but also Western culture.

Seeking to legitimate their presence, and based upon European views of women in society and their own notions of the value of human life, some colonizers and missionaries criticized polygyny and such indigenous women-oriented practices as clitoridectomy, *sati*, foot-binding, and seclusion. In the area of family law, especially relating to marriage and inheritance, Europeans did sometimes seek to provide women with increased individual rights. Among the indigenous Christianized elite in Nigeria, for instance, Christian marriage was initially popular with women for these very reasons; but because it also promoted women's economic dependence and reinforced a pre-existing sexual double standard without the historical protections provided by the extended family, women soon began to chafe under its restrictions. The arbitrariness with which European family law was often administered and its confinement primarily to urban centers combined with other factors to leave a number of states with more than one legal code—European, customary, Islamic, and so on—a situation still in the process of being reconciled in many places.

Gender—the roles, perceptions, ideologies, and rituals associated with sex—is constructed by society. All societies have broad experiences in common (everywhere people construct shelter, trade, procure food, resolve conflict, etc.), but they approach these tasks in vastly different ways. Similarly, with women, writ large, there is much that is the same in the construction of gender; writ small, there is much that is different.

Even accounting for the cultural and historical context, the commonalities in the construction of gender point to women as generally less privileged human beings than men. Women's sexuality has usually been more regulated than that of men. Women have been far more associated with household labor than are men. Women have been less likely to rise to the highest positions of political and/or religious power. Women as a group have exercised less control over wealth than men as a group. Even within the same space and time, gender has been constructed differently for certain women depending on class, race, ethnicity, religion, and other elements. Thus we must view constructions of gender related not only to sex, but to a number of other factors—mode of production, culture, religion, to name a few—that can sometimes operate to bond women and at other times operate to separate them. The fundamental construction of gender everywhere, however, has been to separate women from men—in role, status, privilege, access, and other ways.

Women in Asia

Part I

WOMEN IN SOUTH AND SOUTHEAST ASIA

Barbara N. Ramusack

GLOSSARY

Adat **(plural form of Arabic** *ada***)**: Customary practices or social behavior relating to family relationships, friendship, manners. Among Muslims in South and Southeast Asia, *adat* is contrasted to *shariʿah*, the Islamic law which is based on the Qurʾan, and *sunna*, or tradition.

Adivasi: Aboriginal or indigenous people; tribal people in South Asia.

Antahpur: Bengali term for the women's section of a house, similar to *zenana*.

B.C.E.: "Before the common era." Used in place of B.C.

Begam: Honorific title among Muslim women.

Betel: An aromatic combination of areca nut, lime paste, and spices wrapped in a betel leaf; chewed as a digestive in South and Southeast Asia.

Bhadralok: Bengali word for gentle or respectable people. It designates a cluster of high-caste, educated, urban middle-class Bengalis.

Bhadramahila: Respectable women of the *bhadralok* category.

Bhakti: In the Hindu tradition devotion or love as a path to God.

Brahman: Priests and religious teachers who constitute the highest *varna*.

Caste: Portuguese word meaning "breed"; used to describe the social structure among Hindus in India. Has come to designate a group which claims a common ancestor and status within the social system. See *varna*.

C.E.: "Of the common era." Used in place of A.D.

Dai: Midwife.

Dalit: Oppressed. Name used by some scheduled caste groups in India.

Dargah: Tomb of a Sufi saint or *shaikh*; can become a place of pilgrimage.

Dharma: In the Hindu tradition, moral order, law, justice, duties. In Buddhism *dharma* or *dhamma* (Pali) is the basic teachings of the Buddha.

Dharmasastra: Ancient Hindu legal texts which provide guidance on moral and social duties or *dharma*.

Devadasi: Literally a female servant (*dasi*) of God (*deva*). In Hindu temples an auspicious woman who dances as part of temple ritual and may perform sexual service for temple priests or patrons.

Duppata: In South Asia a rectangular scarf which symbolizes women's modesty, especially when used to cover the hair and breasts.

Endogamy: Practice of marrying within a particular social group.

Fatwa: Legal opinion of a *mufti*, someone who is learned in Muslim jurisprudence. Interprets Islamic law to apply to specific situations.

Harim: Arabic word that designates the women's spaces in a house.

Hukum: Islamic law based mainly on the Qur'an and some traditions associated with the Prophet Muhammad.

Jati: Endogamous subdivision of a caste whose members generally claim a common ancestor and common historic occupation and share geographical proximity.

Kakawin: Javanese and Balinese court poetry in the style of Sanskrit poetry with themes from Indian epics.

Kanyadan: The gift of a virgin daughter in marriage by a Hindu father.

Khadi: Cloth woven from hand-spun yarn.

Kidung: Javanese and Balinese court poetry that incorporates Javanese and Balinese historical characters and events.

Kris: Indonesian sword that has spiritual and magical powers.

Kshatriya: Warriors and administrators who constitute the second *varna*.

Maharaja: Great ruler. See *raja*.

Maharani: Wife of a great ruler.

Matriliny: Kinship system in which descent is traced and sometimes inheritance passes through the mother.

Mestizo: Spanish word designating people of mixed ethnic parentage.

Moksha: Release from the cycle of transmigration in the Hindu tradition.

Nautch: Type of Indian dance. British colonial society in India came to characterize women *nautch* dancers as promiscuous.

Njai: Concubine in Indonesia.

Njonja: Dutch woman married to a Dutch official, more rarely to a Dutch planter or businessman in Indonesia.

Patriliny: Kinship system in which descent is traced and usually inheritance passes through the father.

Patrilocality: System in which a married couple resides with or near the husband's family.

Polyandry: Practice in which women are permitted to have more than one husband simultaneously.

Polygamy: Custom whereby either men or women are permitted multiple spouses simultaneously.

Polygyny: Practice in which men are permitted to have more than one wife simultaneously.

Prajurit estri: Female bodyguard corps attached to a ruler.

Priyayi: Member of the Javanese aristocracy whose status was based upon such personal qualities of character as self-restraint and elegance, artistic accomplishments, and spiritual power, as opposed to hereditary or legal claims.

Purana: Literally, "old." Stories and myths dating from the early centuries of the common era about Hindu gods and goddesses.

Purdah: Persian word which means "curtain" or, by extension, "veil." Therefore women who observe purdah are physically secluded from men.

Purdahnishin: Women who sit behind a curtain or screen.

Raj: Government.

Raja: Sanskrit for king; by the nineteenth century, applied to most Hindu and Sikh rulers.

Rajput: Sanskrit for "king's son." Name of groups who migrated from central Asia into India during the early centuries of the common era, claim *kshatriya* status, and are concentrated in northwestern India in the area known as Rajputana and after 1947 as Rajasthan.

Rani: Wife of a Hindu or Sikh king or ruler, or a female ruler.

Saktism: The Hindu theology which identifies *sakti*, the creative feminine principle, with the Great Goddess (Mahadevi) who is deemed to be the ultimate supernatural reality. Saktism emerged around the sixth century C.E.

Sati: Sanskrit, meaning "one who possesses *sat*"—truth, virtue, purity. Various uses include "a chaste woman": the Hindu widow who burns to death on her husband's funeral pyre through the practice of ritual immolation. During the eighteenth and nineteenth centuries, the British frequently designated the practice and the widow who chose such a death as "suttee."

Satyagraha: Literally, "to grasp the truth." Gandhi based the technique of non-violent resistance on the effort to grasp the truth in a situation.

Shaikh: Originally a descendant of the companions of Muhammad. In Sufism, a *shaikh* is a leader who developed or teaches a particular path *(tariqa)* to achieve union with God.

Stridhan: In Sanskrit *stri* means "woman" and *dhan* means "gift"; hence *stridhan*, gifts which Hindu parents give to a daughter at marriage, usually jewelry, over which she is to retain control. A husband may also give such gifts.

Stridharma: The duties of a chaste Hindu woman.

Stupa: In Buddhism or Jainism a sacred structure, generally dome-shaped, which contains a relic of the Buddha, a great teacher, or a highly respected person. Frequently a place of pilgrimage.

Sudra: Artisans and cultivators, the fourth *varna*, who are to serve the first three *varna*s.

Sufism: The mystical tradition within Islam whereby the believer seeks intimate union with God.

Swadeshi: Use of indigenous products during the nationalist movement in India.

Swayamvara: In ancient India a gathering of suitors from which a woman chooses a husband.

Talak **(Indonesia;** *talaq* **in India):** A form of unilateral divorce in Islam that occurs when a husband pronounces "I divorce thee" at stated intervals. If said three times in succession at once, the wife is particularly vulnerable since there is no possibility of reconciliation.

Vaishya: Merchants, who constitute the third *varna*.

Varna: "Color"; used to designate the four broad, all-India categories within Hindu society—*brahman*, *kshatriya*, *vaishya*, and *sudra*.

Zenana: Persian for "women"; used to indicate the place in a home where women reside, usually in seclusion from unrelated males.

MAPS

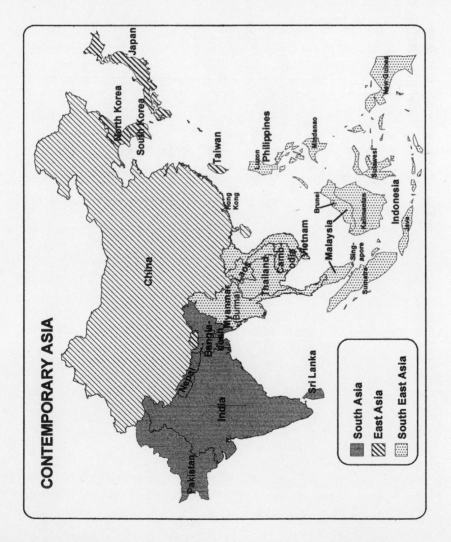

CONTEMPORARY ASIA

South Asia

East Asia

South East Asia

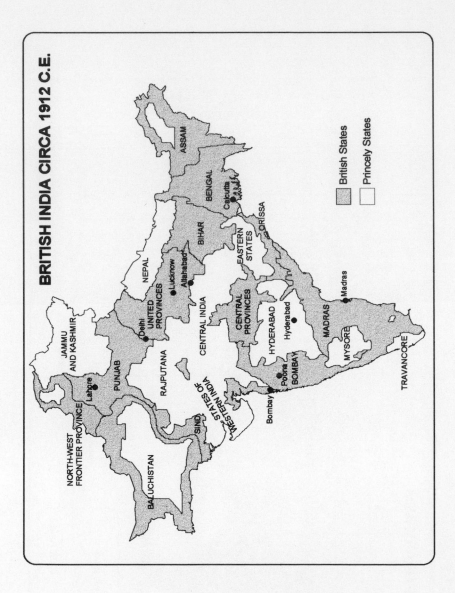

BRITISH INDIA CIRCA 1912 C.E.

British States

Princely States

ASSAM

BENGAL

Calcutta

BIHAR

ORISSA

EASTERN STATES

NEPAL

Lucknow

Allahabad

UNITED PROVINCES

Delhi

CENTRAL INDIA

CENTRAL PROVINCES

HYDERABAD

Hyderabad

MADRAS

Madras

JAMMU AND KASHMIR

RAJPUTANA

MYSORE

NORTH-WEST FRONTIER PROVINCE

Lahore

PUNJAB

SIND

STATES OF WESTERN INDIA

Bombay

Poona

BOMBAY

TRAVANCORE

BALUCHISTAN

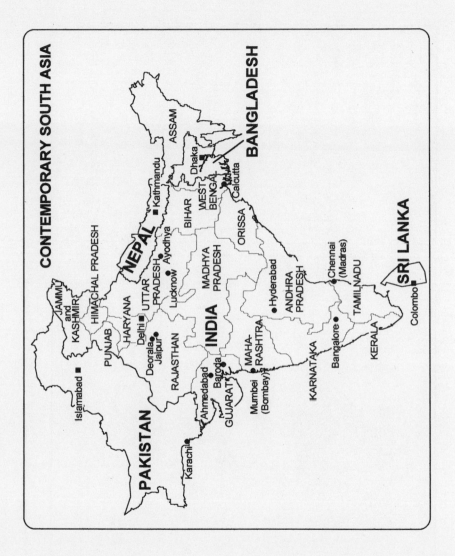

CONTEMPORARY SOUTH ASIA

PAKISTAN

Islamabad ■

Karachi•

JAMMU
and
KASHMIR

HIMACHAL PRADESH

PUNJAB

HARYANA

Delhi ■
Deorala•
Jaipur•
RAJASTHAN

Ahmedabad•
Baroda•
GUJARAT

Mumbei
(Bombay)•
MAHA-
RASHTRA

NEPAL

■ Kathmandu

UTTAR
PRADESH•
Ayodhya
Lucknow•

INDIA

MADHYA
PRADESH

BIHAR

WEST
BENGAL
Dhaka ■
Calcutta

ORISSA

Hyderabad•

ANDHRA
PRADESH

KARNATAKA

Bangalore•

KERALA

ASSAM

BANGLADESH

Chennai
(Madras)•

TAMILNADU

SRI LANKA

Colombo•

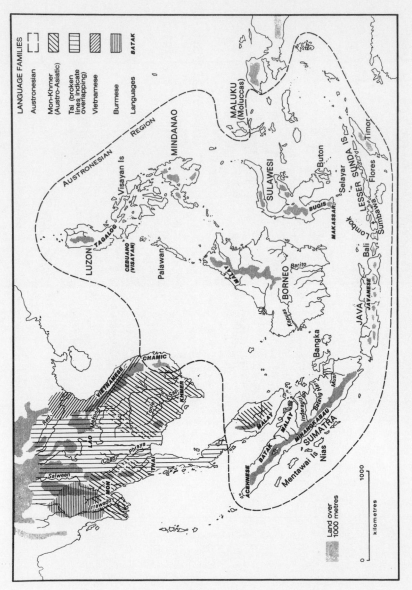

LANGUAGE FAMILIES

Austronesian

Mon-Khmer
(Austro-Asiatic)

Tai (broken
lines indicate
overlapping)

Vietnamese

Burmese

BATAK Languages

AUSTRONESIAN REGION

MINDANAO

Visayan Is

MALUKU
(Moluccas)

LUZON

TAGALOG

*CEBUANO
(VISAYAN)*

Palawan

SULAWESI

Buton

BUGIS

MAKASSAR

Selayar IS

LESSER SUNDA IS

Timor

Flores

Sumbawa

Lombok

Bali

JAVANESE

JAVA

BORNEO

Barito

Kapuas

Bangka

Musi

MALAY

MINANGKABAU

BATAK

SUMATRA

Nias

Mentawai Is

ACEHNESE

Indragiri

Batang Hari

MALAY

CHAMIC

VIETNAMESE

Red

Mekong

LAO

KHMER

Song

Tonle

THAI

Chao
phraya

Salween

Irrawaddy

MON

Land over
1000 metres

0   1000

kilometres

Physical features and language groups in Southeast Asia

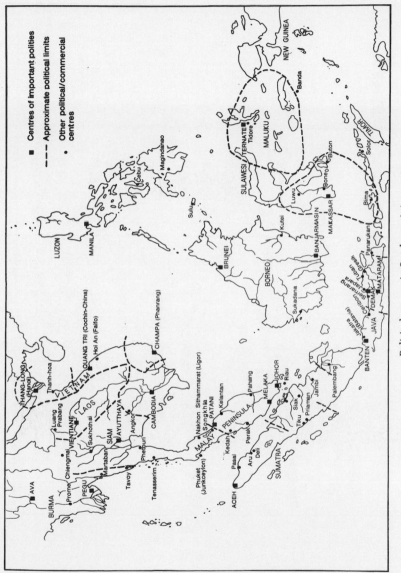

Legend:
- ■ Centres of important polities
- – – – Approximate political limits
- • Other political/commercial centres

Political centres in Southeast Asia, c. 1600

Place names on map:

NEW GUINEA

Banda

MALUKU
TERNATE
Tidore

SULAWESI

BORNEO
TIMOR
Solor

Buton
Boneo
Luwu
Bima
Panarukan
MAKASSAR
BANJARMASIN
Kutei
Sukadana

BRUNEI

Magindanao
Cebu
Sulu
LUZON
MANILA

Gresik
Tuban
Japara
Semarang
Cirebon
Demak
MATARAM
JAVA
Jakarta (Batavia)
BANTEN

Palembang
Jambi
Priaman
Tiku
Siak
Riau
Aru
Deli
Pasai
SUMATRA
ACEH
Perak
Kedah

JOHOR
Pahang
MELAKA
Kelantan
PATANI
Songkhla
Nakhon Sithammarat (Ligor)
MALAY
PENINSULA
Phuket (Junkceylon)

CHAMPA (Phanrang)
QUANG TRI (Cochin-China)
Hoi An (Faifo)
THANG-LONG (Hanoi)
Thanh-hoa
VIETNAM

LAOS
Luang Prabang
VIENTIANE
Sukhothai
SIAM
AYUTTHAYA
Angkor
CAMBODIA
Phetburi

Tenasserim
Tavoy
Martaban
Chiengmai
Prome
PEGU
AVA
BURMA

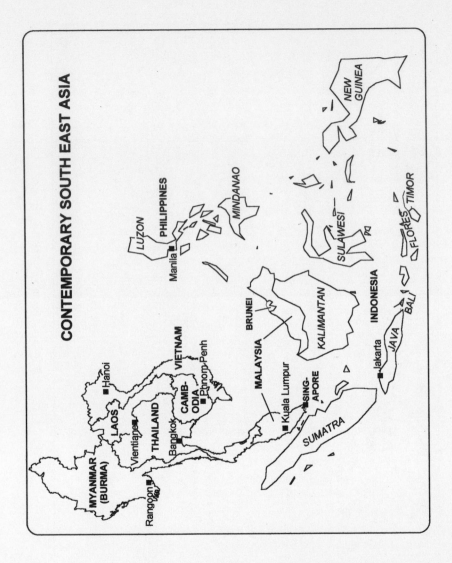

CONTEMPORARY SOUTH EAST ASIA

CHRONOLOGY

B.C.E.

2500–1700	Indus Valley civilization
1700–1000	Coming of Aryans to South Asia
1300–1000	Rig Veda
ca. 563–ca. 483	Siddhartha Gautama-Buddha, founder of Buddhism
ca. 540–ca. 468	Mahavira, founder of Jainism
ca. 600–ca. 200	Evolution of Ramayana
ca. 400–ca. 100	Evolution of Mahabharata
322–183	Mauryan Empire

C.E.

ca. 200–400	Laws of Manu
320–540	Gupta Empire
600–1200	Dominance of regional dynasties in South Asia
ca. 800–ca. 1380s	Khmer state at Angkor
700s	Construction of Borobudur complex on Java
1000–1700	Spread of Islam into South Asia
ca. 1250–1600	Advent of Islam in Southeast Asia
1044–1287	Pagan Empire in Burma
1500s	Arrival of Dutch in Indonesia and Spanish in Philippines
1526–1765	Mughal Empire
1600	Arrival of British in India
1765–1947	British Empire in India
1869–1948	Mohandas K. Gandhi
1885	Formation of Indian National Congress
1899–1946	American rule in the Philippines
1946	Independence of the Philippines
1947	Independence of India and creation of Pakistan
1950	Independence of Indonesia
1971	Creation of Bangladesh

WOMEN IN SOUTH ASIA

Barbara N. Ramusack

INTRODUCTION TO SOUTH ASIA

South Asia is an area of the world containing remarkable ethnic, linguistic, religious, geographical, and political diversity. This cultural
variety makes South Asia a fascinating topic of study, but it also means
that the generalizations intrinsic to a synthesis of its history are more
challengeable than those made about many other areas of the world.
Textbooks try to make its history comprehensible by dividing India
into North-Aryan-Indo-European and South-Dravidian cultural areas and into Hindu and Muslim India. Over the past two millennia
Aryan customs have gradually moved across the Deccan plateau into
south India, but their influence remains uneven. Furthermore, these
broad categories represent only the most obvious differences and ignore many cultural patterns that frequently were and are more mean-
ingful in the lives of individual South Asian men and women. Thus
northwestern India has close cultural ties to western Asia, whereas

northeastern India reflects social arrangements found in Southeast Asia, even though both northwestern and northeastern India are encompassed in the Indo-European language sphere and have populations in which Muslims are a majority. Finally, none of these geographical and cultural categories indicate the intricate mosaic of tribal societies that are concentrated primarily in northeastern and central India but exist throughout the South Asian subcontinent from the Himalayas to the Malabar coast in the southwest. These tribal societies resisted integration into both the Aryan and Dravidian social frameworks until the twentieth century. Consequently, many scholars debate the validity of using the term "Indian" to describe such a multiplicity of cultures and regions.

Nowhere is the problem of making generalizations more hazardous than in a survey of the history of women. Initial Western images of Indian women tended to focus on practices exotic to Westerners, such as physical seclusion (purdah) and the ritual self-immolation of Hindu widows (*sati*). Purdah and *sati* were customs associated primarily with north India and particular classes but came to be considered typical of all Indian women, who were reduced to one undifferentiated category. Some Indian nationalists reacted with theories of a golden age for Indian women before the arrival of either Muslim or British imperialists. Recent scholarship on women in South Asia has analyzed the manner in which class, religion, caste, ethnicity, and colonial political and economic structures have influenced the condition of women. There have also been efforts to understand how South Asian women themselves view their options and positions (R. Kumar 1994; Forbes 1996).

Yet the work of most scholars on women, while it has recorded complex variations in the lives of South Asian women, has had limited influence on the general writing of South Asian history. Feminist scholars, such as those included in a compelling collection of essays edited by Kumkum Sangari and Sudesh Vaid (1990), have made women and gender significant categories of analysis for some historians of nineteenth-century India. Most influential in this volume are articles by Uma Chakravati on the erasure of lower-class women from the nationalist reconstruction of ancient Indian history, Lata Mani on the ways in which Indian and British men debated social reforms on the ground of women's bodies in the controversy over *sati*, and Partha Chatterjee on the nationalist closure of debate on women's status. However, there have been no major shifts in periodization or in categories of South Asian historiography resulting from this research on gender (Ramusack and Burton 1994).

One example of the inertia in historical discourse is the school of subaltern historiography, which focuses on the autonomous politics of subalterns, or the people, as opposed to the elites studied by colonialist and neo-colonialist historians. In the first eight volumes of their collected essays, the subalterns have included only four contributions on Indian women and their representation in fiction and scholarship (R. Guha 1987a; Krishnaraj n.d.; Spivak 1987; Stephens 1989; Tharu 1989; Visweswaran 1996) and two on the concept of domesticity (P. Chatterjee 1992; Chakrabarty 1994). In the ninth volume (Amin and Chakrabarty 1996), there is change; the majority of the essays now include women and/or gender as categories of analysis. In this volume Kamala Visweswaran has noted how the subaltern project has previously subsumed gender under the categories of caste and class, named women as a social group distinctive from subalterns who are presumed to be male, or denied women their agency when confining them to the domestic sphere (1996). Thus the historiography of women in India is alive and well but still struggling for recognition and incorporation into the myriad patterns of Indian history.

Although this survey attempts to indicate the diverse situations of women in South Asia, it too makes regrettable compromises because available scholarship deals primarily, though certainly not exclusively, with north India, the social frameworks associated with Hinduism and Islam, and the colonial and post-colonial periods. There are three readily apparent compromises: there is more coverage of north rather than south India; there is disproportionate attention to the period from 1800 on; and there is no coverage of Bhutan, Nepal, Sri Lanka, and Tibet because of spatial constraints.

INDUS VALLEY CIVILIZATION, 2500–1700 B.C.E.

The archeological remains of the Indus Valley civilization were first unearthed during the 1920s and are still being excavated. This incomplete record and the difficulty of deciphering the Indus script, which is available only in short texts, has limited the information that we have on women or on many aspects of social and intellectual life during this period. From the material remains that have been dated from 2500 to 1700 B.C.E., archaeologists have argued for the prevalence of fertility goddesses based on figurines with full breasts and hips—an ideal of female beauty and movement that influenced the Indian classical dance tradition, which in modern times is preserved in the *bharatnatayam* school with its emphasis on delicate movements and the use of mime—and a delight in jewelry as personal adornment that continues into the present era.

ARYANS AND THE VEDIC AGE, 1700–500 B.C.E.

The arrival of the Aryans during the centuries after 2000 B.C.E. represented the displacement of an agriculturally based, literate society by one whose economy was based on cattle herding. In Western historiography the most distinctive institutions of the Aryans were their social organization and their religious hymns. The importance of the Vedas as the religious expression and historical record of the Aryans is indicated by the frequent designation of this era as the Vedic period.

Aryan society had three main divisions—priests, warriors, and commoners—and provided the basic outline for what Westerners, first the Portuguese and then the British, described as the caste system. As it evolved over millennia, the Aryan social framework came to include four broad categories known as *varna*, which means "color." The *brahmans*, who were priests and teachers, came to be acknowledged as having the primary position. The *kshatriya*, warriors and administrators, cooperated with the *brahmans* in the organization and administration of political structures and cultural institutions and were acknowledged to be equal to *brahmans*, or second only to them. The *vaishya*—merchants, artisans, and eventually cultivators—were third. These three divisions, which the Portuguese labelled *casta* (breed), traced their origin to Aryan society and claimed status as the twice-born or clean castes. As such they enjoyed a physical birth and a later ritual birth when they donned the sacred thread that signified their entrance into adulthood and religious learning. The fourth *varna*, labelled *sudra*, were the servants of the three higher *varna* and probably the indigenous people conquered by the Aryans. Below the four *varna* were the "untouchables," relegated to occupations considered physically demeaning and spiritually polluting, which generally meant anything dealing with human emissions and death. This division had its own hierarchy that ranged from landless agricultural laborers at the top to midwives, who directly handled the polluting afterbirth substances, at the bottom. Each *varna* was divided into caste groups that claimed descent from a mythic founder, and each caste group was further subdivided into *jati* that formed the endogamous unit within which one married. Within a *jati*, men and women were born into a *gotra* or specific endogamous lineage. These categories were not immutable and frequently reflected geographical and ethnic variations. Mobility within the structure also occurred through ritual, political, and economic interactions among *jatis* or other groups.

Indian historians commonly view the Vedic period, which extended from about 1500 to 700 B.C.E., as the heart of the golden age of Indian culture. It was an era of territorial expansion as the semi-nomadic, cattle-herding Aryans moved from northwestern India into the fertile Gangetic plain and then gradually southward into the jungly recesses of central India. The Aryans also began to cultivate cereal grains and to use wooden and later iron plows to work the soil. There were economic surpluses to support a priestly class who produced the Vedas, four major collections of religious hymns, that they then transmitted orally for centuries.

But what was the condition of women during the Vedic period?

Prior to the 1980s, many historians of ancient India, both Indian and Western, concluded that the position of women in Vedic India was "fairly satisfactory" (Altekar 1978: 338), but they tended to treat the condition of women in a topical manner that did not pay much attention to continuity and change through chronological periods. Since they were transmitted orally, the Vedas, the main source of information for these scholars, did not provide a firm temporal context. Historians of religion sometimes reach opposing conclusions about the religious activities of women. Wendy O'Flaherty has characterized the Rig Veda—the earliest collection of Aryan religious hymns, dating from about 1300 to 1000 B.C.E.—as "a book by men about male concerns in a world dominated by men [, and] one of these concerns is women." O'Flaherty divides the hymns about women into conversation hymns and marriage hymns. Both types are concerned with sexual rejection of the female by the male, but the marriage hymns end happily whereas the conversation ones frequently do not (O'Flaherty 1981). Julia Leslie thinks that some Vedas were composed by women who performed sacrifices to the Aryan gods and probably wore the sacred thread that signified their knowledge of the Vedas and participation in sacrifice, the key religious act of the Aryans. She argues that three of the most notable hymns composed by women are Ghosa (Rig Veda [RV] X, 39 and 40), Apala (RV VIII, 80), and Visvavara (RV V, 28). Apala sacrificed to Indra, the god of storms and monsoons, telling him, "Drink thou this Soma [a still-unidentified ritual liquid which may be translated literally as "moon juice"] pressed with teeth, accompanied with grain and curds, with cake of meal and song of praise." Visvavara offered sacrifice to Agni, the fire god and a major rival of Indra, pouring oil on the fire and chanting, "Thy glory, Agni, I Adore, Kindled, exalted in thy strength" (Leslie 1983: 91–92). Thus the evidence is mixed on the status of women in Vedic religious practice (Upadhyaya 1974).

Recently Giti Thadani has argued that patriarchal interpretations of the Vedas have obscured the existence of dual feminine principles that reflect non-generative sexual relationships and the shift from woman-focused to male-dominated cosmologies. This transformation is encapsulated in the rape of Usha, the goddess of dawn and light, by the warrior god, Indra, who eventually slays his enemy, Vitra, and his enemy's mother. Thadani also reinterprets the sexual relationship between Urvashi, a goddess associated with the moon and mares, and the human Pururvas as signifying that lesbian* feminine desire brings immortality while heterosexual relationships are progenitive and lead to mortality (Thadani 1996). Thadani then delineates the evolution of legal and social constraints on female sexuality, especially female sexual desire for and pleasure with other women.

The later Vedic period, dated from the eighth century B.C.E. onward, witnessed a series of religious challenges to the Vedic emphasis on sacrifice and the growing dominance of *brahmans*. These revolts paralleled key economic changes in Aryan society. After a gradual shift to agriculture, Aryans, who increasingly intermarried with indigenous peoples, had the surplus wealth to support cities and new forms of political organization. Religious activity shifted from the worship of many gods to the contemplation of one underlying principle or truth and an emphasis on personal self-control. The Upanishads, which were collections of treatises composed by professional philosophers between 700 and 500 B.C.E., explored metaphysical issues and introduced the concepts of karma (that actions have consequences) and transmigration (that essences or souls move through many existences). By the sixth century B.C.E., Buddhism and Jainism provided heterodox means of achieving release from the cycle of transmigration through individuals following the correct life.

All of these traditions allowed for religious participation by women. In the first Upanishad (the Brhadaranyaka), Gargi Vacaknavi,

---

*The use of the term "lesbian" in the South Asian context is problematical. In Euro-American sources, "lesbian" began to be used to describe relationships between women from the early twentieth century. These bonds might include social, sexual, economic, and/or political support. During the 1970s feminist analysis of lesbian relationships emerged. It viewed lesbianism as including attraction to sexual relationships with women, differentiated between homosociality, which focused on social bonds, and homosexuality, which might encompass genital sexual relations, and critiqued heterosexuality as perpetuating patriarchy. By the 1980s feminists of color questioned the culture-specific character of lesbianism. South Asia seems to present a powerful challenge to Western feminist scholarship, since South Asian women traditionally have significant and complex relationships with women in both their natal and marital families. Empirical research on the existence and nature of sexual attraction and relationships among women in South Asia is limited and theoretical analysis has not produced alternative terms for this relationship.

a woman who represents the tradition of Vedic scholarship among women, debated publicly at the court of King Janaka around 600 B.C.E. Her bold questioning of the concept of negative regression pushed a male counterpart to enunciate the basic doctrine that the ultimate principle or supreme *Brahman* may be defined only by negatives (Findly 1985). In Jainism women were allowed to pursue the monastic life that was considered the preferred life-style. The two major Jain sects, however, had differing views on whether women could attain *moksha*, release from the cycle of transmigration. The Digambara monks, who argued that total renunciation included nakedness, held that women could not achieve *moksha*; the Svetambaras, who viewed renunciation as an interior process or condition, saw such external factors as the absence of clothes as irrelevant and allowed that women might reach *moksha*. Both sects agreed that women were not to accept nudity as a monastic practice (Jaini 1990).

The Buddha sanctioned the establishment of Buddhist nunneries, although reputedly with reluctance and after imposing eight special rules that subordinated nuns of any age to male monks. Reinforcing this unequal status, the Buddha reportedly said that his doctrine would last only half as long in India since he permitted the ordination of women. Within the Theravada or orthodox Buddhist tradition that dominated in India, Buddhist nuns were known as teachers of Buddha's *dharma* to other women and are given credit for composing a text known as the *Therigatha* or *The Psalms of the Sisters* (Gross 1993; Horner 1975; Willis 1985). But Buddhist laywomen were perhaps more honored. Both queens (such as the unnamed aunt of Virpurisadata, an Ikshvaku king in the Andhra region of south India during the early third century C.E.) and courtesans (such as Ambapali) were celebrated for the construction of *stupas* that housed Buddhist relics, temples, and monasteries. Nancy Falk has attributed this seeming Buddhist preference for laywomen over nuns to the Buddhist effort to reconcile itself with the indigenous Hindu *dharma* that emphasized women's role as childbearers. Thus laywomen fulfilled their basic *dharma* as mothers and still benefited the Buddhist community through their patronage (Falk 1980).

During the last centuries of the pre-Christian era, the more orthodox Vedic tradition associated with the *brahmans* began to impose restrictions on women as well as lower social groups (Jamison 1996). The sacrificial tradition had become more complex, and knowledge of the Vedas and their ancillary literature was increasingly limited to male *brahmans*. There was a growing social differentiation as the four major *varna* of Hindu society became more bounded; intermarriage across *varna* boundaries was proscribed; and a hierarchy with *brahmans* at the top evolved. By the late Vedic period women were gradually assigned the same low status as *sudras*, forbidden to wear the sacred thread, and prohibited from autonomous participation in sacrificial rituals. In an intensive analysis of Vedic texts on *srauta*—sacrificial rituals that involved offerings of food (including ghee, or clarified butter) and flowers on auspicious occasions, such as the occurrence of the new and full moons—Frederick Smith has delineated the reduction of the role of the wife of the male sacrificer. This role was considered necessary for the sacrifice to be efficacious for the generation of children, the continuation of the cosmos, and the spiritual release of the sacrificer and his wife. The sacrificer's wife participated only in connection with male officiants and performed subsidiary functions that resembled household tasks such as caring for implements that the husband alone used. Increasingly, however, male attendants displaced her at critical moments in the ritual, especially those that celebrated her sexuality and procreative powers (Smith 1991). Werner Menski claims that a shift of marriage rituals, from a family-dominated ceremony to one gradually conducted by a priest who transforms the polluting substance of the bride's blood and its potentially destructive attributes into auspiciousness, is another indication of changing conceptions of women (Menski 1991).

Various hypotheses have been proposed to explain these growing restrictions on the rights and status of women in the religious sphere. Altekar, probably the most influential historian on the subject, links them to the growing prevalence of men taking non-Aryan—that is, *sudra*—wives, who had to be excluded from sacrifices because of their impurity. Thus it was a small step to exclude all wives from such religious participation (Altekar 1978). Uma Chakravarti and Kumkum Roy attack Altekar's focus on non-Aryan wives as racist and call for more attention to the "connections between women's status and their participation in productive activities, both as producers and as controllers of production" (Chakravarti and Roy 1988b: WS–8). Leslie argues that the eroding right of women to religious education and sacrificial participation is related to the effort to restrict such activities to the first three *varna*, to the redefinition of the masculine noun as specifically excluding women, and to the restricted ability of women to own property—one qualification of the performer of sacrifice (Leslie 1983). Smith proposes that perhaps such Vedic rituals were divided along gender lines, and because men compiled the Vedic texts, they recorded only male rituals (Smith 1991: 43–44).

More recently, scholars have begun to explore how social, political, and economic changes from the eighth to the third centuries B.C.E. created a structural framework that increasingly subordinated women in spheres besides religion. The shift from hunting-gathering and pastoralism to an agricultural economy and growing urbanization after 800 B.C.E. supported the development of class and caste divisions. As occurred in most patriarchal societies, Indian men sought to control female sexuality, which was responsible for social reproduction, to ensure patrilineal succession to property (Bhattacharji 1991; Chakravarti 1993a). However, Indian society is distinctive for its restraints on female sexuality in order to maintain the ritual purity associated with high-caste status. Using prescriptive texts produced by *brahmans* and literary narratives including epics, Uma Chakravarti traces the evolution of "brahmanical patriarchy," which she defines as "a set of rules and institutions in which caste and gender are linked, each shaping the other, and where women are crucial in maintaining the boundaries between castes" (Chakravarti 1996b: 9). Women came to be controlled through socialization in the ideology of *stridharma* (the ideal of wifely fidelity), through laws and customs which sanctioned familial control of women (including physical punishment), and finally through kings, who had authority to punish wayward wives. Thus a combination of consent and coercion secured the compliance of upper-caste women in the perpetuation of caste divisions that subordinated them while they simultaneously provided spiritual and material rewards (Chakravarti 1993a).

Kumkum Roy elaborates on the connection between political and social changes in fostering the subordination of women. The emergence of monarchy from around 700 B.C.E. onward at the expense of other forms of political association was intimately related to the process of social differentiation and the privileging of the *grha*, a form of household organization that "was characterized by patriarchal control, exercised on the procreative powers of the wife, and over productive resources, which were ideally transferred from the father to the son(s)" (K. Roy 1994: 300). The *raja*, or ruler, supported the *grha* since it was easier to negotiate with single heads of households than corporate groups. In turn the head of a household seeking dominance was strengthened by the external support of the *raja*. This patriarchal hierarchy in the public and private spheres was then reflected in and legitimated by the increasing marginalization and control of women's sexuality and procreative powers in religious rituals. Although this scholarship has significantly deepened our understanding of the complexity of the condition of women in ancient India, its dependence on sources produced by *brahmans* means the condition of lower-class/caste women in all areas of India and of elite women in non-Aryan controlled regions remains obscure.*

THE MAURYAN EMPIRE, 320–ca. 185 B.C.E.

The Mauryan empire was the first major centralized state in India and would remain the most extensive example of such a political achievement until the great Mughal Empire, founded in C.E. 1526. For this period there exists a major secular source on the legal rights of women. Chandragupta Maurya, the founder of the dynasty, was reputedly assisted by Kautilya, a *brahman* prime minister, who provided the core of the *Arthasastra*, a handbook of statecraft that is often compared to Machiavelli's *The Prince*. This compendium documents that women had property rights to *stridhan*, the gift made to a woman at the time of her marriage by her parents and afterward augmented by her husband. *Stridhan* was usually jewelry, which among many cultural groups was a convenient way of carrying surplus wealth, but could include certain rights to immovable property. Eight forms of marriage were also recorded. They ranged from the most prestigious, involving the gift of a virgin daughter (*kanyadan*) by her father to another male, to the least honorable, which was marriage by abduction while the woman was incapacitated through sleep or intoxication. Marriage was both a secular and sacred institution. Widows could remarry, although when they did so, they lost rights to any property inherited from their deceased husbands. There is also evidence that women were active in such public economic activities as wage-labor in state-owned textile factories as well as serving as temple dancers, courtesans, and court attendants. There is little information on lower-class women other than some comments on laboring women and the need to give work as spinners to such disadvantaged women as widows and "defective girls" (*Arthasastra* 1992).

The *Arthasastra* may be seen as the practical guide for dealing with women, but ideal prescriptions for women were also being formulated during the extended period from the Mauryan empire to the Gupta empire (ca. C.E. 320-540). These centuries, the classical era of Hindu culture, were marked by the effort of cultural elites to classify and codify all branches of knowledge. From 300 B.C.E. to around C.E. 300, three great prescriptive sources evolved. The first two are the

---

*In addition to the works cited within this section, see Basham 1954; Leslie 1986, 1991b; O'Flaherty 1980; Paul 1985.

epics of the *Mahabharata*, an accumulation of almost one hundred thousand verses that relates the conflict between two sets of cousins, the Kauravas and Pandavas, for control of the fertile territory north of Delhi, and the shorter *Ramayana* that has as its centerpiece the ideal king, Rama, and his ideal wife, Sita (Jayal 1966). The third is the Laws of Manu, which belongs to the category of *dharmasastras*, or legal treatises.

The *Mahabharata* has a cast of hundreds who display a fascinating, human combination of high virtue and moral weakness. Several women characters play key roles in the action that portrays the futility of war and the desirability of peace as turbulent Aryans gradually expand into the Indo-Gangetic plain and fight over land, which became more valuable as it was utilized for agriculture rather than cattle herding. Draupadi is probably the best-known woman, but she is also the most atypical of the prescriptive literature that was emerging simultaneously. She was beautiful, educated at her father's court, able to make an independent choice of husband at a *swayamvara* (a convocation of suitors), and the wife of the five Pandava brothers. Since polyandry was not practiced in Aryan society, her marriage reflects the influence of tribal customs from possibly the foothills of the Himalayas, which provided a boundary to Aryan expansion. A bold personality, Draupadi is usually held up as a strong woman who remained modest.

Other women characters from the *Mahabharata* recur in Indian culture, generally refashioned in a more submissive form. In the epic bearing her name, Shakuntala, the daughter of an ascetic, is a simple young woman who meets a prince hunting near her father's forest retreat. When he proposes marriage by mutual consent (a form of marriage that did not require religious rites), she audaciously asks that her son be the heir to his throne. After their marriage, the husband returns to his princely occupation and forgets his promise. Several years later Shakuntala boldly travels to the prince's kingdom and demands that he recognize their son as his heir. In his highly acclaimed play entitled "Shakuntala and the Ring of Remembrance," Kalidasa, the great Sanskrit dramatist of the Gupta period, transformed Shakuntala into a shy, submissive girl who becomes a symbol of love in separation.

Neither Draupadi nor Shakuntala were deemed ideal wives (Sutherland 1991a, 1991b), but Sita, of the epic *Ramayana*, came to be idolized in that role in renditions by Valmiki in Sanskrit compiled possibly around 200 B.C.E. and by Tulsidas (1532–1623) in Hindi. In these two re-tellings Sita is extolled for her chastity, obedience, loyalty, and faithfulness to her husband despite a remarkable series of trials, including an unjust accusation of infidelity by her husband's subjects. Following her husband from a royal palace into a difficult forest exile, she remains faithful despite temptation by an evil king and agrees to an ordeal by fire, at her husband's request, to prove her sexual purity. Even after emerging unscathed from the flames, Sita is forced into forest exile, this time with her sons. She eventually secures recognition of her sons as the legitimate heirs of Rama, and then returns to Mother Earth, where she had been born in a furrow. These events and images are transmitted across time and space through countless oral performances and re-tellings and, during the 1980s, in a television series that dominated the Sunday morning schedule of millions of Indians.

Several scholars, including Romila Thapar and A. K. Ramanujan, have pointed out that there are many different versions or tellings, including Buddhist and Jaina ones, of the Ramayana story (Coburn 1995; Ramanujan 1991; Richman 1991; Thapar 1987). In these alternatives, such as the Tamil telling by Kamban (about the ninth to tenth century C.E.), Sita is portrayed as angry, willful, and so powerful that the fire of her chastity (*karpu*) burns up Agni, the Vedic fire god, during her fire ordeal (Shulman 1991). In Telugu songs sung by both *brahman* and non-*brahman* women, female characters enjoy agency, and occasionally even revenge; the blemishes of male characters are subtly observed; and the tensions within joint families are poignantly delineated (Narayana Rao 1991). Still Sita continues to be celebrated as the ideal woman along with Savitri, the wife who skillfully bargained to rescue her husband from Yama, the god of death. Subsequent myths tend to ignore Savitri's intelligent bargaining and to emphasize instead her capacity for endurance and her offer to exchange her own life for that of her husband.

There is also a Tamil epic, *Cilappatikaram* or *The Tale of an Anklet*, from about C.E. 450, in which the primary heroine is Kannaki, a devoted wife. She suffers the loss of her husband to a beautiful courtesan but still offers to sell a gem-encrusted ankle bracelet to help him repay his debts. When he is beheaded because of an unjust accusation, Kannaki, in her wrath, destroys by fire the city where her husband met his fate. Eventually the goddess Parvati pacifies Kannaki, who is reunited with her husband in heaven. The husband suffers because of bad actions in an earlier life, but Kannaki demonstrates the power of chastity and righteousness.*

*In addition to the works cited in this section, see M. Chandra 1973; Erndl 1991; Shattan 1989.

THE TARNISHED AGE OF THE GUPTAS, C.E. 320–540

Although its territorial extent was about half of that of the preceding Mauryan empire, the Gupta empire is seen as the classical age of Indian culture because of its literary and artistic accomplishments. It was the great age of Sanskrit poetry and drama, of sculpture, and of cave temple architecture as seen at Ajanta and Ellora in western India. The available sources yield relatively little enlightenment about specific women, whether elite or non-elite. But some information on elite women as a category comes from the *Kamasutra*, a manual about the many ways to acquire pleasure, a legitimate goal for Hindu men in the householder, or second stage, of their lives. Women were expected to be educated, to give and to receive sexual pleasure, and to be faithful wives. Courtesans were trained in poetry and music as well as the skills of sexual pleasure and were esteemed members of society. Since visual artists in India usually remained anonymous until the twentieth century, we know nothing as yet about the possible role of women in the creation of the great sculpture and painting of the Gupta period.

Another secular view of women is provided in such popular stories as the collection *Tales of Ancient India*, translated by J. A. B. van Buitenen, which portrays faithful wives, decadent Buddhist nuns, and scheming courtesans. Courtesans were the one category of women who were likely to be educated and sometimes were known to have spoken Sanskrit. A prime example of a noble-hearted courtesan was Vasantasena, the heroine of the "The Little Clay Cart," a popular play in Sanskrit ascribed to Sudraka (ca. C.E. 400). Vasantasena is an exception to the stereotype of greedy courtesans in her willingness to sacrifice her jewelry for her lover. She, however, achieves respectability only by becoming his wife. The other major dramatic female heroine of classical Indian literature is Shakuntala, who is now represented as a docile young woman who yearns for her distant lover in Kalidasa's "Shakuntala and the Ring of Remembrance." Barbara Stoler Miller (1984: 36) has emphasized how Kalidasa's play seeks a balance between duty and passion. Only after the king and Shakuntala have learned to control their passions is the king able to recognize Shakuntala as his wife and the mother of his son Bharata, who will rule his empire. Once again a sexually active woman must be contained with the bounds of marriage.

Legal Rights of Women

The legal rights, as well as the ideal images, of women were increasingly circumscribed during the Gupta era. The Laws of Manu, compiled from about 200 to 400 c.e., came to be the most prominent evidence that this era was not necessarily a golden age for women. Through a combination of legal injunctions and moral prescriptions, women were firmly tied to the patriarchal family, much as Confucianism in China enjoined women to observe the three obediences to father, husband, and son. The following extracts from the Laws of Manu (translated by Wendy Doniger, 1991) reflect the effort of the brahmanical elite to restrict the legal independence of women, to establish the moral subordination of wives to husbands, and to socialize women in self-control.

> In childhood a woman should be under her father's control, in youth under her husband's, and when her husband is dead, under her sons'. She should not have independence. (Chap. 5, verse 148, Doniger, p. 115)

> A virtuous wife should constantly serve her husband like a god, even if he behaves badly, freely indulges his lust, and is devoid of any good qualities. (Chap. 5, verse 154, Doniger, p. 115)

> A virtuous wife who remains chaste when her husband has died goes to heaven just like those chaste men, even if she has no sons. (Chap. 5, verse 160, Doniger, p. 116)

> But a woman who violates her (vow to her dead) husband because she is greedy for progeny is the object of reproach here on earth and loses the world beyond. (Chap. 5, verse 161, Doniger, p. 116)

> A wife, a son, and a slave: these three are traditionally said to have no property; whatever property they acquire belongs to the man to whom they belong. (Chap. 8, verse 416, Doniger, p. 196)

> The bed and the seat, jewellery, lust, anger, crookedness, a malicious nature, and bad conduct are what Manu assigned to women. (Chap. 9, verse 17, Doniger, p. 198)

> The appointment of widows is never sanctioned in the Vedic verses about marriage, nor is the remarriage of widows mentioned in the marriage rules. (Chap. 9, verse 65, Doniger, p. 205)

> A thirty-year-old man should marry a twelve-year-old girl who charms his heart, and a man of twenty-four an eight-year-old girl; and if duty is threatened, (he should marry) in haste. (Chap. 9, verse 94, Doniger, p. 208)

Thus the Laws of Manu severely reduced the property rights of women, recommended a significant difference in ages between husband and wife and the relatively early marriage of women, and banned widow remarriage. Manu's preoccupation with chastity reflected possibly a growing concern for the maintenance of inheritance rights in the male line, a fear of women undermining the increasingly rigid caste divisions, and a growing emphasis on male asceticism as a higher spiritual calling (Chakravarti 1993a). Although the Laws of Manu represent the effort of *brahmans* to impose their ideals as the dominant practice in Hindu society, the authority of these injunctions would be modified in practice by the continuity of customary laws, especially in geographically isolated areas where tribal customs prevailed (Chaki-Sirkar 1984). The impact was also limited in areas where the Sanskritic tradition was relatively weak, such as Kerala, where matrilineal descent among the Nayars prevailed until the late nineteenth century.

In India the legal right of women to hold property is further differentiated by the presence of two legal traditions, the Mitsksara and the Dayabhaga, which regulate the division of property among Hindus. In the Dayabhaga school, which is unique to Bengal, widows have the right to inherit *stridhan* and a limited estate in property (which they may use but not alienate) as members of joint families. These provisions might be one factor accounting for *sati* becoming more prevalent in Bengal than in other parts of India. The Mitskara school that prevails throughout the rest of India awards ownership in property at birth to males in a joint family; widows have very restricted rights to inherit. For example, in this school, a widow may inherit property only after her last great-grandson; by then, she would be long deceased (S. N. Mukherjee 1982).

Prescriptive Roles for Women

During this era we have increasing evidence of the practice of child marriage, the physical seclusion of women, and *sati*. The age of women at marriage during the early Vedic period seems to have hovered around sixteen, but by the Gupta period there appeared to be a growing preference for younger brides, as indicated in the Laws of Manu. Early marriages were designed to protect the family honor and to maintain caste divisions that were deemed dependent on the chastity of women. Although such marriages were not consummated until puberty, the residence of young brides in their in-laws' home possibly meant that it was easier to engender loyalty to the patriarchal extended family unit among girls of six or seven than among mature women of sixteen. Early marriages might also have been an unconscious response to high rates of maternal mortality and low median ages.

The Laws of Manu acknowledge the same eight forms of marriage as outlined in the *Arthasastra*, but they discount as base the last four, which involved some individual initiative (P. Mukherjee 1978). *Kanyadan*, or the gift of a virgin daughter in marriage, emerges as the act through which a man gains the greatest spiritual merit. This transaction, which occurs between two males, the father and the groom, also ensures the immortality of the groom's line by providing heirs and enables the young girl to achieve auspiciousness as a mother. Once the marriage of daughters becomes a spiritual necessity, fathers make many concessions in order to effect such transactions. Women become objects to be given, and marriage is their only acceptable social status. *Kanyadan* also establishes a unidirectional flow of gifts from the bride's family to the groom's family, which reflects the lower status of the giver to the receiver (Fruzzetti 1982; Van der Veen 1972). These gifts come to be crudely labelled dowry. In her work in progress on the concept of dowry, Veena Oldenburg claims that these gifts are also evidence of the love of parents for daughters and their desire to care for them throughout their lives. Others emphasize that dowry might be related to the inability of women to inherit property, the need for men to gift their daughters to a restricted pool of men, and increasing hypergamy (Bhattacharji 1991).

Sati is a term of multiple meanings and the focus of much debate (Hawley 1994; Nandy 1975). It may refer to a virtuous woman so dedicated to her husband that she burns to death on his funeral pyre; it may refer to the act of self-immolation itself; or Sati may be a goddess (Hawley 1994). The first recorded instance of *sati* as the act of self-immolation is not certain, but Elizabeth Leigh Stutchbury (1982) notes that Greek chronicles relate that in 316 B.C.E. the wife of Meteus, an Indian general who died fighting Antigonus, burned herself and that this custom prevailed among the "Kathia" tribe of Punjab. The origin of *sati* as a social custom has been ascribed both to the Aryans and to later tribes migrating from Central Asia into South Asia. In the *puranas*, a class of religious literature that dates from the fourth to the fourteenth centuries C.E. and that integrates indigenous myths with elaboration of the Vedic tradition, Sati is first mentioned as a goddess. She is the initial wife of Lord Siva and commits self-immolation because of an insult to her God-Husband. Many scholars argue that she does not serve as the inspiration for the ritual suicide of a widow, since she died before her husband (Dehejia 1994; Kinsley 1986; Oldenburg 1994). The practice of *sati* is most dramatically associated with higher-caste Rajputs, especially *kshatriyas*, and *brahman* groups in Bengal, but it was also known in other areas, including south India. Vociferous debate over the religious basis for this practice arose first in the early nineteenth century, when the British moved to outlaw the custom, and more recently after an alleged *sati* occurred at Deorala near Jaipur, Rajasthan, in September 1987 (Hawley 1994). Orthodox supporters of the custom continue to cite passages from the *dharmasastra* that enjoin a wife to be *sati*, or pure, and claim that death unequivocally ensures purity and prevents a woman from becoming an inauspicious widow. Opponents of the practice rely on the same passage and argue that to be *sati*, or chaste, does not require a widow to commit suicide.

The tradition gradually developed that through *sati* a widow would earn thirty-five million years of bliss for her deceased husband and for herself and would bring auspiciousness for three to seven generations for her marital and sometimes even her natal family. A *sati* stone erected on the site of a widow's immolation was a perpetual reminder of the woman's sacrifice and a popular place of pilgrimage (Courtright 1994).

There is little evidence about the function of *sati* from the widow's viewpoint or that of orthodox Hindus who promoted the practice. Many of the most-quoted accounts of *sati* have come from foreign observers, beginning with Ibn Battuta in the thirteenth century, through the French physician François Bernier in the seventeenth century, to numerous British officials and travelers in the nineteenth century. Their accounts have portrayed instances of both voluntary and involuntary *sati* and have been the filter for women's voices. Scholars have tended to relate *sati* to the increasingly low status of women in general and widows in particular and to the desire of high castes to maintain their ritual purity. As widows were increasingly held responsible for their husbands' death, *sati* became a form of personal expiation. For the woman it also presented an escape from the harsh life prescribed for a widow, in which she was to wear white *saris* and no jewelry, eat only one meal daily, and avoid all celebratory occasions, especially weddings, since she was considered inauspicious. Some commentators have labeled such an existence "cold *sati*." However, the research of Anand Yang (1989) has revealed the use of *sati* by lower-caste/class women in Bihar long after the death of their husbands as an honorable means of suicide in desperate economic situations. *Sati* also brought spiritual and social prestige to a woman's family and in-laws as well as economic relief, since they did not have to provide for the widow who could no longer remarry.

Women in Religion

Although the prescriptive literature of the Gupta period urged sub-missiveness, chastity, and even ritual suicide for women, the religious literature was more ambivalent about women. The *Devi-Mahatmya*, a Sanskrit text dating from the fifth or sixth century c.e. that is part of the Markandevya *purana*, codified the non-Aryan, non-Vedic tradi-tion of seeing the ultimate principle of the universe as feminine (Coburn 1985). This cult of envisioning the divine as feminine is known as Saktism in India. It is associated with the tribal groups and possibly the Indus Valley and Dravidian cultures that existed in India prior to the coming of the Aryans and that survived on the geographical fringes of the Aryan conquests. The emergence of the *Devi-Mahatmya* reflects the continuing dynamic interaction between Aryan and non-Aryan traditions.

Stated in the simplest terms, these female personifications of the divine are usually portrayed in three major incarnations. Most ba-sic is the Mother Goddess, known simply as Devi, who protects and nurtures her devotees. The second form is Durga, a goddess created by male gods and given all their weapons in order to destroy Mahisa, the buffalo demon, whom the gods in their separate existences can-not contain. Durga, whose historical origin appears to be non-Aryan, first appears as unmarried around the fourth century c.e. and was frequently associated with mountains that fringed Aryan society. Al-though her aggressive and bloody behavior violate prescriptive Hin-du norms for the ideal woman, Durga eventually is married to Siva both in her form as Durga (where she becomes the focus of Durga Puja, a major autumn festival in Bengal) and as Parvati, a goddess who exists to bring the ascetic Siva into marriage and settled society (Kinsley 1986; O'Flaherty 1982). The most horrific and potent form of the female goddess is Kali, the black goddess of Time and Destruc-tion, who is created to help Durga in her battle with Mahisa. Kali is represented initially as autonomous but is eventually viewed as a con-sort of Siva, the powerful god of the Hindu trinity who destroys the world when its inhabitants can no longer observe their caste duty or *dharma*. Wearing a necklace of skulls as symbolic of her destructive power, Kali has a long tongue that licks up the blood of a demon who creates new beings from drops of his blood. She embodies the disor-derliness of life as well as the existence of death (Kinsley 1986).

These images of female goddesses have been analyzed as evidence of the male fear of female potency, as the embodiment of ambiguous attitudes toward women and female power in a society that was becoming increasingly sex-segregated, and as symbols of female empowerment. For the historian they reflect the re-emergence of female goddesses from pre-Aryan cultures and the continuing interaction among the multiple cultures eventually labeled "Hinduism" by outside observers (Brown 1990; Harman 1989; Hawley and Wulff 1996; Kinsley 1986; Larson et al. 1980; Maury 1969; Pintchman 1994). The divine as female also re-emerged in a new form of Buddhism.

In northeastern India during the Pala period, from the eighth to the twelfth centuries c.e., Tantric Buddhism evolved in reaction to institutionalized Buddhism (Kinsley 1997). This new form of Buddhism taught that enlightenment can be achieved through everyday activities and that if one is spiritually prepared, the senses, desire, and sexual intimacy can be significant aspects of the spiritual journey. Many scholars of Tantric Buddhism have characterized women as ancillary in male yogic practices leading to enlightenment. But Miranda Shaw claims that women were equal to men as divinities, teachers, and devotees. There were women Tantric teachers: for example, Bhiksuni Lakshmi of Kashmir (ca. tenth to eleventh centuries c.e.), who developed a widely practiced fasting ritual to achieve purification and salvation (Shaw 1994), and women who organized ritual communal feasts which included sacramental food and drink, spiritual instruction, and music and dancing as means to a higher understanding of the ultimate reality. Shaw argues that men and women are complementary and equal partners in the esoteric practice of Tantric sexual union through which both women and men seek "passionate enlightenment" by surrendering to egoless freedom (Shaw 1994: 140–78). Shaw's creative scholarship, combining textual analysis and anthropological fieldwork with extended discipleship with a Tantric guru (teacher), reveals the possibilities of feminist reinterpretation of religious traditions. By discarding Western categories of body and soul, sublimation and passion, her analysis attempts to understand words, actions, and deities within the more fluid conceptual diagrams of the religious tradition being studied.*

SPREAD OF ISLAM INTO SOUTH ASIA, c.e. 1000–1700

Many Indian scholars claim that the major impact of Islamic culture on Indian women came from the imposition of purdah or veiling. This view maintains that Muslim women were veiled and that Hindu men began to veil their wives first as protection from possible dis-

---

*In addition to the works cited in this section, see O'Flaherty 1980; Orr 1994, 1999.

honor by Muslim men and then as a form of social prestige. There is, however, growing evidence that elite Indian women were confined to inner apartments in palace complexes as early as the Gupta period. Such physical seclusion seems to be related to growing legal restrictions (for example, the Laws of Manu); to an emphasis on the importance of female chastity for the maintenance of family honor; and to the prestige resulting from the withdrawal of women from economically productive, public activities (Vasantasena in "Little Clay Cart"). With the arrival of Turkish Muslim conquerors in the late twelfth century, the physical seclusion of Hindu women intensified. Peasant women moved around in the public sphere from economic necessity and probably covered their heads or faces with the ends of their *saris* or a separate piece of cloth when they passed a stranger.

Purdah and the Zenana in South Asia

Whatever the origins of the adoption of purdah and physical seclusion in South Asia, the rules of its observance were significantly different between Hindus and Muslims. In Hindu households physical distance was practiced toward certain related males, especially fathers-in-law and older brothers-in-law; toward non-related males; and toward older females (Varsha Joshi 1995). Among Muslims physical seclusion was practiced primarily toward non-related males.

Hanna Papanek (1973), Doranne Jacobson (1976), and Sylvia Vatuk (1982) have explored the function of purdah in contemporary India. In the absence of historical research on the practice of purdah in the earlier centuries, we must extrapolate backward from their conclusions and from modern literary sources. Purdah means "veil" but also refers to the physical seclusion of women in a particular section of a dwelling, either the *harim* (Arabic) or the *zenana* (Persian). In Western literature on women in the Middle East and South Asia that portrayed women as the exotic, these two terms conjured up images of women who are sexually exploited by their husbands or overlords. Current research establishes the *harim* or *zenana* as a women's abode where various activities take place: sexual relationships, reproduction of the family, socialization of children and daughters-in-law, and management of the household. There is very limited scholarship on lesbian relationships within the *zenana* (Thadani 1996), but Ismat Chugtai (b. 1915) wrote a short story, "The Quilt," during the 1940s that depicts a lesbian relationship between a woman in the *zenana* and her maidservant, as seen through the eyes of a child.

Most social science research portrays the *zenana* as an arena of power in which the widest authority was vested in the oldest female, usually the wife of the eldest male. Sylvia Vatuk (1987) has pointed out that Indian women may be legally under the authority of fathers, husbands, and sons, but on a daily basis they experience cultural norms being implemented by mothers, mothers-in-law, and daughters-in-law. Trying to explain why women impose practices which might oppress other women, Hanna Papanek states that "where women perceive no alternatives to living by these norms, they may see no other way to assure a good life for their children than by continuing to enforce inequality" (1990: 181). The tenderness of mothers toward their daughters but also their frustration at social responsibilities is poignantly captured by Ambai (C. S. Lakshmi, b. 1944) in her Tamil short story, "Fall, My Mother." Here a woman despairs over the difficulty of arranging a marriage for a daughter whose darker skin is deemed less desirable because of the high status accorded to fair skin (Arkin and Shollar 1989). This preference for fair skin is reflected in the term *varna*, which means "color" and designates the four all-India categories of Hindu society. Thus the *harim* or *zenana* might be an arena of oppression for women by women as well as men, but it also provided protection and support for women as well as ambivalent opportunities to exercise power.

Despite the practice of purdah among Muslims, the Turkish Muslims who established the Sultanate at Delhi in 1206, which was continued by various dynasties until 1526, illustrated the manner in which tribal social customs mediated religious precepts. Within ruling Turkish Muslim families, women sometimes acquired a literary education, were physically active, and frequently influenced political events. Among Turkish sultans, succession was a major problem because tribal supporters had the right to approve a ruler, and multiple wives produced numerous contenders. There was no established pattern of primogeniture, and so women in a sultan's *harim* were particularly active in pressing the claims of their sons to succession.

Women in Politics

Shah Turkan, the wife of Iltutmish (ruled c.e. 1210–1236), who had risen from slave to sultan, promoted the fortunes of her incompetent son, Rukn-ud-din. However, Iltutmish wanted his more capable daughter Razia declared his successor. Insubordinate Turkish nobles in Delhi soon imprisoned the ambitious queen-mother and her decadent son and accepted Razia as the lesser evil. She ruled from 1236 to 1240. Ibn Battuta, the noted chronicler of Sultanate India, recorded that she appeared in public without a veil, was known as a good horsewoman, and led her troops into military battle. She was murdered in a fight with rebellious nobility who challenged the authority of any Delhi sultan who attempted to exert authority over these rapacious supporters.

In 1526 Babur established the great Mughal dynasty that gradually extended Muslim political power over much of India. Women continued to play key roles in imperial politics. His mother and her relatives frequently advised and monetarily assisted Babur during the twenty years he spent wandering in Central Asia before he settled in India. Gulbadan, one of Babur's daughters, has left a sympathetic account, entitled *Humayanama* (1902), of the reigns of her father and his less decisive son, Humayan, which includes an insightful portrayal of the rivalries and friendships among the imperial women (Gulbadan Begam 1902; Godden 1981). The most powerful and controversial Mughal woman was Nur Jahan (1577–1645), a thirty-four-year-old Persian widow who married the emperor Jahangir and was an active participant in imperial tigershoots and hunting expeditions (Findly 1993). She managed to have her father and brother appointed to key political offices, thereby strengthening the Persian element at the Mughal court, and served her husband as an important conduit of requests. Many of her enemies and later scholars have portrayed Nur Jahan as the strong-willed manipulator of Jahangir.

Chakravarti and Roy have argued that women who ruled in their own right, such as Razia, or acted on behalf of their husbands, such as Nur Jahan, receive negative treatment because they seem to threaten the established order. Women who have preserved power for their sons, however, are deemed praiseworthy (Chakravarti and Roy 1988b: WS–7). But Mughal imperial women played a variety of roles. Mumtaz Mahal (ca. 1593–1631), the wife of Shah Jahan, was the woman for whom the Taj Mahal was built when she died after the birth of her fourteenth child. Not only was she much loved by her husband, she was also knowledgeable about major policies and keeper of the imperial seal, which authenticated imperial decrees. Her daughters were also active in imperial politics. Jahanara Begam (ca. 1613–ca. 1683), the eldest, was in charge of her siblings after her mother's death, supervised the imperial household, and became a political confidante of her father and her brother, Dara Shikoh. Interested in literature and music, Jahanara also shared a commitment to Sufism with Dara. When their brother Aurangzeb triumphed in a bloody war of succession in 1658, Jahanara chose to accompany her father, Shah Jahan, into his prison in the Red Fort in Agra, where he had a room with a view of the Taj Mahal. After her father's death in 1666, Jahanara was permitted to move to her own house outside of the fort and remained one of the few people able to speak frankly to Aurangzeb (Misra 1967; Pal 1989; Richards 1993).

Some elite Hindu women had political roles both within and outside the Mughal Empire. As in many cultures, foreign conquerors used marriage to consolidate political power. Akbar sought to reaffirm his alliance with Rajput opponents by marrying a daughter from the princely house of Amber-Jaipur. Their son was the emperor Jahangir. There are also instances of Hindu women ruling in kingdoms on the periphery of the Indo-Gangetic plain in medieval Orissa, Kashmir, and Andhra. Cynthia Talbot has recovered the life of queen Rudrama-devi, of the Kakatiya dynasty, based at Warangal in the Telangana region of Andhra. Having no son, Rudrama-devi's father appointed her as his heir and ruled jointly with her for several years. Confronted with external and internal military challenges upon the death of her father in 1261, Rudrama-devi became a heroic ruler, leading her troops to victory, possibly even dying in battle in 1289. Talbot emphasizes how the gap between a female ruler and a patrilineal society that ideologically excluded women from political power was bridged by Rudrama-devi's construction of a public male persona. Although she is physically represented in sculpture as a woman, she assumed a male name and wore masculine clothing while fulfilling both the warrior role of the male ruler and the patronage activities of a female consort (Talbot 1995).

Six centuries later Rani Lakshmi (ca. 1835–1858) of Jhansi, another warrior queen, was even more widely mythologized in the historical record. When her husband—the ruler of Jhansi, a small state in central India—died in 1853, the British refused to recognize an adopted heir and declared that Jhansi had lapsed to British control. For the next four years the Rani tried to secure the rights of her adopted son, and eventually she joined the revolt of Indian troops in 1857. An effective organizer and an inspirational leader, she actively participated in military engagements against the British forces and died from wounds received in battle. At her death General Hugh Rose, her British opponent in that last battle, declared that "here lay the woman who was the only man among the rebels." The Rani quickly emerged as the Indian equivalent of Joan of Arc. There was a significant difference in that Lakshmi was first a wife and a mother and Joan was a virgin, but both became potent female symbols of courageous resistance and national identity. Lakshmi's military exploits were echoed almost a century later in 1943, when Subhas Chandra Bose named a female volunteer contingent of his Indian National Army (based in Singapore and fighting with the Japanese against the British) the Rani of Jhansi Regiment. The Rani of Jhansi thus combined the traditional maternal role of working for the rights of a son with renown as a military leader, thereby being an incarnation of the Hindu goddesses Durga and Parvati (Lebra-Chapman 1986).

Women and Religious Practice

By the arrival of the Muslims, Hindu women were excluded from education and participation in the Sanskritic tradition of Hinduism. However, they increasingly found emotional sustenance in *bhakti*, or devotional Hinduism. Krishna, an incarnation of Vishnu, first enunciated the essence of *bhakti*, the approach to god through pure love, in the *Bhagavad Gita*. *Bhakti* saints, frequently from lower castes, propagated this message through vernacular poetry from the third century onward in south India and from the tenth century in north India. They attracted wide audiences among dispossessed groups such as *sudras*, untouchables, and women; extraordinary individuals among these followers became *bhakti* poets and saints themselves (*Manushi* 1989; Ramanujan 1982). The earliest recorded female *bhakti* poet and saint is Antal (ninth century C.E.), whose Tamil poems laud the surrender of female devotees to Krishna (Dehejia 1990). Antal was not an exception in south India. Mahadevi Akka (twelfth century C.E.), a worshipper of Siva, is especially well-known among the several female *bhakti* poets composing in Dravidian languages. After reputedly abandoning an earthly husband, Mahadevi Akka described her adulterous love-making with Siva in earthy, erotic poems composed in popular Kannada (Ramanujan 1973). Revathi Krishnaswamy has argued that Mahadevi Akka's explicitly sexual relationships with Siva, the divine lover who is clearly superior to any human lover, satirized religious and social conventions and provided an emotional and psychological refuge for other women bound in unsatisfactory sexual relationships (1993).

The most famous woman *bhakti* poet is Mirabai (ca. 1498–ca. 1546), whose life and legacy have been interpreted in diverse ways (Mukta 1994; Pandey 1965). According to biographies from the seventeenth and eighteenth centuries, Mira was born in 1498 in a Rathor Rajput princely family in Marwar (Jodhpur) state in western Rajasthan. After being educated in such womanly arts as music, dance, and manners and such manly arts as hunting and sports, Mira was married in a political alliance to a son of the powerful Sisodia Rajput, Rana Sanga of Mewar (Udaipur) state. Her marriage was far from ideal: she refused to worship the family goddess, declared herself a devotee of Lord Krishna (an incarnation of the god Vishnu), and possibly eschewed sexual relations with her husband. When he died, she rejected the pleas of her in-laws to bring honor to their family by performing *sati*. Instead she revealed her marriage to Lord Krishna, abandoned her marital family, and spent the remainder of her life in the public sphere singing hymns of praise to Krishna. Because there are no contemporaneous written sources documenting her life, John Hawley has questioned whether Mirabai ever existed as a historical person, while acknowledging the potency of the devotional poetry that has been ascribed to her (Hawley and Juergensmeyer 1988).

Feminist scholars have sought to analyze the impact of Mira's example and poetry on the lives of Hindu men and women through the subsequent centuries. On the one hand, Kumkum Sangari, working from a close textual analysis of Mirabai's poetry, concludes that "Mira represents a struggle, not a victory" (Sangari 1990: 1551), since her willing sacrifice of herself to Krishna as a husband-god reinscribed elements of patriarchy. Thus Mira deviated from her subject position as widow in the human social order to become a servant of a husband-god who could control both her female body and the social body described as female. Her self-willed servitude is seen as claiming rights and reciprocity, while acknowledging duties. Sangari grounds her analysis of Mira's poetry in the temporal context of sixteenth-century Rajasthan, where Rajput men imposed norms of brahmanical patriarchy, such as strict control of female sexuality, on Rajput women as part of their efforts to create powerful states and a high-status ritual identity (Sangari 1990). On the other hand, Parita Mukta combines extensive participant-observer fieldwork in contemporary Gujarat and Rajasthan with textual analysis to conclude that Mira provides a means by which lower-class men and women in Gujarat and some areas of Rajasthan can express and criticize their oppression. She reveals how in the region of the former princely state of Mewar-Udaipur, Mira is not publicly worshiped, how her name is a synonym for "promiscuous woman," and how she can function as a symbol of lower-class resistance to current Rajput efforts to fortify high-status identity (Mukta 1994).

The corpus of poems that can be attributed reliably to Mirabai is relatively small, although tradition ascribes numerous poems and hymns to her (Alston 1980). Mirabai's life not only demonstrates the acceptance of women as *bhakti* saints, but also illustrates how *bhakti* provided an outlet for women who chose to defy social conventions and family injunctions. At the same time her life story reveals the dominance of certain patriarchal patterns. The Muslim counterpart in India of the *bhakti* movement was Sufism, a mystical movement that preached the need for direct union with God. Although the existence of female Sufi *shaikhs* who led Sufi orders in South Asia is uncertain, there were female Sufi saints whose spiritual perfection was manifested in extraordinary events (Rizvi 1978). Calling their path of proclaiming a passionate love for God as one beyond the Qur'an, Sufi *shaikhs* served as spiritual and psychological advisers to their devotees, and women found an emotional and religious refuge in their advice. In the context of Bijapur, a Muslim kingdom in the Deccan, Richard Eaton (1974, 1978) has described Sufism as the folk religion of Islam. It reflected the dualism of Islam, with men going to the mosques while women went to the *dargahs* or tombs of Sufi *shaikhs*, where they made votive offerings of flowers or food. In Bijapur and elsewhere in India, women, both Muslim and Hindu, made pilgrimages to these *dargahs* to seek cures for infertility or resolution for family disputes. Such religious activity reflected the intense pressure that all Indian women felt to produce sons as well as the absence of perceived, fixed boundaries between the two religions among lower-class women. Sufi *shaikhs* also taught the basic doctrines of Islam, and their call for love of God through vernacular poetry, which included lullabies and work songs, at times contained sentiments similar to those in the poems of the *bhakti* saints (Eaton 1974).

Although some historians have viewed the establishment of Islam in India as an unmitigated disaster for women because of the increasing prevalence of purdah, the period from 1000 to 1700 still witnessed diverse conditions for women. Hindu women had access to the *bhakti* tradition, which softened the strictures of socially circumscribed roles and even allowed some to evade them altogether. Eaton's work on Sufism indicates that the boundaries between Hindu and Muslim cultures remained permeable for many women. In the political sphere, women at the Sultanate and especially the Mughal courts participated in the imperial decision-making process as mothers, wives, sisters, and daughters (Tirmizi 1979). Our knowledge of non-elite women during this period remains scanty.*

ARRIVAL OF EUROPEANS, 1600–1800

When the British first arrived in India in the early seventeenth century, they were humble petitioners for trade privileges at the opulent court of the Mughal emperor and the lesser establishments of semi-

*In addition to the works cited in this section, see Hiebert 1985.

autonomous kings on the periphery of the Mughal empire. These merchants viewed their position in India as transitory, came without British women, and frequently entered into loose sexual alliances with indigenous women, some of whom were *nautch* (a type of Indian dance) dancers, reputedly easily available for sexual relations. As the control of the Mughal Empire declined, many Indian rulers as well as the English East India Company attempted to extend their territorial base and political power. By 1765 the English Company emerged as a regional Indian state with its assumption of the right to collect revenues in Bengal.

During the intensified political conflict of the second half of the eighteenth century, several Indian women emerged as major political leaders. Stewart Gordon has outlined how three successful women rulers (Ahilyabai Holkar, of Indore; Begum Samru, the widow of an Austrian military adventurer who had an estate east of Delhi; and Mamola Begam, of Bhopal) proved their legitimacy and gained the favor of their subjects. Each of these women had been trained by her father or husband, acted authoritatively (including leading troops in military battles and rendering decisive legal settlements), and created supportive new elites. Ahilyabai built a "performance-oriented, non–kin-based bureaucracy" in Indore, and the Begams of Bhopal would control their state until 1947 (Gordon 1978: 296).

WOMEN IN COLONIAL SOUTH ASIA, 1800–1947

Reform Movements and Indian Women

By the early nineteenth century the British sought to legitimize their military seizure and retention of political power in India with moral and legal principles. Claiming that the position of women reflected the level of development of a civilization, British officials constructed a hierarchy based on the status of women. They expressed the dominant Western view that Indian women had an inferior position compared to European women and placed British women at the apex of their paradigm and Indian women toward the bottom. The British then reasoned that the oppressed condition of Indian women was a strong moral justification for British imperial rule in India. British policies, they argued, would "improve" the lives of Indian women. Christian missionaries and Western-educated Indian male social reformers soon joined British officials in this venture. Evangelical missionaries wanted to implant Christian ideals in Indian family life to provide a support system for religious conversion. Claiming that they were stung by British accusations, inspired by such Western social philosophers as Jeremy Bentham and John Stuart Mill, and aroused by concern about the fate of their female relatives, Indian male reformers focused on education and legal reforms (V. Mazumdar 1976). Some Indian reformers used Western liberal arguments, but many maintained that they were merely restoring to women the rights and status that they had enjoyed in a vaguely defined golden age before the arrival of foreign—either Muslim or British—invaders (Chakravarti 1989; Forbes 1976; S. N. Mukherjee 1982; Shridevi 1965). The major objectives of these male reformers were to promote education for girls, later marriages, a prohibition on *sati* and female infanticide, and the relaxation of purdah restrictions on the physical mobility of women.

The British construction of the role of women within Indian society and the actual benevolence of transferring Victorian ideals, which were constricting English women, to the diverse cultures of India has been increasingly interrogated. Some historians consider British efforts at reform of women's position as attacks on the masculinity of Indian men and on their control of their family relations (Engels 1983; Sinha 1989). Mrinalini Sinha has decisively argued that British officials as well as Indian nationalists, both reformers and revivalists, would utilize the bodies and minds of Indian women to legitimate their claims to power and to buttress their masculinity. British officials felt challenged in the metropole by British feminists and new sexual identities, and Indian nationalists were impugned by British rhetoric about Indian (especially Bengali) effeminacy, and by tentative efforts of some Indian reformers to encroach on patriarchal control of female sexuality (1995). Other scholars view Indian male reformers as more interested in refuting British charges of being personally unworthy to govern themselves and in co-opting a nascent women's movement than in instituting basic social changes that would alter patriarchal social relations and increase the autonomy of women (S. Banerjee 1989a; G. Pearson 1981). While both British and Indian leaders claimed to be the more dedicated champions of Indian women, neither group consulted extensively with Indian women about how they perceived their own needs.

More recently there has been a lively debate on how attitudes and conceptions of the ideal Indian woman changed during the late nineteenth century and into the twentieth century. Partha Chatterjee (1989) has argued that Indian male nationalist reformers had resolved the women's question to their own satisfaction by the end of the nineteenth century. Culture was divided into the world, where colonial power dominated, and the home, a refuge from humiliation in the world, where Indian men retained the authority accorded to them by a patriarchal, extended family structure. The home and especially women embodied the spiritual values of Indian (conceived implicitly as Hindu) culture, which must be preserved at all costs from colonial legislative and physical encroachment. Encouraging conjugal marriages, widow remarriage, and secular education for girls, liberal Indian reformers fostered a domesticity combining Victorian qualities of cleanliness and punctuality with Indian ones of modesty, humility, and self-sacrifice that effectively subordinated women within a patriarchal nuclear family (Bannerji 1993; P. Chatterjee 1992; Chakrabarty 1994; T. Sarkar 1992). This new domesticity as practiced by their women became a sign of the cultural superiority of the emerging Bengali middle class, who sought dominance within Indian society through their mediation between the Indian masses and the British colonial power. Reforms in the condition of women were closely linked not only to nationalism but also to class and religious agendas (Amin 1996b; N. Desai 1957; Devji 1994).

After distinguishing between liberal, reformer nationalists and revivalist nationalists, Tanika Sarkar (1993b) asserts that the latter subjected Hindu women to a reconfigured Hindu patriarchy as part of their nationalist project to resist colonial intervention. Revivalist nationalists defined a new Hindu conjugality based on a love freely given as opposed to coerced submission of women as wives. They continued to valorize early marriage, a ban on widow remarriage, and even the ultimate self-sacrifice of *sati* as evidence of Indian, but essentially Hindu, superiority to the militarily and politically dominant colonial power. Indian women were fashioned as icons of Indian nationalism. Once again male reformers and revivalist nationalists contested their visions of the Indian nation on the bodies of Indian women without paying much attention to women's concerns. Women's voices in folk tales, published works, and public actions disputed these male constructions of Hindu conjugal life.

Two examples are illustrative. In her autobiography first published in 1868 and subsequently revised and enlarged in 1897, Rashsundari Debi (ca. 1809–ca. 1900), an upper-caste Bengali, recounted the emotional trauma and hard work of her conjugal life as trials which she was able to bear only with divine assistance. As Tanika Sarkar relates, Rashsundari "had it both ways. She proclaimed her predicament to the whole world through the print-medium and she reserved the image of the self-effacing Hindu wife who suffers her deprivations with smiling forbearance" (T. Sarkar 1993a: 46). In western India, Tarabai Shinde (ca. 1850–ca. 1910) wrote a powerful critique of Indian male reformers who exhorted Indian women to conform to ideals that they themselves did not follow and ascribed faults to Indian women that they themselves exhibited in greater depth. Rosalind O'Hanlon, who has translated Tarabai's commentary, claims that "as caste groupings searched for new ways of expressing identity and social distinction . . . the public conduct of their women became paramount, and was judged according to standards increasingly brahmanical in character" (1994: 12). Thus Indian women might be subjected to reified patriarchal standards in an attempt by their male relatives to achieve dominance as an emerging middle class within Indian society as well as to undergird Indian male efforts to challenge British legitimacy. It can be argued that, in both Bengal and western India, nationalists sought to reconstitute a Hindu patriarchy that "subordinated women more firmly to caste and family authority, and consigned them to a domain of 'private life' supposedly outside politics" (ibid.). At the same time, Indian nationalists shifted their image of Indian women from that of companionate wives to that of mothers. Increasingly Indian women personified the nation conceived of as Mother India at the same time they were exhorted to produce healthy sons who would defend Mother India from rapacious colonialists (J. Bagchi 1990; T. Sarkar 1987; S. Sen 1993).

During the last decades of the nineteenth century, as revivalist nationalists sought to screen women's issues from the purview of the state, British women and Indian women emerged as participants in the social reform movement which focused on the condition of Indian women. Initially British women portrayed themselves as benevolent catalysts for a women's movement in India. Recent scholarship is more ambivalent about British feminists who in their efforts to participate in British politics and to further professional careers as publicists, teachers, and physicians constructed oppressed, helpless Indian women whom they could uplift, educate, and cure. Women ranging from Mary Carpenter to Josephine Butler functioned as maternal imperialists, although by the twentieth century some, such as Margaret Cousins, preferred the image of universal sisterhood (Burton 1994, 1995; Candy 1994; Jayawardena 1995; Nair 1992; Ramusack 1981a, 1990a). As Indian male reformers shifted their interest from social issues to political protest from the 1870s on, Indian women gained more authority in reform organizations devoted to improving the condition of Indian women (Borthwick 1984). Reform movements focusing on Indian women operated through three types of institutions: government, private associations, and the press. Several distinct groups utilized these institutions to promote particular reforms: British officials, Christian missionaries, Indian male reformers, British female reformers, and Indian female reformers.

British officials, Christian missionaries, and some Indian reformers urged the government of India to enact legislation to "improve" the condition of women. In many cases such legislation revealed sharp disjunctures between rhetoric and action and had contradictory results for Indian women. Initially reformers sought legislation ostensibly to preserve the lives of women through prohibitions on *sati* and on female infanticide. In 1813, the year in which missionaries were first permitted legally to proselytize in British territory, the British Company issued a regulation defining *sati* as legal if various criteria were met, mainly that the *sati* had been voluntary (Mani 1989). During this same period evangelical missionaries and Indian reformers, principally Ram Mohan Roy (1774–1833)—the distinguished Bengali *brahman* reformer who founded the rationalist Hindu reform society of the Brahmo Samaj in Calcutta in 1828—supplied data indicating that the practice of *sati* was not strictly enjoined in Hindu scriptures. Roy was an early representative of the Bengali *bhadralok*, a high-status group known as "gentlemen" or "the respectable," who provide many leaders of religious and social reform movements. In a persuasive analysis of the discourse around *sati*, Lata Mani highlights how Indian proponents and opponents of legislation prohibiting *sati*, as well as its British supporters, accorded primacy to the injunctions of Hindu scripture. All three groups of men claimed to be the most authentic interpreters of Hindu tradition that was being defined on the site of Hindu women (Mani 1986, 1989, 1998). Few reformers spoke about women as the subjects of *sati* who might be exercising some agency. After extensive lobbying, Lord Bentinck, the governor-general (who was himself influenced by Jeremy Bentham) issued the regulation prohibiting *sati* in 1829 regardless of whether it was voluntary or involuntary (V. Mazumdar 1978). Legislation explicitly prohibiting female infanticide was not put into effect until 1870. It proved to be easier to apply the prohibition on *sati*, which was a quasi-public ceremony, than on female infanticide, which was a private act. The next phase of legislation attempted to change the negative status of daughters and widows.

Widows of the first three *varna*, but especially *brahmans*, had been prohibited from remarrying. *Sudra* and "untouchable" women were generally allowed to remarry. Uma Chakravarti has described how the Peshwa government in eighteenth-century Maharashtra forbade certain lower castes from implementing a prohibition on widow re-marriage in order to undercut possible claims from lower castes for high caste status (1996b). After he had observed the harsh fate of young widows in Calcutta, Ishwar Chandra Vidyasagar (1820–1891) lobbied intensively, and the British passed the Widow Remarriage Act of 1856, which allowed Hindu widows to remarry legally but stipulated that remarried widows forfeited any rights in their deceased husbands' estates.

The Widow Remarriage Act illustrates the mixed impact of legal reform designed to support social reform. On the one hand high-caste, especially *brahman*, widows gained the right to remarry. On the other hand lower-caste widows who had been able to and did remarry ac-cording to their customary law now came to forfeit their rights to the property of their deceased husbands upon remarriage. Thus lower-caste women lost a right they had formerly enjoyed. As Lucy Carroll argues, the British courts served to extend *brahman* and Hindu norms through all areas of Indian society (Carroll 1989). The British, how-ever, endorsed customary law where it reenforced its political con-trol. In Haryana, the Hindi-speaking area of Punjab nearest to Delhi, Prem Chowdhry relates how the British supported the custom of *karewa*, whereby a widow would remarry a male relative, usually a younger brother, of her deceased husband in order to prevent parti-tion of landed property. Although many widows had no choice in such remarriages, the British encouraged them to prevent land frag-mentation and resultant social unrest (Chowdhry 1994, 1995). Thus British legislative reforms usually were not based on the needs ar-ticulated by Indian women, who tended to be viewed as objects of legislative reforms rather than its subjects. Since the British would not actively nurture widow remarriages and Indian reformers failed to mobilize the support and participation of women in this campaign, the impact of this legislation was limited (Bandyopadhyay 1995).

Probably the most famous, yet ultimately ineffectual, legislative action of the colonial state made allegedly to improve the condition of women was the Age of Consent Act of 1891 (Kosambi 1991). It raised the age of consent to sexual relations for married and unmar-ried girls from ten to twelve and thereby provided a statutory foun-dation for later marriages. As many more women entered early mar-riages than committed *sati*, this legislation had potentially much wider impact. However, once again "authentic" Hindu traditions and now both Indian and British masculinity within the imperial structure would be defined on the bodies of Indian women. Mrinalini Sinha

(1995) reveals how British official proponents and Indian revivalist opponents of the Consent Act, especially in Bengal, sought to "revitalize" colonial masculinity by reaffirming patriarchal control over women's sexuality. In their desire to retain Indian male control over Indian female sexuality, British officials and Indian nationalists, both reformers and revivalists, collaborated to limit the terms of the Age of Consent Act and its implementation. For example, the British included a marital rape clause in this Consent Act in India, which implied that Indian men could not be trusted to refrain from sexual relations with an underage wife, although marital rape was excluded from the Consent Act in Britain, implying that British men could be so trusted. The British in India never enforced the marital rape clause; hence they reaffirmed Indian men's control of Indian women's sexuality.

Another example of the willingness of the colonial government to extend the authority of Indian men over Indian women's sexuality is the inclusion of a provision for the restitution of conjugal rights in the Civil Procedure Code in 1859. In Hindu tradition, a wife could refuse to live with a husband if she were willing to accept a denigrated image, live with her natal family, and never remarry. Under Christian ecclesiastical law as transplanted to India, a husband could sue his wife for restitution of *his* conjugal rights (Engels 1989). Rukhmabai (1864–1955) in Bombay (later Mumbai) became the most celebrated example of how British judges might enforce new legal bases for Indian men's control of women's sexuality. Married at eleven, Rukhmabai remained at her natal home, did not consummate her marriage, and was educated. By 1884 she refused to join her husband because of his lack of education and dissolute life. He filed a suit to obtain his conjugal rights. Although a lower court found in her favor, a higher court affirmed her husband's claim and sentenced her to six months imprisonment if she did not return to her husband. Eventually her husband agreed to a settlement, and they were divorced in 1888. Subsequently Rukhmabai pursued a medical degree in London and had a lengthy and productive medical career in India. Her case demonstrates how laws had negative effects on the lives of Indian women as well as extended patriarchal control over them in new ways (Anagol-McGinn 1992; Burton 1998; S. Chandra 1996, 1998; Kosambi 1996b).

In contrast to the debates over legislation on *sati* and widow remarriage, some Indian women emerged in the public sphere as propagandists supporting Rukhmabai and the Age of Consent legislation. They wrote, organized meetings that passed resolutions of support for Rukhmabai and the legislation, and formulated petitions. In Bengal women were less active, possibly because of greater orthodoxy or because the effort to reaffirm colonial masculinity, for which male control over female sexuality was seen as integral, erased the public participation of Bengal women from the record (Sinha 1995). In western India, women's voices emerged more forcefully. In an analysis of Maharashtrian women's participation in the campaign against child marriage during the 1880s, Padma Anagol-McGinn (1992) contrasts women's critiques with those of men. These women attacked early marriages, arguing that they psychologically damaged women by denying them education and freedom of expression and were the source of significant unhappiness because of a lack of conjugal compatibility. Men opposing early marriages emphasized economic consequences, mainly poverty, and eugenic factors, especially the physical degeneration of Indians. Thus women evolved a gendered assessment of the impact of early marriages on themselves and sought significant changes, such as adult marriages, while men expressed concern about economic, medical, and political consequences. Men did not consider the impact of these marriages on women and were anxious to maintain male dominance within slightly later marriages. Ultimately the British government of India could avoid extensive prosecutions for illegal consummation of early marriages under the 1891 act since there was no legal requirement for the registration of births. Because governmental intervention had such limited impact, changes in public opinion would be essential in order to achieve reforms.

Associations created to improve the physical and social conditions of life for Indian women constituted the second vehicle for reformers (Thakkar 1997). Indian male reformers tried to influence other Indian males through several means. D. K. Karve (1858–1962), a *brahman* educator from Poona (later Pune), founded a home for widows and used personal example, marrying a widow (Karve 1963). Kandukuri Virasalingam (1848–1919) campaigned in south India for widow remarriage and female education. Others, such as M. G. Ranade (1842–1901), who founded the Prarthana Samaj in Poona, provided organizational support systems for those willing to commit themselves to these new practices. At the same time, because of family opposition the widowed thirty-two-year-old Ranade declined to marry a widow and married Ramabai, an eleven-year-old virgin. Muslim men were not involved in campaigns around *sati* or the promotion of widow remarriages, since the former was a practice specific to particular Hindu groups and widow remarriage was not prohibited in Islam. However,

Muslim men, particularly those of the emerging middle class, formed associations to promote female education so that their daughters and wives could become companionate wives and wise mothers (Amin 1995, 1996a, 1996b; Minault 1997, 1998).

Gradually British and Indian women took the initiative to influence public opinion and values. They ranged from educated widows such as Pandita Ramabai (1858–1922) in western India to middle-class Bengali women such as Dr. Kadambini Ganguly (1861–1923), the first Western-educated woman physician in Bengal (1886), who belonged to the Brahmo Samaj, a rationalist Hindu reform society in Calcutta. Educated in Sanskrit literature by her *brahman* parents at home, Pandita Ramabai remained unmarried until twenty. Widowed a few years later, she campaigned for the education of women, testifying before the Hunter Commission in 1881 about the need for education of women; she went to England and the United States for advanced studies, wrote a book (*The High-Caste Hindu Woman*), and became a questioning convert to Christianity (Burton 1997; Chakravarti 1996a, 1998; Kosambi 1988, 1992). Upon her return to India in 1889, she opened a home in Poona for widows, the Sharada Sadan, which provided education and employment for widows and other women in need. By 1900, she had established another institution at Kedgaon that housed over two thousand women and children who attended school or received industrial training and subsequently engaged in industrial production. Pandita Ramabai is just one prominent example of an Indian woman who established institutions that supported amelioration in the life-styles of other Indian women. Her fund-raising tours in the United States and her writings on Indian women were an important counterbalance to British women's constructions in their journals (Burton 1994, 1997; Nair 1992) of Indian women as oppressed sisters who needed to be uplifted.

The writing of Indian women (as opposed to male reformers) on women's issues began in the mid-nineteenth century. Besides autobiographical works and tracts such as those by Rashsundari Debi and Tarabai Shinde, women increasingly wrote in journals circulated both privately and publicly. In Bengal Indian women contributed to male-edited journals such as the *Bamabhodhini Patrika*, which Brahmo reformists started in 1863 and continued until the 1920s as a forum for women's issues. In 1898 women founded *Antahpur* (in Bengal *antahpur* designated the *zenana* or women's section of a house), which was "edited and conducted by the ladies only" (Borthwick 1984; Murshid 1983). In the Hindi-speaking area of the United Provinces, Rameshwari Nehru (1886–1966) began *Stree Darpan* in 1909 (Borthwick 1984; Talwar 1990). Since *Antahpur* was in Bengali and *Stree Darpan* was in Hindi, both publications spoke to Indian women directly and further contested the right of British women to represent Indian women. Similar Indian-language journals edited by Indian women existed in Bombay, Gujarat, and Madras (later Chennai), but copies of them are even more elusive than of *Antahpur* and *Stree Darpan*. Two Muslim women wrote voluminously for women's journals edited by their husbands: Muhammadi Begam (ca. 1878–1908), in Lahore, and Waheed Jahan Begam (1886–1939), in Aligarh. Their journals (*Tahzib un-Niswan* and *Khatun*, respectively) and others were generally in Urdu, the lingua franca of upper- and middle-class Muslims throughout India, and their contents ranged from articles on the advantages of education for women, to household hints, to creative writing (Minault 1998). In the twentieth century, English-language journals edited by women, such as the *Indian Ladies Magazine* and *Stri Dharma* (which had Telugu and Tamil supplements) that were published in Madras, would have greater impact on British views and a wider all-India circulation but probably at the cost of less exposure among Indian women not literate in English.

Reformers sought to have Indian men, and secondarily Indian women, accept the legitimacy of certain practices and opportunities for women—for example, education for women or moving out from physical seclusion—through journals, books, public speeches, personal example, and associations. Propaganda rather than formal legislation was the initial step, because no secular laws prohibited such activity by women (Hossain 1988). Christian missionaries, Indian religious reformers, and British officials were the first groups to promote the education of Indian girls. They shared common objectives and all wanted to educate Indian women so that they would be more suitable companions for their educated husbands and better mothers for their sons (Forbes 1996). Religious educators, whether Hindu, Muslim, or Christian, wished to deepen Indian women's understanding of their specific religious traditions so that they would preserve the family commitment to religion during stressful periods (Kishwar 1989; Minault 1998).

By the middle of the nineteenth century, three educational formats were available for Indian women: home education, *zenana* education, and formal schools. In the beginning, home education was the most popular, since fathers could teach daughters, brothers could teach sisters, husbands could teach wives, or a hired tutor could visit the home. Although this system of education could be sporadic, it could also be extremely effective when both parties were willing and able to participate. In her autobiography, tellingly entitled *Himself*, Ramabai Ranade (1862–1924) reported that education by one's husband often exposed the wife to being shunned by her female in-laws (Ranade 1938). Uma Chakavarti (1993b) has emphasized that the young Ramabai Ranade was overtly challenging the power relationships within the female domain of the household, especially the position of widowed sisters-in-law who might have slowly acquired some degree of authority because of their age and their brother's affection. Another evocative image of such exclusion appears in Satyajit Ray's film of Rabindranath Tagore's novel, *The Home and the World*, where the heroine, Bimala, educated by a governess at the behest of her husband, is mocked by her widowed sister-in-law.

Christian missionaries pioneered *zenana* education in which a missionary woman would visit periodically a small group of girls, usually relatives or friends from the surrounding neighborhood, in the women's quarters of the home of an upper-class Hindu male. The education consisted of reading, writing, and simple arithmetic necessary to oversee household accounts, but it also included compulsory Bible stories and sometimes needlework. There was a story that H. C. Mullens "opened the *zenanas* at the point of her embroidery needle" when an Indian male invited her to teach his wife this art after admiring the slippers for her husband that Mullens was decorating (Forbes 1986: WS–3). Many Indians criticized *zenana* education because of its evangelical content and a few well-publicized conversions to Christianity.

Education in schools would have been the most efficient method in terms of resources and curriculum, but it encountered strong social constraints. Going out to a public place meant abandoning or modifying purdah, relaxing purity/pollution rules by Hindus, and trusting professional teachers. Many students also left school after a few years because of early marriages. These factors meant that schools for women had major difficulties in attracting and retaining students. Founded in 1849 by a member of the governor-general's council, Bethune College in Calcutta was the first secular school for girls. Missionary schools date from the mid-nineteenth century; Isabella Thoburn, an American Methodist, took in pupils in 1869 in Lucknow and laid the foundation for the first Christian college for Indian women (Flemming 1989; Jayawardena 1995). Two other major Christian women's colleges that also had high school divisions were Kinnaird College in Lahore (Maskiell 1984) and Madras Christian Women's College in Madras. Many Indian men were concerned about the threat of conversion to students in these schools, and so Indian social reform associations founded their own institutions beginning in the 1870s. In Calcutta, the Brahmo Samaj supported the Victorian Institution and the Brahmo Girls School; the Arya Samaj set up the Kanya Mahavidyalaya in Jullunder, Punjab (Kishwar 1989); and schools for Muslim girls were established at Aligarh in 1906, Calcutta in 1911, Lucknow in 1912, and Jullunder in 1926 (Amin 1995; Minault 1982, 1983, 1998). These institutions were to educate girls to become suitable wives for Western-educated Indian males and capable mothers for a new generation of children, much as education in nineteenth-century Japan sought to produce good wives and wise mothers. In India the impact of these institutions was limited to a small elite. The Indian census recorded a literacy rate for women in any language of 0.7 percent in 190l and 6 percent in 1946.

Even so, Indian women who pursued literary, especially English-language, education were viewed with ambivalence by both elite and non-elite men, at least in Bengal. For many elite Bengali men, Western-educated "modern" women were a challenge to the moral purity of the home, which Bengali nationalists deemed the essential site of Indian cultural superiority in contrast to the material superiority of British in the world. Tanika Sarkar argues that "the archetypal evil woman . . . was not the immoral or the economically independent one, but one who, inspired by modern education, has exchanged sacred ritual objects (the conchshell bangle, the ritually pure fabric, sindur) for foreign luxury ones" (1992: 222). Morality and consumption were related, and Western education of women threatened both the nationalist project and patriarchal control in the family. It also apparently challenged Bengali concepts of masculinity, since many men wanted to deny the kind of education they had had to their female relatives. Thus by the late nineteenth century many Bengali men sought to confine the education of *bhadramahila*, or respectable women, to religious epics and child care. Although they shared their husbands' acceptance of Victorian ideals about the importance of women's roles as housewives and mothers in the conjugal household, Bengal women writing in journals used these functions as the rationale for access to a broad education. They needed a worldly education in order to prepare sons for the world (Bannerji 1991). This debate over the appropriate education for women was largely confined to the emerging middle class, but the backlash against women crossed class boundaries.

In his study of folk culture in Calcutta in the nineteenth century, Sumanata Banerjee demonstrates that English-educated men and women were ridiculed in popular songs but that women were special targets, as in the following song:

> Housewives no longer have any sense of shame,
> They always dress in Anglicized fashion.
> They've left cooking and are fond of knitting.
> Wearing gowns they move around,
> Singing all sorts of nonsense.
> Men have lost their power,
> They're tied to their wives' apron-strings.
> It's a world of women all around.
> (Banerjee 1989b: 111)

Such mockery was not limited to oral culture. English-educated Bengali women were depicted visually as henpecking their husbands in *pat* paintings, which were also known as Kalighat paintings because these boldly outlined watercolors on cheap paper were produced around the Kalighat temple devoted to Kali, the patron goddess of Calcutta. Kalighat paintings, which had religious and secular subject matter, included images of both educated wives and prostitutes striking men or leading them like sheep (Archer 1971; Banerjee 1989b). These popular stereotypes indicated that non-elite men were as concerned as elite men about challenges to patriarchal power. But there are also *pat* paintings with Bengali *bhadralok* beating women (Archer 1971).

Professional and Economic Opportunities for Indian Women

The practice of purdah in India restricted women from active participation in the public sphere, but it provided the foundation for some professional work among certain categories of Indian women. The two major areas were education and medicine. Originally, older Indian men were teachers of Indian girls before the age of puberty. Then missionaries and unmarried Western women such as Annette Ackroyd Beveridge (1842–1929) became the dominant component of the educational effort, but they were expensive. Gradually Indian women, widows, Christian converts, and a few Brahmo women entered the teaching profession as the schools expanded. Some Brahmo women taught because their marriages were relatively late, but salaried work was not considered suitable for either single or married Indian women until much later in the twentieth century. Still, teaching girls was a socially acceptable form of employment for those few women who preferred or were socially constrained to remain single (Southard 1984).

Indian women dominated the practice of medicine on Indian women, particularly in the specialties of obstetrics and gynecology. Western women were an early and continuing presence, initially associated with missionary groups. Clara McSwain, a graduate of the Women's Medical College, Philadelphia, arrived in India in 1870 and was soon followed by a long series of American and British women physicians, of whom the most prominent would be Ida B. Scudder, who founded a major medical complex at Vellore in South India. (Americans came first since women were not admitted to British medical schools until the 1870s.) The usual manner for Indian women to consult with Indian male medical personnel was through intermediaries, including the use of a doll to indicate parts of the body that were experiencing pain. Even that contact was rare for most women. Childbirth was the major event in a woman's medical history, and there she was attended by a midwife (*dai*), who was considered an "untouchable" because she had to handle the ritually polluting afterbirth. Some Bengali Brahmo women studied modern means of delivery with an emphasis on sanitation and assisted relatives and friends.

The Madras Medical College was the first such institution in India to admit women, in the winter of 1875. Four women entered, and they graduated in 1878. By 1890, women had secured admission to medical colleges or schools (the latter offering a less prestigious degree than the former) in Bombay, Calcutta, Agra, and Lahore. As Western medicine developed in India, obstetrics and gynecology became female-dominated, in contrast to the West, where male gynecologists gradually usurped the position of female midwives (Kosambi 1996a; Ramanna 1994). In 1884 Vicereine Harriot Dufferin founded a charitable institution, colloquially labeled the Dufferin Fund, which aimed to provide medical relief for *purdahnishin* women and, incidentally, employment for British and Indian women physicians and nurses in its various hospitals (Arnold 1993; Burton 1996; S. Guha 1996; Lal 1994). Racial discrimination pervaded the Dufferin Fund, as Indian women physicians were generally relegated to smaller hospitals and lower pay scales (Forbes 1994b). In turn these Indian women, known as "lady doctors," joined the chorus of voices that denigrated the techniques of midwives. While traditional midwives remained the sole medical resource for the vast majority of Indian women, elite women turned to Indian women practitioners who transmitted Western medical practices to them (Forbes 1994a).

Relatively little scholarly attention has been paid to the economic activity of women in colonial India, so our knowledge is sketchy. Some elite women were *zamindarins*, or landholders, in Bengal and had vary-ing degrees of authority in managing their estates. But most elite wom-en who worked for pay were in the professions that catered to other women, such as education and medicine. Among non-elite women there were a variety of occupations, including paid sexual labor. Co-lonial imperatives (such as the desire to limit military expenditures by providing prostitutes rather than wives for non-commissioned British troops) and economic changes (such as the growing pauper-ization of agricultural workers) shaped the practice of prostitution. Women who needed to provide for their own and their family's sur-vival migrated to military cantonments where they were subjected to callous government regulation or urban centers where they provided sexual service for both lower- and upper-class Indians (Ballhatchet 1980; Dang 1993; Levine 1994). In a distinctive category were cour-tesans, most prominently those in Lucknow, who were preservers of an elite culture and entrepreneurs who owned property and paid taxes (Oldenburg 1984; 1990; Post 1987). Increasingly, however, Indian nationalists portrayed most women who worked outside of the house-hold as prostitutes. Characterized as willful and sexually deviant, pros-titutes became the binary opposite of the good, chaste, and submissive Hindu woman whom the revivalist nationalists idealized as spiritual and physical mothers (Archer 1971; R. Chatterjee 1993).

Women were employed in some manufacturing areas, most no-tably jute (Engels 1996), match-making, and textiles (Forbes 1996). In Bombay the number of women employed in the textile industry peaked in 1926 and declined during the 1930s. The worldwide de-pression triggered retrenchment of the work force, and rationaliza-tion of production to reduce costs led to increased mechanization. This in turn eliminated many of the unskilled jobs, such as winding and reeling, done by women. New social benefits such as maternity leaves made women seem more expensive than male workers, and an emerging focus on the role of women as reproducers of the labor force also channeled women into the home (R. Kumar 1983). In Ben-gal the proportion of women in the work force declined sharply as modernized industries expanded because of the preference for male workers and social constraints on female mobility; the number of women workers was also low in the agricultural sector (N. Banerjee 1989; M. Mukherjee 1995).

The vast majority of non-elite women were employed in the ag-ricultural sector (K. Kumar 1989). The most visible women agricul-tural laborers worked on tea and coffee plantations. Janaki Nair has revealed how low birth and high death rates on tea plantations led to some minimal reforms, including short maternity leaves for women workers and measures to encourage family units in which women would reproduce at a higher rate (1996b). But women laborers were generally hidden from statistical surveys. In many areas they processed food, such as cleaning or grinding grain within the *zenana*, or worked in the fields on an irregular basis. Their male relatives and the colonial officials who produced the categories for the decennial censuses did not deem such tasks to be part of the economic process. Hence these women were not included in the censuses that formed the basis for later research and policy decisions. One case study in Bengal reveals the detrimental effect of the introduction of rice-husking machines from the 1940s on women's earnings from hand rice-husking, which women traditionally did within the home (M. Mukherjee 1989).

Indian Women's Organizations

In the late nineteenth century Indian women began to form associations on their own initiative. Many of these groups met intermittently, conducted their meetings in Indian languages, and have left few documents. The available records indicate that Indian women were acquiring the organizational skills needed to call meetings, formulate resolutions, debate them, and then forward them to appropriate authorities. The difficulty in sustaining these associations reflects the fact that their organizers still maintained their primary commitment to their roles as mothers and wives. Thus organizational involvement was subject to family responsibilities: preparation for weddings, education of children, and maintenance of the household as their elite husbands were transferred to various locations. There is relatively little research on such organizations beyond the Bengal area, but they certainly existed in western India and probably elsewhere (Forbes 1979c, 1982a).

In Bengal, the first women's organizations were linked to the two factions within the Brahmo Samaj and generally emphasized the need for "improvement" rather than emancipation of women. The emphasis was on women becoming more responsible wives and mothers and gradually supporting appropriate charitable activities outside the home (Borthwick 1984). Moreover, women not associated with the Brahmo Samaj engaged in similar activities. Shudha Mazumdar (1899–1994), a member of a Bengali middle-class family, gives a graphic portrayal of her widening involvement in women's organizations in rural Bengal. Mazumdar first became involved in 1916 in what Indian women called social work and acquired speaking and organizational skills working with women. By 1919 she reluctantly agreed to come out of purdah by going to a garden party, but she soon went to an annual session of the Indian National Congress in Calcutta (Shudha Mazumdar 1986). Mazumdar's experiences reveal how the opportunity to accompany her husband to his various postings in rural Bengal enabled her to form a close bond with him, to participate in women's organizations, and to emerge from purdah without facing the immediate strictures of older male and female relatives.

Most scholarly accounts of Indian women's organizations tend to begin with the twentieth century and to focus on the All-India Muslim Ladies Conference (AIMLC), the Women's Indian Association (WIA), the National Council of Women in India (NCWI), and the All-India Women's Conference (AIWC) (Forbes 1981b; Minault 1981a). All of these organizations demonstrate the close ties between social reform, education for women, and nationalist politics, but they also reflect the differing orientations of their founders and chronology of their foundation. The All-India Muslim Ladies Conference, established in 1914, was connected with the inauguration of a new residence hall for the Aligarh Girls School, an early institution for Muslim women. Its principal supporters were an Indian male reformer and his wife, Shaikh and Begum Abdullah, and Sultan Jahan Begum of Bhopal, the only woman ruler among the princes of India. The Conference remained associated with the Aligarh group in Muslim politics. Failing to expand during the 1920s, it had ended by 1931 (Minault 1981a). Muslim women would not form a distinctly Muslim organization until 1949 with the creation of the All Pakistan Women's Association (Chipp-Kraushaar 1970).

The Women's Indian Association reflected the growing political involvement of Indian women and the work of sympathetic British feminists. Margaret Cousins (1878–1954), an Irish feminist and a Theosophist, helped to organize a deputation of Indian women in 1917 to petition for an extension of the franchise to Indian women (Candy 1994; Jayawardena 1986; Ramusack 1981a). Sarojini Naidu (1879–1949), a poet and political activist who in 1925 would become the first Indian woman president of the Indian National Congress, led the delegation (Paranjape 1997). In the same year, 1917, Cousins and Dorothy Jinarajadasa, an English feminist married to a Ceylonese Buddhist leader of the Theosophical Society, called the first meetings of the Women's Indian Association. This group was based in Madras, utilized the network of the Theosophical Society, and worked for political ends, such as the franchise, as well as social reforms.

The All-India Women's Conference evolved in response to the call from the governor of Bengal for suggestions on what was an appropriate educational curriculum for Indian women (Aparna Basu and B. Ray 1990). The indefatigable Margaret Cousins did much of the initial organizing work but closely collaborated with Indian women activists. At their meeting in Poona in 1927 the women realized that education could not be discussed in isolation and so decided to meet annually and to expand their consideration of other social issues. Seeking a broad base of membership, the AIWC specifically decided to remain apolitical. Much of its initial energy was devoted to the establishment of Lady Irwin College of Home Sciences in New Delhi. Although many of its resolutions related to the preparation of women for roles in an extended family of public activity, the AIWC also debated controversial social issues. As early as 1932 it called for public clinics to dispense information on contraception (Ramusack 1989). During the extensive negotiations over constitutional reform and the civil disobedience movement in the early 1930s, the AIWC cooperated with other women's organizations to demand a more radical extension of the franchise to women. In 1934 it also began to lobby for a uniform civil code that would guarantee legal rights to all women, regardless of their religious affiliation, in such key areas as marriage, divorce, adoption, and inheritance (Forbes 1984). During the late 1930s many of the AIWC officers became absorbed in the struggle for independence. Consequently organizational activity dwindled significantly when, by the early 1940s, officers such as Rajkumari Amrit Kaur (1889–1964) and Vijayalakshmi Pandit (b. 1900), the sister of Jawaharlal Nehru, were jailed for political activity (Pandit 1979). World War II further disrupted its organizational network.

There are varying interpretations of the autonomy of Indian women activists, organizations, and the formal women's movement in India prior to independence. Vijay Agnew emphasizes their close ties to the nationalist movement and argues that women "perceived their participation in politics as being supportive of the activity of their male family members . . . and did not change the ideals of Hindu womanhood" (1979: 140, 144). In other words women became active as mothers, wives, daughters, and sisters and did not seek power for themselves. Jana Everett outlines two dominant ideologies. One was a women's uplift approach, which emphasized "reform of social practices so as to enable women to play a more important and more constructive role in society." The other was a "women's rights" strategy, most clearly exemplified by the AIWC, which sought "the extension of the civil rights enjoyed by men in the political, economic, and familial spheres to women" (Everett 1981: 82). Geraldine Forbes emphasizes that Indian women pursued a social feminism, which she defines as "an interest in women's rights combined with an acceptance of the traditional definition of womanhood that justified women's public role in terms of biological and psychological uniqueness. . . . Indian women sought to extend their housekeeping role to the world outside the walls [of their homes]" (Forbes 1982b: 238–39).

Indian women reformers have been lauded generally as self-sacrificing individuals who achieved major gains for women within the context of a nationalist struggle (Agnew 1979; Forbes 1982a, 1982b; Kaur 1985; R. K. Sharma 1981; Southard 1995). Increasingly some scholars question the class bias of these women activists, their willingness to be co-opted by the British governmental establishment or by Indian political parties, and their decision not to challenge patriarchal values (Caplan 1985; Everett 1981; Jayawardena 1986; Liddle and Joshi 1986). In the 1990s other scholars, such as Chandra Mohanty (1991a, 1991b) and Mrinalini Sinha, have argued that Indian women who sought as individuals and through organizations to critique and challenge both the imperialist and the nationalist discourses on women must be examined in relation to categories of class, race, religion, ethnicity, and gender and situated in specific historical contexts of time and place. Only then can one assess the possibilities for and the accomplishments of these women activists in addressing gender issues that affected women as women. In an analysis of the response of Indian women to the controversy over Katherine Mayo's *Mother India*, a highly inflammatory critique of women's position in India published in 1927, Sinha argues that Indian women both refuted the claims of British women and their organizations to speak for Indian women (Sinha 1995b: 28–29) and sought to create a space for "challenging the patriarchal closure of the 'home' as a site for women's struggle" (Sinha 1994a: 260). Thus Indian women's organizations used the controversy over *Mother India* to campaign successfully for the passage of the Sarda Act of 1929, which raised the minimum age of marriage for girls to fourteen and thereby defied revivalist nationalists and conservative legislators who had opposed such legislation (Forbes 1979b; Ramusack 1981b; Sinha 1994b).

Indian Women and Political Activity

The founding of the Indian National Congress in 1885 is frequently seen as inaugurating the nationalist movement in India, although political protest against British rule began far earlier. Because of physical seclusion, the elite Indian women most likely to be involved in the Congress had little contact with the colonial administrative structure except through the experiences of their fathers, brothers, and husbands. Depending on the location of the annual meetings of the Congress, women began to attend as observers and even delegates as early as 1889. They, however, did not participate in the debates. By 1900 women in Bengal and western India were becoming more vocal. The protest against the 1905 partition of Bengal by the British in defiance of Bengali opposition mobilized many new groups. Women became particularly involved in the *swadeshi* movement, which promoted the use of indigenous instead of foreign products. Since they were in control of consumption in the domestic sphere, women could participate in *swadeshi* activity, purchasing local products without challenging their traditional roles (Borthwick 1984; Forbes 1988).

Mahatma Gandhi is credited with greatly expanding the participation of women in nationalist political activities. Many scholars have emphasized the importance of Gandhi's ideology and program, which called upon women as mothers, wives, and daughters to join the nationalist struggle. Gandhi directed women to spin yarn, to wear *khadi* (the cloth woven from such yarn), and to promote temperance. These activities protested against British economic dominance and could be performed within the home, long deemed the legitimate sphere for women. Thus, political activity did not necessarily demand a break with custom or the disruption of the household (Agnew 1979; K. Ahmad 1984; Aparna Basu 1976; Kishwar 1985). In an insightful essay, Sujata Patel (1988) has analyzed how Gandhi's undeniable empowerment of women, occurring within the context of family and marriage, was closely related to his own background as a middle-class, urban Indian. Thus Gandhi's rhetoric, although it provided the justification for masses of women to become involved in the nationalist struggle, did not demolish the separate spheres of Indian women and men.

Gandhi's appeal brought significant numbers of women into the public arena during the 1919 non-cooperation movement. Basanti Devi (1880–1974) and Urmila Devi (1883–1956)—the wife and the sister, respectively, of C. R. Das, the leader of the Congress in Bengal —were among the first women to sell *khadi* and to be arrested for their efforts. Women intensified their public commitment during the 1930 civil disobedience movement. Gandhi had barred women from participating in the Salt March that opened that 1930 campaign because he did not want to be accused of using Indian women as a shield against British repression. Once he was arrested, however, women openly challenged British authority through protest marches in Bombay as well as through the socially constructive work of picketing toddy or foreign cloth shops, promoting hand-spinning, and the wearing of the coarse, itchy *khadi*. Gandhi's use of religious rhetoric to describe such activity enabled many women to participate without threatening the patriarchal social structure. Some contemporary scholars, however, have been critical of Gandhi's claim that women were better able than men to practice *satyagraha* or non-violent resistance because of their greater capacity for self-sacrifice, because the claim tended to reinforce traditional stereotypes of ideal feminine qualities that subordinated the individual to the group (Mies 1980; Patel 1988).

During the 1920s, subaltern (lower-class) political leaders mobilized women in their movements and attacked women's sexual subordination more radically than Gandhi did. Two examples are illustrative. In the Pratapgarh district of the United Provinces, Baba Ram Chandra, a peasant activist, called for peasant-tenants to avoid denigrating women who lived with men outside of wedlock and to renounce early marriages and polygyny. He also supported the efforts of his wife, Jaggi, to organize women peasants and their participation in protest meetings and *satyagraha* campaigns (K. Kumar 1989). In Madras, Periyar (a title meaning "the great one") E. V. Ramasamy Naicker, who founded the Self-Respect Movement among non-*brahman*s in 1926, attacked patriarchal control of women's lives through three means. First, he promoted self-respect marriages shorn of Hindu rituals, where the couple pledged friendship and equality and called each other comrades. Second, he organized conferences where women were encouraged to discuss women's issues. Third, he urged women to participate independently of their male relatives in public politics. Unfortunately, Periyar's efforts did not eradicate patriarchal attitudes within the non-*brahman* movement in Madras, and they resurfaced in the 1940s, especially after Periyar himself, at age sixty, married a woman of twenty (Anandhi S. 1991; V. Geetha 1998).

During the 1920s women also participated in a more elitist form of political action. In Bengal a few young women in their late teens and early twenties joined their brothers in terrorist attacks on British officials and British institutions. Because the older revolutionary groups were in disarray, the newer revolutionary organizations acknowledged that women could perform the same activities as men: smuggling messages and weapons, manufacturing bombs, raiding British armories, and assassinating British officials. Bina Das (b. 1911), a student first at Bethune and then at Diocesan College in Calcutta, is a well-known example because of her dramatic but unsuccessful attempt to assassinate the governor of Bengal in February 1932. Her contemporaries Santi Ghose (b. 1916) and Suniti Choudhury (b. 1917) had been successful in their attack on the district magistrate in Comilla in 1931, and Pritilata Waddedar led a group of fifteen men who raided the Chittagong Club, killing one person and injuring twelve others. These women stressed the importance of political freedom, which would bring about social change for all of Indian society, including women (Forbes 1981a; R. Kumar 1994).

While women terrorists thought that political freedom would bring improvement in gender relations, women active in the communist movement generally subordinated gender issues to class struggle. In Bengal communist women worked to secure food rationing and other relief measures during the devastating man-made famine of 1943–45. In 1946 they were active in the *tebhaga* movement, which demanded an increase from one-half to two-thirds, or *tebhaga*, of crops for the sharecroppers' own use (Chakravartty 1980; Custers 1987). From 1945 to 1947 in the Thane district of Maharashtra, Warli *adivasi* (tribal) women participated along with men in a revolt to end forced labor and bonded-indebtedness that oppressed them as *adivasi*. Although the Kisan Sabha (Peasant Society) of the Warlis was successful in alleviating the worst aspects of forced labor, including much of the sexual exploitation of tribal women by landlords, it ultimately failed to ameliorate the gender oppression of Warli women within their own community, especially the practice of labeling women as witches (Saldanha 1986). Moreover, after the political agitation ended, Warli women were relegated from public politics to the home and field. Although it occurred largely in the early 1950s after independence was achieved, the women activists of the Telangana revolt, in the Andhra region of the princely state of Hyderabad, suffered a similar fate. After they had participated in the militant struggle to end forced and bonded labor and to gain land rights and legal guarantees of permanent tenancy, they were urged to return to the domestic sphere (Stree Shakti Sanghatana 1989).

At the other end of the spectrum of political activity, the involvement of Indian women with the British government of India was much more restricted than that of their male counterparts. Indian women received a prompt, positive, although limited, response to their request for the franchise from Indian male-dominated legislative councils and consequently did not feel the antipathy toward male legislators that British and American suffragists did. During the 1920s a narrow franchise was granted to Indian women, province by province (Forbes 1996; Southard 1993). Bombay and Madras led the way in 1921, and Kamaladevi Chattopadhyaya (1903–90) and Hannah Angelo ran for the Madras Legislative Council in 1926 (Chattopadhyay 1986). Neither won. Muthulakshmi Reddi (1886–1968), a physician, was nominated as the first woman legislator and was selected as deputy speaker of the Madras Council. Although she was interested in a broad range of issues, she was most noted for advocating legislation to end the institution of *devadasis* (M. Reddy 1930).

Devadasis were women dedicated in their youth to service in Hindu temples and were based in centers of Hindu orthodoxy, particularly Madras (later Tamilnadu), Mysore princely state (later Karnataka), and Orissa (Kersenboom-Story 1987; Marglin 1985; Nair 1994a; M. Reddy 1930, [1964?]; Srinivasan 1983, 1985). Their ritual function was to dance before the temple deity, and they also had sexual relations with temple priests and patrons. Embodying auspiciousness and becoming highly skilled singers and dancers, they received material compensation from Hindu rulers and other male patrons, including property rights, for their artistic and sexual services. However, by the 1890s the new moral order being forged in the context of Indian nationalism had little room for the exercise of female sexuality outside of the patriarchal family and for independent women controlling property (Parker 1998). Bureaucrats in the princely state of Mysore undercut the financial base of *devadasis* when, in 1909, they prohibited employment of *devadasis* in temples that received allowances from the state. The moral order of a new middle class sought to confine female sexuality to the family. As Janaki Nair has pointed out, even though Muthulakshmi Reddi was anxious to develop women's autonomy, she "resolved the troubling question of *devadasi* sexuality within the parameters set by male nationalists by encouraging them to marry and domesticate themselves" (Nair 1994a: 3164; Nair 1996b: 166–69). In Madras the legal abolition of *devadasis* came in 1947. As they lost the material basis for developing their musical skills, *devadasis* migrated to larger urban centers, especially Bombay, and became sex workers (Nair 1994a). Women as well as men would sponsor legislation that would have ambivalent effects on other women.

Women achieved the franchise in all provinces by 1930. The Government of India Act of 1935 extended the franchise among women but through terms that most Indian women's organizations found unacceptable. For example, in an effort to get around the fact that few married Indian women owned property, the British offered the vote to the wives of certain classes of male property owners and military personnel. This practice followed the pattern of gradual extension of the franchise to women pursued in Great Britain, but Indian women wanted universal franchise and not partial steps based on a woman's relationship to a man (Forbes 1979a, 1996; Nair 1996b; Southard 1993). In the 1936–37 elections women won 56 out of approximately 1,500 seats in the provincial legislatures. Only one woman legislator became a minister: Vijayalakshmi Pandit, a sister of Jawaharlal Nehru, was selected as the Minister for Local Government and Public Health in the United Provinces (Pandit 1979). Three women became deputy speakers and two parliamentary secretaries (Forbes 1996). Although the results were significant, these elections unfortunately presaged the difficulty that women candidates would have in obtaining the party ticket and then engaging in the bruising and expensive campaigning necessary to win an election in independent India.

British colonial officials had made what they perceived as the degraded position of women in India into a major ideological argument legitimating British rule in India. They passed legislation that extended certain rights to women, for example enabling Hindu widows to remarry. Although, as Uma Chakravarti (1996b) has shown, they were not the first to do so, the British enshrined the underlying spirit of the *brahmanic* Laws of Manu in the Gentoo Code of 1772. Gradually the British evolved an expensive legal system that enforced a legal code severely restricting the independence of women and their right to property and control over their children. Because of their ignorance of the complexity of competing legal systems in India, the British actually reduced the flexibility that customary law had provided for many women.

Recent scholarship has revealed how both reformist and revivalist Indian nationalists accepted various aspects of Victorian ideology that strengthened patriarchal control over women within a reconfigured nuclear family. The reformers argued that women in India had had a golden age before the arrival of the Muslims and that reform efforts were attempting to recapture the lost eminence of women. The revivalists glorified the self-sacrifice, devotion, and obedience of Indian women as superior to Western emphases on independence and alleged self-centeredness. By the late nineteenth century, elite Indian women challenged the glorification of early marriage and lamented their lack of access to education and the physical and emotional cost of idealized wifely self-sacrifice and devotion. In the twentieth century, women were one of many groups politicized by the independence struggle, and they subordinated women's rights issues to the demand for political freedom and class equality. Elite women

tended to hope that independence would bring full equality with Indian men, and non-elite women, such as those participating in the
Warli or Telangana movements, thought that successful class struggles
would bring relief from gender oppression as well.*

WOMEN IN POST-COLONIAL SOUTH ASIA, 1947 TO THE PRESENT

Women in Independent India

Independence brought a significant improvement in the legal status
of Indian women, but initially it also produced unprecedented disruption in the lives of Hindu, Sikh, and Muslim women who migrated to
and from the new states of India and Pakistan. Until the 1990s there
had been little research on the human impact of the partition of the
British empire into the two states of India and Pakistan (Butalia 1998).

Recently feminist scholars have focused on how women were
affected by state-imposed communal identities. For example, the government of India launched a far-reaching program to recover Hindu
and Sikh women abducted in Pakistan and to "return" or bring them
to India while simultaneously sending Muslim women abducted by
Hindus and Sikhs in India to Pakistan. Although many of these women
had suffered sexual and other physical and emotional abuse, some
had established long-term relationships with their abductors, who
were sometimes the fathers of their children. In general, government
legislation and social workers did not take into account personal preference and forcibly repatriated these women without much attention to how their natal families would receive them. Thus the so-called
Recovery Program of the Government of India represents one further
stage in the imposition of communal identity on women and a state-
imposed patriarchal vision of appropriate female sexuality (Aparna
Basu 1996; Butalia 1994; Major 1995; Menon and Bhasin 1996, 1998).
The River Churning, written in 1947 by Jyotirmoyee Devi (1894–1988),
is a poignant novel about a young Hindu girl initially sheltered by a
Muslim family in East Pakistan during the partition riots. When she is
sent to her relatives in Calcutta, they ostracize her as ritually polluted
because she was possibly raped and then had lived with Muslims for
six months (1995).

*In addition to the works cited in this section, see Allen and Mukherjee 1982; J.
Bagchi 1995; Chaudhuri 1997; Das 1921; Dehejia 1997; Engels 1990; Jayawardena
and de Alwis 1996; Krishnamurty 1989; MacMillan 1988; Masani 1988; Metcalf 1991;
Minault 1981b; Nair 1994b; Nanda 1976; Oldenburg 1990; Price 1994; Ramusack
1990b; L. Sahgal 1997; M. Sahgal 1994; Sangari and Vaid 1989; T. Sarkar 1997.

The 1950 constitution granted women the right to vote and included an equal rights provision that banned discrimination on the basis of sex. But it did not inaugurate a uniform civil code. Jawaharlal Nehru had promised reforms in the personal laws for Hindu women but encountered strong opposition from orthodox Hindu groups (N. Banerjee 1998). It took him until 1954 and 1955 to secure a series of legislative acts, known collectively as the Hindu Marriage Code, that most importantly prohibited polygamy and established divorce by mutual consent. Many women activists were disappointed, however, by the decision to allow Muslims to follow their personal law in an effort to reconcile the 10 percent Muslim minority that stayed within India after the creation of Pakistan (N. Desai and Krishnaraj 1987; L. Sarkar 1976).

Muslim women in India remained under Qur'anic injunctions, which permitted a man to have four wives as long as all were treated equally. There is much controversy over the security afforded to women in marriage and for inheritance by Qur'anic law and the four schools of Muslim law (Agnes 1996; Bhatty 1976; Carroll 1979, 1982a, 1982b). Some Muslim reformers in India have argued for a uniform civil code. They cite Muslim states in the Middle East that have them and claim such codes afford protection to women who are relatively uneducated and without the support of sympathetic male kin. Orthodox Muslim groups, reaffirming the validity of Qur'anic injunctions, have been strengthened by the growing support for Muslim fundamentalism which emerged in the late 1970s. The case of Shah Bano, a Muslim woman who sued for support from her former husband under the Indian Penal Code, brought these issues to public attention. In 1985 she received a positive verdict from a Hindu judge, but his action raised a widespread protest from orthodox Muslim political and religious leaders. After some initial hesitation, Rajiv Gandhi supported a bill, named, ironically, the Muslim Women's (Protection of Rights on Divorce) Act, which essentially prevents Muslim women from utilizing the Indian Penal Code to redress a marital issue. Divorced Muslim women are to rely upon their natal families or the Muslim community for support, not their former husbands (Pathak and Ranjan 1989).

The 1950s and 1960s represented a period in which elite women reaped the rewards of independence in India. Vijayalakshmi Pandit, serving as speaker of the UN General Assembly and as ambassador to the Soviet Union, the United States, and Great Britain, achieved international distinction. Padma Naidu, the daughter of Sarojini Naidu, was appointed the governor of the state of West Bengal. Hansa Mehta achieved prominence as vice-chancellor of M. S. University in Baroda. Sucheta Kripalani even served as chief minister of Uttar Pradesh (formerly the United Provinces), the most populous Indian state. Women were elected to state legislatures and the Lok Sabha, the lower house of the Indian Parliament, earning 5.9 percent of the seats in 1967 and 7.07 percent in 1996. These numbers are slightly higher than the female representation in similar bodies in Western countries, including the United States. Most notably, Indira Gandhi became prime minister of India in 1966. Although being Nehru's daughter aided her initial selection, she demonstrated her ability to remain in power through several elections until her assassination in 1984.

Middle-class women, a minority of about 10 percent of Indian women, found new opportunities for employment and public service. The professions of teaching, medicine, and government service absorbed increasing numbers of educated women. Those women who preferred to combine volunteer social service with their family responsibilities were coopted onto the Central Welfare Board, which oversaw social service institutions that received government funding. In an analysis of what these women activists did after 1947 in Madras, Patricia Caplan has pointed out that "women play an active part in class formation, not only as housewives and workers, but also as members of voluntary organizations and dispensers of social welfare" (Caplan 1985: 5). In other words, some Indian women activists reinforced class boundaries and had yet to focus on the fundamental social changes needed to improve the condition of the vast majority of Indian women.

Personalized images of elite Indian women can be found in literature, memoirs, and autobiographies, and of non-elite women in ethnographical studies and short stories. The work of R. K. Narayan (b. 1907), a south Indian novelist who created the fictional town of Malgudi, encompasses a broad range of women. In *The Dark Room* (1938), Savitri, the heroine, cannot escape from a stifling family situation because of her lack of economic independence and self-confidence. Daisy, the heroine of *The Painter of Signs* (1976), is a government birth control worker who refuses marriage proposals and ties to her natal family. Anita Desai (b. 1937) has focused on the lives of urban women and has etched the divergent paths of two sisters in *Clear Light of Day* (1980). Memoirs of major political figures, such as those by Kamaladevi Chattopadhyaya (1986), Gayatri Devi of Jaipur (1976), Vijayalakshmi Pandit (1979), and Begum Shaista S. Ikramullah (1969) are important expressions of their authors' autonomy. *The Nectar in the Sieve* (1954), by Kamala Markandaya, is the most readily available novel about peasant women. All of these novels and memoirs were written originally in English. Some accounts of the lives of peasant women are in anthropological studies and analyses of folk tales told by women. An example of the former is *Behind Mud Walls* (1989), in which William and Charlotte Wiser studied the same north Indian village over four decades from 1930 to 1970, and one of the latter is Raheja and Gold's *Listen to the Heron's Words* (1994).

There is a much more extensive literature by Indian women writing in Indian languages, and English translations of their novels, short stories, and poems are becoming increasingly available (Hosein 1989a, 1989b; Lakshmi 1984). Prime examples are the Bengali short stories of Mahasweta Devi, which Kalpana Bardhan (1990) and Gayatri Chakravorty Spivak (1995) have translated; *Truth Tales*, edited by a collective in Delhi (1990); the massive two-volume anthology by Susie Tharu and K. Lalita of the writings of Indian women from 600 B.C.E. to the present (1990, 1991); and *The Inner Courtyard*, a collection edited by Lakshmi Holmström (1990).

Resurgence of Women's Activism in India

An assessment of what happened to Indian women after independence was one factor that launched a new women's movement in India during the 1970s. The United Nations declaration of 1975 to 1985 as the Decade for Women stimulated the appointment of a government commission to prepare a report on the current status of women in India for submission to the UN. The Committee on the Status of Women, composed of nine women and one man, was shocked by their research, which documented distressing conditions for many women in independent India. Their report, *Towards Equality*, revealed that the ratio of women to men had begun to decline from the 1901 census, when it was 971 women to 1,000 men, to the 1971 census, when it reached 930 women to 1,000 men. (After rising to 934 women in 1981, the ratio was 929 women to 1,000 men in the 1991 census.) Further research ascertained that despite legal equality, this drop reflected continuing malnutrition and higher rates of mortality among women, girl babies, and very young girls. Another startling finding was the declining number of women in paid employment, particularly in the agricultural and unorganized manufacturing sector, where unskilled women had the greatest scope for employment. Professional women had increased their employment and seemed the one group of women rewarded by independence. Yet at this time journalists, such as Promilla Kapur (1974), and social scientists, most notably

Rama Mehta (1970), were publishing books and articles suggesting that middle-class women had numerous complaints (Liddle and Joshi 1986; Mies 1980).

Shortly after *Towards Equality* was submitted in December 1974, Indira Gandhi imposed an Emergency in June 1975, which restricted the exercise of civil rights because of an alleged threat to national security. Women activists soon were protesting against the suspension of civil rights, the stringent promotion of birth control measures by Sanjay Gandhi (the younger son of Mrs. Gandhi), police rape of women detained in local jails ("custodial rape"), and the newly emerging phenomena of bride burnings or dowry deaths (Katzenstein 1989; R. Kumar 1994; Omvedt 1980). Campaigns on the latter two issues resulted in legislation but revealed once again the often ambivalent impact of legal acts. In the 1980s a feminist campaign for more stringent laws punishing rape, focusing on the brutal impact of violence against women, was taken over by politicians who sought legislation to protect the honor of women and their families. When a law was enacted in 1983, it defined custodial rape, which carried a mandatory sentence of ten years, but remained silent on familial or marital rape (R. Kumar 1994).

Although a Dowry Prohibition Act had been passed in 1961, the giving of dowry spread during the 1960s and 1970s to groups further down the social hierarchy and to new areas in south India where dowry had not been given. This extension seems to be related to growing affluence in certain groups and the desire to translate economic gains into increased social prestige by marrying daughters into higher social groups and by following the customs of those social groups. In the Delhi area there was increased press coverage of instances where a new bride was burned to death, supposedly because of an accident while cooking. Because of the Hindu practice of cremation within twenty-four hours of death, it was frequently difficult to obtain evidence needed to establish the probability of murder. Still, investigations of some bride burnings and the actions of courageous parents of dead brides, with the support of some women's groups, have focused attention on this phenomenon.

Protest against police rape and bride burnings coalesced with protest against the Emergency to create a new wave of feminist activism during the late 1970s. Neera Desai and Maithreyi Krishnaraj (1987) have outlined six types of women's organizations besides mainstream groups such as the AIWC and the YWCA. They include agitational consciousness-raising groups; mass-based organizations, including trade unions and tribal associations; groups that provide services to needy women; professional women's organizations; women's wings of political parties; and research networks that include both academics and activists working to provide documentation on women's issues. Like its early twentieth-century predecessors, this women's movement utilized legislation, new associations, and the press as its instruments to improve the condition of women. Examples of legislation are the efforts to secure tighter laws to stop the giving and the taking of dowry. Associations took new forms, such as *Saheli* ("girl-friend"), a Delhi collective which seeks to inform women of their legal rights and assist them in obtaining employment, especially when they decide to divorce. The use of the press includes articles in general newspapers but also in newly established feminist journals such as *Manushi* (*Woman*) and books issued by a feminist press, Kali for Women. There are also new institutions. Women's Studies emerged first at SNDT Woman's University in Bombay in 1973 and has developed as a field of teaching and research that focuses primarily, though not exclusively, on issues with policy implications. By the mid-1990s there were twenty-three women's studies centers in India. On the theoretical level, women activists have debated sharply about the validity of characterizing this women's movement as feminist since feminism is seen as embedded in socio-economic conditions in Europe and the United States and distinctly middle class in its composition and goals. More recently some Indian women have contended that there are multiple feminisms, some of which can supply modes of analysis useful in the Indian context. A second point of difference is the desirability of autonomy or separation of the women's movement from political parties on both left and right, because these organizations are judged to subordinate women's issues to party objectives (Krishnaraj n.d.).

The revived women's movement which dates from the early 1970s differs from earlier ones because of the emergence of grass roots women's groups among lower-class women which include organizations among tribal and *dalit* (oppressed-untouchable) women in Maharashtra; women in Himachal Pradesh who participated in Chipko, an effort to conserve forests; and peasant women in Andhra Pradesh, Bengal, and Bihar (Amrita Basu 1992; Bhushan 1989; Everett 1986; Gulati 1981; Jain 1980; Jain and Banerjee 1985; Kishwar and Vanita 1984; R. Kumar 1994). Although both leftist political parties (Marxist and socialist) and feminists have sought to shape the direction of these mass movements, the groups have courageously tried to evolve programs which seek to address the condition of women qua women, as well as *dalits* or peasants. Thus they raise such topics as gender oppression within classes because of such factors as alcoholism and lack of women's access to land when land rights are redistributed. They also tackle difficult issues like the double sexual standard and sexual terrorism, which make it hard for women to participate in political organizing. They criticize Marxists for subsuming women's issues under class struggle and feminists for their lack of sustained attention to economic issues (most notably equal wages and property rights), their disinterest in political power, and their unproductive theoretical debates (Omvedt 1993). Many of these lower-class mass movements exist for relatively short periods because they work against overwhelming material constraints. One relatively long-lived effort to organize lower-class urban women for the purpose of obtaining legal rights and improving their access to economic resources is the Self-Employed Women's Association (SEWA) in Ahmadabad. In 1972 Ela Bhatt began to organize women ragpickers and sidewalk vegetable vendors to obtain access to low-cost credit and education, and SEWA has expanded its range of activities to include organizing women workers in the informal sector to bargain for better working conditions (Everett 1983; Selliah 1989).

By 1990 new areas of concern emerged. One key issue revolves around amniocentesis. In the Delhi area and in the surrounding states of Punjab and Haryana, clinics began to do amniocentesis primarily to determine the sex of the fetus, and then performed abortions if the sex was not the one desired. Since estimates that up to 99 percent of such abortions are of female fetuses, some women activists have demanded the prohibition of amniocentesis and secured passage of such legislation in Maharashtra in 1988. Others call for a ban on advertising by such clinics. Women's control over their reproductive activities remained highly contested in other ways. The state-supported family planning program has retreated from the coercive measures utilized during the Emergency from 1975 to 1977. Still, some feminists are disturbed by its orientation toward lower class women, its carelessness about women's health, and its willingness to experiment with controversial contraceptives. Furthermore, the greater preference for female sterilization as opposed to male sterilization reflects a continuing undervaluing of women's health (Parikh 1990).

During the 1990s the recurrence of religious fundamentalism—or what some feminist scholars have defined as religious nationalism, which emphasizes the political manipulation of religious symbols—

has affected women adversely. Among Muslim women in India as well as Pakistan and Bangladesh, there is increasing stress on the need for veiling and for the imposition of Muslim laws on all personal relationships in order to reaffirm religious commitment. The Shah Bano case discussed above is only the most recent example of how the individual rights of women are circumscribed in campaigns to construct a communal identity in a post-modern nation-state (Pathak and Rajan 1989; Hasan 1993).

For Hindu women in India, religious fundamentalism, religious nationalism, and ethnic honor have merged in two spectacular episodes. One was Roop Kanwar's alleged *sati* in Deorala, about fifty miles from Jaipur, in September 1987. Upon the death of her husband of six months, the eighteen-year-old widow allegedly joined her husband on his funeral pyre. About ten thousand people witnessed the illegal event, of which the local police claimed to be unaware and therefore did nothing to prevent. Women's groups protested strongly to the Rajasthan state government and to the central government, and legislation was consequently passed to prevent future *satis* (Oldenburg 1994; Sangari and Vaid 1996).

The other instance is the growing involvement of Hindu women in the revival of Hindu nationalism associated with the Ram Janambhoomi movement (Sarkar and Butalia 1995). On December 6, 1992, Hindu militants destroyed a mosque (Babri Masjid) at Ayodhya in north India, constructed in the sixteenth century by the Mughal emperor Babur after he supposedly destroyed a temple on the site of the alleged birthplace (Ram Janambhoomi) of Ram, the god-hero of the epic *Ramayana*. Three interlocking institutions—the Rashtriya Swayamsevak Sangh (RSS), a paramilitary Hindu nationalist organization; the Bharatiya Janata Party (BJP), an electoral party; and the Vishwa Hindu Parishad (VHP), a world Hindu cultural association that appeals to Indian Hindus living abroad—promote the Hindutva movement, which seeks to transform India into an avowedly Hindu nation. Hindutva propaganda, disseminated through modern media such as tape cassettes and films, articulates hatred toward a secular state characterized as corrupt and repressive and a Muslim minority constructed as pampered and abusive. Individual women are prominent in the BJP, most notably Vijayraje Scindia and Uma Bharati, and Sadhvi Rithamabara is a fiery preacher for the VHP. Amrita Basu (1993) has probed how this trio of women leaders have been able to utilize the Hinduvta movement to achieve personal and political goals, while at the same time they displace frustrations with Hindu patriarchal practices from Hindu to Muslim men and render Muslim women invisible. The RSS has also developed an extensive women's wing with an impressive base among high-caste, middle-class, urban Hindu women. Although their members enter the public sphere of politics through Hindu nationalism, their activism does not necessarily challenge gender inequality or create feminist consciousness or solidarity (Bacchetta 1993, 1996; T. Sarkar 1993c). In the aftermath of devastating communal rioting in Bombay in January 1993, in which Hindu women actively collaborated with the Shiv Sena in attacks on Muslim neighborhoods and Muslim women sought to protect their male relatives from attacks, Flavia Agnes acknowledged that gender solidarity could not overcome communal tensions and called for the evolution of a new secular framework (Agnes 1994).

Women in Pakistan

Created in 1947 with the specific goal of becoming an Islamic republic, Pakistan provides a legal and social setting for women in which they are subject to Qur'anic law as it has been modified by legislation (Willmer 1996). The All Pakistan Women's Association (APWA) promoted the passage of the Muslim Family Laws Ordinance (MFLO) of 1961 in an effort to restrict polygyny and to equalize the opportunity of women to divorce (Chipp-Kraushaar 1981). The elite members of the APWA, however, could have little impact on the implementation of such modernist legislation. During the 1970s and 1980s the government of General Zia ul-Huq attempted to bring the civil law into closer congruence with Islamic law. In 1973 the Council of Islamic Ideology was formed to ensure that civil laws, including the MFLO, were interpreted in accordance with Islamic principles, and its rulings do not always favor women. It has eight to ten members, but only one must be a woman. Women's groups, especially the Women's Action Forum, and professional associations, particularly those of lawyers, have protested against efforts to reduce the scope of the MFLO (Alavi 1988).

The efforts to promote an Islamic culture also resulted in injunctions on dress and suitable occupations for women (Mumtaz and Shaheed 1987). Conservative women wear the *burqa* (a long cloak which covers the head and face as well as the body) and moderate women veil themselves with a *chaddar* (a large shawl) or a *duppata* (a rectangular scarf). Educated women are channeled into occupations dealing with women, such as education and medicine. They also staff female banks that deal only with women. Restrictions on their public activities include a prohibition on Pakistani women's participation in such international sports competitions as the Olympic Games.

Women have the right to vote, belong to political parties, and run for office. Benazir Bhutto (b. 1953), who first became prime minister in 1988 and was ousted in August 1990 on charges of mismanagement and corruption, is the most famous woman in Pakistani politics. The elder daughter and first child of a former prime minister who founded the Pakistan People's Party (PPP), her participation is similar to that of women in India and Bangladesh who enter politics through relationships with prominent males (Bhutto 1988). Bhutto reflects the ambiguous position of even elite women and the imperatives of political power in contemporary Pakistan (Zakaria 1990). Educated at Harvard and Oxford, she assented to an arranged marriage in 1988, fulfilled her role as a mother, producing two sons and a daughter, and wears a *duppata* over her head whenever she appears in public. Her personal charisma and skill as an orator (first developed as president of the Oxford Union) enabled her to regain power as prime minister in October 1993 despite the weak organizational base of the PPP. However, she once again was ousted in November 1996 on charges of maladministration and corruption, and her party suffered an overwhelming defeat in elections in February 1997.

Women in Bangladesh

Created in 1947 as East Pakistan, Bangladesh achieved its independence from Pakistan in 1971. Although patriarchal institutions such as patriliny and patrilocality are firmly rooted in Bangladesh, Bengali culture, which has some ties to Southeast Asian cultures as well as the Bengali Hindu culture of India, has attenuated the legal position of Islamic institutions and injunctions in Bangladesh. Furthermore, Sheikh Mujib, the popularly acclaimed liberator, first president, and later prime minister of Bangladesh, was firmly committed to secularism. Naila Kabeer has argued that "secular states allow more negotiable frameworks for the politics of gender than imaginable in states where legitimacy is ultimately derived from religious texts which codify the principle of gender inequality" (Kabeer 1991: 44). So while many aspects of women's lives—such as marriage, divorce, and inheritance—are decided according to religious law, women were declared equal to men under the constitution of 1972. Purdah or gender segregation remains an ideal, but public veiling is less pervasive than in Pakistan. Poorer women who must work maintain evidence of the ideal in their shyness and their efforts to avoid contact with unrelated males (Chowdhury 1994).

After the assassination of Mujib in 1975, his military successors, Generals Zia-ur-Rahman and Hussain Muhammad Ershad, set the country on a more pro-Islamic road to secure an influential source of legitimacy for their seizure of power. Neither, however, issued public injunctions as General Zia-ul-Huq did in Pakistan, which forbade women to wear the *sari* or the *bindi* (the red dot on the forehead which Hindu women wear upon marriage but which many South Asian women now wear as a beauty mark), which the Pakistani leader viewed as un-Islamic. Both men continued to court international aid, which after 1975 increasingly came with stipulations that women be specifically targeted in development schemes. To gain international aid, both generals publicly articulated that women were significant for the development of the country. The Women in Development or WID programs tended to be narrowly constructed and to benefit rich peasant women whose families profited or middle-class women who were employed as administrators, or to focus on population control. But the government found itself in a dilemma as some aid providers, apparently those from the Middle East such as Saudi Arabia, sought a more Islamic orientation, with a reaffirmation of separate spheres, less public participation by women in development schemes, and an end to population control measures that allegedly led to sexual chaos.

Despite some signs of optimism, the situation of Bangladeshi women remains vulnerable (Abdullah and Zeidenstein 1982). Their subordinate position is reflected in life expectancy, which in 1981 was 49 years for women and 53 for men. The maternal mortality rate is one of the highest in the world, being responsible for 27 percent of deaths among females from 10 to 49 years (Rozario 1998). At the same time, some elite women are visible in professions dealing with women, such as education and medicine (Jahan and Papanek 1979; Feldman and McCarthy 1984), and women have legal and political rights to vote and hold office. Many political parties have women's organizations; the most active is the Mahila Parishad of the Communist party. The latter has agitated for the rights of women factory workers and bank employees, campaigned against violence toward women and the growing demand for dowry, and opposed the nomination of women to reserved seats since this provision gives the ruling party (who makes the nominations) a strengthened voting bloc. In this ambiguous situation, some non-governmental organizations (NGOs) have begun to organize during the 1980s among lower-class rural and urban women. Focusing on gender rather than class or legal issues, the NGOs seek to organize women into collectives, to make women aware that they are oppressed as women and not only because of their class position, and to empower them to take actions themselves to improve their situation. Thus they differ from WID programs, which target immediate needs and concentrate on improving material conditions without addressing gender and ideological issues (Kabeer 1988, 1991).

As has occurred throughout South Asia, wives and daughters of assassinated politicians emerged during the 1990s as leaders of the political parties of their male relatives. Khaleda Zia, the widow of the assassinated military dictator, was prime minister in the early 1990s. Despite her rhetorical sympathy with women, her government undertook the prosecution of Taslima Nasrin, a feminist author, for writings which allegedly defamed Islam. In 1996 Sheikh Hasina Wajed, the daughter of Sheikh Mujib, replaced Khaleda Zia as prime minister. Although many perceive women prime ministers in South Asia as contradictions to the prevailing patriarchal structures, the entry of these women into politics has been based primarily on kinship ties and not on firm political organizational bases. Moreover, as religious nationalism gains strength throughout South Asia, its political impact on women as individuals and as a group is highly ambivalent.*

*In addition to the works cited in this section, see Afshar 1991; Agarwal 1988; Arkin and Shollar 1989; Bumiller 1990; Charlton et al. 1990; Dube et al. 1986; Fernandes 1994; L. Gulati 1984; Hasan 1994; Hashmi 1995; Jeffery 1979, 1989; Kalpagam 1994; Kapur 1977; Mies 1982; Mukhopadhyay 1984; Papanek 1990; A. Pearson 1996; Raju et al. 1998; Ram 1998; Ratti 1993; N. Sahgal 1989; Sakala 1980; U. Sharma 1980; Shiva 1988; Singer 1993a, 1993b, 1997; Stephens 1989; Suleri 1989; Swarup et al. 1994; Tharu 1989; Vyas 1993; Wieringa 1995.

WOMEN IN SOUTHEAST ASIA

Barbara N. Ramusack

WOMEN IN SOUTHEAST ASIA PRIOR TO 1500

Most world history textbooks cover the entire panorama of South-east Asian history in around twenty pages, with usually less than five pages devoted to the era before C.E. 1500 and the arrival of Europe-ans. This meager consideration probably reflects the difficulties of syn-thesizing effectively the diversity that exists in a world area with many language families; few large, centralized, bureaucratic empires; and a complex array of indigenous and world religions, including Hindu-ism, Buddhism, Islam, and Christianity. In these surveys, Southeast Asia is generally categorized as a mainland that includes the modern states of Burma (later Myanmar), Thailand, Cambodia, Laos, Viet-nam, and the archipelagoes (now the island nations of Indonesia and the Philippines). Malaysia and Singapore are frequently considered island nations, since both had long-standing ties to the islands that now form Indonesia (or the so-called "lands below the winds") and the former includes both islands and the elongated peninsula that bridges the islands and the mainland of Southeast Asia. Since Southeast Asia lies strategically across sea routes between two prominent world cultures—the Indian and the Chinese—historians have also focused on the impact of Indian and Chinese religious, social, and political forms on the local societies of this region.

During the last half of the twentieth century historians have shifted from a paradigm of binary geographical divisions and the hegemony of external forces to the concept of an underlying Southeast Asian culture and have argued for an autonomous history of Southeast Asian peoples, societies, and states (Smail 1961). Anthony Reid, for example, has described Southeast Asia as sharing geographical characteristics, including abundant water, rainfall, and forests; nutritional characteristics, such as a diet in which rice and fish dominate and the chewing of betel (an aromatic combination of areca nut, lime paste, and spices wrapped in a betel leaf) was widespread; and economic similarities, especially participation in extensive intra- and inter-regional commercial relations over water (Reid 1988b: 1–7; Brownrigg 1991). The numerous languages of Southeast Asia are now divided into four families: the Austroasiatic (perhaps with its origins in northeastern Thailand) with the Mon-Khmer group, including Mon, Khmer, and Vietnamese on the mainland; the Austronesian (possibly with its home in Taiwan) prevailing in the Philippines, Indonesia, parts of the Malay peninsula, and southeastern Vietnam; the Tai, whose principal languages are Thai and Lao; and the Tibeto-Burman, of which Burmese is the chief example (Bellwood 1992: 106–115). By the fifteenth century, Malay, an Austronesian language, would spread through commercial activity and become a lingua franca throughout much of the region.

Furthermore, historians have moved beyond the thesis of primitive peoples in Southeast Asia being the passive recipients of sophisticated institutions from India and China. A more nuanced view has emerged, in which Southeast Asian political leaders and social elites consciously borrowed cultural forms which would support or enhance their social status, political control, economic dominance, or spiritual potency. Thus Malay traders shrewdly utilized the Chinese tributary system and courted merchants from South Asia to expand their mercantile networks. In the religious sphere, Hindu deities (first Siva and then Vishnu) and Buddhism became amalgamated with each other and with indigenous traditions. *Brahman* priests, probably both Indian and local, devoted to Siva and Vishnu contributed to myths explaining the universe and performed rituals legitimating monarchical power. Elites in Cambodia and Java adopted aspects of the caste structure associated with Hindu culture in India (such as *varna* and occupational categories and some elements of hierarchy) that reinforced their superior status. In the first century C.E., the Chinese empire moved into northern Vietnam and for many centuries sought to impose its political control and cultural patterns there. Although they assimilated some facets of Confucian culture, the Vietnamese resisted wholesale incorporation into the Chinese sphere. Ultimately Vietnam was a buffer that stalled further Chinese incursions by land into Southeast Asia.

Early European observers and many scholars have characterized gender relationships in Southeast Asia as complementary and more equal than those observed in the neighboring Indian and Chinese civilizations. Although there was only limited research on women and gender issues in Southeast Asian history prior to the 1990s (Dobbin 1980), historians have begun to devote more attention to both the lived experience and the representation of women in Southeast Asia in specialized articles and monographs as well as synthetic overviews. Compared with historians, however, anthropologists, literary critics, sociologists, and multidisciplinary scholars in women's and development studies have produced a more extensive literature. Their work analyzes the condition and status of women since the 1950s and has been directed primarily toward policy issues, such as the impact of multinational corporations that employ millions of Southeast Asian women, of changing relationships between urban and rural sectors of national economies, of differential rates of infant and maternal mortality among various segments of populations, and of the development of international networks promoting prostitution in Southeast Asia. Several influential collective volumes provide insightful new ways to conceptualize gender, especially how what is deemed appropriate behavior for men and women evolves, from within Southeast Asian cultures rather than from Euro-American perspectives. These include Jane Atkinson and Shelley Errington's *Power and Difference: Gender in Island Southeast Asia* (1990); Sita van Bemmelen et al., eds., *Women and Mediation in Indonesia* (1992); Elsbeth Locher-Scholten and Anke Neihof's *Indonesian Women in Focus* (1987); Aihwa Ong and Michael Peletz's *Bewitching Women and Pious Men: Gender and Body Politics in Southeast Asia* (1995); and Laurie J. Sears's *Fantasizing the Feminine in Indonesia* (1996). Still, this research leaves unexplored much of the lived experience of women prior to 1900, and these titles reflect the greater current availability of secondary sources in English on women in Indonesia than for other areas of Southeast Asia. Because of the lack of coverage on early Southeast Asian history in world history textbooks, my account will provide some background on this era as a basis for understanding women's roles and gender relationships in subsequent periods.

Early state formation in Southeast Asia occurred from the eighth to the fourteenth centuries C.E., and the principal units were Angkor for the Khmers, Pagan for the Burmese, Ayutthaya for the Thai, the Ly state for the Vietnamese, Srivijaya for the Malay, and Majapahit for Indonesia.

In the territory now included in Cambodia, Chinese sources record the existence of a kingdom named Funan that sent tribute to China between C.E. 253 and 519. Some historians now consider that Funan was not a unified kingdom but rather a period that possibly witnessed the introduction of systematic irrigation. Irrigation enabled dry rice-growing principalities to integrate with hunting and gathering societies to form small states that collectively might have forwarded tribute to the Chinese. The peoples of these states were worshippers of Siva, although Buddhist concepts were present—for example, the influence of actions in previous lives on subsequent ones and the acquisition of merit as a central concern of life.

Khmer and Sanskrit inscriptions from C.E. 600 onward indicate the continued co-existence of Hindu and indigenous deities, caste categories such as *varna*, and hereditary servitude. By the ninth century C.E., Khmer leaders were consolidating a state based at Angkor. They built extraordinary Hindu and Buddhist temples, Buddhist *stupa*s and monasteries, and royal palaces at Angkor; proclaimed themselves universal monarchs; affirmed their ties to Siva (an ancestral deity who watered the earth) and occasionally to Vishnu (most notably Suryavarman II [r. ca. C.E. 1113–50], who constructed Angkor Wat, which depicted many stories of Vishnu and his incarnations); personified virtue; and extended patronage to all classes. Buddhist ideas gradually became more prominent, and during the thirteenth century most Cambodians converted to Theravada Buddhism (Chandler 1983; de Casparis and Mabbett 1992a).

In Burma, Mon and Pyu peoples formed the first historical political centers in the lower Irrawaddy basin with the Pyus at Prome prominent during the centuries prior to C.E. 850. During the Pyu period, Burmese sources record that women were admitted to Buddhist monasteries, although many scholars claim that the ordination of women as nuns had ceased in Theravada Buddhism before it spread to Southeast Asia. Inscriptions record that Buddhist women of the political elite donated Buddha images to cave and free-standing temples. There is also a story of a young Mon woman who is said to have converted a king of Pegu to Buddhism (Mi Mi 1984). Thus in Burma, as well as in Buddhist enclaves in south India, women were active as patrons of Buddhism.

According to Michael Aung-Thwin, the Pagan state that existed from 1044 to around c.e. 1300 coincides with the classical age of Burmese history, when the institutional foundations of the modern Burmese society and state were laid. The six fundamental components of this classical age were Theravada Buddhism, which supported merit as the path to salvation; an economy of redistribution; a state based on agriculture, in which control of labor was more crucial than control of land; a society where horizontal occupational classes coexisted within a vertical structure of patron-client relationships; codified law; and a kingship that was legitimated by acquiring merit for king and people through gifts of resources (mainly land, tax exemptions, and people) to Buddhist monasteries (Aung-Thwin 1985). Relatively little is known about the condition of most women during this era, although royal women were significant in determining succession and appeared to control considerable resources.

Pagan kings had four queens; the chief one, designated the "Southern Queen," was of royal birth, usually a half-sister or cousin of the king. Only her sons were considered legitimate heirs, and her eldest daughter became the "Princess of the Solitary Post," the female counterpart of the male heir apparent. Succession could pass among the king's brothers as well as his sons, as long as they were sons of the chief queen. Militarily successful, charismatic claimants could legitimate succession to kingship through marriage to the chief queen of their predecessor or the "Princess of the Solitary Post" (ibid.). Besides functioning as the link between kingly succession, Pagan queens also sought to acquire merit through gifts to Buddhist institutions. In c.e. 1271, Queen Phwa Jaw (Pwazaw) of Pagan declared that

> [W]henever I am born, I wish to be fully equipped with *dana*, precepts, faith, wisdom, nobility, which are virtues, and not know a bit of misery. At the end, having enjoyed bliss as man [*sic*] and *nat* [spirit], I wish the state of *arahant*ship which is noble, having internalized the doctrine of release and the tranquil and serene peace of *nibbana* [release from cycle of transmigration]. Thus I donate these lands, gardens, *kywan* (bondsmen), cows, and properties. All of these endowed properties are bona fide, none will have cause for argument later. (Ibid.: 41)

Thus Queen Phwa Jaw seemed to accept a hierarchy of rebirths from woman to man to spirit on the way to *arahant*ship or buddhahood, but emphasized that she had clear control of moveable and immoveable properties.

There is some indication that Burmese women were active in agriculture, in the spinning of yarn and the weaving of cloth, and in trade. They were particularly identified with the trade of items associated with the production of betel and the elaborate rituals involved with the chewing of betel, such as jewelled betel containers (Mi Mi 1984).

In 1351, a male member of a Chinese merchant family who had married into ruling families of neighboring Thai kingdoms formally established a Thai state based at Ayutthaya. Situated in the Mekong and Chao Phraya river valleys, Ayutthaya had to contend with challenges from other Thai rivals as well as Burmese, Khmer, and Vietnamese neighbors.

After centuries of contested incorporation into the Chinese empire, the Ly dynasty established an autonomous Vietnamese state based at Thang-long (modern-day Hanoi) by the early eleventh century c.e. It patronized Buddhist monks who adapted Chinese Buddhist sects to the Vietnamese context. Although Vietnamese women might have been active donors to Buddhist institutions, our knowledge of women in Vietnam prior to c.e. 1500 is scant. Most sources cite three women who were honored as heroines challenging Chinese control. In c.e. 40, the two Trung sisters led an army, including female officers, that won independence for three years. Upon the victorious return of the Chinese, the Trung sisters committed suicide. In c.e. 247, Trieu Thi Trinh, a nineteen-year-old peasant girl, similarly led resistance to the Chinese and chose suicide when defeated (Marr 1981).

From the seventh to the twelfth centuries C. E., Srivijaya, based at Palembang in southeastern Sumatra, dominated trade through the Malacca (Melaka) and Sunda Straits. The Malay rulers of this entrepôt state forged their power through a special relationship with China; the provision of such services as loading, sorting, and distribution of foreign and local products (mainly from forests, such as aromatic woods and spices, and from seas, such as coral) for traders; the control of piracy; and extensive patronage of religious and educational institutions. Invasions from Java, changing attitudes in China toward trade, and tensions between Srivijaya and its vassal ports weakened its dominance in the thirteenth and fourteenth centuries. Malacca, established around 1400, laid claim to the heritage and position of Srivijaya as the dominant entrepôt of the Straits. From around the thirteenth century, Indian traders displaced Arab traders. They came primarily from Gujarat but also from the west and east coasts of Malabar and Coromandel, respectively, and probably from Bengal. These Indian traders carried Chinese and Southeast Asian products first to India and then to Middle Eastern ports. They became the primary agents of the spread of Islam in the Malayan peninsula and the Indonesian archipelago (Andaya and Andaya 1982). Only the Balinese resisted acceptance of Islam, because of their opposition to Javanese encroachments; they maintained their integration of Hindu social and religious institutions with indigenous ones (Andaya and Yoneo Ishii 1992).

In central Java, the Sailendra dynasty of Mahayana Buddhist kings constructed the awe-inspiring series of graduated terraces at Borobudur in the early ninth century C.E., while a Saivite dynasty constructed a great temple complex at Prambanan about one century later. In 1292, the state of Mahapahit was established in central Java and would gradually claim hegemony eastward to Bali, northward to Borneo and the Celebes, and westward to Sumatra and even the straits of Malacca, thus laying the basis for the modern state of Indonesia (K. Taylor 1992).*

WOMEN IN SOUTHEAST ASIA, 1500–1880

Women and Indigenous Cultures in Early Modern Southeast Asia

Depicted by foreign travelers (ranging from Chinese Buddhist monks on pilgrimage to India, to the ubiquitous Ibn Battuta, to European merchants, missionaries, and adventurers) as being either bright butterflies or shrewd traders, women are frequently stereotypical characters in Southeast Asian historiography. Many outsider sources on women in Southeast Asia comment on their relatively high social position and link it to their economic autonomy, the veneration of fertility in indigenous religions, and bilateral kinship systems in which descent and property may pass through both the female and male lines (Andaya 1994; van Esterik 1982). Moreover, the existence of matriliny among the Minangkabau in Sumatra, where both descent and inheritance passed through women, also attracts attention. A more detailed examination of the status and rights of women in early modern Southeast Asia indicates that cultural borrowing from other civilizations can be selective and that pre-existing cultural patterns that represent indigenous belief systems and successful adaptation to environmental conditions might incorporate foreign elements but still

*In addition to the works cited in this section, see Fan 1982; Reid 1993.

84   Barbara N. Ramusack

remain dominant. However, recent research also suggests that the acceptance of world religions and the development of larger, centralized states led to a uneven reduction in the autonomy of Southeast Asian women and their consequent ability to participate in religious, political, and economic activities.

In the sphere of kinship and sexual relationships, the status of women as daughters and wives in Southeast Asia must be correlated with particular times and places. *Adat*, indigenous customary law and practices, could mitigate the constraints of the three dependencies of Indian women (despite the spread of the Laws of Manu to some areas, such as Cambodia), the three obediences of Confucian ideology (in northern Vietnam), and Islamic Qur'anic law (*hukum*) (in much of Malaysia and Indonesia). In his Braudelian-inspired survey of early modern Southeast Asia, Anthony Reid asserts that the value of daughters was never questioned in Southeast Asia as it was in China, India, and the Middle East, although sons were preferred in such areas as Vietnam. In his description of marriage, Reid relates that "the pattern of monogamy was reinforced by the ease of divorces, the preferred means of ending an unsatisfactory union" (1988b: 152). Moreover, "the pan-Southeast-Asian pattern of female autonomy . . . meant that divorce did not markedly reduce a woman's livelihood, status or network of kin support" (ibid.: 153) Reid claims that European visitors expressed surprise at two other aspects of sexual relations in Southeast Asia: first, the prevalence and lack of condemnation of premarital sexual activity, which, if it resulted in a pregnancy, led to the marriage of the couple and thus precluded illegitimacy; and second, the mutual respect and constancy of couples, because the autonomy of women apparently induced husbands as well as wives to try to maintain satisfying martial relations. But these generalizations might reflect European exaggeration and misperception of Southeast Asian customs and attitudes that appeared to differ widely from those which the observers remembered from home.

Utilizing indigenous sources, especially literature, as well as European sources, scholars have begun to modify and specify various aspects of these broad generalizations about female autonomy in early modern Southeast Asia. On the one hand, Barbara Andaya has commented that romantic love between husband and wife was highly valued in seventeenth-century Sumatra and that "it was considered appropriate for a husband to be stricken with grief when his wife died, to spend long periods weeping by her grave, and for a dead wife to appear to her husband in dreams with words of warning or advice" (Andaya 1993: 24–25).

On the other hand, indigenous sources reveal women subordinate and treated as objects. In a feminist analysis of *Sejarah Melayu*, a Malay court chronicle dated from around the sixteenth century but describing events in the mid-fifteenth century, Ruzy Suliza Hashim (1998) highlights how Tun Kudu, the daughter of a chief minister of Malacca, is divorced by Sultan Muzaffar Syah to be given in marriage to his treasurer in order to heal a rupture between two court factions, one of which is headed by Tun Kudu's brother. This Muslim woman was divorced according to Muslim protocols—except for the crucial one of asking for her consent—and used as an instrument to achieve political stability.

To overcome a lack of conventional, indigenous historical sources for early modern Bali, Helen Creese analyzes *kakawin* and *kidung* court poetry from the seventeenth and eighteenth centuries to decipher the ideals for Balinese elite women. Although the more stylized *kakawin* poetry incorporated Sanskrit poetic conventions and myths such as the Ramayana and Mahabharata, and the more direct *kidung* genre utilized epic tales of Javanese princes and historical battles, both of which employ battle imagery to describe sexual relationships, with the man as victor and the woman overcome by the arrow of love. Virginity before marriage was prized, but sexual relations ideally were to be a source of pleasure for both partners (Creese 1998; forthcoming a and b). *Kakawin* and *kidung* poetry also laud shyness and loyalty in elite women and the practice of ritual suicide by Balinese women, especially widows—surely a sign of subordinate status. Related to the Indian practice of *sati* and reported in Cambodia and Siam as well as elsewhere in island Southeast Asia, ritual suicide was committed by *satya* (fire) or by stabbing with a *kris* (sword) (ibid.). It is difficult to determine how widespread through Balinese society were the values and practices celebrated in this court poetry, but these literary texts were performed in relatively accessible public spaces.

In many areas of Southeast Asia, as in South Asia before and after the arrival of Europeans, daughters and women were valued as marriage partners since inter-state relationships were closely correlated with kinship ties (Andaya 1993; Carey and Houben 1987). Multiple wives and concubines in royal families could, however, spawn jealousy among women competing for the idealized relationship of romantic love with their mutual husband (Andaya 1993).

In the economic sphere, women were significant as local traders and produced some formidable exporters, including a pepper trader in Cochin-China and a tin merchant in Aceh, at the northern tip of Sumatra, who inspired fear in the Dutch. Women of royal families participated extensively in international trade: for example, the wife of Sultan Hasanuddin of Makassar on Sulawesi and those who occupied the thrones of three port principalities (Aceh, Jambi, and Indragiri) on Sumatra (Carey and Houben 1987; Reid 1988b).

Utilizing such skills as negotiation and fluency in several languages, learned through commercial activities, women in Southeast Asia were also notable diplomats. The king of Cochin-China dealt with the first Dutch mission to his state through a Vietnamese woman who spoke Portuguese and Malay. In Jambi on Sumatra, a prince's consort and his mother invited the wife of the Dutch resident to a tea party to settle the debts of the son with the Dutch East India Company (VOC) (Andaya 1993). Women were also used as envoys in peace-making missions, since they could bargain adroitly and were willing to subordinate their own sense of honor to the need to compromise in order to achieve settlements (Reid 1988a).

Perhaps the most spectacular exercise of public power by women in early modern Southeast Asia occurred in Aceh on Sumatra and Mataram on Java, where at least two rulers maintained female bodyguard corps (*prajurit estri*), including a group trained in the use of arms (Carey and Houben 1987; A. Kumar 1997). Remarking on the sultan of Mataram in the mid-seventeenth century, Rijklop van Goens estimated that his corps

> contained about 150 young women altogether, of whom thirty escorted the ruler when he appeared in audience. Ten of them carried the ruler's impedimenta—his water vessel, *sirih* [containers and instruments for making betel] set, tobacco pipe, mat, sun-shade, box of perfumes, and items of clothing for presentation to favored subjects—while the other twenty, armed with bare pikes and blow-pipes, guarded him on all sides. . . . [They] were trained . . . in dancing, singing, and playing musical instruments; and . . . , although they were chosen from the most beautiful girls in the kingdom, the ruler seldom took any of them as a concubine, though they were frequently presented to the great nobles of the land as wives. They were counted more fortunate than the concubines, who could never entertain an offer of marriage so long as the ruler lived, and sometimes not even after his death. (A. Kumar 1980: 5)

Valentijn, an eighteenth-century visitor, added "that the young women proved 'not a little high-spirited and proud' when given as wives, knowing as they did that their husbands would not dare to wrong them for fear of the ruler's wrath" (ibid.).

An extraordinary but unnamed member of the *prajurit estri* of Mangkunegara I (1726–96) of Java wrote a diary for the decade from

1781 to 1791 that documents how some women were literate and had extensive knowledge of court politics. In a comparison of the diary as a record of events with letters of male members of the VOC covering the same period and episodes, Ann Kumar found that "the area where the two records coincide is greater than where they diverge, and their divergence can be attributed more to the necessity of both sides keeping certain secrets, and to the imperfections in their means of gathering information, than to differences in their perception of the overall situation" (ibid.: 101). The female corps spawned another exotic image of Asian women among foreign observers, namely that of amazon warriors in Southeast Asian culture. More importantly, the existence of such female corps in Siam as well as Java indicates the continuing physical mobility of women and an alternative to marriage as a means of entering the orbit surrounding political power.

In some areas women actually ruled in their own right. Austronesian societies, which ranged from Polynesia to Madagascar and included Indonesia and the Philippines, did not have myths that were common to Hindu, Buddhist, Muslim, and Confucian traditions about the negative consequences when women exercised political power. Reid has noted that between 1400 and 1600 "there is a remarkable tendency for just those states participating most fully in the expanding commerce of the region to be governed by women" (1988b: 640). Examples range from Shin Saw Bu (1453–71) in Burma to Patani on the east coast of the Malay peninsula where the rule of women (1584–1688) coincided with the era when that port was a major entrepôt for the China trade. In Muslim Aceh, four queens (1641–99) maintained its status as the leading independent port in insular Southeast Asia, although in 1699 a *fatwa*, or decree (allegedly from Mecca) enjoined that the practice was against the laws of Islam (Andaya and Yoneo 1992). Although women as rulers were not unchallenged, they appear to have been chosen and governed successfully because of their knowledge of market conditions and their ability to both bargain skillfully and maintain their capital (Mi Mi 1984; Reid 1988a, 1988b; Tarling 1992a; Vreede-de Stuers 1960).

Although women in Southeast Asia enjoyed higher status and greater autonomy when compared to their counterparts in Indian and Chinese societies, Barbara Andaya has argued that the advent and assimilation of world religions in Southeast Asia had mixed effects on conceptions of divinity as female and on the participation of women in religious rituals, as well as on their social status and sexuality. As had occurred in South Asia, the Hindu god Siva acquired indigenous female deities as spouses when he arrived in Southeast Asia.

In India, his partners included Parvati, a mountain goddess; Durga, a warrior goddess; and Kali, a goddess of time, destruction, and death. In Cambodia, Po Nagar, an early spirit goddess, married him as Bhagavati; and in Java and Bali, Dewi Sri, a rice goddess, married Siva as Uma. Similarly, as noted in India, iconographic representations tended to portray Siva as physically much larger than his newly acquired consorts and to emphasize phallic symbols over those of the *yoni*, the female generative organ (Andaya 1994). However, compared to the growing literature on the persistence of worship of the Mother Goddess in her own image and in such manifestations as Durga and Kali in India, little is currently known about the continued veneration of indigenous female deities in Southeast Asia. Women's role in indigenous spirit possession rituals in the Malay-Indonesian sphere and later in the Philippines was increasingly denigrated. Women in Southeast Asia also seemed to experience restricted access to spiritual knowledge in Hinduism, Buddhism, and Islam; hence their participation in religious rituals was attenuated (Andaya 1994; Brewer 1997).

The penetration of world religions, especially Hinduism and Islam, into Southeast Asia also diminished women's position within marriage, their physical mobility, and autonomous expressions of their sexuality. There was a growing emphasis on the duties of a wife to her husband as well as a concern over the propensity of women to tempt men from the pursuit of spiritual achievements (Andaya 1994). By the late eighteenth century in Java, where Islam co-existed with earlier Javanese customs, husbands were restricted to four wives and could divorce them by proclaiming *talak* ("I divorce thee") three times. Women could only seek dissolution of their marriages if their husbands had some defect such as loss of reason, but wives were able to remarry after divorces or the death of their husbands (A. Kumar 1997).

European Colonial Policies and Southeast Asian Societies

As in South Asia, the Portuguese were the first Europeans, in the early 1500s, to establish outposts in Southeast Asia, most notably at Malacca (Melaka on the Malaya peninsula), on Java, and in eastern Indonesia, particularly the Moluccas (Maluku) and the Spice Islands. Soon the Spanish in the Philippines and the Dutch in Java challenged their Portuguese rivals. Although these outsiders had relatively limited interaction with indigenous societies from the sixteenth to the eighteenth centuries, they developed major urban centers, most notably the Portuguese at Malacca (1511), the Spanish at Manila (1571), and the Dutch at Batavia (1619), where their economic and political institutions would profoundly affect the lives of Southeast Asian men and women. These changes ranged from increased monetarization of the economy, to the evolution of plantation agriculture to meet the demands of the export trade, to greater disparities in the sex ratio (with overwhelming proportions of men in the urban populations), to intensified poverty and increased domestic slavery.

European practices triggered changes that soon impacted the sexuality and economic options of women in Southeast Asia. At the same time, the spread of world religions, especially Islam and Christianity, into Southeast Asia introduced new prescriptions on female chastity and physical mobility that further circumscribed female sexual and economic autonomy. In regard to sexuality, Barbara Andaya (1998) has analyzed how the custom of "temporary" marriages was transmuted into commodified sexual service. When European traders first arrived in Southeast Asia, societies from Burma to the Philippines had long permitted local women to cohabit with foreign traders in "temporary" marriages where both partners had rights and benefits. The men provided gifts and contacts to outside trading networks, and the women reciprocated with links to local economies, knowledge of indigenous conditions, family support groups, and sexual relations. Since such women might themselves be active in retail marketing and wholesale commerce, they had value as both economic and sexual partners. If their families were nearby, they had social resources that ensured their equitable treatment. When the trader-spouses departed, the relationships could be terminated with suitable gifts and support for any children produced who would stay with their mothers. The women were then free to enter other such marriages or sexual relationships without loss of social status.

In seventeenth-century Ayutthaya, a major entrepôt and capital of Siam, Osoet Pegua is an unusual example of this practice of concubinage or "temporary marriage." An entrepreneurial Mon woman (therefore marginal in Siamese society), raised in the Dutch settlement at Ayutthaya, Osoet had successive liaisons with three Dutch trader-officials from around 1630 to 1651, which produced one son and three daughters. Because of her close ties with a high official in the royal court of Siam and his wife, Osoet was able to facilitate Dutch access to local products. Her multiple networks also helped her to obtain favorable contracts for her commercial services, which at times included a monopoly on supplying provisions for the Dutch establishment in Ayutthaya. Even after the departure of her third Dutch partner, Osoet controlled enough financial resources to be able to send expensive gifts such as elephants to the Dutch governor-general in Batavia and thus prevent the repatriation of her children to their fathers. These men succeeded in reclaiming their Dutch-Mon offspring only after her death in 1658 (Dhiravat 1998). Thus Osoet epitomized the Southeast Asian woman who could acquire significant economic assets and personal autonomy from European trade because of her local contacts, economic acuity, and sexual services. Changing conditions would reduce future such possibilities for other women.

During the seventeenth century, as the numbers of European and especially Chinese men increased in international entrepôts and their economies became more monetarized, temporary marriages were reduced to commercial exchanges of sexual services for cash. Wives metamorphosed into concubines and then into prostitutes, with fewer rights and increasingly degraded status. Indigenous families who could afford not to do so became reluctant to have their daughters involved in these relationships. Consequently, European and Chinese traders increasingly sought sexual services from female slaves who were without familial support and desperately in need of economic subsistence. In some instances these women might sell their sexual services in order to provide support for their impoverished families. Moreover, European and Chinese men sometimes maintained several slave-concubines who earned money for their owners through their sexual work or could be sold to raise cash. Those who analyze prostitution in contemporary Southeast Asia increasingly emphasize the long-term origins of this phenomenon.

In a case study of the pepper trade on the west coast of Sumatra, Barbara Andaya (1995) has delineated how European economic demands, coupled with restrictive ideals of female modesty, resulted in the economic marginalization of women. When pepper was first brought from India to Southeast Asia, women cultivated it as one of several crops in family gardens. However, as export demands fostered larger-scale plantations, male laborers displaced women, for whom plantation labor was incompatible with other domestic duties or contrary to religious ideals of female modesty. Moreover, these prescriptions of appropriate womanly behavior also constrained women from taking their pepper crops to coastal centers for sale to Europeans, since, as noted above, these ports were becoming notorious as sites of prostitution. Thus in Sumatra, the center of the export trade in pepper, some women found their economic autonomy and resources reduced when they could not compete equally in the production or the marketing of pepper (ibid.). As European traders and colonizers extended their political control and transmitted their cultural forms to Southeast Asia, they influenced the lives of indigenous women in even more complex ways.

The Philippines, which Magellan claimed for the Spanish Crown in 1521, did not face effective colonization until the beginning of the seventeenth century and was an appendage to the more lucrative Spanish provinces of Latin America. Colonial policies encouraged first the lower levels of the small Spanish official hierarchy and later the Chinese traders to intermarry with local women, but the resulting *mestizo* community was much smaller than the one in Latin America. Concubinage and prostitution in urban centers gradually became more visible, as noted above, in the Indonesian archipelago. The introduction of Roman Law to the Philippines formally reduced the legal rights of indigenous women, particularly in regard to their children, to property, and to divorce. Spanish Christian prescriptions regarding premarital and marital sexual morality eroded the sexual freedom of Filipino women. Parents were urged to guard the chastity of their daughters, and at school elite girls were socialized to protect their virtue (Andaya 1997, Szanton 1982). The Catholic sacrament of oral confession also facilitated clerical efforts to ascertain and to condemn sexual practices contrary to Christian morality (Rafael 1988).

The impact of Spanish Christianization was most profound on those indigenous, usually older, women who functioned as animist shamans or "priestesses" (*baylan* in Visayan or *catalonan* in Tagalog). These women communicated with the world of spirits through drama, song, and dance and performed rituals at birth, during illnesses, and at death. Spanish missionaries, labeling these powerful women idolaters and witches, enjoined young male converts to desecrate and destroy their images or "idols" and ritual instruments. Furthermore, the missionaries promoted Christian sacraments (especially baptism), images, and institutions such as hospitals in order to usurp the shamans' roles as midwives, healers, and specialists dealing with death (Andaya 1994; Brewer 1997).

An alternative but subordinated religious commitment for Filipino women eventually emerged. In 1621 Mother Jerónima de la Asuncion, a sixty-five-year-old Spanish Poor Clare, arrived in Manila and founded a cloistered community. Because of the sharp contrast in its practices (such as silent prayer, the cutting of its members' hair, the abstention from sexual relations) from those of shamans, this community had little local appeal. A century later, Ignacia del Espiritu Santo founded an order later known as the Religious of the Virgin Mary, designed to accommodate indigenous women (Brewer 1997).

Although both Portuguese and Spanish encouraged some intermarriage of their officials with indigenous women, the Dutch in Indonesia created the most substantial *mestizo* community in Southeast

Asia (Blusse 1986; J. G. Taylor 1983, 1996). After an unsuccessful effort to encourage the export of Dutch girls from orphanages in the metropole to become brides of its Dutch officers in Java, in 1652 the VOC restricted official marriages between Dutch men and women. It permitted marriages between Dutch men and Javanese women but only if the latter had converted to Christianity. It then enjoined its other servants to live as bachelors or allowed them to form unofficial unions with Asian women. If Dutch men recognized the children of these liaisons, they would be considered legitimate and given legal status as Europeans. Jean Gelman Taylor (1983) has described how Eurasian daughters remained in Indonesia to provide marriage partners for senior Dutch officials. In their mid-teens these women generally married well-established Dutch men, two decades or more older than themselves. Creators of a *mestizo* culture in which they wore an Indonesian sarong and blouse, chewed betel, and lived in semi-seclusion, these women—known as *njai*—served the Dutch authorities as intermediaries between cultures (Locher-Scholten 1992; J. G. Taylor 1992) and as guardians of the social order in a frontier society. They produced children for employment and marriage within the Dutch establishment and possibly influenced their husbands against excessive drunkenness, lavish displays of wealth, and sexual practices (such as homosexual relationships) which Dutch officials deemed unacceptable. Consequently, in Indonesia, the category "European" included Eurasian children, in sharp contrast to British India, where such children were never officially categorized as British or European. Ann Stoler asserts that official Dutch support for concubinage "revealed how deeply the conduct of private life, and the sexual proclivities which individuals expressed were tied to corporate profits and to the security of the colonial states" (1989: 638). Thus the boundaries between public and private spheres were fluid if colonial political and economic interests benefited.

By the 1920s Dutch colonial policy sought to replace concubinage and marriage between Dutch officials and Eurasian and Indonesian women with marriage among "full-blooded" Europeans, or even sexual relations with prostitutes (Ming 1983) in an attempt to maintain cultural boundaries vis-à-vis nationalist incursions. This effort was only partly successful, since 27.5 percent of the Europeans in Indonesia still married either indigenous or "mixed-blood" women in 1927 and 20 percent still chose such women as late as 1940 (Gouda 1995: 165).

Still, a new category of *njonja*s, or colonial matrons, emerged, similar to *memsahib*s in British India. Frances Gouda has delineated how Dutch "colonial men mobilized their wives and daughters to shoulder the task of upholding the internal hierarchy and moral dignity of the white community, but were quick to blame women for any reputed loss of white status" (1993b: 334). Despite their duties to regulate morality and to buttress white prestige in the private world through proper relationships with their Indonesian servants (Locher-Scholten 1994), Dutch women along with Indonesian men and women were also viewed as "emotional, irrational, naive, lazy, or self-indulgent" (Gouda 1993b: 320). Consequently, they required the protection and the strong paternal-patriarchal guidance of Dutch men. As occurred in other colonial contexts such as India, Fiji, and Africa, white men entrusted their white female partners with responsibility for helping to maintain colonial authority, viewed any sexual attraction and relations between white women and indigenous men as threatening to that authority and their own masculinity, restricted their female relatives to domestic space, and then condemned these women as being racist in their lack of empathy for indigenous culture. Many white Dutch women benefited from their complicity with the imperial enterprise, but their position was ambiguous since they were clearly subordinate associates (Gouda 1995).

Although the colonial policies of the British in Burma and Malaya and the French in Indochina did not encourage the development of *mestizo* societies, intermarriages and less formalized liaisons occurred. Historical research is much more sparse on these regions than on India and Indonesia about this topic. Fiction, however, provides some insights about contemporary colonial attitudes. F. Tennyson Jesse wrote a fascinating novel, *The Lacquer Lady* (1929), about the final British annexation of Burma in 1885 as told by a *mestizo* woman with a Greek father and a Burmese mother. Jesse had traveled to Burma in 1923 and interviewed a few survivors from the end of the nineteenth century, including a *mestizo* woman who had served as "European" lady-in-waiting at the Burmese court. Although her novel carries a strong overlay of the fantasy of the East, her narrative contains a rich description of details of court rituals and personal rivalries among royal women.

More recently, Penny Edwards has analyzed two novels by French men about French women as well as sexual relationships between French colonial officials and Cambodian women. During the second half of the nineteenth century, it was socially acceptable for French men to have extended sexual relationships with Khmer women. However, in 1898 Governor-General Doumer sought to strengthen colonial control over Indochina, including the private lives of officials. So

French men were encouraged to marry French women, whose role was to produce children and thereby maintain the purity of the French culture, race, and nation. But French men remained ambivalent toward Cambodian women, whose reputed moral decadence and sexual wiles supposedly threatened their virility while their embodiment of womanly submissiveness seemed an attractive alternative to so-called New (modern) French women. These images of Cambodian women ignored the active participation of Cambodian women in agricultural and petty-trading economic activities and their autonomy in some areas of family relationships. As in India, indigenous women were urged to avoid imitating educated French women, who were seen as undermining French masculinity and culture (P. Edwards 1998). Unfortunately we know little from the perspective of Cambodian men or women about Cambodian women during this period.

There are two articles on women in Vietnam that illustrate what can be gleaned from indigenous, as opposed to colonial, sources. Ta Van Tai (1981) has described how the Le Code (1428–1788) embodied elements of customary Vietnamese law that softened the impact of Confucian injunctions and the later Nguyen laws (1802–1945). In Vietnam, as in India and Indonesia, customary law offered some recognition of women's rights that might be severely diminished under more "modern" legal codes. Literature provides one Vietnamese woman's extraordinary voice. Ho Xuan Huong, a poet active during the last decades of the eighteenth century and in the early decades of the nineteenth century, lived mainly in the urban precursor of modern Hanoi. Her poems use explicit references to sex as "a weapon against male humbug and supremacy" (Thong 1979: xlii). One example is "The Cake-that-drifts-in-water":

> My body is both white and round.
> In water I now swim, now sink.
> The hand that kneads me may be rough—
> I still shall keep my true-red heart.
> (ibid.: 99)

Although little is known about her life except that she married twice as a concubine and was widowed twice, she seems to reflect on her life in her poem "On Being a Concubine":

> One gal lies under quilts, the other chills.
> To share a husband—damn it, what a fate!
> I'd settle for just ten, nay five mere times.
> But fancy, it's not even twice a month!

I take it all for rice; some musty rice.
I labor as a maid: a wageless maid.
Had I but known I should end up like this,
I would have sooner stayed the way I was.
(ibid.: 100)

Her lament reflects growing restrictions on the sexual and economic
options available to women during the early modern period in Southeast Asia. From the end of the nineteenth century the rise of nationalist movements protesting against foreign political, cultural, and
economic domination offered ambivalent opportunities for women.
Indonesia is the most studied area probably because of an extraordinary woman who championed women's education and left an extraordinary testament of her views.*

WOMEN IN COLONIAL SOUTHEAST ASIA, 1880–1950

Reform Movements and Southeast Asian Women

Indonesians and many foreigners celebrate Raden Ajeng Kartini
(1879–1904) as the leading female advocate of women's and national
liberation because of numerous collections of her letters (Kartini 1964;
Coté 1992, 1995; Rutherford 1993; J. G. Taylor 1974, 1984, 1993; J.
S. Taylor 1976; Tiwon 1996; Zainu'ddin 1980a and 1980b). The daughter of a *priyayi*, an aristocratic Javanese who functioned as a Dutch
civil servant, and his secondary wife, Kartini was among the first Indonesian women to attend a European primary school, where she
became proficient in Dutch and met European girls. While her brothers went to secondary school, Kartini had to retreat into seclusion
from 1891 to 1895 in preparation for marriage. During those years
she read the works of Pandita Ramabai as well as some by Dutch feminists and became a friend of the Dutch wife of an assistant resident
in Japara. By 1898, her fame as an educated Indonesian woman who
appeared in public led to an invitation to attend the governor-general's
reception in honor of the coronation of Queen Wilhelmina. The next
year Kartini began to write to Dutch and Indonesian friends reflecting
on the condition of women in Indonesia and arguing for education
as a means of self-improvement, of escape from arranged marriages
and polygyny, and of preparation for motherhood (Coté 1995). These
themes were similar to those that elite women in India had begun
advocating in autobiographies, journals, and letters a few decades ear-

*In addition to the works cited in this section, see Abdurachman 1988; Reid
1993.

lier. For some feminists, the great paradox in Kartini's life was that, after strongly championing education for women and declaring her desire not to marry, Kartini first declined a scholarship to study in the Netherlands and shortly thereafter in 1903 agreed to an arranged marriage with an elderly widower who had three secondary wives. Their marriage lasted for only ten months; Kartini died on September 17, 1904, four days after the birth of her son.

Although well-known in Dutch and Indonesian elite circles during her lifetime, Kartini acquired lasting fame when J. H. Abendanon, a former director of education, religion, and industry in the Netherlands East Indies, published a selection of her letters in 1911. He wanted to demonstrate the value of educational reforms under the so-called Ethical Policy. To serve these goals, he excluded her letters to Indonesians and excised references to conflicts between Kartini and her relatives as well as her negative comments about colonial rule.

Dutch reformers sympathetic to Kartini's ideas on education formed the Kartini Foundation in 1913 to establish basic schools in which *priyayi* daughters could be educated as better housewives and mothers while retaining traditional Javanese values that were equated with aristocratic values—for example, self-restraint and graceful elegance. Frances Gouda has argued that this Dutch-sponsored education of elite Javanese and later Balinese girls was related to the Dutch policy of stripping *priyayi* men of their sacral and personal bases of authority and co-opting them into a constructed, hereditary hierarchy subordinated to Dutch political and cultural authority (1995). After the death in 1915 of her husband, Coenraad Theodoor, Elizabeth (Betsy) van Deventer-Maas (d. 1942) set up the Van Deventer Foundation in 1917 to launch boarding schools where *priyayi* women could be trained as teachers to transmit an approved blend of Javanese and Western values to lower-class women in urban and rural areas. However, *priyayi* class values that confined women after marriage to the home militated against the effectiveness of this trickle-down theory. Consequently, the mass of women—peasants, plantation laborers, and servants—remained non-literate and economically exploited within the colonial system (Gouda 1995).

Post-colonial scholars, both abroad and in Indonesia, continue to analyze and shape the persona and legacy of Kartini. Cora Vreede-de Stuers (1960) and Ailsa Thomson Zainu'ddin (1980a) pioneered the resuscitation of Kartini as an individual woman and her contextualization within a developing Indonesian women's movement. Responding to the contention that Kartini was a creation of the West, Jean

Gelman Taylor (1993) focuses on Kartini as a member of the *priyayi*. She concludes that Kartini was symptomatic of the *priyayi*'s effort to buttress their social position with the Dutch by educating their daughters so that they could establish congenial social relations with the Dutch wives of colonial officials. Nonetheless, Kartini challenged *priyayi* values in her campaign for personal freedoms for unmarried girls and her desire for a career.

Scholars have also delineated how Indonesian authors and political leaders have interpreted and used the legacy of Kartini. In an analysis of two influential works on Kartini, Danilyn Rutherford (1993) asserts that ambiguities in Kartini's life and writings permit reconstructions that respond to contemporary political issues. In an introduction to Kartini's life published in 1962 during the Old Order of Sukarno, Pramoedya Ananta Toer—Indonesia's greatest living novelist, whose works were banned in his own country—portrayed Kartini as able to challenge traditional values and transcend differences between classes. Thus Rutherford argues that Pramoedya sought to portray Kartini as "the first 'Indonesian thinker' able to represent her people in modern terms" (1993: 26). In a biography published in 1977 during the New Order of Suharto, Soeroto (Sitisumandari Suroto) collated scholarly data with oral interviews to construct Kartini as having a *priyayi* sense of benevolent responsibility for peasants, thus functioning as an inspiration for patriotic loyalty to the benevolent authoritarian New Order Indonesian state.

More recently, Sylvia Tiwon (1996) underscores how the New Order Indonesian government has apotheosized a woman who lived only four days after childbirth as *Ibu* ("Mother") Kartini. It now promotes Hari Ibu Kartini, Mother Kartini Day, when young girls wear tight, fitted jackets, batik skirts, elaborate hairstyles, and ornate jewelry to school, supposedly replicating Kartini's attire but in reality wearing an invented and more constricting ensemble than she ever did (Sears 1996a: 37–38). Thus Kartini validates the New Order policy of State Ibuism, "which defines women as appendages and companions to their husbands, as procreators of the nation, as mothers and educators of children, as housekeepers, and as members of Indonesian society—in that order" (Suryakusuma 1996: 101). In neither colonial nor independent Indonesia is there room for the Kartini who proclaims "I long to be free, to be allowed, to be able to make myself independent, to be dependent on no-one else, . . . to never have to marry" (As quoted in Tiwon 1996: 55, ellipsis Kartini's). Despite the scholarly cottage industry devoted to Kartini, other Indonesian women activists remain in historiographical purdah.

In 1980, Christine Dobbin lamented that three influential political historians of twentieth-century Indonesia did not integrate elite or non-elite women into their analyses. Although more research on women in social and political reform movements and nationalist movements throughout Southeast Asia has been initiated and published during the 1990s, it has yet to be incorporated into broader syntheses. There are occasional references to the role of Filipino women in the revolutionary movement against Spain and then the United States and to the impact of the American educational system, which provided equal access to both sexes. Thus the literacy rate among women in the Philippines was 82 percent by 1970, but the education was in English.

One significant exception to the invisibility of women in political histories is the work of David Marr on Vietnam. He writes, "By the 1920s, 'women and society' had become something of a focal point around which other issues often revolved. . . . Women became conscious of themselves as a social group with particular interests, grievances, and demands." But then "[d]ebates over women's rights (*nu guyen*) led rapidly to the question of distinctions among women (as well as men)" (1981: 191). Perhaps more quickly than elsewhere, the two sides of traditionalist and modern feminists were joined by social radicals concerned about women working on plantations, in mines, in factories, and as concubines and prostitutes. By 1925, Ho Chi Minh recognized the oppression of women by men, and five years later the newly formed Indochinese Communist Party numbered the fight for equality between the sexes among its ten principal tasks. In the late 1930s, the party urged reforms appropriate to various classes of women, such as equal pay for equal work for employed women, equal inheritance rights for middle-class women, the elimination of polygyny, and the right to free choice in marriage and divorce.

Economic and Professional Opportunities for Women

There is little historical research directly on women's economic situation during the colonial period. In general works there are sporadic references to the role of women as traders within both villages and urban areas. Most women worked in the agricultural sector, but there are only superficial comments on their participation. Moving beyond perfunctory description, Ann Stoler has argued that colonial rule and the introduction of private property in Java did not result in sexual dichotomy "but rather an increased scarcity and concentration of strategic resources . . . [that] adversely affected both men and women in the lower strata of village society" (1977: 89). By the 1930s, women came to constitute about 50 percent of the laborers on rubber plantations in Malaya (Heyzer 1986) and Vietnam and were a major factor on the tea, coffee, rubber, tobacco, and sugar plantations of Indonesia (Coolie Budget Commission 1956; Manderson 1980a). Women also worked under exploitative conditions in the textile mills of Vietnam (Eisen 1984). Prefiguring research on prostitution during the late twentieth century, James Warren recreated the lives of Japanese prostitutes in Singapore during the early 1900s and sought "to emphasize the dynamic nature of their struggle to find happiness or the factors which conditioned their failure, in contrast to the usual interpretation of these women as 'victims'" (1987a: 163).

During the nineteenth century women in Manila worked in new occupations, such as cigar makers in state-run tobacco factories and teachers in schools established by the Spanish colonial government, and in traditional ones as vendors, shopkeepers, seamstresses, embroiderers, prostitutes, and midwives. In contrast to other colonial powers, religious officials, namely the Spanish friars or priests, supervised women in some of these occupations, especially as inspectors of schools and as character witnesses for female applicants in tobacco factories and for reformed prostitutes. Ma. Lusia Camagay has emphasized that female economic activity, which included strikes at the tobacco factories, refutes the Spanish construction of Filipino women as coy, shy, and frail (1995). By the end of the nineteenth century, the Spanish government had provided institutions to credential women as teachers and midwives. Reversing the pattern in India, a School for Midwives was established first in 1879; a Superior Normal School for Women followed in 1892. The advent of the Americans in the early twentieth century brought coeducation and the opening of other professions, such as medicine and law, to elite women (Alzona 1933; Jayawardena 1986).

Women's Organizations in Southeast Asia

Initial efforts to form associations to improve the condition of women started in Southeast Asia, as they had in South Asia, in the early 1900s. Although most women in Southeast Asia possessed greater economic autonomy and physical mobility than did women in South Asia, their organizations were similar in structure and goals. Both used the press to propagandize for changes in social attitudes. To promote women's efforts to obtain education and to move into public arenas, Indonesian men and women formed associations such as the Putri Mardika

(The Independent Woman) in 1912. Articles in its weekly journal dealt with arranged marriages, child marriages, polygyny, and the women's congress in Paris in 1919. Several other women's associations were formed in the 1910s, and their publications proliferated. In Minangkabau, where matriliny prevailed, Rohana Kudus established a school for women in 1905 and began writing articles for journals, which her father and then her husband edited. Eventually she established *Sunting Melayu* (*Malayan Headdress*), the first women's paper in Indonesia. Areas of concern were the negative impact on women of polygyny, colonial control, and beauty contests. Rohana Kudus also formed the Union of Sumatran Women in 1911, which sent delegates to the first Indonesian Women's Congress (Wieringa 1995a). Emphasizing their limited class base, Vreede-de Stuers declares that these early groups wanted to improve the position of women through education, and they "flung open the doors of the 'domestic prison' in which women of the middle and upper classes were imprisoned like birds" (1960: 64–65).

Indonesian women were initially indifferent to suffrage. In 1908, Dutch women in Batavia, including Charlotte Jacobs, had formed a branch of the Vereeniging voor Vrouwenkiesrecht (Women's Suffrage Association, based in the Netherlands, hereafter VVV). Personifying the continuum between metropole and colony, Aletta Jacobs (1854–1929), sister of Charlotte and president of the VVV in the Netherlands, visited the Dutch East Indies in 1912 as part of a world tour with Carrie Chapman Catt, her American colleague who was president of the International Women's Suffrage Alliance (IWSA). Their goals were to promote women's suffrage, primarily in their home countries, and to learn about conditions of women in countries that were not represented at the IWSA. Jacobs was not particularly concerned with Indonesian nationalism or suffrage for Indonesian women, since there seemed to be little opportunity for the latter (Blackburn 1997). Although it had been first proposed in 1912, the Dutch colonial government established a Volksraad (People's Council) only in 1918. In general, the VVV was relatively unsuccessful in attracting Indonesian, Chinese, Arab, or Eurasian women in the Netherlands Indies to its membership (Blackburn 1995).

Indonesian nationalist and religious organizations created female sections that had greater appeal to middle- and lower-middle-class women than did suffrage associations. The impact of these subsidiary groups on women was mixed. The Aisjijah female section of the Muhammadijah, formed in 1912, sought to excise the influence of *adat* or customary law that preserved indigenous traditions. Over the centuries, Indonesians and other Malay peoples had melded *adat* and *hukum*, or Qur'anic law, into a synthesis in which neither was dominant. In some instances, *adat* worked to protect women, as when it limited the use of the *talak* form of divorce (by which a man could pronounce a divorce without any third party present) among Muslim men. Sometimes *adat* reenforced Muslim law, as in supporting the right of Muslim men to have four wives. Occasionally, Islamic law modified the operation of *adat*, as when it allowed Muslim women and men to assert their individuality and independence vis-à-vis family responsibilities prescribed and reinforced by *adat*. But the changing balance between *adat* and Islamic law could also weaken the autonomy of women in such areas as inheritance. The Aisjijah also sought to extend Islamic practices in more concrete ways. It prescribed a headdress for its members that left the face bare but covered the head and the neck. This partial veiling occurred during the twentieth century in a culture where most Muslim women previously had not worn any head-covering. Thus religious reform for women might bring some restrictions on their legal rights and dress, while simultaneously providing more opportunities for education and participation in religious activities, as in women's mosques (Vreede-de Stuers 1960).

In 1928, the representatives of over thirty women's associations met at the first Indonesian Women's Congress in Jog Jakarta (Yogyakarta) to discuss education and marriage as they affected women. Like the All India Women's Conference, which began in January 1927, the Indonesian women eschewed the consideration of political issues in an effort to obtain the broadest possible unity. They, too, proceeded to establish a type of coalition, the Perikatan Perempuan Indonesia (PPI), a federation of Indonesian women. Its elite membership asked the colonial government (1) to increase the number of girls' schools; (2) to ensure that an official explanation of the *talak* be given to the bride at the time of the marriage settlement; and (3) to aid the widows and orphans of Indonesian civil servants. Its social orientation was further reflected in the celebration of December 22, the day it first met, as Mother's Day (Hari Ibu). The Isteri Sedar (Alert or Aware Women) soon challenged the moderate position of the PPII, successor to the PPI. Established in 1930, the Isteri Sedar declared itself a political organization committed to the freedom of Indonesia and to improving the situation of proletarian women (especially their working conditions), and in favor of national education. The Isteri Sedar thought that a broad-based federation such as the PPII could never effect significant social reform because some constituent group was likely to be against most reforms. For example, in 1931 Muslim members of the PPII refused to send delegates to the First Conference of Asian Women at Lahore in India because that conference was on record as opposing polygyny. Many Indonesian Muslim women saw this position as contrary to Islamic law.

Debates over the appropriate age for marriage illustrate continuing differences among Indonesian women's organizations and between Indian and Indonesian cultures and colonial systems. In Indonesia, public discussion of so-called child marriages began in the early 1900s and involved Dutch colonial officials, Indonesian civil servants, Indonesian women (beginning with Kartini), Dutch feminists, and one male nationalist leader. Reformers generally sought to raise the age of marriage to ensure that girls would have an adequate period of childhood, access to education, more stable marriages, and improved health and maternal health care. A few reformers also wanted girls to have some choice in their marriage partner. Dutch officials were concerned about early consummation of marriages that might physically harm young wives, but Indonesian civil servants claimed that the practice of *kawin gantung*, where young wives resided with their parents until adulthood or menstruation, prevented such damage. Furthermore, some Dutch and Indonesian officials argued that the possibility of divorce to terminate difficult marriages reduced negative consequences of early marriages. Although child marriage was discussed at the 1928 Women's Congress, opposition of conservatives within the PPII and from the Aisjijah meant that women's organizations did not present a united front. There would be no legislation on minimum ages of marriage until 1974, twenty years after similar legislation in independent India—despite strong propaganda from the Isteri Sedar, a book by Dr. Soetomo (a secular nationalist who sought to answer objections from Muslims and nationalists), support from Dutch feminists, and efforts by the colonial government to pass legislation in the 1930s. By 1974, the New Order program of family planning to slow population growth became a major impetus for later marriages. The 1974 Marriage Law set the minimum ages of sixteen for girls and nineteen for boys, but census statistics indicate a rising age at marriage had already begun to occur, especially in urban areas (Blackburn and Bessell 1997).

Indonesian women's organizations did not begin to demand the right to vote until July 1938, although a few Indonesian women, most notably Mrs. Abdoel Rachman and Mrs. Datoe Toemenggoeng, had joined the VVV and sought to broaden its programs to include the interests of Indonesian women. The colonial government's willing-ness to nominate women to certain elective offices ("passive suffrage") but not to allow them to vote ("active suffrage") precipitated action by Indonesian women's organizations. In 1935, instead of Maria Ul-fah Santoso (later Soebadio) (1911–88), an Indonesian law graduate of the University of Leiden and the able leader of a constituent group of the PPII (Kahin 1989), Mrs. Razoux Schultz, a Eurasian woman, was nominated to the People's Council that had been inaugurated in 1918. In September 1941, her replacement, Mrs. J. Ch. Neuyen-Hakker, a Dutch physician, spoke against a government bill granting active suffrage only to Dutch women. A month later, the Dutch co-lonial government granted limited active suffrage to all women, but the threatening Pacific War rendered this advance void (Blackburn 1995).

During the 1920s and 1930s, women's groups and liberal men's associations issued a continuing series of demands for legislation on marriage. The government eventually responded with a "Marriage Ordinance Project" that permitted but did not require registration of marriages. The partners in such marriages had to accept monogamy, and women in registered marriages were able to apply for divorces if their husbands took a co-wife, or for other specified reasons. Opposi-tion from Muslim reform groups arose because of the prohibition on polygyny. Although the Isteri Sedar supported the project, radical women nationalists such as Rasuna Said were against it because it represented interference of the colonial government in the personal sphere. Maria Ulfah Santoso personally supported the project, but in 1938 she made an lengthy speech at the Third Congress of Indone-sian Women which placed the issue of marital legislation in a broader perspective. She called for compulsory education, argued for the ulti-mate disappearance of polygyny, and advised orthodox Muslim wom-en to seek the protection of the more liberal Maliki Islamic law school as opposed to the Shafi'i one followed in Indonesia. Santoso also claimed that Muslim men had to consider the emotional satisfaction of women as well as their material comfort, and the difficulty of emo-tionally satisfying four wives made it probably impossible to follow the Qur'anic prescription that all wives had to be treated equally. Modernist Muslims elsewhere cited similar arguments when they ad-vocated a uniform civil code that would proscribe polygyny for Mus-lim men.

The Japanese occupation restricted the women's movement dur-ing the first half of the 1940s (Lucas 1997). The struggle of Indone-sian nationalists for independence from the Netherlands, achieved in

1950, represented the high point of a partnership between men and women in public life. Afterward there was a deterioration in the position of women, as elite men began to look upon elite women as competitors for jobs and political positions, and non-elite women continued to fear repudiation by their husbands or the entrance of secondary wives. As occurred in other nationalist, anti-colonial struggles, women who had moved timidly and then boldly into public arenas were pushed back into their homes as newly independent governments sought to extend state control over families and secure social stability, ostensibly to promote national development. As mentioned earlier, General Suharto made State Ibuism, which confined women to the roles of wives and mothers, a key element of the New Order. Women in other colonized states had somewhat different experiences.

Women's organizations emerged in Vietnam during the 1920s. In the royal capital at Hue, a stronghold of traditionalism, Madame Nguyen Khoa Tung, whose pen name was Dam Phuong, led in founding the Women's Labor-Study Association (Nu Cong Hoc Hoi) in 1926, which elite women dominated, despite its name. Dam Phuong traveled through Vietnam to stimulate the organization of other women's groups and worked for better educational opportunities for women, while still defending the importance of family responsibilities for women. She also promoted a "buy-Vietnamese" campaign, similar to the *swadeshi* work of Indian women, that reinforced women's role as consumers and as controllers of household expenditures. This association organized a women's handicrafts fair in 1931 in order to build a bridge to other classes, but this activity failed to mollify critics, who called for basic institutional changes that would grant fundamental rights to women.

As in India and Indonesia, Vietnamese women also utilized the press to debate women's issues. In May 1929 *Women's News* (*Phy Nu Tan Van*), a weekly periodical, was established in Saigon. Attracting a wide audience (with a circulation of 8,500 copies during its early years), *Women's News* had an eclectic and increasingly radical editorial policy. It propagandized for improved female education, presented a wide variety of information for and about women, and attacked sexual segregation, polygyny, wife-abuse, religious escapism, and superstition. By 1934, it labeled the tendency of educated women to separate themselves from their working sisters as "feminism" and called for a basic reordering of the economic system, hinting that only socialism would bring true equality. When the *Women's News* ceased publication in 1934, the moderate position came under increasing attack for its lack of attention to class exploitation. Moderate women went in two different directions: a retreat to traditionalism, with an emphasis on devotion to family roles; an espousal of Marxism and the need for a fundamental restructuring of Vietnamese society. Nguyen Thi Minh Khai (1910–1941) became a "professional revolutionary" in 1930 and joined the Communist party, becoming the secretary of the party branch in Saigon-Cholon before she was executed by the colonial government. Women party members were active in general organizing work but achieved particular recognition for efforts to organize other women during the late 1930s. By the end of 1946, about one-quarter of the adult female population of Vietnam belonged to the Vietnam Women's Union of the Viet Minh. Women were willing to pay with their lives in the effort to expel first French and then American political control and to restructure Vietnamese society (Eisen 1984; Jayawardena 1986; Marr 1981; Nguyen 1994; Turner 1998).

In the Philippines, women's organizations emerged shortly after the American occupation and had the twin objectives of social work and achieving the franchise. Founded in 1905 by Concepción Felix, the Asociación Feminista Filipino was soon joined by the Asociación Feminista Ilonga; both were based in Manila. Two broader groups were the National League of Filipino Women, started in 1920, and the Women Citizens League, which María Pax Mendoza-Guazon, the first woman medical school graduate and the first woman to hold a chair at the University of the Philippines, organized in 1928. These Filipino women's organizations had to lobby a Filipino male legislature and received a less-sympathetic response than did women in India. Despite the support of President Quezon, Filipino women did not achieve the franchise until 1937 (Jayawardena 1986).

Thailand was the one country in Southeast Asia not subjected to direct colonial rule, and so women there did not encounter a political sphere dominated by an imperial-colonial dynamic. An authoritarian Thai elite carried out a modernization program during the nineteenth and twentieth centuries. Legal reforms affecting women began with new family codes during the 1920s and then the Monogamy Law of 1935, which legally ended polygamy and prohibited husbands from physically punishing their wives or killing adulterous lovers. Gail Omvedt (1986) has argued that these reforms actually worsened the position of women because socially polygyny was still tolerated, while secondary wives lost any legal protection. Now it was more difficult for a woman to obtain a divorce, and the law required the husband to consent whenever his wife entered any contract. Such consent had

not been necessary earlier. Once again, modernization and its influences, such as legal reforms, might have ambiguous effects on the
actual situation of women.

The current state of historical scholarship in English on women
in Burma, Malaya, Cambodia, and Laos supplies only snippets of information on legal and social reforms regarding women's rights and
autonomy, women's education, or women's organizations since 1800.*

WOMEN IN SOUTHEAST ASIA,
1950 TO THE PRESENT

This section is the shortest, despite the fact that this period commands
the most extensive scholarly literature on women in Southeast Asia.
Although much of this work is both informative and innovative, it
tends to focus on women's lives and representations of women from
the 1960s forward. What follows here is only a summary of the broad
trends regarding the position of women and a list of the major sources
that an interested reader might peruse for more specific data and insights. In all countries, independence from colonial rule has brought
significant improvement in the legal and sometimes social status of
women. These changes are usually most noticeable among elite wom-
en, who were able to take advantage of new professional opportunities because of their education, economic resources, or family network.
After independence each country passed a family or marriage law
that recognized the right of women to free choice in marriage, to
divorce, to retain custody of their children to some extent, and to inherit property. Educational opportunities increased, with a correspond-
ing rise in literacy among women; such rates tend to be higher in
Southeast Asia than in South Asia. The economic situation of women
is more ambiguous. As in South Asia, the percentage of women in
professions such as teaching and medicine has increased significantly. Until the 1990s, there was an important difference in the economic opportunities available to lower-class women in Southeast Asia,
because of the penetration of multinational economic enterprises. Elec-
tronic and textile industries are the most prominent in their exploitation of young, unmarried women, who are viewed as docile, transient
workers. In Thailand, prostitution that caters to an international as

*In addition to the works cited in the section, see Clancy-Smith and Gouda 1998;
Coppel 1997; P. Edwards 1998; Gouda 1993a, 1993b, 1997; Hassan and Cederroth
1997; Hellwig 1994; Jesse 1979; Kepner 1996; Kipp 1998; Lie and Lund 1994; Locher-
Scholten 1992, 1994; Manderson 1992, 1998; Ming 1983; Rimmer and Allen 1990;
Sears 1996a; Stoler 1989, 1992; Tarling 1992b; J. G. Taylor 1997a, 1997b; Toer 1991;
Van Bemmelen 1992; Wieringa 1988a.

well as an indigenous clientele has become a major source of employment for young women, especially from lower economic groups. The 1970s and 1980s witnessed a new wave of women's organizations that are more sensitive than earlier ones to class differences and more oriented to building class solidarity among women and other disadvantaged economic groups. Elite women are trying to build permanent bridges across class lines, while non-elite women demonstrate their ability to organize and to demand changes in social attitudes as well as economic structures. Women in Southeast Asia are mobilizing to counter the questionable effects of modernization and development on their legal rights, social options, and economic opportunities.*

*Suggestions for further reading: Agarwal 1988; Atkinson and Errington 1990; Bell et al. 1993; Brenner 1998; Dancz 1987; Eberhardt 1988; Ebihara 1974; N. Edwards 1988; Eisen 1984; Eisen-Bergman 1975; Evoita 1992; Heyzer 1986; H. Jacobson 1974; Karim 1992, 1995; Koskoff 1987; Laderman 1983; Lewis et al. 1997; Lim 1980; Manderson 1980a, 1980b, 1983; Muller 1994; Murray 1991; Nguyen 1994; Omvedt 1986; Ong 1987, 1995; Ong and Peletz 1995; Peletz 1996; Phongpaichit 1986; Potter 1977; Reyes [1951]; Roseman 1987; Salaff 1988; Sears 1993, 1996a, 1996b; Stivens 1991, 1994, 1996, 1998; Stoler 1977; Strange 1981; Sutton 1987; Thorbeck 1987; Troung 1990; Van Esterick 1982; Wieringa 1988a; White 1989; Wolf 1992.

SOURCES

Any list of sources is selective, and this one is no exception. Because there is an extensive literature from the social sciences and journalism on women in contemporary South and Southeast Asia, this bibliography is particularly limited in the sources cited for the period after 1960. Many books on India are available from South Asia Books, Box 502, Columbia, Missouri 65205 (FAX 573-474-8124, e-mail sabooks@juno.com), which both publishes books in India and sells a wide variety of books published in India. They also can order books in quantity for use as texts if they have three to four months' notice. A brief list of videos is given at the end of the bibliography. If not otherwise indicated, they may be rented or purchased at relatively modest cost from the Center for South Asian Studies, Film and Video Distribution Office, 203 Ingraham Hall, 1155 Observatory Drive, University of Wisconsin, Madison, Wisconsin 53706; FAX 608-265-3062. Information is available at 608-262-9690. Other interesting teaching materials are Indian comic books that focus on episodes from epics, on folk tales, and on historical figures. These illustrated materials are informative for presenting contemporary versions of myths and history and are published by Amar Chitra Katha (http://indiaworld.co.in/open/rec/ack/index.html).

An asterisk (*) indicates readings especially suitable for students.

Abdullah, Tahrunnessa A., and Sondra A. Zeidenstein. 1982. *Village Women of Bangladesh: Prospects for Change*. Oxford: Pergamon Press.
Abdurachman, Paramita R. 1988. "'Niachile Pokaraga': A Sad Story of a Moluccan Queen." *Modern Asian Studies* 22, no. 3: 571–92.
Afshar, Haleh, ed. 1991. *Women, Development and Survival in the Third World*. London: Longman.
Agarwal, Bina. 1994. *A Field of One's Own: Gender and Land Rights in South Asia*. Cambridge: Cambridge University Press.
———, ed. 1988. *Structures of Patriarchy: The State, the Community and the Household*. London: Zed Books.
*Agnes, Flavia. 1994. "Redefining the Agenda of the Women's Movement within a Secular Framework." *South Asia* 17, Special Issue: 63–78. Also published as "Women's Movement within a Secular Frame-

work: Redefining the Agenda" in *Economic and Political Weekly*, 7 May 1994, 1123–28.

*———. 1996. "Economic Rights of Women in Islamic Law." *Economic and Political Weekly* 31, nos. 41 and 42 (12–19 October): 2832–38.

*Agnew, Vijay. 1979. *Elite Women in Indian Politics*. New Delhi: Vikas.

Ahmad, Imtiaz, ed. 1976. *Family, Kinship and Marriage among Muslims in India*. New Delhi: Manohar.

———, ed. 1983. *Modernization and Social Change among Muslims in India*. New Delhi: Manohar.

Ahmad, Karuna Chanana. 1984. "Gandhi, Women's Roles and the Freedom Movement." Occasional Papers on History and Society, no. 19. New Delhi: Nehru Memorial Museum and Library.

Alavi, Hamza. 1988. "Pakistan: Women in a Changing Society." *Economic and Political Weekly* 23 (June 25): 1328–30.

*Allen, Michael, and S. N. Mukherjee, eds. 1982. *Women in India and Nepal*. Australian National University Monographs on South Asia No. 8. Canberra: Australian National University.

Allen, N. J., R. F. Gombrich, T. Raychaudhuri, G. Rizvi, eds. 1986. *Oxford University Papers on India*. Vol. 1, Pt. 1. Delhi: Oxford University Press.

Alston, A. J., trans. 1980. *The Devotional Poems of Mirabai*. Delhi: Motilal Banarsidass.

Altbach, Philip G., and Gail P. Kelly, eds. 1984. *Education and the Colonial Experience*. 2nd rev. ed. New Brunswick, N.J.: Transaction Books. Originally published 1978.

Altekar, A. S. 1978. *The Position of Women in Hindu Civilisation*. 2nd ed., 3rd rep. Delhi: Motilal Banarsidass. Originally published in 1938; second edition originally published in 1958.

Alzona, Encarnacion. 1933. *The Social and Economic Status of Filipino Women, 1565–1932*. Manila: Institute of Pacific Relations.

Amin, Shahid, and Dipesh Chakrabarty, eds. 1996. *Subaltern Studies IX: Writings on South Asian History and Society*. Delhi: Oxford University Press.

*Amin, Sonia Nishat. 1995. "The Early Muslim *Bhadramahila*: The Growth of Learning and Creativity, 1876 to 1939." In Ray, *From the Seams of History*.

———. 1996a. "Childhood and Role Models in the *Andar Mahal*: Muslim Women in the Private Sphere in Colonial Bengal." In Jayawardena and de Alwis, *Embodied Violence*.

*———. 1996b. *The World of Muslim Women in Colonial Bengal, 1876–1939*. Leiden: E. J. Brill.

*Anagol-McGinn, Padma. 1992. "The Age of Consent Act (1891) Reconsidered." *South Asia Research* 12, no. 2: 100–118.

Anandhi S. 1991. "Women's Question in the Dravidian Movement c. 1925–1948." *Social Scientist* 19, nos. 5–6 (May–June): 24–41.

*Andaya, Barbara Watson. 1993. *To Live as Brothers: Southeast Sumatra in the Seventeenth and Eighteenth Centuries*. Honolulu: University of Hawaii Press.

———. 1994. "The Changing Religious Role of Women in Pre-Modern South East Asia." *South East Asia Research* 2, no. 2 (September): 99–116.

*———. 1995. "Women and Economic Change: The Pepper Trade in Pre-Modern Southeast Asia." *Journal of the Economic and Social History of the Orient* 38, no. 2: 165–90.

————. 1997. "Thinking about the Philippine Revolution in a Gendered Southeast Asian Environment." Paper presented to the Fourth International Congress of the Spanish Association of Pacific Studies, Valladolid, Spain, 26–29 November. Copy supplied courtesy of the author.

*————. 1998. "From Temporary Wife to Prostitute: Sexuality and Economic Change in Early Modern Southeast Asia." *Journal of Women's History*: 9, no. 4: 11–34.

Andaya, Barbara Watson, and Leonard Y. Andaya. 1982. *A History of Malaysia*. New York: St. Martin's Press.

Andaya, Barbara Watson, and Yoneo Ishii. 1992. "Religious Developments in Southeast Asia, c. 1500–1800." In Tarling, *Cambridge History* I.

Anderson, Nancy Fix. 1994. "Bridging Cross-Cultural Feminisms: Annie Besant and Women's Rights in England and India, 1874–1933." *Women's History Review* 3, no. 4: 563–80.

*Aquino, Belinda A. 1994. "Philippine Feminism in Historical Perspective." In Nelson and Chowdhury, *Women and Politics Worldwide*.

Archer, W. G. 1971. *Kalighat Paintings*. London: Her Majesty's Stationery Office.

Arkin, Marian, and Barbara Shollar. 1989. *Longman Anthology of World Literature by Women: 1875–1975*. New York: Longman.

Arnold, David. 1993. *Colonizing the Body: State Medicine and Epidemic Disease in Nineteenth-Century India*. Berkeley and Los Angeles: University of California Press.

Arnold, David, and David Hardiman, eds. 1994. *Subaltern Studies VIII: Essays in Honour of Ranajit Guha*. Delhi: Oxford University Press.

The Arthasastra. 1992. Edited, rearranged, translated, and introduced by L. N. Rangarajan. New Delhi: Penguin.

*Atkinson, Jane Monnig, and Shelly Errington, eds. 1990. *Power and Difference: Gender in Island Southeast Asia*. Stanford: Stanford University Press.

Aung-Thwin, Michael. 1985. *Pagan: The Origins of Modern Burma*. Honolulu: University of Hawaii Press.

Bacchetta, Paola. 1993. "All Our Goddesses Are Armed: Religion, Resistance, and Revenge in the Life of a Militant Hindu Nationalist Woman." *Bulletin of Concerned Asian Scholars* 25, no. 4: 38–52.

————. 1996. "Hindu Nationalist Women as Ideologues: The Sangh, the Samiti and Differential Concepts of the Hindu Nation." In Jayawardena and de Alwis, *Embodied Violence*.

Bagchi, Deipica, and Saraswati Raju, eds. 1994. *Women and Work in South Asia: Regional Patterns and Perspectives*. New York: Routledge.

*Bagchi, Jasodhara. 1990. "Representing Nationalism: Ideology of Motherhood in Colonial Bengal." *Economic and Political Weekly* 25 (October 20–27): WS 66–71.

*————, ed. 1995. *Indian Women: Myth and Reality*. Hyderabad: Sangam Books.

Ballhatchet, Kenneth. 1980. *Race, Sex and Class under the Raj: Imperial Attitudes and Policies and Their Critics, 1793–1905*. London: Weidenfeld and Nicolson.

Balzani, Marzia, and Varsha Joshi. 1994. "The Death of a Concubine's Daughter: Palace Manuscripts as a Source for the Study of the Rajput Elite." *South Asia Research* 14, no. 2: 136–62.

Bandyopadhyay, Sekhar. 1995. "Caste, Widow-remarriage and the Reform of Popular Culture in Colonial Bengal." In Ray, *From the Seams of History*.

*Banerjee, Nirmala. 1989. "Working Women in Colonial Bengal: Modernization and Marginalization." In Sangari and Vaid, *Recasting Women*.

———. 1998. "Whatever Happened to the Dreams of Modernity? The Nehruvian Era and Woman's Position." *Economic and Political Weekly* (25 April): WS-2–WS-7.

*Banerjee, Sumanta. 1989a. "Marginalization of Women's Popular Culture in Nineteenth Century Bengal." In Sangari and Vaid, *Recasting Women*.

———. 1989b. *The Parlour and the Streets: Elite and Popular Culture in Nineteenth Century Calcutta*. Calcutta: Seagull Books.

*Bannerji, Himani. 1991. "Fashioning a Self: Educational Proposals for and by Women in Popular Magazines in Colonial Bengal." *Economic and Political Weekly* 26 (October 26): WS-87–WS-90.

———. 1993. "Textile Prison: The Discourse on Shame (*Lajja*) in the Attire of the Gentlewoman (*Bhadramahila*) in Colonial Bengal." *South Asia Research* 13, no. 1: 27–45.

*Bardhan, Kalpana, ed. and trans. 1990. *Of Women, Outcastes, Peasants, and Rebels: A Selection of Bengali Short Stories*. Berkeley and Los Angeles: University of California Press.

Bartholomeusz, Tessa. 1994. *Women under the Bo Tree: Buddhist Nuns in Sri Lanka*. Cambridge: Cambridge University Press.

Basham, A. L. 1954. *The Wonder That Was India: A Survey of the Culture of the Indian Sub-Continent before the Coming of the Muslims*. New York: Grove Press.

*Basu, Amrita. 1992. *Two Faces of Protest: Contrasting Modes of Women's Activism in India*. Berkeley and Los Angeles: University of California Press.

———. 1993. "Feminism Inverted: The Real Women and Gendered Imagery of Hindu Nationalism." *Bulletin of Concerned Asian Scholars* 25, no. 4: 25–36.

Basu, Aparna. 1976. "The Role of Women in the Indian Struggle for Freedom." In Nanda, *Indian Women*.

———. 1996. *Mridula Sarabhai: Rebel with a Cause*. Delhi: Oxford University Press.

*Basu, Aparna, and Bharati Ray. 1990. *Women's Struggle: A History of the All India Women's Conference 1927–1990*. New Delhi: Manohar.

Bedi, Susham. 1994. *The Fire Sacrifice*. Translated from Hindi by David Rubin. Portsmouth, N.H.: Heinemann.

Bell, Diane, Pat Caplan, and Wazir Jahan Karim, eds. 1993. *Gendered Fields: Women, Men, and Ethnography*. London: Routledge.

Bellwood, Peter. 1992. "Southeast Asia before History." In Tarling, *Cambridge History*, I.

Bhattacharji, Sukumari. 1991. "Economic Rights of Ancient Indian Women." *Economic and Political Weekly* 26 (March 2–9): 507–12.

Bhatty, Zarina. 1976. "Status of Muslim Women and Social Change." In Nanda, *Indian Women*.

Bhushan, Madhu. 1989. "Vimochana: Women's Struggles, Nonviolent Militancy and Direct Action in the Indian Context." *Women's Studies International Forum* 12, no. 1: 25–33.

Bhutto, Benazir. 1988. *Daughter of the East*. London: Hamish Hamilton.

Black, Naomi, and Ann Baker Cottrell, eds. 1981. *Women and World Change: Equity Issues in Development*. Beverly Hills: Sage Publications.

*Blackburn, Susan. 1995. "Political Relations among Women in a Multi-Racial City: Colonial Batavia in the Twentieth Century." Paper presented to CNWS Workshop: The History and Identity of Jakarta, Leiden University, 12–13 April.

*————. 1997. "Western Feminists Observe Asian Women: An Example from the Dutch East Indies." In Taylor, *Women Creating Indonesia*.

*Blackburn, Susan, and Sharon Bessell. 1997. "Marriageable Age: Political Debates on Early Marriage in Twentieth-Century Indonesia." *Indonesia* no. 63 (April): 107–41.

*Blusse, Leonard. 1986. *Strange Company: Chinese Settlers, Mestizo Women and the Dutch in VOC Batavia*. Dordrecht, Holland, and Riverton, N.J.: Foris Publications.

*Borthwick, Meredith. 1984. *The Changing Role of Women in Bengal, 1849–1905*. Princeton: Princeton University Press.

Brenner, Suzanne April. 1998. *The Domestication of Desire: Women, Wealth, and Modernity in Java*. Princeton: Princeton University Press.

Brewer, Carolyn. 1997. "From *Baylan* to *Bruha*: Hispanic Impact on the Animist Priestess in the Philippines." In Enrica Garzilli, *Journal*.

Brown, C. Mackenzie. 1990. *The Triumph of the Goddess: The Canonical Models and Theological Visions of the* Devi-Bhagavata Purana. Albany: State University of New York Press.

Brownrigg, Henry. 1991. *Betel Cutters from the Samuel Eilenberg Collection*. Stuttgart: Edition Hansjorg Mayer.

Bumiller, Elisabeth. 1990. *May You Be the Mother of a Hundred Sons: A Journey among the Women of India*. New York: Random House.

*Burton, Antoinette. 1994. *Burdens of History: British Feminists, Indian Women and Imperial Culture, 1865–1915*. Chapel Hill: University of North Carolina Press.

————. 1995. "Fearful Bodies into Disciplined Subjects: Pleasure, Romance and the Family Drama of Colonial Reform in Mary Carpenter's *Six Months in India*." *Signs* 20, no. 3: 545–74.

*————. 1996. "Contesting the Zenana: The Mission to Make 'Lady Doctors for India,' 1874–1885." *Journal of British Studies* 35 (July): 368–97.

————. 1997. *At the Heart of the Empire: Indians and the Colonial Encounter in Late-Victorian Britain*. Berkeley and Los Angeles: University of California Press.

*————. 1998. "From Child Bride to 'Hindoo Lady': Rukhmabai and the Debate on Sexual Respectability in Imperial Britain." *American Historical Review* 103, no. 4 (October): 1119–46.

*Butalia, Urvashi. 1994. "Community, State and Gender: Some Reflections on the Partition of India." *Oxford Literary Review* 16: 31–67.

*————. 1998. *The Other Side of Silence: Voices from the Partition of India*. Delhi: Oxford University Press.

Camagay, Ma. Luisa. 1995. *Working Women of Manila in the Nineteenth Century*. [Manila]: University of Philippines Press and University Center for Women's Studies.

Candy, Catherine. 1994. "Relating Feminisms, Nationalism and Imperialisms: Ireland, India and Margaret Cousins's Sexual Politics." *Women's History Review* 3, no. 4: 581–94.

*Caplan, Patricia. 1985. *Class and Gender: Women and Their Organizations in a South Indian City.* London: Tavistock.

Caplan, Patricia, and Janet M. Bujra, eds. 1978. *Women United, Women Divided: Cross-Cultural Perspectives on Female Solidarity.* London: Tavistock.

*Carey, Peter, and Vincent Houben. 1987. "Spirited Srikandhis and Sly Sumbadras: The Social, Political and Economic Role of Women at the Central Javanese Courts in the Eighteenth and Early Nineteenth Centuries." In Locher-Scholten and Niehof, *Indonesian Women in Focus.*

Carroll, Lucy. 1979. "The Muslim Family Laws Ordinance, 1961: Provisions and Procedures: A Reference Paper for Current Research." *Contributions to Indian Sociology,* New Series, 13, no. 1: 117–43.

*———. 1982a. "*Nizam-i-Islam*: Processes and Conflicts in Pakistan's Programme of Islamisation, with Special Reference to the Position of Women." *Journal of Commonwealth and Comparative Politics* 20 (March): 57–95.

———. 1982b. "*Talaq-i-Tafwid* and Stipulations in a Muslim Marriage Contract: Important Means of Protecting the Position of the South Asian Muslim Wife." *Modern Asian Studies* 16, no. 2: 277–309.

———. 1989. "Law, Custom and Statutory Social Reform: The Hindu Widows' Remarriage Act of 1856." In Krishnamurty, *Women in Colonial India.*

de Casparis, J. G., and I. W. Mabbett. 1992. "Religion and Popular Beliefs of Southeast Asia before c. 1500." In Tarling, *Cambridge History* I.

Chaki-Sircar, Manjusri. 1984. *Feminism in a Traditional Society: Women of the Manipur Valley.* New Delhi: Shakti Books, Vikas.

Chakrabarty, Dipesh. 1992. "Postcoloniality and the Artifice of History: Who Speaks for 'Indian' Pasts?" *Representations* 37 (Winter): 1–26.

———. 1994. "The Difference-Deferral of a Colonial Modernity: Public Debates on Domesticity in British India." In Arnold and Hardiman, *Subaltern Studies VIII.* Originally published in *History Workshop Journal,* Issue 36, 1993.

*Chakravarti, Uma. 1989. "Whatever Happened to the Vedic *Dasi*? Orientalism, Nationalism and a Script for the Past." In Sangari and Vaid, *Recasting Women.*

*———. 1993a. "Conceptualising Brahmanical Patriarchy in Early India: Gender, Caste, Class and State." *Economic and Political Weekly* 28 (April 3): 579–85.

———. 1993b. "Social Pariahs and Domestic Drudges: Widowhood among Nineteenth Century Poona Brahmins." *Social Scientist* nos. 244–246, [v. 21, nos. 9–11]: 130–58.

*———. 1996a. "The Myth of 'Patriots' and 'Traitors': Pandita Ramabai, Brahmanical Patriarchy and Militant Hindu Nationalism." In Jayawardena and de Alwis, *Embodied Violence.*

*———. 1996b. "Wifehood, Widowhood and Adultery: Female Sexuality, Surveillance and the State in Eighteenth Century Maharashtra." In Uberoi, *Social Reform, Sexuality and the State.*

*———. 1998. *Rewriting History: The Life and Times of Pandita Ramabai.* New Delhi: Kali for Women.

Chakravarti, Uma, and Kum Kum Roy. 1988a. "Breaking Out of Invisibility: Rewriting the History of Women in Ancient India." In Kleinberg, *Retrieving Women's History.*

*Chakravarti, Uma, and Kumkum Roy. 1988b. "In Search of Our Past: A Review of the Limitations and Possibilities of the Historiography of Women in Early India." *Economic and Political Weekly* 23 (April 30): WS-2–WS-10.

Chakravartty, Renu. 1980. *Communists in Indian Women's Movement 1940–1950.* New Delhi: People's Publishing House.

Chan, F. Yik-W. 1991. "Mrs. Tjoa Hiu Hoeij (1907–1990): Profile of an Enterprising Peranakan Chinese Woman Writer in Late Colonial Indonesia." *Archipel* 42: 22–28.

Chandler, David P. 1983. *A History of Cambodia.* Boulder, Colo.: Westview Press.

Chandra, Moti. 1973. *The World of the Courtesan.* New Delhi: Vikas.

Chandra, Sudhir. 1996. "Rukhmabai: Debate Over Woman's Right to Her Person." *Economic and Political Weekly* 31 (November 2): 2937–47.

———. 1998. *Enslaved Daughters: Colonialism, Law and Women's Rights.* Delhi: Oxford University Press.

Charlton, Sue Ellen M., Jana Everett, and Kathleen Staudt, eds. 1990. *Women, the State and Development.* Albany: State University of New York Press.

*Chatterjee, Partha. 1989. "The Nationalist Resolution of the Women's Question." In Sangari and Vaid, *Recasting Women.*

———. 1992. "A Religion of Urban Domesticity: Sri Ramakrishna and the Calcutta Middle Class." In Chatterjee and Pandey, *Subaltern Studies VII.*

———. 1993. *The Nation and Its Fragments: Colonial and Postcolonial Histories.* Princeton: Princeton University Press.

Chatterjee, Partha, and Gyanendra Pandey, eds. 1992. *Subaltern Studies VII: Writings on South Asian History and Society.* Delhi: Oxford University Press.

*Chatterjee, Ratnabali. 1993. "Prostitution in Nineteenth Century Bengal: Construction of Class and Gender." *Social Scientist* nos. 244–246, [v. 21, nos. 9–11]: 159–72.

Chattopadhyay, Kamaladevi. 1986. *Inner Recesses Outer Spaces: Memoirs.* New Delhi: Navrang.

Chaudhuri, Nupur. 1997. "Nationalism and Feminism in the Writings of Santa Devi and Sita Devi." In Ghosh and Bose, *Interventions.*

*Chipp-Kraushaar, Sylvia. 1970. "The Role of Women Elites in a Modernizing Country: The All-Pakistan Women's Association." Ph.D. dissertation, Social Sciences, Syracuse University.

———. 1981. "The All Pakistan Women's Association and the 1961 Muslim Family Laws Ordinance." In Minault, *The Extended Family.*

*Chowdhry, Prem. 1994. *The Veiled Women: Shifting Gender Equations in Rural Haryana 1880–1990.* Delhi: Oxford University Press.

*———. 1995. "Popular Perceptions of Widow-remarriage in Haryana: Past and Present." In Ray, *From the Seams of History.*

*Chowdhury, Najma. 1994. "Bangladesh: Gender Issues and Politics in a Patriarchy." In Nelson and Chowdhury, *Women and Politics Worldwide.*

Chowdhury-Sengupta, Indira. 1992. "Mother India and Mother Victoria: Motherhood and Nationalism in Nineteenth-Century Bengal." *South Asia Research* 12, no. 1: 20–37.

*Clancy-Smith, Julia, and Frances Gouda, eds. 1998. *Domesticating the Empire: Race, Gender and Family Life in French and Dutch Colonialism.* Charlottesville: University Press of Virginia.

*Coburn, Thomas B. 1985. Devi Mahatmya: *The Crystallization of the Goddess Tradition*. Columbia, Mo.: South Asia Books.

———. 1995. "Sita Fights While Ram Swoons: A Shakta Version of the Ramayan." *Manushi* no. 90 (September–October): 5–16.

Cohn, Bernard S. 1971. *India: The Social Anthropology of a Civilization*. Englewood Cliffs, N.J.: Prentice-Hall.

Coolie Budget Commission. 1956. *Living Conditions of Plantation Workers and Peasants on Java in 1939–1940*. Dutch East Indies, December 30, 1941. Translation Series, Modern Indonesia Project. Ithaca, N.Y.: Southeast Asia Program, Cornell University.

Coppel, Charles A. 1997. "Emancipation of the Indonesian Chinese Woman." In Taylor, *Women Creating Indonesia*.

*Coté, Joost, trans. and introduction. 1992. *Letters from Kartini: An Indonesian Feminist, 1900–1904*. Clayton, Victoria: Monash Asian Institute, Monash University.

*———. 1995. *On Feminism and Nationalism: Kartini's Letters to Stella Zeehandelaar, 1899–1903*. Clayton, Victoria: Monash Asia Institute, Monash University.

*Coughlin, Richard J. 1950. *The Position of Women in Vietnam*. Cultural Report Series. New Haven: Southeast Asia Studies, Yale University.

Courtright, Paul B. 1994. "The Iconographies of Sati." In Hawley, *Sati, the Blessing and the Curse*.

Creese, Helen. 1998. "Inside the Inner Court: The World of Women in Balinese Kidung Poetry." Paper presented at the conference on "Engendering Early Modern Southeast Asian History," at the East-West Center of the University of Hawai'i at Manoa, March 20–22.

———. Forthcoming a. "Images of Women and Embodiment in Kakawin Literature." In Mackie, *Disorientations*.

———. Forthcoming b. *Women of the Kakawin World*. Armonk, N.Y.: M. E. Sharpe.

Custers, Peter. 1987. *Women in the Tebhaga Uprising*. Calcutta: Naya Prokash.

Dallapiccola, Anna Libera, ed. 1985. *Vijayanagara—City and Empire: New Currents of Research*. Vol. 1. Wiesbaden: Franz Steiner Verlag.

Dancz, Virginia H. 1987. *Women and Party Politics in Peninsular Malaysia*. Singapore: Oxford University Press.

Dang, Kokila. 1993. "Prostitutes, Patrons and the State: Nineteenth Century Awadh." *Social Scientist*, nos. 244–246, [v. 21, nos. 9–11]: 173–96.

Das, Harihar. 1921. *Life and Letters of Toru Dutt*. London: Humphrey Milford, Oxford University Press.

Datar, Chhaya. 1995. "Deterrents in Organizing Women Tobacco Workers in Nipani." In Wieringa, *Subversive Women*.

Datta, V. N. 1988. *Sati: A Historical, Social and Philosophical Enquiry into the Hindu Rite of Widow Burning*. New Delhi: Manohar.

Dehejia, Vidya. 1990. *Antal and Her Path of Love: Poems of a Woman Saint from South India*. Albany: State University of New York Press.

———. 1994. "Comment: A Broader Landscape." In Hawley, *Sati, the Blessing and the Curse*.

———, ed. 1997. *Representing the Body: Gender Issues in Indian Art*. New Delhi: Kali for Women.

*Desai, Anita. 1980. *Clear Light of Day*. Harmondsworth: Penguin.

Desai, Neera. 1957. *Women in Modern India*. Bombay: Vora.

*Desai, Neera, and Maithreyi Krishnaraj. 1987. *Women and Society in India*. Delhi: Ajanta Publications.

Desai, Neera, and Vibhuti Patel. 1985. *Indian Women: Change and Challenge in the International Decade*. Bombay: Popular Prakashan.

Devi, Gayatri, and Santha Rama Rau. 1985. *A Princess Remembers: The Memoirs of the Maharani of Jaipur*. Reprint. Garden City, N.J.: Anchor Books. Originally published 1976.

*Devi, Jyotirmoyee. 1995. *The River Churning*. Translated by Enakshi Chatterjee. New Delhi: Kali for Women.

Devi, Mahasweta. 1987. "Appendix A: 'Breast-Giver.'" Translated by Gayatri Chakravorty Spivak. In Guha, *Subaltern Studies V*.

*———. 1995. *Imaginary Maps: Three Stories by Mahasweta Devi*. Translated by Gayatri Chakravorty Spivak. New York: Routledge.

Devji, Faisal Fatehali. 1994. "Gender and the Politics of Space: The Movement for Women's Reform, 1857–1900." In Hasan, *Forging Identities*. Originally published in *South Asia* (1991).

Dhiravat na Pombejra. 1998. "VOC Employees and Their Relationships with Mon and Siamese Women: A Case Study of Osoet Pegua." Paper presented at the conference on "Engendering Early Modern Southeast Asian History," at the East-West Center of the University of Hawai'i at Manoa, March 20–22.

Dobbin, Christine. 1980. "The Search for Women in Indonesian History." In Zainu'ddin, *Kartini Centenary*.

Dube, Leela, Eleanor Leacock, and Shirley Ardener, eds. 1986. *Visibility and Power: Essays on Women in Society and Development*. Delhi: Oxford University Press.

Duley, Margot I., and Mary I. Edwards, eds. 1986. *The Cross-Cultural Study of Women: A Comprehensive Guide*. New York: Feminist Press.

Eaton, Richard Maxwell. 1974. "Sufi Folk Literature and the Expansion of Indian Islam." *History of Religions* 14 (November): 117–27.

———. 1978. *Sufis of Bijapur 1300–1700: Social Roles of Sufis in Medieval Islam*. Princeton: Princeton University Press.

Eberhardt, Nancy, ed. 1988. *Gender, Power, and the Construction of the Moral Order: Studies from the Thai Periphery*. Madison, Wis.: Center for Southeast Asian Studies, University of Wisconsin.

*Ebihara, May. 1974. "Khmer Village Women in Cambodia: A Happy Balance." In Matthiasson, *Many Sisters*.

Edwards, Nancy. 1988. "The Balance of the Sexes in the Philippines." In Kolenda, *Cultural Constructions of "Woman."*

*Edwards, Penny. 1998. "Womanizing Indochina: Fiction, Nation, and Cohabitation in Colonial Cambodia, 1890–1930." In Clancy-Smith and Gouda, *Domesticating the Empire*.

*Eisen, Arlene. 1984. *Women and Revolution in Viet Nam*. London: Zed Books.

Eisen-Bergman, Arlene. 1975. *Women of Viet Nam*. San Francisco: People's Press.

Elson, Vickie C. 1979. *Dowries from Kutch: A Women's Folk Art Tradition in India*. Los Angeles: Museum of Cultural History, University of California, Los Angeles.

*Engels, Dagmar. 1983. "The Age of Consent Act of 1891: Colonial Ideology in Bengal." *South Asia Research* 3 (November): 107–34.

———. 1989. "The Limits of Gender Ideology: Bengali Women, the Colonial State, and the Private Sphere, 1890–1930." *Women's Studies International Forum* 12, no. 4: 425–27.

*———. 1990. "History and Sexuality in India: Discursive Trends." *Trends in History* 4, no. 4: 15–42.

*———. 1996. *Beyond Purdah? Women in Bengal 1890–1939*. Delhi: Oxford University Press.

Engels, Dagmar, and Shula Marks, eds. 1994. *Contesting Colonial Hegemony: State and Society in Africa and India*. London: British Academic Press, Publication of the German Historical Institute London.

*Erndl, Kathleen M. 1991. "The Mutilation of Surpanakha." In Richman, *Many Ramayanas*.

———. 1993. *Victory to the Mother: The Hindu Goddess of Northwest India in Myth, Ritual and Symbol*. New York: Oxford University Press.

Esterline, Mae Handy, ed. 1987. *They Changed Their Worlds: Nine Women of Asia*. Lanham, Md.: University Press of America.

Everett, Jana. 1986. "We Were in the Forefront of the Fight: Feminist Theory and Practice in Indian Grass-roots Movements." *South Asia Bulletin* 6, no. 1: 17–24.

*Everett, Jana Matson. 1981. *Women and Social Change in India*. New Delhi: Heritage Publishers.

*———. 1983. "The Upsurge of Women's Activism in India." *Frontiers* 7, no. 2: 18–26.

Evoita, E. U. 1992. *The Political Economy of Gender: Women and the Sexual Division of Labour in the Philippines*. London: Zed Books.

*Falk, Nancy Auer. 1980. "The Case of the Vanishing Nuns: The Fruits of Ambivalence in Ancient Indian Buddhism." In Falk and Gross, *Unspoken Worlds*.

———. 1994. *Women and Religion in India: An Annotated Bibliography of Sources in English 1975–92*. Kalamazoo, Mich.: New Issues Press, College of Arts and Sciences, Western Michigan University.

*Falk, Nancy Auer, and Rita M. Gross, eds. 1980. *Unspoken Worlds: Women's Religious Lives in Non-Western Cultures*. San Francisco: Harper and Row.

Fan Kok Sim. 1982. *Women in Southeast Asia: A Bibliography*. Boston: G. K. Hall.

Fatima, Altaf. 1994. *The One Who Did Not Ask*. Translated from Urdu by Rukshana Ahmad. Portsmouth, N.H.: Heinemann.

Feldhaus, Anne. 1995. *Water and Womanhood: Religious Meanings of Rivers in Maharashtra*. New York: Oxford University Press.

*Feldman, Shelley, and Florence E. McCarthy. 1984. *Rural Women and Development in Bangladesh: Selected Issues*. Oslo: NORAD, Ministry of Development Cooperation.

Fernandes, Leela. 1994. "Contesting Class: Gender, Community, and the Politics of Labor in a Calcutta Jute Mill." *Bulletin of Concerned Asian Scholars* 26, no. 4: 29–43.

Fildes, Valerie, Lara Marks, and Hilary Marland, eds. 1992. *Women and Children First: International Maternal and Infant Welfare 1870–1945*. London: Routledge.

Findly, Ellison Banks. 1985. "Gargi at the King's Court: Women and Philosophic Innovation in Ancient India." In Haddad and Findly, *Women, Religion, and Social Change*.

———. 1993. *Nur Jahan: Empress of Mughal India*. New York: Oxford University Press.

Flemming, Leslie A., ed. 1989. *Women's Work for Women: Missionaries and Social Change in Asia*. Boulder, Colo.: Westview Press.

Florida, Nancy K. 1996. "Sex Wars: Writing Gender Relations in Nineteenth-Century Java." In Sears, *Fantasizing the Feminine*.

Forbes, Geraldine H. 1976. "'Awakenings' and 'Golden Ages': Writings on Indian Women." *Views and Reviews* 2 (Spring): 61–74.

———. 1979a. "Votes for Women: The Demand for Women's Franchise in India, 1917–1937." In V. Mazumdar, *Symbols of Power*.

———. 1979b. "Women and Modernity: The Issue of Child Marriage in India." *Women's Studies International Quarterly* 2, no. 4: 407–19.

———. 1979c. "Women's Movement in India: Traditional Symbols and New Roles." In Rao, *Social Movements in India*.

*———. 1981a. "Goddesses or Rebels? The Women Revolutionaries of Bengal." In Seely, *Women, Politics and Literature in Bengal*.

*———. 1981b. "The Indian Women's Movement: A Struggle for Women's Rights or National Liberation?" In Minault, *The Extended Family*.

*———. 1982a. "Caged Tigers: 'First Wave' Feminists in India." *Women's Studies International Forum* 5, no. 6: 525–36.

*———. 1982b. "From Purdah to Politics: The Social Feminism of the All-India Women's Organizations." In Papanek and Minault, *Separate Worlds*.

———. 1984. "In Pursuit of Justice: Women's Organisations and Legal Reforms." *Samya Shakti* 1, no. 2: 33–54.

———. 1986. "In Search of the 'Pure Heathen': Missionary Women in Nineteenth Century India." *Economic and Political Weekly* 21 (April 26): WS-2–WS-8.

*———. 1988. "The Politics of Respectability: Indian Women and the Indian National Congress." In Low, *The Indian National Congress*.

*———. 1994a. "Managing Midwifery in India." In Engels and Marks, *Contesting Colonial Hegemony*.

*———. 1994b. "Medical Careers and Health Care for Indian Women: Patterns of Control." *Women's History Review* 3, no. 4: 515–30.

*———. 1996. *Women in Modern India*. New Cambridge History of India, series 4, vol. 2. Cambridge: Cambridge University Press.

Fruzzetti, Lina M. 1982. *The Gift of a Virgin: Women, Marriage, and Ritual in a Bengali Society*. New Brunswick, N.J.: Rutgers University Press.

*Gandhi, Mohandas Karamchand, Mahatma. 1941. *To the Women*. Edited by Anand T. Hingorani. Karachi: Anand T. Hingorani.

Gandhi, Nandita. 1995. "Masses of Women, but Where Is the Movement? A Case Study of the Anti Price Rise Movement in Bombay, 1972–1975." In Wieringa, *Subversive Women*.

Ganguli, B. N., ed. 1977. *Social Development: Essays in Honour of Smt. Durgabai Deshmukh*. New Delhi: Sterling Publishers.

Garzilli, Enrica, ed. 1997. *Journal of South Asia Women Studies, 1995–1997*. Milan, Italy: Asiatica Association. (This began as an on-line publication at ftp://ftp.shore.net/members/india; it is no longer available there.)

Geetha, V. 1998. "Periyar, Women and an Ethic of Citizenship." *Economic and Political Weekly* (25 April): WS-9–WS-15.

Ghosh, Bishnupriya, and Brinda Bose, eds. 1997. *Interventions: Feminist Dialogues on Third World Women's Literature and Film*. New York: Garland Publishing.

*Godden, Rumer. 1981. *Gulbadan: Portrait of a Rose Princess at the Mughal Court*. New York: Viking Press.

Gordon, Stewart. 1978. "Legitimacy and Loyalty in Some Successor States of the Eighteenth Century." In Richards, *Kingship and Authority in South Asia*.

Gouda, Frances. 1993a. "The Gendered Rhetoric of Colonialism and Anti-Colonialism in Twentieth-Century Indonesia." *Indonesia* no. 55 (April): 1–22.

*———. 1993b. "*Nyonyas* on the Colonial Divide: White Women in the Dutch East Indies, 1900–1942." *Gender and History* 5, no. 3: 318–42.

*———. 1995. *Dutch Culture Overseas: Colonial Practice in the Netherlands Indies, 1900–1942.* Amsterdam: Amsterdam University Press.

———. 1997. "Languages of Gender and Neurosis in the Indonesian Struggle for Independence, 1945–1949." *Indonesia* no. 64 (October): 45–76.

Gould, Harold A., and Sumit Ganguly, eds. 1993. *India Votes: Alliance Politics and Minority Governments in the Ninth and Tenth General Elections.* Boulder, Colo.: Westview Press.

*Gross, Rita M. 1993. *Buddhism after Patriarchy: A Feminist History, Analysis, and Reconstruction of Buddhism.* Albany: State University of New York Press.

*Guha, Ranajit. 1987a. "Chandra's Death." In Guha, *Subaltern Studies V.*

———, ed. 1987b. *Subaltern Studies V: Writings on South Asian History and Society.* Delhi: Oxford University Press.

———, ed. 1989. *Subaltern Studies VI: Writings on South Asian History and Society.* Delhi: Oxford University Press.

Guha, Supriya. 1996. "A History of the Medicalisation of Childbirth in Late Nineteenth and Early Twentieth Century Bengal." Ph.D. dissertation, University of Calcutta.

*Gulati, Leela. 1981. *Profiles in Female Poverty: A Study of Five Poor Working Women in Kerala.* Delhi: Hindustan Publishing Corporation.

*———. 1984. *Fisherwomen on the Kerala Coast: Demographic and Economic Impact of a Fisheries Development Project.* Albany, N.Y.: International Labor Office.

Gulati, S. 1985. *Women and Society.* Delhi: Chanakya.

Gulbadan Begam. 1902. *The History of Humayun or Humayun-nama.* Translated by Annette S. Beveridge. London: Royal Asiatic Society.

Gupta, Sanjukta. 1991. "Women in the Saiva/Sakta Ethos." In Leslie, *Roles and Rituals for Hindu Women.*

Haddad, Yvonne Yazbeck, and Ellison Banks Findly, eds. 1985. *Women, Religion and Social Change.* Albany: State University of New York Press.

Haggis, Jane. 1998. "'Good Wives and Mothers' or 'Dedicated Workers?' Contradictions of Domesticity in the 'Mission of Sisterhood,' Travancore, South India." In Ram and Jolly, *Maternities and Modernities.*

Hainsworth, Geoffrey B., ed. 1981. *Southeast Asia: Women, Changing Social Structure and Cultural Continuity.* Ottawa, Canada: University of Ottawa Press.

Hansen, Kathryn. 1992. "Heroic Modes of Women in Indian Myth, Ritual and History: The *Tapasvini* and the *Virangana.*" In Sharma and Young, *Annual Review of Women in World Religions.*

Harlan, Lindsey. 1992. *Religion and Rajput Women: The Ethic of Protection in Contemporary Narratives.* Berkeley and Los Angeles: University of California Press.

Harlan, Lindsey, and Paul Courtright, eds. 1994. *From the Margins of Hindu Marriage: Essays on Gender, Religion, and Culture.* New York: Oxford University Press.

Harman, William P. 1989. *The Sacred Marriage of a Hindu Goddess.* Bloomington: Indiana University Press.

Hart, George L., III. 1973. "Women and the Sacred in Ancient Tamilnadu." *Journal of Asian Studies* 32, no. 2: 233–50.

*Hasan, Zoya. 1993. "Communalism, State Policy, and the Question of Women's Rights in Contemporary India." *Bulletin of Concerned Asian Scholars* 24, no. 4: 5–15.

*———, ed. 1994. *Forging Identities: Gender, Communities and the State*. New Delhi: Kali for Women.

Hashim, Ruzy Suliza. 1998. "Bringing Tun Kudu Out of the Shadows: Interdisciplinary Approaches to Understanding Female Presence in *Sejarah Malayu*." Paper presented at the conference on "Engendering Early Modern Southeast Asian History," at the East-West Center of the University of Hawai'i at Manoa, March 20–22.

Hashmi, Taj ul-Islam. 1995. "Women and Islam: Taslima Nasreen, Society and Politics in Bangladesh." *South Asia* 18, no. 2: 23–48.

Hasna Begum. 1986. "Mass Media and Women in Bangladesh." *South Asia*, New Series, 9 (June): 15–23.

Hassan, Sharifah, Zaleha Syed, and Sven Cederroth. 1997. *Managing Marital Disputes in Malaysia: Islamic Mediators and Conflict Resolution in the Syariah Courts*. NIAS Monographs, no. 75. Richmond: Curzon Press.

Hawley, John Stratton, ed. 1994. *Sati, the Blessing and the Curse: The Burning of Wives in India*. New York: Oxford University Press.

Hawley, John Stratton, and Mark Juergensmeyer. 1988. *Songs of the Saints of India*. New York: Oxford University Press.

*Hawley, John Stratton, and Donna Marie Wulff, eds. 1982. *The Divine Consort: Radha and the Goddesses of India*. Berkeley and Los Angeles: Lancaster-Miller.

*———, eds. 1996. *Devi: Goddesses of India*. Berkeley and Los Angeles: University of California Press.

Hellwig, Tineke. 1994. *In the Shadow of Change: Women in Indonesian Literature*. Berkeley: Center for Southeast Asian Studies, University of California at Berkeley.

Heyzer, Noeleen. 1986. *Working Women in South-East Asia: Development, Subordination and Emancipation*. Milton Keynes: Open University Press.

Hiebert, Julie Hamper. 1985. "Sanskrit Poetry by Three Vijayanagara Queens." In Dallapiccola, *Vijayanagara—City and Empire: New Currents of Research*.

Hockings, Paul, ed. 1987. *Dimensions of Social Life: Essays in Honor of David Mandelbaum*. Berlin: Mouton de Gruyter.

Holden, Pat, ed. 1983. *Women's Religious Experience*. London: Croom Helm.

*Holmström, Lakshmi, ed. 1990. *The Inner Courtyard: Stories by Indian Women*. London: Virago Press.

Horner, I. B. 1975. *Women under Primitive Buddhism: Laywomen and Almswomen*. Reprint. Delhi: Motilal Banarsidass. Originally published 1930.

Hosein, Attia. 1989a. *Phoenix Fled*. Introduction by Anita Desai. Harmondsworth: Penguin/Virago.

———. 1989b. *Sunlight on a Broken Column*. Introduction by Anita Desai. Harmondsworth: Penguin/Virago.

*Hossain, Rokeya Sakhawat. 1988. *Sultana's Dream and Selections from The Secluded Ones*. Translated and introduced by Roushan Jahan. Afterword by Hanna Papanek. New York: Feminist Press.

Ibn Battuta. 1929. *Travels in Asia and Africa*. Translated by H. A. R. Gibb. London: George Routledge.

Ikramullah, Begum Shaista S. 1969. *From Purdah to Parliament*. London: Crescent Press.

*Jacobson, Doranne. 1974. "The Women of North and Central India: Goddesses and Wives." In Matthiasson, *Many Sisters*. Reprinted in Jacobson and Wadley, *Women in India* (1977).

———. 1976. "The Veil of Virtue: *Purdah* and the Muslim Family in the Bhopal Region of Central India." In Ahmad, *Family, Kinship and Marriage among Muslims in India*.

*———. 1980. "Golden Handprints and Red-Painted Feet: Hindu Childbirth Rituals in Central India." In Falk and Gross, *Unspoken Worlds*.

*Jacobson, Doranne, and Susan S. Wadley. 1977. *Women in India: Two Perspectives*. Columbia, Mo.: South Asia Books.

Jacobson, Helga E. 1974. "Women in Philippine Society: More Equal than Many." In Matthiasson, *Many Sisters*.

Jahan, Rounaq, and Hanna Papanek. 1979. *Women and Development: Perspectives from South and Southeast Asia*. Dhaka: Bangladesh Institute of Law and International Affairs. Distributed by South Asia Books.

Jain, Devaki. 1986. "Gandhian Contributions towards a Theory of Feminist Ethic." In Jain and Eck, *Speaking of Faith*.

Jain, Devaki, and Nirmala Banerjee, eds. 1985. *Tyranny of the Household: Investigative Essays on Women's Work*. New Delhi: Shakti Books, Vikas.

Jain, Devaki, and Diana L. Eck, eds. 1986. *Speaking of Faith: Cross-Cultural Perspectives on Women, Religion and Social Change*. London: Women's Press.

*Jain, Devaki, assisted by Nalini Singh and Malini Chand. 1980. *Women's Quest for Power: Five Case Studies*. New Delhi: Vikas.

Jaini, Padmanabh S. 1990. *Gender and Salvation: Jaina Debates on the Spiritual Liberation of Women*. Berkeley and Los Angeles: University of California Press.

*Jamison, Stephanie. 1996. *Sacrificed Wife, Sacrificer's Wife: Women, Ritual and Hospitality in Ancient India*. New York: Oxford University Press.

Jayal, Shakambari. 1966. *The Status of Women in the Epics*. Delhi: Motilal Banarsidass.

*Jayawardena, Kumari. 1986. *Feminism and Nationalism in the Third World*. London: Zed Books.

———. 1995. *The White Woman's Other Burden: Western Women and South Asia during British Rule*. New York: Routledge.

*Jayawardena, Kumari, and Malathi de Alwis, eds. 1996. *Embodied Violence: Communalising Women's Sexuality in South Asia*. London: Zed Books.

*Jeffery, Patricia. 1979. *Frogs in a Well: Indian Women in Purdah*. London: Zed Books.

*Jeffery, Patricia, Roger Jeffery, and Andrew Lyon. 1989. *Labour Pains and Labour Power: Women and Childbearing in India*. London: Zed Books.

Jesse, F. Tennyson. 1979. *The Lacquer Lady*. Reprint. London: Virago Press. Originally published 1929.

Johnson-Odim, Cheryl, and Margaret Strobel, eds. 1992. *Expanding the Boundaries of Women's History*. Bloomington: Indiana University Press.

Joshi, V. C., ed. 1975. *Rammohan Roy and the Process of Modernization in India*. New Delhi: Vikas.

Joshi, Varsha. 1995. *Polygamy and Purdah: Women and Society among Rajputs*. Jaipur: Rawat Publications.

*Kabeer, Naila. 1988. "Subordination and Struggle: Women in Bangladesh." *New Left Review* no. 168 (March/April): 95–121.

———. 1991. "The Quest for National Identity: Women, Islam and the State in Bangladesh." *Feminist Review,* no. 37 (Spring): 38–58.

Kahin, George McT. 1989. "In Memoriam: Maria Ullfah Soebadio, 1911–1988." *Indonesia* no. 49 (April): 119–20.

Kalidasa. 1984a. "Malavika and Agnimitra." In Miller, *Theater of Memory.*

*———. 1984b. "Shakuntala and the Ring of Recollection." In Miller, *Theater of Memory.*

———. 1984c. "Urvasi Won by Valor." In Miller, *Theater of Memory.*

Kalpagam, U. 1994. *Labour and Gender: Survival in Urban India.* Thousand Oaks, Calif.: Sage Publications.

The Kama Sutra of Vatsyayana. 1962. Translated by Richard F. Burton. New York: E. P. Dutton.

Kapadia, Karin. 1994. "Impure Women, Virtuous Men: Religion, Resistance and Gender." *South Asia Research* 14, no. 2: 184–94.

Kapur, Promilla. 1974. *The Changing Status of the Working Woman in India.* New Delhi: Vikas.

———. 1977. "Problems of Urban Working Women." In Ganguli, *Social Development.*

Kapur, Ratna, ed. 1996. *Feminist Terrains in Legal Domains: Interdisciplinary Essays on Women and Law in India.* New Delhi: Kali for Women.

*Karim, Wazir Jahan. 1992. *Women and Culture: Between Malay* Adat *and Islam.* Boulder, Colo.: Westview Press.

*———, ed. 1995. *"Male" and "Female" in Developing Southeast Asia.* Oxford and Washington, D.C.: Berg Publishers.

*Karlekar, Malavika. 1982. *Poverty and Women's Work: A Study of Sweeper Women in Delhi.* New Delhi: Vikas.

*———. 1991. *Voices from Within: Early Personal Narratives of Bengali Women.* Delhi: Oxford University Press.

*Kartini, Raden Adjeng. 1964. *Letters of a Javanese Princess.* Translated by Agnes Louise Symmers. Edited and with an introduction by Hildred Geertz. Reprint. New York: W. W. Norton. Originally published 1920.

*———. 1995. *On Feminism and Nationalism: Kartini's Letters to Stella Zeehandelaar, 1899–1903.* Translated with an introduction by Joost Coté. Clayton: Monash Asia Institute, Monash University.

Karve, D. D., ed. and trans. 1963. *The New Brahmans: Five Maharashtrian Families.* Berkeley and Los Angeles: University of California Press.

Katzenstein, Mary Fainsod. 1989. "Organizing against Violence: Strategies of the Indian Women's Movement." *Pacific Affairs* 62, no. 1 (Spring): 53–71.

Kaur, Manmohan. 1985. *Women in India's Freedom Struggle.* New Delhi: Sterling Publishers. (Earlier edition published in 1968 was entitled *Role of Women in the Freedom Movement [1857–1947].*)

*Kautilya. 1992. *The Arthasaastra.* Edited, rearranged, translated and introduced by L. N. Rangarajan. New Delhi: Penguin.

Kepner, Susan Fulop, ed. and trans. 1996. *The Lioness in Bloom: Contemporary Thai Fiction.* Berkeley and Los Angeles: University of California Press.

Kersenboom-Story, Saskia C. 1987. Nityasumangali: *Devadasi Tradition in South India.* Delhi: Motilal Banarsidass.

*Kinsley, David. 1986. *Hindu Goddesses: Visions of the Divine Feminine in the Hindu Religious Tradition.* Berkeley and Los Angeles: University of California Press.

———. 1997. *Tantric Visions of the Divine Feminine: The Ten Mahavidyas.* Berkeley and Los Angeles: University of California Press.

Kipp, Rita Smith. 1998. "Emancipating Each Other: Dutch Colonial Mission-
    aries' Encounter with Karo Women in Sumatra, 1900–1942." In
    Clancy-Smith and Gouda, *Domesticating the Empire*.
*Kishwar, Madhu. 1985. "Women and Gandhi." *Economic and Political Weekly*
    20 (October 5 and 12): 1691–1702, 1753–1758.
*———. 1989. "The Daughters of Aryavarta." In Krishnamurty, *Women in Co-
    lonial India*.
*Kishwar, Madhu, and Ruth Vanita, eds. 1984. *In Search of Answers: Indian
    Women's Voices from Manushi*. London: Zed Books.
Kleinberg, S. Jay, ed. 1988. *Retrieving Women's History: Changing Perceptions of
    the Role of Women in Politics and Society*. Berg: UNESCO.
Kolenda, Pauline, ed. 1987. *Regional Differences in Family Structure in India*.
    Jaipur: Rawat.
———, ed. 1988. *Cultural Constructions of "Woman"*. Salem, Wis.: Sheffield
    Publishing.
*Kosambi, Meera. 1988. "Women, Emancipation and Equality: Pandita Rama-
    bai's Contribution to the Women's Cause." *Economic and Political Week-
    ly* 23 (October 29): WS-38–WS-49.
———. 1991. "Girl-Brides and Socio-Legal Change: Age of Consent Bill (1891)
    Controversy." *Economic and Political Weekly* 26 (August 3–10):
    1857–68.
*———. 1992. "Indian Response to Christianity, Church and Colonialism: Case
    of Pandita Ramabai." *Economic and Political Weekly* 27 (October 24–
    31): WS-61–WS-71.
———. 1996a. "Anandibai Joshee: Retrieving a Fragmented Feminist Im-
    age." *Economic and Political Weekly* 31, no. 49 (7 December): 3189–
    3197.
———. 1996b. "Gender Reform and Competing State Controls over Women:
    The Rakhmabai Case (1884–1888)." In Uberoi, *Social Reform, Sexu-
    ality and the State*.
Koskoff, Ellen, ed. 1987. *Women and Music in Cross-Cultural Perspective*. Westport,
    Conn.: Greenwood Press.
*Krishnamurty, J., ed. 1989. *Women in Colonial India: Essays on Survival, Work
    and the State*. Delhi: Oxford University Press.
Krishnaraj, Maithreyi, ed. N.d. *Feminism: Indian Debates 1990*. Bombay: SNDT
    University.
Krishnaswamy, Revathi. 1993. "Subversive Spirituality: Woman as Saint-
    Poet in Medieval India." *Women's Studies International Forum* 16, no.
    2: 139–47.
Kruks, S., et al., eds. 1989. *Promissory Notes*. New York: Monthly Review Press.
Kumar, Ann. 1980. "Javanese Court Society and Politics in the Late Eigh-
    teenth Century: The Record of a Lady Soldier." Pt. 1: "The Reli-
    gious, Social and Economic Life of the Court." *Indonesia* no. 29
    (April): 1–49. Pt. 2: "Political Developments: The Courts and the
    Company, 1784–1791." *Indonesia* no. 30 (October): 67–111.
———. 1997. *Java and Modern Europe: Ambiguous Encounters*. Richmond:
    Curzon.
Kumar, Kapil. 1989. "Rural Women in Oudh 1917–1947: Baba Ram Chandra
    and the Women's Question." In Sangari and Vaid, *Recasting Women*.
Kumar, Nita, ed. 1994. *Women as Subjects: South Asian Histories*. Charlottesville:
    University Press of Virginia.
*Kumar, Radha. 1983. "Family and Factory: Women Workers in the Bombay

Cotton Textile Industry, 1919–1939." *Indian Economic and Social History Review* 20, no. 1: 81–110.

*———. 1994. *The History of Doing: The Women's Movement in India*. New Delhi: Kali for Women. Reprint. New York: Verso. Originally published 1993.

Laderman, Carol. 1983. *Wives and Midwives: Childbirth and Nutrition in Rural Malaysia*. Berkeley and Los Angeles: University of California Press.

Lakshmi, C. S. 1984. *The Face behind the Mask: Women in Tamil Literature*. New Delhi: Shakti Books, Vikas.

Lal, Maneesha. 1994. "The Politics of Gender and Medicine in Colonial India: The Countess of Dufferin's Fund, 1885–1888." *Bulletin of the History of Medicine* 68: 29–66.

Larson, Gerald James, Prataditya Pal, and Rebecca P. Gowen. 1980. *In Her Image: The Great Goddess in Indian Asia and The Madonna in Christian Culture*. Santa Barbara: UCSB Art Museum, University of California, Santa Barbara.

The Laws of Manu. 1991. Translated by Wendy Doniger with Brian K. Smith. London: Penguin.

Lay, Ma Ma. 1991. *Not Out of Hate: A Novel of Burma*. Translated by Margaret Aung-Thwin. Edited by William H. Frederick. Athens: Ohio University Press.

Lebra-Chapman, Joyce. 1986. *The Rani of Jhansi: A Study of Female Heroism in India*. Honolulu: University of Hawaii Press.

*Leslie, I. Julia. 1983. "Essence and Existence: Women and Religion in Ancient Indian Texts." In Holden, *Women's Religious Experience*.

———. 1986. "*Strisvbhava*: The Inherent Nature of Women." In Allen et al., *Oxford University Papers on India*.

———. 1989. *The Perfect Wife: The Orthodox Hindu Woman According to the Stridharmapaddhati of Tryambakayajvan*. Delhi: Oxford University Press.

———. 1991a. "Suttee or *Sati*: Victim or Victor?" In Leslie, *Roles and Rituals for Hindu Women*.

*Leslie, I. Julia, ed. 1991b. *Roles and Rituals for Hindu Women*. Rutherford, N.J.: Fairleigh Dickinson University Press.

Levine, Philippa. 1994. "Venereal Disease, Prostitution, and the Politics of Empire: The Case of British India." *Journal of the History of Sexuality* 4, no. 4: 579–602.

Lewis, Milton, Scott Bamber, and Michael Waugh, eds. 1997. *Sex, Disease, and Society: A Comparative History of Sexually Transmitted Diseases and HIV/AIDS in Asia and the Pacific*. Westport, Conn.: Greenwood Press.

Liddle, Joanna, and Rama Joshi. 1986. *Daughters of Independence: Gender, Caste and Class in India*. London: Zed Books.

Lie, Merete, and Ragnhild Lund. 1994. *Renegotiating Local Values: Working Women and Foreign Industry in Malaysia*. NIAS Studies in Asian Topics, no. 15. Richmond: Curzon Press.

*Lim, Catherine. 1980. *Or Else, The Lightning God and Other Stories*. Portsmouth, N.H.: Heinemann/Methuen.

Locher-Scholten, Elsbeth. 1992. "Njai in Colonial Deli: A Case of Supposed Mediation." In Van Bemmelen, *Women and Mediation in Indonesia*.

———. 1994. "Orientalism and the Rhetoric of the Family: Javanese Servants in European Household Manuals and Children's Fiction." *Indonesia* no. 58 (October): 19–39.

*Locher-Scholten, Elsbeth, and Anke Niehof, eds. 1987. *Indonesian Women in Focus: Past and Present Notions*. Dordrecht, Holland and Providence: Foris Publications.

Low, D. Anthony, ed. 1988. *The Indian National Congress: Centenary Hindsights*. Delhi: Oxford University Press.

Lucas, Anton. 1997. "Images of the Indonesian Woman during the Japanese Occupation, 1942–45." In Taylor, *Women Creating Indonesia*.

Mackie, V., ed. Forthcoming. *Disorientations: Embodiments of Women in Asian Cultural Forms*. Sydney: Wild Peony Press.

*MacMillan, Margaret. 1988. *Women of the Raj*. London: Thames and Hudson.

Mageli, Eldrid. 1996. *Organising Women's Protest: A Study of Political Styles in Two South Indian Activist Groups*. NIAS Monographs, no. 72. Richmond: Curzon Press.

The Mahabharata. 1973, 1975, 1978. Translated and edited by J. A. B. Buitenen. Vols. I, II, III. Chicago: University of Chicago Press.

Major, Andrew J. 1995. "'The Chief Sufferers': Abduction of Women during the Partition of the Punjab." *South Asia* 18, Special Issue: 57–72.

Malhotra, Anshu. 1994. "'Every Women Is a Mother in Embryo': Lala Lajpat Rai and Indian Womanhood." *Social Scientist* nos. 248–49, [v. 22, nos. 1–2]: 40–63.

Mandelbaum, David G. 1988. *Women's Seclusion and Men's Honor: Sex Roles in North India, Bangladesh, and Pakistan*. Tucson: University of Arizona Press.

*Manderson, Lenore. 1980a. "Right and Responsibility, Power and Privilege: Women's Roles in Contemporary Indonesia." In Zainu'ddin, *Kartini Centenary*.

*———. 1980b. *Women, Politics, and Change: The Kaum Ibu UMNO, Malaysia, 1945–1972*. Kuala Lumpur: Oxford University Press.

*———. 1992. "Women and the State: Maternal and Child Welfare in Colonial Malaya, 1900–1940." In Fildes et al., *Women and Children First*.

———. 1998. "Shaping Reproduction: Maternity in Early Twentieth-Century Malaya." In Ram and Jolly, *Maternities and Modernities*.

*———, ed. 1983. *Women's Work and Women's Roles: Economics and Everyday Life in Indonesia, Malaysia and Singapore*. Development Studies Centre Monograph No. 32. Canberra: Australian National University.

*Mani, Lata. 1986. "Production of an Official Discourse on *Sati* in Early Nineteenth Century Bengal." *Economic and Political Weekly* 21 (April 26): WS-32–WS-40.

*———. 1989. "Contentious Traditions: The Debate on *Sati* in Colonial India." In Sangari and Vaid, *Recasting Women*.

*———. 1998. *Contentious Traditions: The Debate on Sati in Colonial India*. Berkeley and Los Angeles: University of California Press.

Manushi: A Journal about Women and Society. Published by the *Manushi* Collective in New Delhi.

Manushi. 1989. Special Issue on Women Bhakta Poets, nos. 50–51 (January–June).

Marglin, Frederique Apffel. 1985. *Wives of the God-King: The Rituals of the Devadasis of Puri*. Delhi: Oxford University Press.

Markandaya, Kamala. 1954. *Nectar in a Sieve*. New York: John Day.

*Marr, David G. 1981. *Vietnamese Tradition on Trial, 1920–1945*. Berkeley and Los Angeles: University of California Press.

Masani, Zareer. 1988. *Indian Tales of the Raj*. Berkeley and Los Angeles: University of California Press.

Maskiell, Michelle. 1984. *Women between Cultures: The Lives of Kinnaird College Alumnae in British India*. Foreign and Comparative Studies, South Asian Series, no. 9. Syracuse, N.Y.: Maxwell School of Citizenship and Public Affairs, Syracuse University.

Masselos, Jim. N.d. "The Artist as Patron: Women's Embroidery in Gujarat." In Masselos, *Popular Art*.

———, ed. N.d. *Popular Art in Asia: The People as Patrons. The Visual Arts*. Working Papers: No. 1. Sydney: Center for Asian Studies, University of Sydney, pp. 34–46.

*Matthiasson, Carolyn J., ed. 1974. *Many Sisters: Women in Cross-Cultural Perspective*. New York: The Free Press.

*Maury, Curt. 1969. *Folk Origins of Indian Art*. New York: Columbia University Press.

*Mazumdar, Shudha. 1989. *A Pattern of Life: The Memoirs of an Indian Woman*. Edited with an introduction by Geraldine Forbes. Armonk, N.Y.: M. E. Sharpe, An East Gate Book. Originally published in 1977.

Mazumdar, Sucheta. 1995. "Women on the March: Right-wing Mobilization in Contemporary India." *Feminist Review* 49 (Spring): 1–28.

Mazumdar, Vina. 1976. "The Social Reform Movement in India: From Ranade to Nehru." In Nanda, *Indian Women*.

———. 1978. "Comment on Suttee." *Signs* 4, no. 2: 269–73.

*———, ed. 1979. *Symbols of Power: Studies on the Political Status of Women in India*. Bombay: Allied Publishers.

*Mehta, Rama. 1970. *The Western Educated Hindu Woman*. Bombay: Asia Publishing House.

*———. 1977. *Inside the Haveli*. New Delhi: Arnold-Heinemann.

*Menon, Ritu, and Kamla Bhasin. 1996. "Abducted Women, the State and Questions of Honour: Three Perspectives on the Recovery Operation in Post-Partition India." In Jayawardena and de Alwis, *Embodied Violence*.

*———. 1998. *Borders and Boundaries: Women in India's Partition*. New Delhi: Kali for Women. Paperback edition. Rutgers, N.J.: Rutgers University Press.

Menski, Werner F. 1991. "Marital Expectations as Dramatized in Hindu Marriage Rituals." In Leslie, *Roles and Rituals for Hindu Women*.

Metcalf, Barbara Daly. 1984. "Islamic Reform and Islamic Women: Maulana Thanawi's *Jewelry of Paradise*." In Metcalf, *Moral Conduct and Authority*.

———, ed. 1984. *Moral Conduct and Authority: The Place of Adab in South Asian Islam*. Berkeley and Los Angeles: University of California Press.

———, ed. and trans. 1991. *Perfecting Women: Maulana Ashraf 'Ali's Bihishti Zewar*. Berkeley and Los Angeles: University of California Press.

Mi Mi Khaing. 1984. *The World of Burmese Women*. London: Zed Books.

Mies, Maria. 1980. *Indian Women and Patriarchy: Conflicts and Dilemmas of Students and Working Women*. New Delhi: Concept.

———. 1982. *The Lace Makers of Narsapur: Indian Housewives Produce for the World Market*. London: Zed Books.

Miller, Barbara D. 1981. *The Endangered Sex: Neglect of Female Children in Rural North India*. Ithaca, N.Y.: Cornell University Press.

Miller, Barbara Stoler, ed. and trans. 1984. *Theater of Memory: The Plays of Kalidasa*. New York: Columbia University Press.

*Minault, Gail. 1981a. "Sisterhood or Separation? The All-India Muslim Ladies' Conference and the Nationalist Movement." In Minault, *The Extended Family*.

———. 1982. "Purdah's Progress: The Beginnings of School Education for Indian Muslim Women." In Sharma, *Individuals and Ideas in Modern India*.

———. 1983. "Shaikh Abdullah, Begum Abdullah, and *Sharif* Education for Girls at Aligarh." In Ahmad, *Modernization and Social Change Among Muslims in India*.

———. 1986. "Making Invisible Women Visible: Studying the History of Muslim Women in South Asia." *South Asia*, New Series, 9 (June) 1: 1–14.

*———. 1990. "Sayyid Mumtaz Ali and 'Huquq un-Niswan': An Advocate of Women's Rights in Islam in the Late Nineteenth Century." *Modern Asian Studies* 24, no. 1: 147–92.

———. 1993. "The School for Wives: The Ideal Woman as Educated Muslim." The Aziz Ahmad Lecture. Toronto: University of Toronto, Centre for South Asian Studies.

———. 1997. "Women, Legal Reform and Muslim Identity." *Comparative Studies of South Asia, Africa and the Middle East* 17, no. 2: 1–10.

*———. 1998. *Secluded Scholars: Women's Education and Muslim Social Reform in Colonial India*. Delhi: Oxford University Press.

*Minault, Gail, ed. 1981b. *The Extended Family: Women and Political Participation in India and Pakistan*. Columbia, Mo.: South Asia Books.

Ming, Hanneke. 1983. "Barracks-Concubinage in the Indies, 1887–1920." *Indonesia* no. 35 (April): 65–93.

Misra, Rekha. 1967. *Women in Mughal India (1526–1748 A.D.)*. Delhi: Munshiram Manoharlal.

*Mohanty, Chandra Talpade. 1991a. "Cartographies of Struggle: Third World Women and the Politics of Feminism." In Mohanty et al., *Third World Women*.

———. 1991b. "Under Western Eyes: Feminist Scholarship and Colonial Discourses." In Mohanty et al., *Third World Women*. Originally published in *Boundary 2* (1984).

*Mohanty, Chandra Talpade, Ann Russo, and Lourdes Torres, eds. 1991. *Third World Women and the Politics of Feminism*. Bloomington: Indiana University Press.

Morgan, Susan. 1996. *Place Matters: Gendered Geography in Victorian Women's Travel Books about Southeast Asia*. New Brunswick, N.J.: Rutgers University Press.

Mukherjee, Mukul. 1989. "Impact of Modernisation on Women's Occupations: A Case Study of the Rice-husking Industry of Bengal." In Krishnamurty, *Women in Colonial India*.

*———. 1995. "Women's Work in Bengal, 1880–1930: A Historical Analysis." In Ray, *From the Seams of History*.

Mukherjee, Prabhati. 1978. *Hindu Women: Normative Models*. New Delhi: Orient Longman.

Mukherjee, S. N. 1982. "Raja Rammohun Roy and the Debate on the Status of Women in Bengal." In Allen and Mukherjee, *Women in India and Nepal*.

Mukhopadhyay, Maitrayee. 1984. *Silver Shackles: Women and Development in India*. Oxford: OXFAM.

Mukta, Parita. 1994. *Upholding the Common Life: The Community of Mirabai*. Delhi: Oxford University Press.

Muller, Helen J. 1994. "Women in Urban Burma: Social Issues and Political Dilemmas." *Women's Studies International Forum* 17, no. 6: 609–20.

Mumtaz, Khawar, and Farida Shaheed. 1987. *Women of Pakistan: Two Steps Forward, One Step Back?* London: Zed Books.

Murray, Alison J. 1991. *No Money, No Honey: A Study of Street Traders and Prostitutes in Jakarta*. Singapore: Oxford University Press.

*Murshid, Ghulam. 1983. *Reluctant Debutante: Response of Bengali Women to Modernization, 1849–1905*. Rajshahi: Sahitya Samsad, Rajshahi University.

*Nair, Janaki. 1992. "Uncovering the Zenana: Visions of Indian Womanhood in Englishwomen's Writings, 1813–1940." In Johnson-Odim and Strobel, *Expanding the Boundaries of Women's History*.

———. 1994a. "The Devadasi, Dharma and the State." *Economic and Political Weekly* 29 (December 10): 3157–67.

———. 1994b. "On the Question of Agency in Indian Feminist Historiography." *Gender and History* 6, no. 1: 82–100.

———. 1996a. "Prohibited Marriage: State Protection and the Child Wife." In Oberoi, *Social Reform, Sexuality and the State*.

*———. 1996b. *Women and Law in Colonial India: A Social History*. New Delhi: Kali for Women. Published in collaboration with the National Law School of India University, Bangalore.

Nanda, B. R., ed. 1976. *Indian Women: From Purdah to Modernity*. New Delhi: Vikas.

Nandy, Ashis. 1975. "*Sati*: A Nineteenth Century Tale of Women, Violence and Protest." In Joshi, *Rammohan Roy and the Process of Modernization in India*.

*Narayan, R. K. 1976. *The Painter of Signs*. New York: Viking Press.

*———. 1978. *The Dark Room*. Reprint. London: Heinemann. Originally published 1938.

Narayana Rao, Velcheru. 1991. "A *Ramayana* of Their Own: Women's Oral Tradition in Telugu." In Richman, *Many Ramayanas*.

Nehru, Shyam Kumari, ed. N.d. [1938?]. *Our Cause: A Symposium by Indian Women*. Allahabad: Kitabistan.

Nelson, Barbara J., and Najma Chowdhury, eds. 1994. *Women and Politics Worldwide*. New Haven: Yale University Press.

*Nelson, Nici. 1979. *Why Has Development Neglected Rural Women? A Review of the South Asian Literature*. Oxford: Pergamon Press.

Nguyen, Thi Tuyet Mai. 1994. *The Rubber Tree: Memoir of a Vietnamese Woman who was an Anti-French Guerrilla, a Publisher and a Peace Activist*. Edited by Monique Senderowicz. Jefferson, N.C.: McFarland.

O'Flaherty, Wendy Doniger. 1980. *Women, Androgynes, and Other Mythical Beasts*. Chicago: University of Chicago Press.

———. 1981. *The Rig Veda: An Anthology*. Harmondsworth: Penguin.

———. 1982. "The Shifting Balance of Power in the Marriage of Siva and Parvati." In Hawley and Wulff, *The Divine Consort*.

*O'Hanlon, Rosalind. 1994. *A Comparison between Women and Men: Tarabai Shinde and the Critique of Gender Relations in Colonial India*. Madras: Oxford University Press.

*Oldenburg, Veena Talwar. 1984. *The Making of Colonial Lucknow, 1856–1877*. Princeton: Princeton University Press.

———. 1990. "Lifestyle as Resistance: The Case of the Courtesans of Lucknow, India." *Feminist Studies* 16, no. 2: 259–87.

———. 1994. "The Roop Kanwar Case: Feminist Responses." In Hawley, *Sati, the Blessing and the Curse*.

Omvedt, Gail. 1980. *We Will Smash This Prison: Indian Women in Struggle*. London: Zed Books.

———. 1986. *Women in Popular Movements: India and Thailand during the Decade of Women*. Report No. 86.9. Geneva: United Nations Research Institute for Social Development.

———. 1993. *Reinventing Revolution: New Social Movements and the Socialist Tradition in India*. Armonk, N.Y.: M. E. Sharpe, An East Gate Book.

*Ong, Aihwa. 1987. *Spirits of Resistance and Capitalist Discipline: Factory Women in Malaysia*. Albany: State University of New York Press.

*———. 1995. "State versus Islam: Malay Families, Women's Bodies, and the Body Politic in Malaysia." In Ong and Peletz, *Bewitching Women, Pious Men*.

*Ong, Aihwa, and Michael G. Peletz, eds. 1995. *Bewitching Women, Pious Men: Gender and Body Politics in Southeast Asia*. Berkeley and Los Angeles: University of California Press.

Orr, Leslie C. 1994. "Women of Medieval South India in Hindu Temple Ritual: Text and Practice." In Sharma and Young, *Annual Review of Women in World Religions*, III.

———. 1999. *Donors, Devotees, and Daughters of God: Temple Women in Medieval Tamilnadu*. New York: Oxford University Press.

Pal, Pratapaditya. 1989. "Ruler of the World." In Pal et al., *Romance of the Taj Mahal*.

Pal, Pratapaditya, Janice Leoshko, Joseph M. Dye, III, and Stephen Markel. 1989. *Romance of the Taj Mahal*. London: Thames and Hudson, Los Angeles County Museum of Art.

Pandey, S. M. 1965. "Mirabai and Her Contributions to the *Bhakti* Movement." *History of Religions* 5 (Summer): 54–73.

Pandit, Vijayalakshmi. 1979. *The Scope of Happiness: A Personal Memoir*. New York: Crown Publishers.

*Papanek, Hanna. 1973. "Purdah: Separate Worlds and Symbolic Shelter." *Comparative Studies in Society and History* 15 (June): 289–325. (Reprinted in Papanek and Minault, *Separate Worlds*.)

———. 1984. "False Specialization and the Purdah of Scholarship: A Review Article." *Journal of Asian Studies* 44, no. 1: 127–48.

*———. 1990. "To Each Less Than She Needs, From Each More Than She Can Do: Allocations, Entitlements, and Value." In Tinker, *Persistent Inequalities: Women and World Development*.

*Papanek, Hanna, and Gail Minault, eds. 1982. *Separate Worlds: Studies of Purdah in South Asia*. Columbia, Mo.: South Asia Books.

Paranjape, Makarand, ed. 1997. *Sarojini Naidu: Selected Letters 1890s to 1940s*. New Delhi: Kali for Women.

Parikh, Manju. 1990. "Sex-Selective Abortions in India: Parental Choice or Sexist Discrimination?" *Feminist Issues* 10, no. 2: 19–32.

Parker, Kunal M. 1998. "'A Corporation of Superior Prostitutes': Anglo-Indian Legal Conceptions of Temple Dancing Girls, 1800–1914." *Modern Asian Studies* 32, no. 5: 559–633.

*Patel, Sujata. 1988. "Construction and Reconstruction of Woman in Gandhi." *Economic and Political Weekly* 23 (February 20): 377–87.

*Pathak, Zakia, and Rajeswari Sunder Rajan. 1989. "'Shahbano.'" *Signs* 14, no. 3: 558–82.

Pattynama, Pamela. 1998. "Secrets and Danger: Interracial Sexuality in Louis Couperus's *The Hidden Force* and Dutch Colonial Culture around 1900." In Clancy-Smith and Gouda, *Domesticating the Empire*.

Paul, Diana Y. 1985. *Women in Buddhism: Images of the Feminine in Mahayana Tradition*. 2nd ed. Berkeley and Los Angeles: University of California Press. Originally published 1979.

Pearson, Anne Mackenzie. 1996. *"Because It Gives Me Peace of Mind": Ritual Facts in the Religious Lives of Hindu Women*. Albany: State University of New York Press.

*Pearson, Gail. 1981. "Nationalism, Universalization, and the Extended Female Space in Bombay City." In Minault, *The Extended Family*.

———. 1982. "The Female Intelligentsia in Segregated Society: Early Twentieth Century Bombay." In Allen and Mukherjee, *Women in India and Nepal*.

*———. 1989. "Reserved Seats—Women and the Vote in Bombay." In Krishnamurty, *Women in Colonial India*.

*Peletz, Michael G. 1996. *Reason and Passion: Representations of Gender in a Malay Society*. Berkeley and Los Angeles: University of California Press.

Phongpaichit, Pasuk. 1986. *From Peasant Girls to Bangkok Masseuses*. Albany, N.Y.: International Labor Office.

Pintchman, Tracy. 1994. *The Rise of the Goddess in the Hindu Tradition*. Albany: State University of New York Press.

Post, Jennifer. 1987. "Professional Women in Indian Music: The Death of the Courtesan Tradition." In Koskoff, *Women and Music in Cross-Cultural Perspective*.

Potter, Sulamith Heins. 1977. *Family Life in a Northern Thai Village: A Study in the Structural Significance of Women*. Berkeley and Los Angeles: University of California Press.

Pramoedya, Ananta Toer. 1991. *The Girl from the Coast*. Translated by Harry Aveling. Singapore: Select Books.

Premchand. 1979. *Godan*. Bombay: Jaico.

Price, Pamela G. 1994. "Honor, Disgrace and the Formal Depoliticization of Women in South India: Changing Structures of the State under British Colonial Rule." *Gender and History* 6, no. 2 (August): 246–64.

Rafael, Vicente L. 1988. *Contracting Colonialism: Translation and Christian Conversion in Tagalog Society under Early Spanish Rule*. Ithaca, N.Y.: Cornell University Press.

Raheja, Gloria Goodwin, and Ann Grodzins Gold. 1994. *Listen to the Heron's Words: Reimagining Gender and Kinship in North India*. Berkeley and Los Angeles: University of California Press.

Rajan, Rajeswari Sunder. 1993. *Real and Imagined Women: Gender, Culture and Postcolonialism*. London: Routledge.

Raju, Saraswati, Janet Townsend, Peter Atkins, and Naresh Kumar. 1998. *An Atlas of Women and Men in India*. New Delhi: Kali for Women.

Ram, Kalpana. 1998. "Maternity and the Story of Enlightenment in the Colonies: Tamil Coastal Women, South India." In Ram and Jolly, *Maternities and Modernities*.

————, and Margaret Jolly, eds. 1998. *Maternities and Modernities: Colonial and Postcolonial Experiences in Asia and the Pacific.* Cambridge: Cambridge University Press.

Ramabai, Sarasvati, Pandita. 1976. *The High-Caste Hindu Woman.* Reprint. Westport, Conn.: Hyperion Press. Originally published 1887.

Ramanna, Mridula. 1994. "The Establishment of Medical Education and Facilities for Women in the City of Bombay." *Indica* 31, no. 1: 41–50.

————. 1997. "A Voice from the Nineteenth Century: The Story of Dosebai Cowasjee Jessawalla." *Journal of the K. R. Cama Oriental Institute* 61: 1–16.

*Ramanujan, A. K. 1973. *Speaking of Siva.* Baltimore, Md.: Penguin.

*————. 1982. "On Woman Saints." In Hawley and Wulff, *The Divine Consort.*

————. 1991. "Three Hundred *Ramayanas*: Five Examples and Three Thoughts on Translation." In Richman, *Many Ramayanas.*

Ramanujan, A. K., Velcheru Narayana Rao, and David Shulman, eds. and trans. 1994. *When God Is a Customer: Telugu Courtesan Songs by Ksetrayya and Others.* Berkeley and Los Angeles: University of California Press.

*Ramaswamy, Sumathi. 1992. "Daughters of Tamil: Language and Poetics of Womanhood in Tamilnad." *South Asia Research* 12, no. 1: 38–59.

————. 1993. "En/gendering Language: The Poetics of Tamil Identity." *Comparative Studies in Society and History* 35, no. 4: 683–725.

The Ramayana: A Shortened Modern Prose Version of the Indian Epic. 1977. By R. K. Narayan. Harmondsworth: Penguin.

*Ramusack, Barbara N. 1981a. "Catalysts or Helpers? British Feminists, Indian Women's Rights, and Indian Independence." In Minault, *The Extended Family.*

————. 1981b. "Women's Organizations and Social Change: The Age-of-Marriage Issue in India." In Black and Cottrell, *Women and World Change.*

*————. 1989. "Embattled Advocates: The Debate over Birth Control in India, 1920–40." *Journal of Women's History* 1, no. 2: 34–64.

*————. 1990a. "Cultural Missionaries, Maternal Imperialists, Feminist Allies: British Women Activists in India, 1865–1945." *Women's Studies International Forum* 13, no. 4: 295–308.

————. 1990b. "From Symbol to Diversity: The Historical Literature on Women in India." *South Asia Research* 10, no. 2: 139–57.

Ramusack, Barbara N., and Antoinette Burton. 1994. "Introduction." Special Issue on Feminism, Imperialism and Race: A Dialogue between India and Britain. *Women's History Review* 3, no. 4: 469–81.

*Ranade, Ramabai. 1938. *Himself: The Autobiography of a Hindu Lady.* Translated and adapted by Katherine Van Akin Gates. New York: Longmans, Green.

Rao, M. S. A., ed. 1979. *Social Movements in India.* Vol. 2. New Delhi: Manohar.

Ratti, Rakesh, ed. 1993. *A Lotus of Another Color: An Unfolding of the South Asian Gay and Lesbian Experience.* Boston: Alyson Publications.

*Ray, Bharati, ed. 1995. *From the Seams of History: Essays on Indian Women.* Delhi: Oxford University Press.

Ray, Rajat K. 1979. "Man, Woman and the Novel: The Rise of a New Consciousness in Bengal, 1858–1947." *Indian Economic and Social History Review* 16, no. 1: 1–31.

Ray, Reginald A. 1980. "Accomplished Women in Tantric Buddhism of Medieval India and Tibet." In Falk and Gross, *Unspoken Worlds.*

Reddy, M. Atchi. 1983. "Female Agricultural Labourers of Nellore, 1881–1981." *Indian Economic and Social History Review* 20, no. 1: 67–80.

*Reddy, Muthulakshmi. 1930. *My Experiences as a Legislator*. Madras: Current Thought Press.

———. [1964?]. *Autobiography of Dr. Mrs. Muthulakshmi Reddy*. Madras: N.p.

*Reid, Anthony. 1988a. "Female Roles in Pre-Colonial Southeast Asia." *Modern Asian Studies* 22, no. 3: 629–45.

*———. 1988b. *Southeast Asia in the Age of Commerce 1450–1680*. Vol. 1. *The Lands below the Winds*. New Haven: Yale University Press.

———. 1993. *Southeast Asia in the Age of Commerce 1450–1680*. Vol. 2. *Expansion and Crisis*. New Haven: Yale University Press.

Reyes, Felina. [1951]. *Filipino Women: Their Role in the Progress of Their Nation*. Washington, D.C.: United States Department of Labor, Women's Bureau.

Richards, John F., ed. 1978. *Kingship and Authority in South Asia*. Madison: South Asian Studies, no. 3, University of Wisconsin Publication Services.

———. 1993. *The Mughal Empire*. The New Cambridge History of India, series 1, vol. 5. Cambridge: Cambridge University Press.

Richell, Judith. 1992. "Ephemeral Lives: The Unremitting Infant Mortality of Colonial Burma, 1891–1941." In Fildes et al., *Women and Children First*.

*Richman, Paula. 1988. *Women, Branch Stories, and Religious Rhetoric in a Tamil Buddhist Text*. Foreign and Comparative Studies, South Asian Series No. 14. Syracuse, N.Y.: Maxwell School of Citizenship and Public Affairs, Syracuse University.

———, ed. 1991. *Many Ramayanas: The Diversity of a Narrative Tradition in South Asia*. Berkeley and Los Angeles: University of California Press.

The Rig Veda: An Anthology. 1979. Translated by Wendy D. O'Flaherty. Harmondsworth: Penguin.

Rimmer, P. J., and L. M. Allen, eds. 1990. *The Underside of Malaysian History: Pullers, Prostitutes, and Plantation Workers*. Singapore: Singapore University Press.

Rizvi, Saiyid Athar Abbas. 1978. *A History of Sufism in India*. Vol. 1. Delhi: Munshiram Manoharlal.

Roseman, Marina. 1987. "Inversion and Conjuncture: Male and Female Performance among the Temiar of Peninsular Malaysia." In Koshoff, *Women and Music in Cross-Cultural Perspective*.

Roy, Kumkum. 1994. *The Emergence of Monarchy in North India Eighth—Fourth Centuries B.C.: As Reflected in the Brahmanical Tradition*. Delhi: Oxford University Press.

Roy, Manisha. 1972. *Bengali Women*. Chicago: University of Chicago Press.

Rozario, Santi. 1998. "The *Dai* and the Doctor: Discourses on Women's Reproductive Health in Rural Bangladesh." In Ram and Jolly, *Maternities and Modernities*.

*Rutherford, Danilyn. 1993. "Unpacking a National Heroine: Two Kartinis and Their People." *Indonesia* no. 55 (April): 23–40.

*Sahgal, Lakshmi. 1997. *A Revolutionary Life: Memoirs of a Political Activist*. With an Introduction by Geraldine Forbes. New Delhi: Kali for Women.

Sahgal, Manmohini Zutshi. 1994. *An Indian Freedom Fighter Recalls Her Life*. Edited by Geraldine Forbes. Armonk, N.Y.: M. E. Sharpe, An East Gate Book.

*Sahgal, Nayantara. 1989. *Rich Like Us*. New York: New Directions.

Sakala, Carol. 1980. *Women of South Asia: A Guide to Resources*. Millwood, N.Y.: Kraus International.

Salaff, Janet W. 1988. *State and Family in Singapore: Restructuring an Industrial Society*. Ithaca, N.Y.: Cornell University Press.

Saldanha, Indra Munshi. 1986. "Tribal Women in the Warli Revolt: 1945–47: 'Class' and 'Gender' in the Left Perspective." *Economic and Political Weekly* 21 (April 26): WS-41–WS-52.

*Sangari, Kumkum. 1990. "Mirabai and the Spiritual Economy of *Bhakti*." *Economic and Political Weekly* 25 (July 7 and 14): 1464–75, 1537–52.

*Sangari, Kumkum, and Sudesh Vaid. 1996. "Institutions, Beliefs and Ideologies: Widow Immolation in Contemporary Rajasthan." In Jayawardena and de Alwis, *Embodied Violence*.

*———, eds. 1990. *Recasting Women: Essays in Colonial History*. New Delhi: Kali for Women. Reprint. New Brunswick, N.J.: Rutgers University Press. Originally published 1989.

*Sarkar, Lotika. 1976. "Jawaharlal Nehru and the Hindu Code Bill." In Nanda, *Indian Women*.

*Sarkar, Tanika. 1987. "Nationalist Iconography: Image of Women in Nineteenth Century Bengali Literature." *Economic and Political Weekly* 22 (November 21): 2011–15.

*———. 1992. "The Hindu Wife and the Hindu Nation: Domesticity and Nationalism in Nineteenth Century Bengal." *Studies in History* 8, no. 2, n.s.: 213–35.

———. 1993a. "A Book of Her Own. A Life of Her Own: Autobiography of a Nineteenth-Century Woman." *History Workshop Journal* no. 36: 35–65.

*———. 1993b. "Rhetoric against Age of Consent: Resisting Colonial Reason and Death of a Child-Wife." *Economic and Political Weekly* 28 (September 4): 1869–78.

*———. 1993c. "The Women of the Hindutva Brigade." *Bulletin of Concerned Asian Scholars* 24, no. 4: 16–24.

*———. 1997. "Talking about Scandals: Religion, Law and Love in Late Nineteenth Century Bengal." *Studies in History* 13, no. 1, n.s.: 64–95.

*Sarkar, Tanika, and Urvashi Butalia, eds. 1995. *Women and the Hindu Right: A Collection of Essays*. New Delhi: Kali for Women.

Sax, William S. 1991. *Mountain Goddess: Gender and Politics in a Himalayan Pilgrimage*. New York: Oxford University Press.

Schalk, Peter. 1994. "Women Fighters of the Liberation Tigers in Tamil Ilam: The Martial Feminism of Atel Palacinkam." *South Asia Research* 14, no. 2: 163–83.

Schenkhuizen, Marguérite. 1993. *Memoirs of an Indo Woman: Twentieth-Century Life in the East Indies and Abroad*. Translated by Lizelot Stout van Balgooy. Athens: Ohio University Center for International Studies, Monographs in International Studies, Southeast Asia Series, No. 92.

Seager, Joni. 1997. *The State of Women in the World Atlas*. Revised. New York: Penguin. Originally published 1986.

Searle-Chatterjee, Mary. 1981. *Reversible Sex Roles: The Special Case of Benares Sweepers*. Oxford: Pergamon Press.

*Sears, Laurie J., 1996a. "Introduction: Fragile Identities." In Sears, *Fantasizing the Feminine*.

*———, ed. 1993. *Autonomous Histories, Particular Truths: Essays in Honor of John R. W. Smail*. Madison: University of Wisconsin, Center for Southeast Asian Studies.

*———, ed. 1996b. *Fantasizing the Feminine in Indonesia*. Durham, N.C.: Duke University Press.

Seely, Clinton B., ed. 1981. *Women, Politics and Literature in Bengal*. East Lansing: Asian Studies Center, Michigan State University.

Selliah, S. 1989. *The Self-Employed Women's Association, Ahmedabad, India*. Albany, N.Y.: International Labor Office.

Sen, Sumita. 1993. "Motherhood and Mothercraft: Gender and Nationalism in Bengal." *Gender and History* 5, no. 2: 231–43.

Shapiro, Ann-Louise, ed. 1994. *Feminists Revision History*. New Brunswick, N.J.: Rutgers University Press.

Sharma, Arvind, ed. 1987. *Women in World Religions*. Albany: State University of New York Press.

Sharma, Arvind, and Katherine K. Young, eds. 1992. *Annual Review of Women in World Religions*. Vol. 2. *Heroic Women*. Albany: State University of New York Press.

———. *Annual Review of Women in World Religions*. Vol. 3. Albany: State University of New York Press.

Sharma, Jagdish P., ed. 1982. *Individuals and Ideas in Modern India: Nine Interpretive Studies*. Calcutta: Firma KLM.

Sharma, Radha Krishna. 1981. *Nationalism, Social Reform and Indian Women (1921–1937)*. Patna: Janaki Prakashan.

*Sharma, Ursula. 1980. *Women, Work, and Property in North-West India*. London: Tavistock.

———. 1986. *Women's Work, Class, and the Urban Household: A Study of Shimla, North India*. London: Tavistock.

Shattan, Merchant-Prince. 1989. *Manimekhalai (The Dancer with the Magic Bowl)*. Translated by A. Danielou. New York: New Directions.

*Shaw, Miranda. 1994. *Passionate Enlightenment: Women in Tantric Buddhism*. Princeton: Princeton University Press.

*Shiva, Vandana. 1988. *Staying Alive: Women, Ecology and Development in India*. London: Zed Books.

*Shridevi, S. 1965. *A Century of Indian Womanhood*. Mysore: Rao and Raghavan.

Shulman, David. 1976. "The Murderous Bride: Tamil Versions of the Myth of the Devi and the Buffalo Demon." *History of Religions* 16 (November): 120–47.

———. 1991. "Fire and Flood: The Testing of Sita in Kampan's *Iramavataram*." In Richman, *Many Ramayanas*.

———, ed. 1995. *Syllables of Sky: Studies in South Indian Civilization in Honor of Velcheru Narayana Rao*. Delhi: Oxford University Press.

Sinclair-Brull, Wendy. 1997. *Female Ascetics: Hierarchy and Purity in Indian Religious Movements*. Richmond: Curzon Press.

Singer, Wendy. 1993a. "Defining Women's Politics in the Election of 1991 in Bihar." In Gould and Ganguly, *India Votes*.

———. 1993b. "Women's Politics and Land Control in an Indian Election: Lasting Influences of the Freedom Movement in North Bihar." In Gould and Ganguly, *India Votes*.

———. 1997. *Creating Histories: Oral Narratives and the Politics of History-Making*. Delhi: Oxford University Press.

*Sinha, Mrinalini. 1989. "The Age of Consent Act: The Ideal of Masculinity and Colonial Ideology in Nineteenth Century Bengal." In Stewart, *Shaping Bengali Worlds, Public and Private*.

———. 1994a. "Gender in the Critiques of Colonialism and Nationalism: Locating the 'Indian Woman.'" In Shapiro, *Feminists Revision History*.

*———. 1994b. "Reading *Mother India*: Empire, Nation, and the Female Voice." *Journal of Women's History* 6, no. 2: 6–44.

*——. 1995. *Colonial Masculinity: The "Manly Englishman" and the "Effeminate Bengali" in the Late Nineteenth Century*. Manchester: Manchester University Press.

The Slate of Life: More Contemporary Stories by Women Writers of India. 1994. Edited by Kali for Women. Introduction by Chandra Talpade Mohanty and Satya P. Mohanty. New York: The Feminist Press at the City University of New York.

Smail, John J. W. 1961. "On the Possibility of an Autonomous History of Southeast Asia." *Journal of Southeast Asian History* 2, no. 2: 72–102.

Smith, Frederick M. 1991. "Indra's Curse, Varuna's Noose, and the Suppression of the Woman in the Vedic *Srauta* Ritual." In Leslie, *Roles and Rituals for Hindu Women*.

Southard, Barbara. 1984. "Bengal Women's Education League: Pressure Group and Professional Association." *Modern Asian Studies* 18, no. 1: 55–88.

——. 1993. "Colonial Politics and Women's Rights: Woman Suffrage Campaigns in Bengal, British India in the 1920s." *Modern Asian Studies* 27, no. 2: 397–439.

*——. 1995. *The Women's Movement and Colonial Politics in Bengal: The Quest for Political Rights, Education and Social Reform Legislation, 1921–1936*. New Delhi: Manohar.

Spivak, Gayatri Chakravorty. 1987. "A Literary Representation of the Subaltern: Mahasweta Devi's 'Stanadayini.'" In Guha, *Subaltern Studies V*.

Srinivasan, Amrit. 1983. "The Hindu Temple Dancer: Prostitute or Nun?" *Cambridge Anthropology* 8, no. 1: 73–99.

——. 1985. "Reform and Revival: The Devadasi and Her Dance." *Economic and Political Weekly* 20 (November 2): 1869–76.

Stein, Dorothy K. 1978. "Women to Burn: Suttee as a Normative Institution." *Signs* 4, no. 2: 253–68.

Stephens, Julie. 1989. "Feminist Fictions: A Critique of the Category 'Non-Western Woman' in Feminist Writings on India." In Guha, *Subaltern Studies VI*.

Stewart, Tony K., ed. 1989. *Shaping Bengali Worlds, Public and Private*. East Lansing: Asian Studies Center, Michigan State University.

Stivens, Maila. 1996. *Matriliny and Modernity: Sexual Politics and Social Change in Rural Malaysia*. St. Leonards: Allen and Unwin.

——. 1998. "Modernizing the Malay Mother." In Ram and Jolly, *Maternities and Modernities*.

*——, ed. 1991. *Why Gender Matters in Southeast Asian Politics*. Clayton: Centre of Southeast Asian Studies, Monash University.

Stivens, Maila, Cecilia Ng, K. S. Jomo, and Jaharah Bee, eds. 1994. *Malay Peasant Women and the Land*. Atlantic Highlands, N.J.: Zed Books.

*Stoler, Ann. 1977. "Class Structure and Female Autonomy in Rural Java." *Signs* 3, no. 1: 74–89.

*——. 1989. "Making Empire Respectable: The Politics of Race and Sexual Morality in Twentieth-Century Colonial Cultures." *American Ethnologist* 14, no. 4: 634–60.

——. 1992. "Sexual Affronts and Racial Frontiers: European Identities and the Cultural Politics of Exclusion in Colonial Southeast Asia." *Comparative Studies in Society and History* 34, no. 3: 514–51.

Strange, Heather. 1981. *Rural Malay Women in Tradition and Transition*. New York: Praeger.

*Stree Shakti Sanghatana. 1989. *"We Were Making History:" Life Stories of Women in the Telangana People's Struggle*. London: Zed Books.

Stutchbury, Elizabeth Leigh. 1982. "Blood, Fire and Mediation: Human Sac-
    rifice and Widow Burning in Nineteenth Century India." In Allen
    and Mukherjee, *Women in India and Nepal.*
*Sudraka. 1968. "The Little Clay Cart." In *Two Plays of Ancient India.* Trans-
    lated by J. A. B. van Buitenen. New York: Columbia University Press.
Suleri, Sara. 1989. *Meatless Days.* Chicago: University of Chicago Press.
Sunder Raj, M. 1993. *Prostitution in Madras: A Historical Perspective.* Delhi:
    Konarak.
Suryakusuma, Julia I. 1996. "The State and Sexuality in New Order Indone-
    sia." In Sears, *Fantasizing the Feminine.*
Sutherland, Sally J. M. 1989. "Sita and Draupadi: Aggressive Behavior and
    Female Role-Models in the Sanskrit Epics." *Journal of the American
    Oriental Society* 109, no. 1: 63–79.
———. 1991a. "The Bad Seed: Senior Wives and Elder Sons." In Sutherland,
    Bridging Worlds.
———, ed. 1991b. *Bridging Worlds: Studies on Women in South Asia.* Berkeley:
    Center for South Asia Studies, University of California at Berkeley,
    Occasional Paper No. 17, Occasional Paper Series.
Sutton, R. Anderson. 1987. "Identity and Individuality in an Ensemble Tra-
    dition: The Female Vocalist in Java." In Koshoff, *Women and Music in
    Cross-Cultural Perspective.*
Swarup, Hem Lata, Niroj Sinha, Chitra Ghosh, and Pam Rajput. 1994. "Wom-
    en's Political Engagement in India: Some Critical Issues." In Nelson
    and Chowdhury, *Women and Politics Worldwide.*
*Szanton, M. Christina Blanc. 1982. "Women and Men in Iloilo, Philippines:
    1903–1970." In Van Esterick, *Women of Southeast Asia.*
*Ta Van Tai. 1981. "The Status of Women in Traditional Vietnam: A Com-
    parison of the Code of the Le Dynasty (1428–1788) with the Chi-
    nese Codes." *Journal of Asian History* 15, no. 2: 97–145.
*Talbot, Cynthia. 1995. "Rudrama Devi, the Female King: Gender and Politi-
    cal Authority in Medieval India." In Schulman, *Syllables of Sky.*
The Tale of An Anklet: An Epic of South India: The Cilappatikaram of Ilanko Atikal.
    1994. Translated by R. Parthasarathy. New York: Columbia Univer-
    sity Press.
Tales of Ancient India. 1959. Translated by J. A. B. van Buitenen. Chicago:
    University of Chicago Press.
Talim, Meena. 1972. *Women in Early Buddhist Literature.* Bombay: University
    of Bombay.
Talwar, Vir Bharat. 1990. "Feminist Consciousness in Women's Journals in
    Hindi: 1910–1920." In Sangari and Vaid, *Recasting Women.*
Tarling, Nicholas, ed. 1992a. *The Cambridge History of Southeast Asia.* Vol. 1.
    From Early Times to c. 1800. Cambridge: Cambridge University Press.
———. 1992b. *The Cambridge History of Southeast Asia.* Vol. 2. *The Nineteenth
    and Twentieth Centuries.* Cambridge: Cambridge University Press.
*Taylor, Jean Gelman. 1974. "Educate the Javanese!" Translation of an essay
    from the Dutch by R. A. Kartini, with introduction and notes. *Indo-
    nesia* no. 17 (May): 83–98.
*———. 1983. *The Social World of Batavia: European and Eurasian in Dutch Asia.*
    Madison: University of Wisconsin Press.
———. 1984. "Education, Colonialism and Feminism: An Indonesian Case
    Study." In Altbach and Kelly, *Education and the Colonial Experience.*
———. 1992. "Women as Mediators in VOC Batavia." In van Bemmelen et
    al., *Women and Mediation in Indonesia.*

*———. 1993. "Once More Kartini." In Sears, *Autonomous Histories, Particular Truths*.

———. 1996. "*Nyai Dasima*: Portrait of a Mistress in Literature and Film." In Sears, *Fantasizing the Feminine*.

———. 1997. "Official Photography, Costume and the Indonesian Revolution." In Taylor, *Women Creating Indonesia*.

*———, ed. 1997. *Women Creating Indonesia: The First Fifty Years*. Clayton: Monash Asia Institute, Monash University.

Taylor, Jean Stewart. 1976. "Raden Ajeng Kartini." *Signs* 1, no. 3, pt. 1: 639–61.

Taylor, Keith W. 1992. "The Early Kingdoms." In Tarling, *Cambridge History*, I.

Taylor, Sandra. 1999. *Vietnamese Women at War: Fighting for Ho Chi Minh and the Revolution*. Lawrence: University Press of Kansas.

*Thadani, Giti. 1996. *Sakhiyani: Lesbian Desire in Ancient and Modern India*. London: Cassell.

Thakkar, Usha. 1997. "Puppets on the Periphery: Women and Social Reform in Nineteenth Century Gujarati Society." *Economic and Political Weekly* 32 (January 4–11): 46–52.

*Thapar, Romila. 1987. "Traditions versus Misconceptions." *Manushi*, nos. 42–43: 2–14.

Tharu, Susie. 1989. "Response to Julie Stephens." In Guha, *Subaltern Studies IV*.

*Tharu, Susie, and K. Lalita, eds. 1990. *Women Writing in India*. Vol. 1. *600 B.C. to the Early Twentieth Century*. New York: Feminist Press.

*———. *Women Writing in India*. 1991. Vol. 2. *The Twentieth Century*. New York: Feminist Press.

Tharu, Susie, and Tejaswini Niranjana. 1996. "Problems for a Contemporary Theory of Gender." In Amin and Chakrabarty, *Subaltern Studies IX*.

Thong, Huynh Sanh, ed. and trans. 1979. *The Heritage of Vietnamese Poetry*. New Haven: Yale University Press.

Thorbeck, Susanne. 1987. *Voices from the City: Women of Bangkok*. London: Zed Books.

Tilak, Lakshmibai. 1950. *I Follow After: An Autobiography*. Translated by E. Josephine Inkster. Bombay: Oxford University Press.

Tinker, Irene, ed. 1990. *Persistent Inequalities: Women and World Development*. New York: Oxford University Press.

Tirmizi, S. A. I. 1979. *Edicts from the Mughal Harem*. Delhi: Idarah-i Adabi-yat-i Delli.

Tiwon, Sylvia. 1996. "Models and Maniacs: Articulating the Female in Indonesia." In Sears, *Fantasizing the Feminine*.

Towards Equality: Report of the Committee on the Status of Women in India. 1975. New Delhi: Government of India, Department of Social Welfare, Ministry of Education and Social Welfare.

Truong, Thanh-Dam. 1990. *Sex, Money and Morality: Prostitution and Tourism in Southeast Asia*. London: Zed Books.

Truth Tales: Contemporary Stories by Women Writers of India. 1990. Edited by Kali for Women. Introduction by Meena Alexander. New York: Feminist Press.

Turner, Karen Gottschang, with Phan Thank Hao. 1998. *Even the Women Must Fight: Memories of War from North Vietnam*. New York: John Wiley.

*Uberoi, Patricia, ed. 1996. *Social Reform, Sexuality and the State*. New Delhi: Sage Publications.

Upadhyaya, Bhagwat Saran. 1974. *Women in Rgveda*. Reprint. Delhi: S. Chand. Originally published 1933.

Van Bemmelen, Sita. 1992. "Educated Toba Batak Daughters as Mediators in the Process of Elite Formation (1920–1942)." In van Bemmelen, *Women and Mediation in Indonesia*.

*Van Bemmelen, Sita, et al., eds. 1992. *Women and Mediation in Indonesia*. Leiden: KITLV Press.

Van der Veen, Klass W. 1972. *I Give Thee My Daughter: A Study of Marriage and Hierarchy among the Anavil Brahmans of South Gujarat*. Assen: Van Gorcum.

*Van Esterik, Penny, ed. 1982. *Women of Southeast Asia*. Center for Southeast Asian Studies, Monograph Series on Southeast Asia, Occasional Paper No. 9. De Kalb: Northern Illinois University.

Varma, Mahadevi. 1994. *Sketches from My Past: Encounters with India's Oppressed*. Translated by Neera Kuckreja Sohoni. Boston: Northeastern University Press.

*Vatuk, Sylvia. 1982. "Purdah Revisited: A Comparison of Hindu and Muslim Interpretations of the Cultural Meaning of Purdah in South Asia." In Papanek and Minault, *Separate Worlds*.

———. 1987. "Authority, Power and Autonomy in the Life Cycle of the North Indian Woman." In Hocking, *Dimensions of Social Life*.

*Visweswaran, Kamala. 1996. "Small Speeches, Subaltern Gender: Nationalist Ideology and Its Historiography." In Amin and Chakrabarty, *Subaltern Studies IX*.

*Vreede-de Stuers, Cora. 1960. *The Indonesian Woman: Struggles and Achievements*. S'Gravenhage: Mouton.

———. 1968. *Parda: A Study of Muslim Women's Life in Northern India*. New York: Humanities Press, 1968.

Vyas, Anju, and Sunita Singh, eds. 1993. *Women's Studies in India: Information Sources, Services, and Programmes*. Thousand Oaks, Calif.: Sage Publications.

*Wadley, Susan S. 1975. *Shakti: Power in the Conceptual Structure of Karimpur Religion*. Chicago: University of Chicago Studies in Anthropology, Series in Social, Cultural, and Linguistic Anthropology, 2.

*———. 1977. "Women and the Hindu Tradition." In Jacobson and Wadley, *Women in India*.

———. 1980a. "Hindu Women's Family and Household Rites in a North Indian Village." In Falk and Gross, *Unspoken Worlds*.

*———, ed. 1980b. *The Power of Tamil Women*. Foreign and Comparative Studies, South Asian Series, no. 6. Syracuse, N.Y.: Maxwell School of Citizenship and Public Affairs, Syracuse University.

Wallace, Ben J., Rosie Mujid Ahsan, Shahnaz Hup Hussain, and Ekramul Ahsan. 1987. *The Invisible Resource: Women and Work in Rural Bangladesh*. Boulder, Colo.: Westview Press.

Ward, Barbara E., ed. [1963]. *Women in the New Asia: The Changing Social Roles of Men and Women in South and South-east Asia*. [Paris]: UNESCO.

*Warren, James Francis. 1987a. "Placing Women in Southeast Asian History: The Case of Oichi and the Study of Prostitution in Singapore Society." In Warren, *At the Edge*.

———, ed. 1987b. *At the Edge of Southeast Asian History*. Quezon City: New Day.

White, C. 1989. "Vietnam: War, Socialism and the Politics of Gender Relations." In Kruks, *Promissory Notes*.

Wieringa, Saskia. 1988a. "Aborted Feminism in Indonesia: A History of Indonesian Socialist Feminism." In Wieringa, *Women's Struggles and Strategies*.

———. 1995a. "Matrilinearity and Women's Interests: The Minangkabau of Western Sumatra." In Wieringa, *Subversive Women*.

———, ed. 1988b. *Women's Struggles and Strategies*. Aldershot: Gower.

———, ed. 1995b. *Subversive Women: Historical Experiences of Gender and Resistance*. London: Zed Books.

*Willis, Janice D. 1985. "Nuns and Benefactresses: The Role of Women in the Development of Buddhism." In Haddad and Findly, *Women, Religion and Social Change*.

Willmer, David. 1996. "Women as Participants in the Pakistan Movement: Modernization and the Promise of a Moral State." *Modern Asian Studies* 30, no. 3: 73–590.

Wilson, Liz. 1996. *Charming Cadavers: Horrific Figurations of the Feminine in Indian Buddhist Hagiographic Literature*. Chicago: University of Chicago Press.

*Wiser, William H., and Charlotte M. Wiser. 1989. *Behind Mud Walls, 1930–1960: With a Sequel: The Village in 1970 and a New Chapter: The Village in 1984 by Susan W. Wadley*. Revised edition. Berkeley and Los Angeles: University of California Press. Originally published 1930.

Wolf, Diane L. 1992. *Factory Daughters: Gender, Household Dynamics, and Rural Industrialization in Java*. Berkeley and Los Angeles: University of California Press.

Yang, Anand A. 1989. "Whose Sati? Widow Burning in Early Nineteenth Century India." *Journal of Women's History* 1, no. 2: 8–33.

Young, Katherine K. 1987. "Hinduism." In Sharma, *Women in World Religions*.

*Zainu'ddin, Ailsa Thomson. 1980a. "Kartini: Her Life, Work and Influence." In Zainu'ddin, *Kartini Centenary*.

*———, ed. 1980b. *Kartini Centenary: Indonesian Women Then and Now*. Monash Papers on Southeast Asia, Annual Indonesia Lecture Series, no. 5. Clayton: Centre of Southeast Asian Studies, Monash University.

Zakaria, Rafiq. 1990. *Women and Politics in Islam: The Trial of Benazir Bhutto*. New York: New Horizons Press.

VIDEOS

Dadi and Her Family: A Rural Mother-in-Law in North India. Color/45 minutes. Possibly the best video available on women in rural India.

Kamala and Raji. Color/40 minutes. Analyzes the lives of two members of the Self-Employed Women's Association (SEWA) in Ahmedabad.

Mithila Painters: Five Village Artists from Madhubani, India. Color/40 minutes. Video that focuses on five village painters (four women and one man) and illustrates what occurs when a traditional form of painting is transcribed for commercial sale from walls of houses to handmade paper. Filmed in Bihar in 1981 but released in 1994.

Munni. Color/20 minutes. The life of a young girl who is learning the traditional art of Mithali painting in a Bihari village.

No Longer Silent. Color. Overview of women's movement in New Delhi with a primary focus on middle-class women and the issues of brideburning and the debate over amniocentesis. Not distributed by Wisconsin.

Rana. Color/25 minutes. Story of a young female Muslim student living in
Delhi. Not distributed by Wisconsin.

Wedding of the Goddess. Pt. 1. Color/36 minutes. History of the Chittirai festival in Madurai, Tamilnadu. Pt. 2. Color/40 minutes. A record of the
nineteen-day festival in honor of the Goddess.

Who Will Caste the First Stone? Color/52 minutes. Video. Examines impact of
Islamization on women in Pakistan. Available from the Cinema
Guild, 1697 Broadway, New York, NY 10019.

Part II

WOMEN IN EAST ASIA

Sharon Sievers

GLOSSARY

Agnatic: Blood relationship. In the Chinese case, a requirement for the maintenance of the family line through males; elsewhere in Asia, other forms of fictive kinship prevailed, allowing for the continuation of the family through adoption and other means.

Altaic: Refers to the development of cultural and linguistic influences east of the Altai mountain range in Central Asia; Japanese and Korean, for example, are Altaic languages that originated among peoples (probably nomadic) east of the Altai range.

Ama: Descriptive name given to women divers in Japan; the term can be traced to Japan's earliest records indicating the existence of a group of women who were responsible for providing fish and shellfish for their communities. Contemporary *ama* still dive for shellfish, but they are best known in the West as pearl divers put on display for tourists. In fact, they play important roles in the maintenance of pearl farming and fishing in contemporary Japan.

Arctic shamanism: Descriptive term given to a type of shamanism monopolized by women and characterized by "hysteria" and trancelike states that facilitate their roles as mediators between the known and unknown. The term itself was probably first used by M. Czaplicka in *Aboriginal Siberia: A Study in Social Anthropology*, published in 1914.

B.C.E.: "Before the common era." Used in place of B.C.

C.E.: "Of the common era." Used in place of A.D.

Comfort women: A euphemism used by the Japanese army during the war against China (1937–45) to describe women from various parts of Asia (especially Korea, which was a Japanese colony at the time) abducted and forced into providing sex for Japanese troops. Throughout the war, women from all Japanese-controlled parts of Asia, including some Japanese women, were sent wherever the Japanese army went, from Manchuria, to Southeast Asia, to islands in the Western Pacific. Korean women, numbering more than 250,000, bore the brunt of this violence; few of them survived.

Concubine system: Justified by the need to continue the patriline and guarantee the birth of suitable heirs, the system had many variations in East and Northeast Asia, ranging from the large communities of concubines in China's imperial palaces and Tokugawa's Chiyoda castle, to systems of "extra wives" with no legal rights in smaller patrilineal households. In China, Japan, and Korea, the acquisition of additional women in the patriarchal family was considered a mark of status. There is no East Asian equivalent of the Middle Eastern harem, although some would argue that the concubine system of the Chinese imperial court closely approximates it.

Grades of mourning: A hierarchical system based on agnatic lineage that entitled male descendants to participate in family ritual based on their proximity to the main line of the family; also used as a marker of proximity in other contexts that made one eligible for family benefits. An extension of a larger system privileging the (agnatic) male line.

Hakka: Han Chinese who immigrated to south China over several centuries from various other parts of China; thought of as "guest settlers" in part because of language (dialect) differences and cultural habits that they apparently refused to give up, Hakka have long been considered not only different, but inferior, by many Chinese.

Kami: A term used very early in Japanese folk religious tradition to connote someone or something (usually in nature) that was perceived as superior, or blessed with unusual abilities or powers. The sun goddess was a *kami*, as is the sun line represented by Japan's imperial house. However, persons identified as *kami* in what ultimately became the Shinto tradition shared their notoriety with trees, foxes, mountains, and many other "deities." There is no Japanese counterpart to the Judeo-Christian notion of a God representing a monotheistic tradition.

Kiangsi soviet: The Chinese Communists, retreating from the attacks of the Kuomintang, established this "rural soviet" on the rugged Kiangsi-Hunan border in central China; here Mao Tse-t'ung emerged as the ideological and political leader of the Chinese Communist Party, using the Kiangsi base as an opportunity to develop a revolutionary ideology based on the peasantry, as well as a People's Liberation Army under the leadership of Chu Teh.

Kisang: Korean women entertainers often compared to Japanese geisha; however, it is likely that the *kisang* or *kisaeng*, as they are often also called, have a longer history than their counterparts in Japan.

Kuomintang (KMT): Chinese nationalists who claimed the ongoing traditions of the 1911 revolution. Chiang K'ai Shek became the head of the KMT in the twenties, collaborating first with the rival CCP (Chinese Communist Party) in a campaign to reunite all of China; he later turned against them and made them his principal enemies, attacking them throughout the war with Japan and after (1945–49).

Manchurian Incident: An "incident" manufactured and carried out by the Kwantung Army, a branch of the Japanese Army stationed in Manchuria. Led by disgruntled officers acting without government consent, Japanese army personnel exploded a bomb on the South Manchurian railway on September 18, 1931. They blamed the explosion on Chinese troops in the area, and used the ensuing disorder to move into Mukden and other parts of the country. This action eventually led to the Lytton Report and Japan's withdrawal from the League of Nations in 1933, and the annexation of Manchuria that same year.

Manchus: Non-Chinese nomadic peoples from the area north of China's Great Wall; they conquered China in 1644; the resulting Ch'ing dynasty lasted until 1911, making it one of China's most "successful" periods of rule by a non-Chinese group.

May Fourth Movement: Returning Chinese students from Japan and the West organized a massive protest of the failures of the Versailles Peace Conference, including its failure to agree to a racial equality clause in the proposed League of Nations documents, the cession of Germany's former Shantung leasehold to Japan, and Japan's continuing exploitation of China (evidenced by the 21 Demands and Nishihara loans that were considered little more than bribes). Demonstrations and strikes, as well as powerful boycotts of Japanese goods, prevented the signing of the Versailles Peace Treaty. This movement is considered by many to mark the beginning of ongoing revolution in China, culminating with the victory of the Chinese Communist Party over the Kuomintang in 1949.

May Thirtieth Movement: Began with protests over the British shooting of thirteen Chinese who were demonstrating against the treaty port system in Shanghai, May 30, 1925. It quickly mushroomed into a huge anti-foreign movement reaching many other parts of China, and creating strikes and boycotts that were particularly damaging to foreign merchants, manufacturers, and traders in China.

Miko: Term used in Japan's early texts to describe women with mantic, or shamanic powers. There is no specific term for male shamans in the Japanese tradition. *Miko* have traditionally been divided into two categories: those who belong to the imperial court and Shinto shrines, and those (*ichiko* or *sato-miko*) who served communities in the countryside.

Neo-Confucianism: Term used in the West to describe the results of a major Confucian revival in Sung (960–1279) China; it may be seen as, in part, an effort to re-order Chinese society, a society that was becoming much more fluid than before, particularly in terms of basic issues of social status and definitions of virtue. Chu Hsi (1130–1200) is often described as the founder of Neo-Confucianism, but he was only one of many thinkers who contributed to its content. From the standpoint of women's history in China, Japan, and Korea, Neo-Confucianism is often seen as a vehicle for reinforcing restrictive notions of female virtue that focused on duty, responsibility, and sexual purity.

Northern Expedition: Effort by China's Kuomintang, led by Chiang K'ai Shek, to reunify China in the twenties by marching from south to north, reclaiming Chinese territory from the warlords and potentially from Western powers as well; Manchuria was the end point of this expedition, and it set the stage for escalating Chinese–Japanese conflict in the region.

Samurai: Term originally derived from a Heian period verb meaning "to serve"; *samurai* assumed greater roles as the old civil aristocracy built around the imperial court found itself less and less able to control the struggle for land in the countryside. The *samurai* represented a new elite group, a military aristocracy whose relationship to the court remained strong, if ambivalent, for a long period in Japanese history. In the fifteenth and sixteenth centuries, the roles of *samurai* changed dramatically in keeping with the changing nature of warfare and increasing involvement of peasants recruited to serve by various competing families. In the Tokugawa period (1600–1868), *samurai* were given the highest social status, but engaged in few military duties; they became administrators and bureaucrats who helped to build an early modern society.

Shamanism: Folk religious traditions characterized by the use of archaic techniques of ecstasy, performed by "specialists of the sacred" (see works by Mircea Eliade) who know how to employ ecstatic possession for the benefit of the community.

Sinification: The process of acculturation through which Chinese cultural habits come to influence, and sometimes dominate, other cultures in East, Northeast, and Southeast Asia.

Tungus: Early nomadic tribe situated southwest of the Amur river; it represents the Northeast Asian connection to languages and cultures in the Altai mountain range in the steppes of Central Asia; thought to have influenced the culture and language of both Korea and Japan.

Yenan: Mountain base occupied by the Chinese Communist Party after the Long March (6,000 miles through difficult terrain made by the CCP to escape the attacking Kuomintang; only about 10 percent of those who set out from the Kiangsi soviet survived). Yenan became the wartime base of the CCP, from which they were able to continue to organize for the coming revolution and to attack invading forces from Japan after 1937.

MAPS

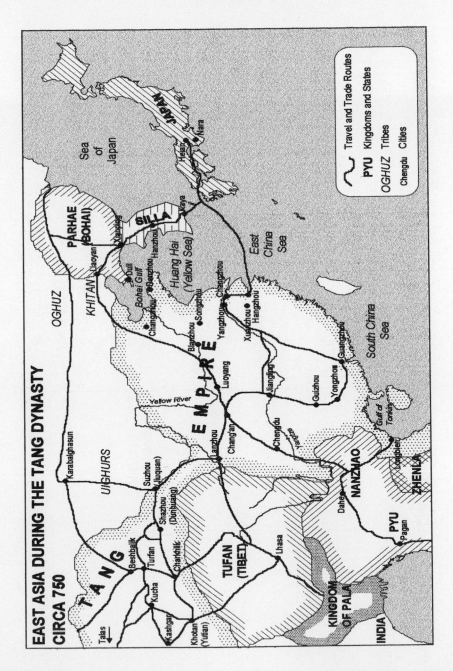

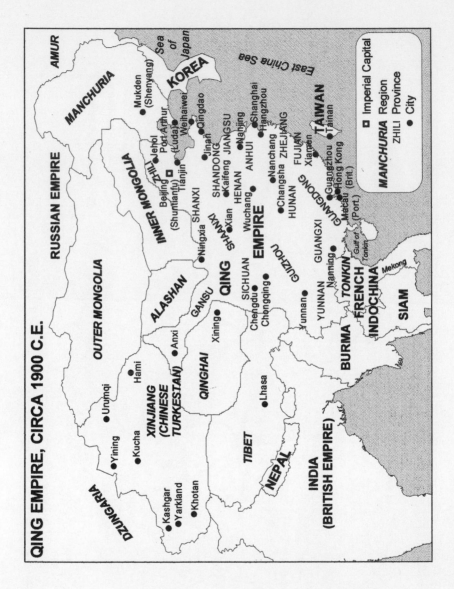

QING EMPIRE, CIRCA 1900 C.E.

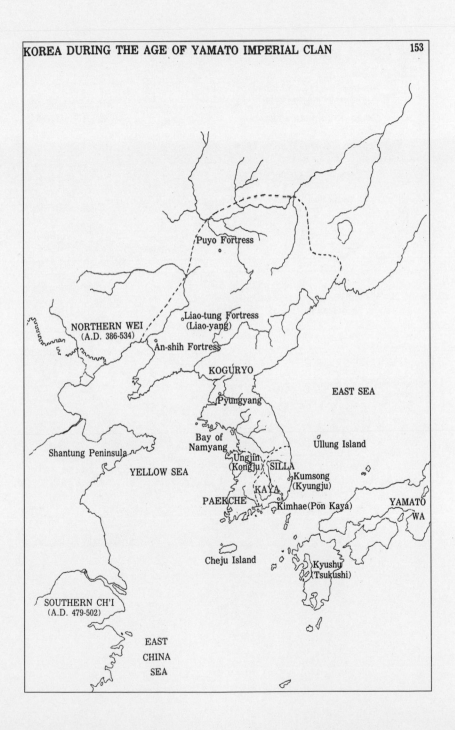

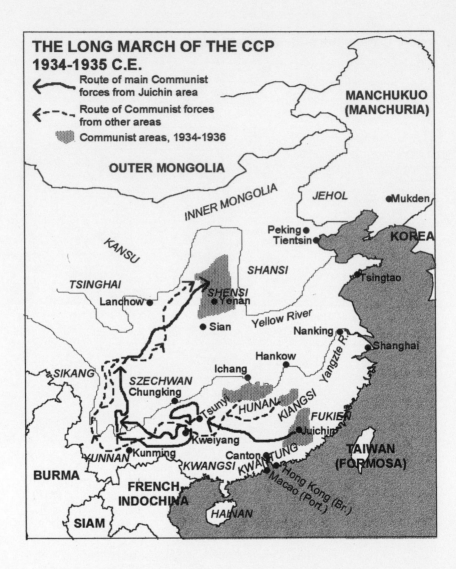

THE LONG MARCH OF THE CCP
1934-1935 C.E.

← Route of main Communist
   forces from Juichin area

←--- Route of Communist forces
      from other areas

▓ Communist areas, 1934-1936

OUTER MONGOLIA

INNER MONGOLIA

MANCHUKUO
(MANCHURIA)

JEHOL

●Mukden

KANSU

TSINGHAI

Peking ●
Tientsin ●

KOREA

Lanchow ●

SHANSI

SHENSI
● Yenan

● Sian

Yellow River

● Tsingtao

Nanking ●

Shanghai ●

Hankow ●

SIKANG

SZECHWAN
Chungking

Ichang ●

Yangzte R.

Tsunyi
●

HUNAN

KIANGSI

FUKIEN

Kweiyang
●

Juichin ●

● Kunming

Canton
●

TUNG

TAIWAN
(FORMOSA)

YUNNAN

KWANGSI

KWA

Hong Kong (Br.)
Macao (Port.)

BURMA

FRENCH
INDOCHINA

HAINAN

SIAM

CHRONOLOGY

DATE	CHINA	KOREA	JAPAN
B.C.E.			
1200–1100	Shang		Jōmon
1100–770	Western Chou		
770–403	Eastern Chou		
403–221	Warring States	Han Tribes	
221–206	Ch'in		Yayoi
206 to C.E. 8	Former Han	Paekche, Koguro, Silla	
C.E.			
8–23	Hsin (Wang Mang)		
25–220	Later Han		
222–280	Three Kingdoms		Kōfun
265–304	Western Chin		
304–386	Sixteen Kingdoms		
386–581	Wei		
581–618	Sui		Yamato
618–907	T'ang	Silla	Taika, Nara, Heian
907–960	Five Dynasties		
960–1126	Sung	Koryo	Fujiwara (Late Heian)
1127–1279	Southern Sung		Taira, Kamakura
1279–1368	Yuan	Mongol Domination	Northern/ Southern Courts

DATE	CHINA	KOREA	JAPAN
1368–1662	Ming	Yi Dynasty	Ashikaga
1662–1912	Ch'ing	Japanese Rule (1910–)	Tokugawa Meiji (1868–1912)
1912–1949	Republic		Taisho (1912–1926) Showa (1926–1989)
1949–	People's Republic	North/South Korea	Heisei (1989–)

WOMEN IN CHINA, JAPAN, AND KOREA

Sharon Sievers

Twentieth-century scholarship has demolished the myth of a monolithic Asia; in its place, we now see an extremely complex and diverse
constellation of civilizations, many of which are as different from each
other as the East and West that Kipling thought would never meet.
We have done far less to dismantle stereotypic assumptions about
women in Asia, even though their history adds significantly to our
understanding of the difference and particularity of life in such countries as China, Japan, and Korea. Women's history underscores our
sense of Korea and Japan as different and discrete cultures, in spite of
very strong Chinese influence.

There is no monolithic Asian women's "experience" for historians; but there are women's histories in Asia, often made more, rather
than less, problematic by what they seem to share. Twentieth-century imperialism is a case in point. Both China and Japan occupied

what might be called a semi-colonial status vis-à-vis the West at different times in the modern period; Korea was, however, later colonized by Japan, and Japan invaded China in 1937. How should we view the shared "experience" of Chinese, Japanese, and Korean women in this setting? Japanese women were part of a colonizing military presence in Asia, but many were also victimized by it. Like Korean women, Japanese women (in much smaller numbers) were sent to service the Japanese military as "comfort women" (prostitutes), carrying with them slightly higher status than Korean women. Films and books published since 1945 testify to the suffering Japanese women experienced in various parts of Asia as a result of the Pacific War. But no one would argue that women of the nation that brought colonial rule to Korea and invaded China in 1937 really shared the experience of Chinese or Korean women, or that all Japanese women would describe their wartime histories the same way. In a less contemporary setting, historians have made it clear that family systems and Confucian ideas are not translatable across these three cultures, if indeed they are translatable from region to region within each culture. The challenge of women's history is to problematize, not homogenize—to talk about women in Asia in ways that explain how compelling and important their stories are—separately and together.

In a number of ways, it is still possible to describe historical research on women in China, Japan, and Korea as having just begun, although even for those who are confined to the use of Western languages, things have improved enormously in the last ten years. Thanks primarily to historians of women in Asia, and the efforts of editors and translators who are bridging the language gap, Western scholarship on women in Asia is now moving forward, and increasing numbers of Asian scholars are publishing in Western languages. Western-language scholarship on Korea is still difficult to find, but that too is beginning to change.

Women's history asks different questions, often demonstrates significantly different priorities, and given the choice, would devise new chronologies that could more adequately describe women's experience. It is still true, for example, that in spite of major changes in twentieth-century historiography, history as a discipline continues to privilege public, political activity. Significance continues to attach to generals who conquer, not women who may build communities and culture, and many of the questions historians consider important still, by definition, exclude women. Chronology is a problem in Asia as in the West: the increased social mobility of the Sung dynasty (960–1279) in China, or Japan's Muromachi (1336–1573) included women, but this story is not yet complete; Japan's "Taisho democracy" (ca. 1918) was a period in which women continued to be denied the most fundamental political rights, even as the parliament approved universal manhood suffrage in 1925.

Women's history in Asia, as elsewhere, resists monochromatic categories; it is not a branch of social or economic or political history. It may often seem little more than family history, because so much of what we have learned about women's lives has been filtered through the study of family institutions. If we are to replace some of the stereotypes of Asian women, many of which come from representations of their lives in the family, we need to begin to see them as both private and public persons in Asian history, people whose contributions, in both private and public worlds, were often different from those of men. The brief outline of the history of women in China, Japan, and Korea that follows will challenge traditional historical categories because it is women's history; the focus will fall primarily on women actors who sometimes operated within clearly defined gender roles, but who could also defy them. Women in Asian history, we will see, could be agents of change, or supporters of a kind of social stasis they felt most advantageous to themselves and their families; they could be creators of consensus, but they were also occasionally in conflict with men, and with each other. Looking at their lives, we can begin to appreciate the importance of studying women and their history, if we are to understand Asia at all.

WOMEN IN CHINA, JAPAN, AND KOREA TO 1800

Women in Early Society

It is a paradoxical fact of East Asian history that, thanks to the curiosity and record-keeping of the Chinese, we know more today about powerful women in Japan's prehistory than in China's. China may be, in terms of basic questions about women in prehistory and antiquity, the most frustrating example of the three societies considered here. The relative lack of information about Chinese women in the oral and folk traditions that preceded the Chou (1122–221 B.C.E.) may be due in part to Confucian influence in the earliest historiographical traditions. By the time a written record emerged in China, Confucian perceptions of women among the elite governors of China were fixed, if not unchanging; consequently, it is difficult to find women in the earliest historical records who do not fit Confucian definitions of "good" or "bad" examples of the ideal Confucian woman. Very early, as with Liu Hsiang's (79-8 B.C.E.) *Biographies of Admirable Women*, the

most important elements of the prescriptive model were in place:
women were to be unselfish, loyal, self-sacrificing, and chaste in the
service of father, husband, and ruler (O'Hara 1955).

The suggestion that communities in many parts of Asia, particularly the nomadic areas of the northeast, were at one time predominantly matrilineal is well known. Few anthropologists take seriously
the existence of matriarchal societies in Asia, although the search for
artifacts that place women at the center of religious tradition is increasing, reinforced by international archaeological discoveries. But
the survival of communities of women divers in Korea and Japan
indicates not only that women in early society made significant contributions to the economy; the survival of matrifocal arrangements
among these groups also raises questions about the dominant roles
women might have played in prehistoric societies.

Japan's *ama*, communities of women divers whose oral traditions
suggest a matrilineal, matrilocal, and perhaps matriarchal society functioning in late Jōmon (ca. 2500–250 B.C.E.), were important enough
to the economy to be mentioned in early Japanese records. *Ama* currently live in Japan in matrilocal communities, as do Korean women
who dive on Cheju Island (Cho 1983). In both examples, the central-
ity of the mother's economic, ideological, and emotional roles has
survived even though there are significant levels of tension with the
dominant society, and compromises have resulted. In spite of that,
the essential element—the importance of women as primary providers—remains:

> While the . . . villagers ignore Confucianism's ethical code, the men
> claim exclusive control of Confucian ritual. They cite Confucian
> scholarly values' contempt for manual labor and respect for knowl-
> edge and nobility—to devalue their working women. But beneath
> this thin veneer, a very different picture emerges. Women in this
> village seem content . . . competent and dedicated social actors, full
> of self-respect. The real "social adults," the women, support their
> families and run the village economy. (Cho 1983: 92)

We also know less about the contributions of Chinese women to
developing religious and ethical traditions than we do about Korean
and Japanese women, but it seems unlikely—at least in Northern
China—that there were no strong parallels to the importance of Korean and Japanese women in the development of shamanism. This is
certainly an implication of Hori's (1968) thesis that northern China
was influenced by peoples living east of the Altai mountains in the
steppes of Asia, as well as the Tungus forested regions in northeast

Asia. These religious practices eventually spread throughout Korea, Hokkaido, and the Ryukyu Islands; southern China shared Polynesian or Melanesian traditions. Korean shamanism seems to have derived predominantly from the northern source, while Japanese shamanism ultimately combined the two. It is difficult to say in precisely what geographic mix various strains of shamanism operated in China, but it is very unlikely that Chinese women were somehow less significant in the development of shamanism, and related folk traditions, than their Japanese and Korean counterparts. North China, for example, would have been influenced by the same "arctic shamanism" that predominated in Korea and some parts of Japan; this strain of shamanism gives enormous power to women, who alone can predict, prophesy, and mediate between this world and others. Arctic shamanism is sometimes also referred to as "arctic hysteria" because of the trancelike state female shamans entered in the performance of their mantic duties.

Suzanne Cahill's efforts to find early records of the Queen Mother of the West do provide some interesting possibilities, from Shang oracle bones to explicit references some one thousand years later, in the Warring States period (403–221 B.C.E.). References to the Queen Mother in the *Chuang-tzu* establish her divine powers and immortality; the *Hsun-tzu* emphasizes her role as teacher. But it is the *Classic of Mountains and Seas* that speaks to her mantic powers:

> The Queen Mother is linked with the native southern shamanism of early China in the songs of the *Ch'u tz'u* (*Elegies of Ch'u*) anthology in which she also figures. Her special headdress, leopard's tail, and tiger's teeth are reminiscent of costumes worn by Chinese shamans. The shaman's hair becomes disheveled in ecstatic communion. The connection with a world mountain and with stars is also shamanistic. Shamans travel back and forth to the heavens by climbing up and down world mountains and other pillars of heaven such as divine trees. . . . The shaman flies through the heavens on a quest for deities, often traveling to the stars, where deities reside. (Cahill 1993: 17)

In the story of Himiko, Japan provides us with the only evidence that such shamanic female authority could be translated into political power. The Wei chronicles describe Himiko as unmarried, residing in relative seclusion, attended by many women; a man, the only male in the palace, transmitted her words to society as a whole. Rendering service to deities who, according to these Chinese observers, conferred on her special powers to "bewitch" people, Himiko bears, in

Blacker's words, "all the stigmata of the shamanic ruler" (Blacker 1986: 28). Nor, according to the Chinese account, was Himiko the last of Japan's early female rulers. When she died, "A great mound was raised, more than a hundred paces in diameter. . . . Then a king was placed on the throne, but the people would not obey him. . . . Finally a relative of Himiko named Iyo, a girl of thirteen, was made queen and order was restored" (Tsunoda 1951: 10). Social scientists still hold differing views of the geographic region of Japan actually visited by the Chinese, but there is universal recognition of the connections between the Japanese myth, the power of female shamans, and the supreme deity in the Shinto pantheon, the sun goddess Amaterasu. The Japanese reading of the characters for Himiko strongly suggests close connections with the sun, as well as the mantic traditions of early Japan.

Though not fully documented, the tradition of the *miko*, a woman capable of hearing and transmitting the instructions and advice of the gods, apparently continued in the imperial family. Jingu, the great warrior empress who is said to have led Japanese troops to Korea, is described in Japan's first mytho-history (The *Kojiki*, or *Records of Ancient Matters*, c.e. 712) in terms that suggest she was a *miko*. As late as the seventh century, long after Buddhism had become a significant influence on the court, the empress Jito is thought to have been "within the broad tradition of royal *miko*; she communicated with the gods (*kami*), and she may have had the rare experience for a shaman of conversing directly with the chief of all [*kami*] at Ise, Amaterasu" (Kidder 1979: 207).

If ritually pure women in the arctic shaman tradition could and did translate their power to the temporal realm, it is also true that folk tradition often turned a very different face to women, one that endured. Folk tradition in all three cultures has stigmatized women for their association with various polluting elements; menstrual blood, postpartum discharge, and sexual activity have been seen at various times as tangible evidence of the power of women for good or evil. But it has been their perceived negative powers that have been given a telling kind of continuity in folk tradition; other religious and ethical systems seem to have borrowed the notion of female pollution as a symbolic rationale for women's subordinate ritual status (Ahern 1975).

Viewed in this light, the riddle of women's diminished political/religious powers over time becomes less puzzling. It was, in all three societies, the supposed power of women to disrupt religious and lineage systems that often justified their loss of private and public authority. This development appears most complete in the case of China; in Korea, as in Japan, women continued to retain what Laurel Kendall (1985) calls a "special prominence" in folk tradition, a circumstance that could ameliorate their status in complex ways. As Martina Deuchler explains, two categories of women have always lived outside the walls of social tradition and Confucian ideology: the professional shaman (*mudang, mansin*) and the professional entertainer (*kisang*). Though treated with contempt, these women rendered indispensable professional services. Early documents hint of their importance in Koryo (c.e. 918–1392) society. The shaman received official recognition, and the state called upon her to pray for rain in time of drought. The shaman's most valued function, however, was healing. This was evident even to a Chinese observer. The Koreans, he writes, never used medicine; instead, they called a shaman to exorcise the bad spirits that are supposed to have caused the sickness. And the shamans were feared for their power to communicate with spirits (Deuchler 1983).

Why, in the Chinese case, women so clearly felt the negative effect of folk tradition without apparently enjoying as many of their residual powers in shamanism, as was the case in Korea and Japan, is an open question. But it is likely that ancestor veneration, particularly its early development in China, holds many of the keys to this issue. Cahill reports, for example, that Hzun-tzu, a follower of Confucius who became a founder of Legalism, transformed the Queen Mother of the West from deity to historical personage in the third century B.C.E.:

> Both the heroic emperor and the Queen Mother are made to look like historical people rather than deities. This is a fine example of the Chinese practice of euhemerization (turning mythical people and events into apparently historical ones). Ancient culture heroes who would be considered gods in another tradition are first turned into human ancestors and only then deified by worship in the ancestral cult. (Cahill 1993: 15)

The Chinese family saw itself as the offshoot of a common descent line, guided and advised by ancestors who would accept only the consecrated sacrifices of a male descendant on the father's side. How and why agnatic, or consanguineous, males became the only acceptable mediators between ancestors and descendants in China is, of course, a central (and unanswered) question for historians of women in Asia.

We know that ancestral rites were common to the Shang (1766–

1027 B.C.E.); both Shang and Western Chou (1027–770 B.C.E.) were periods of intense struggle over land and political power. If female shamans in north China lost power they had originally held, that struggle in China's feudal age could certainly have promoted such a result. In any case, the feeling that female shamans in north China would have played a major role in ancestor worship is inescapable; ancestors were precisely the sort of "ghosts" these shamans placated in the service of family or tribe elsewhere in northeast Asia. But if, in China, the female shaman was displaced by an agnatic male medium, two other possible explanations come to mind: 1) the perceived irrationality of women, demonstrated in this case by the "hysteria" of the arctic shaman, and 2) the "power of pollution" common to all women in folk tradition. We have already looked at the ambivalence of Asian society on the question of women and ritual purity. The perceived irrationality of women is harder to trace in the early Chinese record; there is, for example, no Chinese equivalent to the Aristotelian reference to women as "lesser men" incapable of reason, and, by extension, without the virtue necessary to the performance of civic duties. But, in the Chinese case, it is impossible not to see the development of ancestral rites as, in part, the ordering of ritual to exclude the kind of "hysteria" common to the female shaman in north Asia, and by extension, to provide a rationale for the exclusion of women from public, political arenas. Did ancestor worship in the hands of men become a rational, public rite, one from which women, their pollution, and their mystical communion with ancestors were forever banished? If so, the consequences for Chinese women were enormous, even when one takes into account changes in these rites over time, and geographic variations within China related to this issue. Even the powerful Queen Mother of the West was incorporated into this ordering of the world:

> Wang mu was an honorific posthumous title conferred on female ancestors in the father's line, used in the ancestral cult. . . . The patrilineal ancestral cult was one of the primary reflections in early religion of the Chinese tendency to order the world in terms of kinship. Defining the queen mother in kinship terms in the context of the ancestral cult shows an attempt to incorporate her into the predominating view of the structure of the world. (Cahill 1993: 18)

In Korea and Japan, deviation from Chinese patterns of ancestral rites is marked. The Korean case is more problematic; there was no doubt substantial Chinese influence in the development of ancestor worship from antiquity (Ariga 1956), but how uniform and well-developed that influence was, particularly before the fifteenth century, is still largely an unanswered question. What we do know suggests that, before the introduction of Neo-Confucianism in the fifteenth century, Korean women seem to have been powerful, not marginal, members of their society, and that part of this power seems to have been derived from their central roles in shamanic traditions. Martina Deuchler, commenting on women in the Koryo (C.E. 918–1392) period, indicates that "Residence patterns, inheritance rules, and social and ritual recognition provided women with a firm and independent standing in Koryo society. In fact, the high status of Koryo women indicates that Korean society during that period was structurally quite different from the society that developed later on in the Yi dynasty" (Deuchler 1983).

In both China and Korea, where so much of women's subordinate state seems tied to agnatic custom, practitioners of women's history are also interested in ways women were included in religious practice that confirmed the lineage and solidified the community. This "little" tradition seems at first glance to occupy a central place in the daily lives of Chinese and Koreans; Kendall (1985) points out the importance of Korean women in the ritual of daily life and the preservation of folk religious traditions. Chinese women, too, played significant roles, even within the narrow confines of ancestor worship:

> The rites performed in the halls were conducted by and in the presence of men; their daughters and wives played no direct part in the proceedings. In the home, in contrast, it is clear that whatever the theoretical inferiority of women in the sphere of ancestral worship, they occupied a central position in its performance. The women cared for the domestic shrines and probably carried out the ordinary daily rites of lighting incense. . . . It was the women who had prime charge of the ancestors in the home, remembering their death dates and praying to them in need. . . . It is likely that the senior woman in the house was . . . the main routine link between the dead and members of the family. Of course women addressed themselves to their husbands' ancestors, not their own; but they were performing rites at shrines which would in due course house their own tablets and be served by their sons and daughters-in-law. (Freedman 1958: 85–86)

As a footnote to questions of agnatic lineage and the rites that symbolized its authority, there is Japan, where from at least the seventh century a serious effort was made to establish family registers on Chinese agnatic patterns. But the Japanese system deified, not consanguineous ancestors, but local gods; the priority in Japan was to uphold the family, not the lineage, and as a consequence, adoption into the line was widely practiced. The difference this could make in women's status is readily seen in the fact that, in early Japan, women could hold and transmit leadership of the family, uxorilocal marriage was common, and women, especially in the countryside, continued to play major roles in celebration of community and family religious rites, long after Japan's earliest encounter with Chinese influence.

CONFUCIANISM, THE FAMILY, AND WOMEN

Few intellectual traditions in world history have had a more telling impact on women than Confucianism. That is primarily because Confucianism, with its emphasis on the family as the foundation of the state, incorporated and—as it became increasingly institutionalized—rationalized and conceptualized patrilineal customs that remained central not only to China, but to societies throughout Asia influenced by Chinese culture.

Confucianism is often oversimplified, described in terms that suggest it is both monolithic and unchanging. But the study of women in relation to Confucianism reinforces the opposite impression: that the continuity of Confucian ideas is the result of change, not stasis; and that the complexity of the tradition, one that ranges from the ethical views of a political philosopher (Confucius, ca. 551–479 B.C.E.) to the metaphysical deliberations of Chou Tun-i (C.E. 1012–73), represents accommodation to a constantly changing society. Women comprise an important part of that social change, and even though we still know very little of the story, it is instructive to observe the dynamic between women and Confucian ideas that seek to incorporate and legitimize the experience of all social groups in China.

The Confucianism that emerged in China's Han dynasty (206 B.C.E.–8 C.E.) perhaps had no intrinsic commitment to the subordination of women as morally or biologically inferior persons, but it was clear at the outset that females were at the lower end of the family hierarchy, and that they were not expected to play public roles. There are similarities between the Western exclusion of women from public (political) roles on grounds they lacked rationality, and the Confucian insistence that women provide an inner (private) balance to men's public roles. In both instances, women are perceived as lacking the ability to undertake intellectual pursuits crucial to the highest levels of individual and collective moral development. In general, women in Confucianism must operate in private space in order to exercise the limited moral agency of which they are capable.

In early Confucianism, this requirement seems to have been most closely tied to the cultivation of filial piety and other ethical commitments within the family; it takes time for the "inner" roles of women to be linked with the control of their sexuality in this ideological tradition. One of the better examples of an ideal woman in the early Confucian tradition is "The Mother of Mencius," a classic of Confucian piety taken from Liu Hsiang's *Biographies of Admirable Women*:

When Mencius was young, he came home from school one day and found his mother was weaving at the loom. She asked him, "Is school out already?" He replied, "I left because I felt like it." His mother took her knife and cut the finished cloth on her loom. Mencius was startled and asked why. She replied, "Your neglecting your studies is very much like my cutting the cloth. The superior person studies to establish a reputation and gain wide knowledge. . . . If you do not study now, you will surely end up as a menial servant and will never be free from troubles. It would be just like a woman who supports herself by weaving. . . . If a woman gives up her work or a man gives up the cultivation of his character, they may end up as common thieves, if not slaves!

. . . On another occasion when Mencius was not working, he leaned against the door and sighed. His mother saw him and said, "The other day I saw that you were troubled, but you answered that it was nothing. But why are you leaning against the door sighing?" Mencius answered, "I have heard that the superior man judges his capabilities and then accepts a position. He neither seeks illicit gain nor covets glory or high salary. If the Dukes and Princes do not listen to his advice, then he does not talk to them. If they listen to him but do not use his ideas, then he no longer frequents their courts. Today my ideas are not being used in Ch'i so I wish to go somewhere else. But I am worried because you are getting too old to travel about the country." His mother answered, "A woman's duties are to cook the five grains, heat the wine, look after her parents-in-law, make clothes, and that is all! Therefore she cultivates the skills required in the women's quarters and has no ambition to manage affairs outside the house. . . . The *Book of Poetry* says, 'It will be theirs neither to do wrong nor to do good / Only about the spirits and the food will they have to think.' This means that a woman's duty is not to control or take charge. Instead she must follow the 'three submissions.'* When she is young, she must submit to her parents. After her marriage, she must submit to her hus-

*Dorothy Ko suggests that a better translation of "three submissions" is "thrice following," a translation that emphasizes an ideal of gender relations in Confucianism, "that a woman's social status and self-identity be defined by those of the man in each stage of her life cycle—father, husband, son" (Ko 1994: 119).

band. When she is widowed, she must submit to her son. These are
the rules of propriety. Now you are an adult and I am old; therefore, whether you go depends on what you consider right; whether
I follow depends on the rules of propriety." (Translated in Ebrey
1981: 33–34)

The mother of Mencius combines the moral sense Confucianism
prizes with the wisdom of experience; she has added to these gifts a
smattering of knowledge of the classics—that part of the literature
that teaches and rationalizes her role in the family. She knows that
inside work is for women, and the cultivation of superior character is
an exclusively male occupation/career, but in this passage she does
successfully assist in the cultivation of her son's character. In her way,
she is an example of the "astute and assertive" (Ebrey 1981: xxi) woman whose creative ability to subvert, manipulate, and occasionally
overcome some of the strictures of her life we have come to admire.
But she is also a woman for whom community respect is earned, not
through the cultivation of character, or "considering what is right,"
but through the virtuous, complementary role she plays in support of
father, husband, and son.

We need to know much more than we currently do about variations in the family, economically and geographically, in order to understand the history of women. We need a more sophisticated sense
of the life cycles of women in order to understand how women who
entered the family as strangers often later emerged as respected ma-
triarchs, capable of wielding the kind of authority in the domestic
sphere that can influence external events. Research published in the
last decade has given us some sense of the complexity of the questions, and the significant differences one finds moving from T'ang
and Sung to Yuan/Ming/Ching periods. Patricia Ebrey (1993) has done
a great deal of valuable research on women in the family during the
Sung (960–1279), and suggests that studying what women did to deal
with an oppressive family system is a much more fruitful undertaking for historians of women than concentrating on the oppression
itself:

> The descent line from father to son to grandson was taken to be the
> core of the family: obligation to ancestors, family property, and family
> names were all transmitted along the patriline. Texts that can be
> broadly labeled Confucian presented family and kinship as at bot-
> tom a set of connections among men; indeed, people could and did
> compile family histories that failed to mention any women. . . .
> According to the dominant ethical and legal model, in short, the

Chinese family was thoroughly patrilineal, patriarchal, and patrilo-cal. Women were well aware of that model and their marginality in it. Still, most found it to their advantage to respond to the incentives and rewards that this family system offered women and to work within it. (Ebrey 1993: 7–8)

What women had to work with, it is becoming clear, changed over time, and not always for the better. Kathryn Bernhardt's research on legal issues demonstrates that women from T'ang/Sung (618–1279) periods were better able to maintain bilateral relationships with natal families and families into which they married than Ming/Ch'ing (1368–1912) women; that women in the post-Sung era were much more completely cut off from their natal families, a cause and consequence of declining legal status:

Overall, the transformation in the post-Song era brought about a decline in legal status. Specifically a daughter could no longer inherit her father's property so long as there existed a suitable heir within the five grades of mourning; a widow could no longer take her original dowry with her upon remarriage; a wife had fewer grounds upon which to divorce her husband; a widow had to depend upon her marital family rather than her natal one to arrange a remarriage; and a betrothed daughter came to be treated as a wife in certain criminal matters. . . . More generally, the post-Song changes removed much of the latitude that the law had once provided for a natal family to intervene on a daughter's behalf and placed her more fully under the legal control of her marital family. (Bernhardt 1996: 56)

Chinese lineage patterns privileging agnatic males meant that women would suffer the heavy burdens of a patrilineal, patrilocal society; Margery Wolf's (1972) pioneering research on women in Taiwan paints the following picture of women in the late Ch'ing, a picture whose overall accuracy for the period has still not been seriously challenged. In this analysis, women were often unwelcome daughters in their natal families, and strangers who had to prove their value to the families into which they were married. Their labor in their natal families was often discounted; since out-marriage was the inevitability most Chinese women faced, they were often considered "guests" who had to be fed and clothed, and whose wedding, even though it might raise the social status of the family, was a costly affair. After her marriage, the bride's capacity for producing sons and her willingness to work in a potentially hostile environment were quickly tested; in a sense, she was now completely alone—no longer a part of her natal family, and not yet accepted by her husband's family. Little wonder that so many of the stereotypic descriptions of women's lives that have come down to us—particularly those that emphasize the harsh, unforgiving environment surrounding the new bride—are the descriptions we remember. But it is important to recognize other complex issues, including the roles that wives might play in the division of property in Chinese families. Of course our understanding of women's history in China is skewed by the emphasis on gentry families; it is likely that women's lives in families with little property to distribute among sons would be very different. Here, as Freedman (1979) puts it, the father's control was weak, and each brother stood close to his wife, so that even though she "might be made miserable by poverty and hard work" she had more autonomy and less need to "cope with" senior women in the house. We know very little about the lives of women in peasant families; we can read back into the past the experience of the present, and we can assume, though perhaps we should not, that families with upwardly mobile ambitions tended to pattern themselves on the gentry model. One thing seems probable: generally speaking, the higher the status, the more Confucian the family.

In gentry families, women needed more than wisdom and assertiveness to survive; resilience, toughness, and an ability to engage in what Margery Wolf has called "uterine politics" (1972) were required. In Wolf's analysis, women manipulated two institutions ranged against them—property and Confucian values—in a way that could bring them power and relative security in old age. By successfully tying sons to her, and assisting them in their efforts to achieve power in the family, a woman might acquire reflected authority, plus a commitment to the claims of filial piety that would bring security and respect as she grew older. That such a woman was often brought into direct conflict with other family members, especially other women, was axiomatic. The structure of the Confucian Chinese family system guaranteed conflict among women as a constant.

The literature of Confucianism tells us that women are by nature quarrelsome, jealous, and petty-minded; there are a number of characters in the Chinese language that explicitly proclaim the inability of women to get along together. But what were the structural reasons for the legendary conflicts between mothers-in-law, daughters-in-law, and sisters-in-law? It was often the precipitating conflict over property to be divided among agnatic males who together owned it as a joint person. Ideally, the division of property took place when a senior generation died, but division could take place earlier for any number of reasons, including conflict in fraternal relationships. A senior member of the line could prevent a descendant from removing his share; a brother could not. Generally, it was in the interest of the senior generation to keep property intact, and in complex families the patriarch was often strong enough, aided by a wife who had a similar interest, to do so. Thus, a mother-in-law was not only "patriarchy's female deputy" (Stacey 1983: 54), who disciplined and trained the new bride; she and her daughter-in-law often had diametrically opposed interests in the early division of family property, and they were competitors for the loyalties of husbands and sons. Sisters-in-law too often hoped for an early share of family resources, and, for that reason, were often seen as fostering competition and conflict among brothers. The more conflict, the more likely an early division. Myron Cohen (1976) points to the part married sons played in this conflict by explaining that they often tended to paper over differences when they were economically secure and encouraged divisiveness on their wives' part when they were not.

Younger women who successfully achieved an early division of property against the wishes of a mother-in-law could look forward to setting up a household in which they would be physically removed from her domination: free, in theory, to pursue a more intimate relationship with husband or children, and to achieve a semblance of autonomy. Little wonder that so many women were willing to use whatever wealth they brought with them into the family—money or, in exceptional cases, land—plus any earnings for work in excess of routine household tasks, to assist in setting up a new family. Little wonder that mothers-in-law saw daughters-in-law as serious threats, or that sisters-in-law were suspicious of one another. The gain of each woman always came at the expense of another: this was the structural reality of the Chinese family system, and it was this structure, not the innate garrulousness and jealousy of women, that could produce endless conflict.

Seen from this perspective, Chinese women were neither helpless victims of the family system nor powerful actors primarily responsible for its problems. Chinese women struggled under the weight of enormous contradictions, most of which were built into the system; they were actors caught in the tensions of a family system about whose real "success" even the Confucian state was occasionally ambivalent. In all of this, women—as daughters, wives, and mothers—occupied very difficult, if not untenable, positions.

In both Korea and Japan, the Confucian family model, with its attendant imagery and ideology, did not have a major impact on women's lives until fairly late: in the Korean case, with the establishment of the Yi dynasty in the fifteenth century, and in Japan with the development of Tokugawa rule in the seventeenth century.

TAOISM, BUDDHISM, AND FOLK RELIGIONS

China, Japan, and Korea were all heavily influenced by Buddhism, but all three experienced Buddhism as an import; in Japan and Korea, strong folk traditions existed before the introduction of Buddhism, and in China, folk and Taoist religious practices were well entrenched before the import of Buddhism. In all three cases, Buddhism was seen as a competitor in spite of the fact that one of the great strengths of Buddhist tradition has always been its ability to adapt to, and ameliorate, its impact on other religious traditions. The complex of folk traditions that had existed in Japan, for example, gave themselves the name *Shintō*, or the way of the gods, for the first time in reaction to the arrival of Buddhism. For women in all three societies, the import of Buddhism brought decidedly mixed results, partly because there was no single Buddhist ideology relating to women, and partly because Buddhism both influenced, and was influenced by, native traditions in each case.

Folk traditions in Japan and Korea, as we have seen, have a history of attaching value to women, especially strong women, independent of roles they may play in the family. Neither Japanese nor Korean traditions, before the import of Confucianism and Buddhism, dedicated themselves to prescriptive representations of women or made the family central to women's lives. Powerful women exist in the folk religions of both Japan and Korea, a legacy that continues in spite of enormous changes in both societies over time.

Chinese Taoism, however, presents one of the best examples of a religious tradition in which women played central and honored roles. In her discussions of one of the most powerful women in East Asian religions, Hsi Huang Mu (the Queen Mother of the West), Suzanne Cahill (1993) provides striking images that flatly contradict views of women in Buddhist or Confucian texts:

> Medieval Taoists considered the Queen Mother of the West the embodiment of the ultimate yin, the dark female force. They believed that, along with other high deities of Taoism, she created the world and continued to maintain cosmic harmony. The goddess's name, Queen Mother of the West, reveals three essential components of her character: she was regal, female, and associated with the west. As a ruler, she controlled creation, transcendence and divine passion. As a woman, she was mother, teacher, and lover. . . . It may startle Western readers to learn that the Queen Mother's

followers pass over her role in creation, which they see as an automatic and inevitable process, to emphasize two other themes: transcendence and divine passion. . . . Divine passion is the desire of deities and humans for mutual union and communication. One means to transcendence was marriage with a deity of the opposite sex. The marriage, often described in the most sensual of metaphors, was meant to leave sexuality behind and concentrate on the spiritual advancement of both parties. . . . No matter what other meanings are present, representations of the goddess throughout Chinese history have always evoked the two themes of transcendence and divine passion. (Cahill 1993: 3)

Although she too can be both threatening and compassionate, it is her nurturing side that emerges in relationships with the women she protects, women who do not fit into traditional family patterns in China. This was especially true in the case of dancers, prostitutes, or other women who might hope to become celestial attendants, but it was also true for those women who became Taoist nuns, or those who stayed at home. She was not, as Cahill tells us, an advocate of Confucian family roles for Chinese women; in fact, she is "never mentioned as a granter of children. . . . Hsi Wang Mu . . . legitimizes alternative paths. She embodies a model of women as dynamic and creative, independent forces" (Cahill 1986: 168).

Religious Taoism, as Cahill tells us, had its own hierarchical sense of things; the "Taoist celestial bureaucracy" mirrored "the earthly imperium" (Cahill: 1993: 244). But unlike other Chinese hierarchical structures, one gender was not assumed superior to another. Cahill quotes Tu Kuang-t'ing's *Records of the Assembled Transcendents of the Fortified Wall City*, a biography of mortal women, half of whom became Taoist saints:

". . . a person is raised to virtue and talent, unrestricted by distinctions between male and female." The idea is that the paths are separate, but the goals of practice are identical and the Tao is one. This agrees with Taoist beliefs that yang and yin are both essential, and the Tao itself, resolving all contradictions, does not distinguish between genders. (Cahill 1993: 214–15)

Buddhism in China, Japan, and Korea was not only an import; it was a multi-layered, complex religion. Treating Buddhism as a monolith is very much like explaining Christianity, not simply as a monotheistic tradition, but as a unitary system of beliefs. There is no single Buddhist point of view relative to women, but there is a fundamental ambiguity in the Mahayhana tradition that dominated China, Japan, and Korea focused on female sexuality. As Diana Paul (1985) explains,

> Devolution is the way of the world and ordinary human behavior. Evolution, on the other hand, is the way of Buddhist practice. Buddhism works against the grain of devolution. . . . The religious objective is to reverse the entire process of attachment to the world of desire of which sexuality is one important factor. The question to be raised is whether women have the capacity to reverse or at least control their sexuality and worldly desires. (Paul 1985: xxvii–xxviii)

As a consequence of this fundamental problem, in many Buddhist texts and teachings women came to symbolize all that must be transcended in order to achieve enlightenment. That is one of the reasons that outside of the Judeo-Christian tradition it is difficult to find more misogynist descriptions of women than those found in some Buddhist texts. It is often not simply a case of the "tragedy of being born a woman"—almost always the result of bad karma—but it is often the combination of Buddhist, Hindu, and occasionally folk religious attitudes that makes this language so astonishing. A prime example is Japan's Blood Bowl Sutra (*Ketsubon kyō*), preached specifically for women in the context of Pure Land Buddhism, a powerful form of popular Buddhism developed in the late twelfth and early thirteenth centuries. Its vivid portrait of the Blood Pond Hell is different from other such descriptions used to encourage common people to save themselves, because it is so narrowly focused on a single gender:

> All women fall into this hell because of their karma. . . . The red blood flows seven days every month, this is eighty-four days in twelve months. This is why it is called "moon water." This "moon water" is extremely evil and unclean. However, this evil blood spills upon the ground sullying the heads of the Earth Gods, thus invoking the wrath of those 98,072 gods. If poured into water, it pollutes the Water Gods; if disposed of in the mountain forests, it defiles the Mountain Gods. When women wash their soiled clothing in the rivers, the good folk living downstream, ignorant of their act, draw this water and with it prepare tea and rice to offer to the gods and buddhas. . . . Since women, by nature, soil the gods and buddhas, they will all fall into the Blood Pond Hell after they die. (Minamoto 1993: 95)

It is remarkable that such a sutra could be introduced in the context of a developing agreement that women, too, were capable of salvation, an agreement Japan saw for the first time after the Heian period in Pure Land Buddhism, a vehicle that popularized Buddhism and criticized the esoteric (and elite) practices of an earlier day.

In Korea, where Buddhism was introduced in the fourth century, women freely integrated Buddhist ideas and practice into local shamanistic traditions. That may help to account for the fact that women of many different classes participated in Buddhist rites from the beginning and did not encounter the same hostility Japanese women experienced. At the same time, Korean women were aware that they had much more authority in their own traditions than in Buddhism:

> The role of women in shamanism differed from that in Buddhism. Women were active ritual leaders in shamanism whereas they were mainly part of the "congregation" under Buddhism. Although there were many active nuns, the priesthood was organized around male leadership. Buddhism in many ways was a religion associated with a new kind of patriarchal state. (Kim 1976: 21)

In early Japan, Buddhism was a political as well as a religious vehicle, used by advocates of a centralized state to rationalize and symbolize the power of the center over regional and local authority —authority that was primarily linked to Shintō and other folk traditions. Diluting the connections between Shintō and powerful regional families, Buddhism enhanced the legitimacy of the imperial family, but over time it also diminished the power of women in the folk tradition. That is partly because of the views of women Buddhism brought with it, and partly a result of the fact that Buddhism was a carrier of Chinese culture in Japan; and, as we have seen, an important part of Chinese statecraft was organizing property holding on the basis of male lineage.

Wakita Haruko (1984) underscores the fact that this transformation in landholding took a very long time; the inheritance and marriage practices on which the relatively high status of women in Nara (C.E. 710–84) and Heian (C.E. 784–1185) were based changed slowly, particularly for women in the countryside. We have already seen that the Chinese lineage system did not fit an early Japanese society that emphasized the preservation of the family through connections to Shintō deities and real or fictive kinship. Early Japanese society was neither predominantly patrilineal nor patrilocal.

Still, as Blacker (1986) tells us, Japanese women did lose significant religious/political authority to Buddhism beginning in the seventh century:

> Under the new regime, the appearance of mantic queens such as Pimiko and the Empress Jingu became impossible. Under the new system too the *miko* in the large shrines began to lose her mantic gift, and to become before long the figure she is today. Decorative

in her red trousers and silver crown, she now dances, sings, assists in ritual, but no longer prophesies. The ancient power with which this ancient sybil was endowed passed . . . to the level of the "little tradition," the largely unrecorded, orally transmitted folk religion of the villages. The mantic gift of the ancient *miko* survived in a variety of humbler folk—in the traveling bands of women such as the Kumano *bikuni* who, like strolling minstrels, walked the countryside offering their gifts of prophesy and divination, and in the blind women of the north who, without the music and dance so essentially a part of the older *miko's* shamanic performance, transmit the utterances of the numina and dead spirits. (Blacker 1986: 30)

Before the eighth century, roughly one-half of the reigning sovereigns in Japan's imperial family were women, many of whom would have been described as devout Buddhists; but they also continued to identify themselves with mantic traditions. Kidder (1979) describes the Empress Jito (C.E. 687-97) as a "charismatic personality . . . who provided counsel for the operations of government. . . . She was a medium who communicated the will of the *kami*, whose advice was essential for guiding the affairs of state" (Kidder 1979: 204). But after the eighth century, Buddhism became a singular influence in the Japanese record, and the Empress Kōken (C.E. 749–58) emerged, because of her affair with a Buddhist monk, as the stereotypically dangerous woman of many Buddhist texts.

In spite of the fact that the real struggle in her reign was between important aristocratic families at court, like the Fujiwara and their powerful Buddhist competitors, it was Kōken who was blamed for the fact that, after her death, women never again reigned as empresses. The only exceptions were those who "ruled" during the Tokugawa shogunate (1600–1868), a time when the imperial family was a virtual political prisoner of military authority.

In both Buddhism and Taoism, monastic life could serve many different needs, even though life in these institutions could be very difficult and demanding:

Why would a medieval Chinese woman become a Taoist nun? She might take holy orders for various reasons: as a means of refuge or retreat at the death of a husband, as a purifying intermission between husbands[,] . . . as a survival tactic for members of the imperial harem dismissed during anti-luxury campaigns, as a means of escaping palace intrigue and danger, as a method of avoiding marriage and living an independent life outside the family, and as a way of obtaining an education. Some parents sent sick daughters to a convent in hopes of curing them; in times of famine, parents might hand over starving daughters so they might survive. These motives exist in addition, of course, to genuine religious vocation, which is hard to measure. (Cahill 1993: 216)

With slight variations, these descriptions could fit Japan and Korea as well, although the record shows clearly that in Japan, *enkiridera*, sometimes called "divorce temples," were established specifically to allow women time and space in which to get a publicly sanctioned divorce. One such temple, the *Tōkeiji* in Kamakura, is believed to have been established by Hojo Masako (C.E. 1157–1225), the wife of the shogun Minamoto Yoritomo, a devout Buddhist and very powerful woman who, as Yoritomo's widow, played a major role in Kamakura politics until her death. Kathleen Uno (1991) describes the operation of the *Tōkeiji* much later in Japanese history, in the Tokugawa (1600–1868) period:

> In the last half of the Tokugawa period, some two thousand women apparently sought the services of . . . *Tōkeiji*, in Kamakura. According to custom, if a married woman entered this temple and performed its rites for three years, the bond between her and her husband was broken. For women in a hurry, Buddhist temple officials served as divorce brokers. They would go to the husband's village and camp at the headman's door until he summoned the husband and forced him to agree to an amicable divorce. In most cases, just the news that the temple officials were coming was enough to produce a letter of separation. (Uno 1991: 61)

From the standpoint of women's history, it is important to remember that the combined influence of Confucian and Buddhist ideologies contributed instrumentally to the exclusion of women from public roles. Confucianism legitimized the exclusion of women from overt political power by insisting that such a state of affairs contravened the natural order of things; for a woman to assume the title of Emperor was, to turn a Confucian phrase, "like a hen crowing." The limited capacity for rationality many Confucian thinkers attributed to women meant they must exercise the moral agency of which they were capable in the home—not in statecraft. Buddhist views of women made them equally suspect as candidates for occupations in the public arena, but here the lack of rationality and the specter of danger was more explicitly linked, initially at least, to female sexuality. Throughout Asia, particularly in Japan, Buddhism has generally been praised for its mediating, civilizing influence; Buddhist ideas no doubt humanized many aspects of life in the capital and countryside, but women, it is clear, were often only peripheral beneficiaries of that influence.

WOMEN AND LITERATURE IN HEIAN JAPAN (784–1185)

Murasaki Shikibu is the pen name of the woman who wrote the world's first novel, *The Tale of Genji*, in eleventh-century Japan. Very little is known of her life, except that she was born to a minor branch of the Fujiwara family sometime in the last quarter of the tenth century. Her father, a middle-ranking bureaucrat who held occasional minor posts in the capital and served in a provincial governorship, was probably, like many men of his station, interested in literature. Sei Shōnagon, Murasaki's contemporary and the author of *The Pillow Book*, was best known as the daughter of an outstanding poet/provincial governor in her early days at court; it was a legacy about which she apparently felt some ambivalence.

Murasaki tells us that her father, appreciative of the talent she demonstrated very early, expressed the wish that she had been born a boy (Bowring 1982). The irony is that, had she been born a boy, it is unlikely she would have written the world's first, and one of its most ambitious, novels. Why Heian prose traditions should have been dominated by women is an interesting question, and the answers to it tell us a great deal about the status of aristocratic women at the Heian court who were not official wives. One translator suggests that "Possibly it has something to do with the fact that Japan seems to have been relatively free of the harem politics that so beset other Oriental countries, and talented ladies of leisure therefore found other outlets for their energies. It may have to do also with the fact that they were less conventional than men" (Seidensticker in Murasaki 1976: viii).

Historians of Japan are fond of pointing out that the eleventh century was a time when aristocratic Japanese men wrote bad Chinese poetry and women created a brilliant literary tradition. Chinese was the language of the bureaucracy, and Japanese bureaucrats adopted it not only as a foreign language marking the office they held, but with it a Confucian bias against prose as well. They came to see writing Chinese-style, "public" poetry as a moral exercise, designed to develop character, and prose as mere storytelling. Genji himself, as Murasaki describes him in the novel, is at best ambivalent about such "old stories." Coming upon a lady-in-waiting reading a romance, Genji first derides, then champions this literary art. In what is usually considered the first "defense" of the novel anywhere, Genji comments:

> As a matter of fact I think far better of this art than I have led you to suppose. Even its practical value is immense. Without it what should we know of how people lived in the past. . . . For history-books . . .

show us only one small corner of life; whereas these diaries and romances . . . contain, I am sure, the most minute information about all sorts of people's private affairs. . . . But I have a theory of my own about what this art of the novel is, and how it came into being. To begin with, it does not simply consist in the author's telling a story about the adventures of some other person. On the contrary, it happens because the storyteller's own experience of men and things, whether for good or ill—not what he has passed through himself, but even events which he has only witnessed or been told of—has moved him to an emotion so passionate that he can no longer keep it shut up in his heart. Again and again something in his own life or in that around him will seem to the writer so important that he cannot bear to let it pass into oblivion. There must never come a time, he feels, when men do not know about it. . . . Anything whatsoever may become the subject of a novel, provided only that it happens in this mundane life." (Waley/Murasaki 1960: 501–502)

Donald Keene's comment on this passage reinforces the significance of Murasaki's work. "The ideas in this passage are so familiar to us because of the works of modern writers, particularly Proust, that we cannot perhaps immediately see how extraordinary they really are. . . . We do not find any such intent in *The Decameron*, *Tom Jones*, nor in any other European novels before the nineteenth century" (Keene 1955: 77).

Heian women dominated the literature of their time not simply because they possessed wit, intelligence, and leisure; unlike men, they were free to write using *kana*, a phonetic syllabary much more congenial to the expression of Japanese sensibility than the Chinese language. It was not, as so many commentators have told us, that women in the Heian court did not know Chinese; there is little doubt that Murasaki and many of her contemporaries at court could read and write Chinese, though they may have occasionally preferred to keep it quiet. Still, the important issue is that, in many times and places in Japanese history, the phonetic script was less "women's script" than the language of sentiment. For that reason, men—those selfsame bureaucrats Genji represents—often used *kana* to write private poetry. It is probably true that the closer one comes to seventeenth-century Japan, the more likely it is that even aristocratic women might have been more or less confined to expressing themselves in *kana*, but that was certainly not true earlier. In any case, the identification of *kana* as "women's script" or "women's hand"—often intended to connote inferior intelligence since it was much simpler to learn than Chinese characters—did not become widespread until well after the Heian period.

The relative autonomy aristocratic women in the Heian court enjoyed contributed not only to the freedom they had to write, but also to the experiences out of which they wrote. To some extent, that latitude might have been based on the willingness of the court, especially empresses consort, to give them economic support—the kind of economic support aristocratic families ordinarily might assume for unmarried, widowed, or otherwise "unprotected" women. In a sense, ladies-in-waiting, like Murasaki and Sei Shonagon, fared better than contemporaries who became legal wives, and had to accept—in return for economic support and status—prolonged absences on the part of husbands, the competition of other secondary wives, and a generally lonely, apparently celibate existence. *The Gossamer Years* (Seidensticker 1964) presents an autobiographical account of one such legal wife, who was clearly unhappy with her situation.

Heian literature suggests that unmarried women at court understood the boundaries of their lives; they were relatively free agents who, like Sei Shonagon, could choose their lovers, but could not make their private lives public in a way that invited criticism. Women like Murasaki, who came to court young and recently widowed, could choose, as she apparently did, not to have much to do with men. On the other hand, many women at court, widowed or unmarried, used the opportunity to search for suitable husbands among the aristocracy. There was no equivalent of palace concubines/harem at the Heian court.

Based on preliminary research, it seems that women outside the Heian court also enjoyed relatively high status in this period. First, it was common for women in this and preceding periods to inherit property. Wakita (1984) reminds us that, except for consorts and reigning empresses, women were not allowed to hold office in the Japanese bureaucracy, and that meant they could not amass wealth in land; they could, however, retain some measure of independence if they managed to maintain their property holdings. In the countryside, women continued to hold important offices in community groups apparently because they remained principal celebrants in religious rites; without that authority, they could not have shared policy-making responsibilities with men in their communities.

Takamure Itsue, one of Japan's pioneering feminist historians, was the first to appreciate the implications of diverse marriage patterns in early Japan. McCullough (1967), basing his reports on Takamure, outlines four basic patterns of Heian marriage (virilocal, uxorilocal, duolocal, and neolocal); but as Wakita points out, these categories "only tell part of the story: the conjugal activities of the couple itself, including the very common . . . husband/multiple wives syndrome, must also be considered" (Wakita 1984: 82–83).

Wakita agrees that in Nara and Heian, men and women "enjoyed relative equity in marriage, along with property rights and membership in the village communal organization," but she reminds us that the fact that uxorilocal marriage dominated among the aristocracy does not, in and of itself, reflect high status. When husbands moved in with wives and their wives' families, it was often, as Wakita points out, because "the woman's father—that is to say, the patriarchal authority of her family—was sufficiently powerful to demand it" (Wakita 1984: 83).

Social Change and Ideology, 1200–1600

NEO-CONFUCIANISM

One of the challenges historians of women in China have faced is accounting for the development of two institutions considered most repressive of women: footbinding and widow chastity. There are other issues to be addressed, of course, including an apparent loss of legal status on the part of women in China, but they all seem somehow related to the development of Neo-Confucian ideas in the Sung (960–1279). The generation of these ideas in turn is thought to have had substantial impact on women in Korea and Japan.

Recent scholarship has, however, done a great deal to revise our views of T'ang/Sung (618–907/960–1279) relative to women. Historians of women have perhaps done more than any other group to challenge the notion of a monolithic Neo-Confucianism, demonstrating, for example, that some Sung Neo-Confucianists supported a complementary, not hierarchical, view of gendered roles in society and the family (Birge 1989). And Kathryn Bernhardt has shown that, from the standpoint of marriage and property rights, T'ang/Sung women fared considerably better than women in Ming (1368–1644) and Ch'ing (1644–1912) periods (Bernhardt 1996). Women in the Sung seem to have had greater control over dowry than women in later periods, and they did occasionally hold property as well (Ebrey 1993).

One of the repressive institutions attributed to the Sung was the practice of honoring faithful widows. Mark Elvin summarizes the Confucian virtues "that stabilized a society that was ordered according to a hierarchy of age, and divided into kin-groups based on male dominance and male descent-lines" (Elvin 1984: 111). The Confucian virtues most typically honored were (a) filial behavior toward parents and grandparents, (b) the harmonious cohabitation of many generations within a kin-group without any division of property, (c) the fidelity of widows to their husbands, (d) the safeguarding of sexual purity by a woman, through self-mutilation or suicide if necessary, and lastly (e) longevity:

> Though a widow's loyalty to a deceased husband (demonstrated either by assuming her husband's work herself, or by refusing to remarry) was honored in the Sung period, precise definitions of the "virtuous widow" and the prescriptions for state honors did not begin until 1304 under the Yuan, when the Ministry of Rituals proposed that honorific insignia be given to widows bereaved before 30 and living until at least 50 years of age. (Elvin 1984: 23)

Over time, the practice of honoring faithful widows was extended, reaching full development in Ming and Ch'ing periods; what later became the "cult of widow chastity" was an important vehicle in the repression of women of every social class in China.

FOOTBINDING

By now it seems well established that the practice of footbinding in China began in late Sung, although Ebrey tells us that the Sung writer Chou Mi (1232–1308) "attributed to an anonymous source the story that three centuries earlier a dancer in the palace of the ruler of the Later T'ang (923–935) had bound her feet to make them small and curved up like new moons" (Ebrey 1993: 38). That we should know so little of the motivating origins of a practice affecting the daily lives of millions of people over time, in spite of the fact that it had substantial impact on the Chinese economy, is symptomatic of the treatment of women in the historical record. Women certainly exist in the Chinese record in large numbers; what is missing is writing *by* women, rather than writing *on* women by male scholars whose priorities were likely to be different, particularly on an issue like this one.

The practice of footbinding is, however, one of the first things about women's lives in Asia routinely reported in introductory history classes; occasionally, students are presented with slides showing what happens to the feet of a five- or six-year-old girl when they are bound ever more tightly by her mother, until the toes and heels are in close proximity. Occasionally students are told that the practice began as an erotic fetish, or that bound feet were devised to immobilize concubines in the women's quarters who might want to escape. Tiny, three-inch "lotus petals" or "golden lilies" were prized by those who found them erotically stimulating, and bound feet certainly limited mobility. The problem is that too often the story of footbinding is left here, allowing students to regard it as yet another example of "exotic" Asian behavior, with little or no connection to other historical developments, in China or elsewhere.

It is significant that footbinding was not universally practiced in China and did not take root in Korea or Japan. In China, Hakka women (see glossary) did not bind their feet, nor did women of most ethnic minorities, including Manchu women. To what extent footbinding compromised the ability of agrarian women to contribute to farm production remains the subject of ongoing research. It is likely that where rice culture dominated, as in southern China, the practice of footbinding was not always allowed to interfere with the productive lives of women; however, we are left with the strong impression that a lack of mobility made it difficult for women to contribute to "outside" economic work in other regions. The fact that women often compensated for this with "inside" work that contributed significantly to the household economy should be taken into account, but the general conclusion that footbinding had a major impact on China's economy is inescapable.

How was it possible for such a practice to be built into the life cycle of most Chinese women, whatever their class and whatever the impact on the economy? Ebrey, who describes the practice as "firmly entrenched" by the end of Sung, comments that

> Footbinding was an alteration of the body that changed everything about a woman's physical being. She would move about less, sitting rather than standing, staying home rather than going out. With less exercise, she would be softer, more languid. From poetry, we know of men's attraction to languid women, especially unhappy beauties longing for absent men. For women to be smaller, softer, more stationary, and more languid would of course enhance the image of men as larger, harder, more active. (Ebrey 1993: 40–41)

Still, as Ebrey and others have pointed out, this does not answer the larger question of women's apparently eager participation; it was, she reminds us, "mothers, not suitors, who bound little girls' feet despite the pain it caused" (Ebrey 1993: 42). Dorothy Ko (1994) tells us that by the seventeenth century, footbinding separated young girls of six from their brothers; that "Through footbinding, the doctrine of separate spheres was engraved onto the bodies of female children" (Ko 1994: 149).

Finally there is the part played by the commodification of women's bodies in a period (Sung/Yuan/Ming) of economic growth and social change. Ebrey points to the growing market for concubines in the Sung explained by the increasing numbers of men in gentry families who could afford them. And Ko describes a "thriving market in girls" in the Ming in which footbinding played a major role: "Catering to the men they were intended to serve, women groomed for the market regarded the size and shape of their feet as the hallmark of their personhood. The elaborate female-exclusive rituals honoring the Tiny-Foot maiden or the Boddhisattva Guanyin that launched the binding procedure for gentry girls were just as central to the lives of [girls sold on the market]" (Ko 1994: 263).

Chinese society, hierarchal and seemingly closed as it was, offered many more opportunities for upward social mobility throughout much of its history than, for example, Japan, where rank and status were more permanently fixed by a system that privileged inheritance, not merit or office-holding based on one's performance in civil service examinations. Marrying up and out of one's class was very difficult, if not impossible, in the Japanese system, but in the Chinese case, marriage could provide that opportunity for young women with suitably bound feet. Footbinding was even more critical to the prospects of would-be concubines who might rise from low levels of Chinese society to a place, perhaps an important place, in a gentry family and, as we have seen, to the daughters sold into prostitution by their families.

There is perhaps no other institution in Chinese culture that so vividly demonstrates the ironies and inconsistencies of Confucian demands on women. Dorothy Ko suggests that we should not be surprised by this: "It highlights the conflicting demands that men placed on women—as moral guardians and sex objects. Footbinding served the goals of safeguarding a woman's purity while accentuating her sensuousness, both of which rendered her desirable in men's eyes" (Ko 1994: 264).

There is little disagreement among historians of women that footbinding in China was an exploitative, oppressive practice that caused enormous suffering; it is, on one level, a stunning example of misogyny and economic exploitation played out in Chinese institutions. But it also an important story Chinese women tell us about themselves, a story that suggests we need to establish a clearer appreciation of footbinding as a part of the life cycle; that we need to be very careful to place the practice in a wider institutional context that confronts "exotic" representations we too often see when this issue is presented in the classroom.

KOREA AND JAPAN

Historians have often assumed that Neo-Confucianism became the dominant ideology in Korea with the establishment of the Yi dynasty (1392-1910), but recent research on Korean women has raised important questions about that assumption. It is quite clear that Korean Neo-Confucians intended to change the habits of Korean women by limiting their freedom to move in public spaces, emphasizing the legitimacy of the patriline through exclusion of women from family registers, and prohibiting their participation in ancestral rites. It is possible that these changes became a part of the lives of some aristocratic women (Kim 1976). On the other hand, commoners and many aristocratic women often seem to have ignored these prescriptions. Mark Peterson reports that, in spite of the self-conscious adoption of Confucian principles by the founders of the Yi dynasty, the status of women in the family was relatively unaffected prior to 1600. He outlines for us the basic elements of that status before the seventeenth century:

> 1. The patrilineage was not the basic unit of society. 2. . . . The principle that men were superior to women did not apply. Daughters were listed with sons in the order of their birth, both in the genealogy and the inheritance documents. 3. Inheritance was equally divided among sons and daughters. Women held equal rights to property and could give or receive property on an equal footing with men. 4. Ancestor ceremonies were not the responsibility of the male children alone. Daughters also had responsibility for the ceremonies and held land to support them. 5. Adoption was seldom practiced. When an adoption took place, representatives of the woman's natal lineage were involved in the decision-making process. 6. Female lines were as important as male lines. In record keeping and in recognition of relationships, affinal ties seem to have been as significant as those between lineage members. 7. Remarriage was not unusual. Prejudices against, or limitations on married women were minimal in the first century of the dynasty, but hardened thereafter. (Peterson 1983: 42)

The connection between landholding and participation in ancestral rites seems to have been a crucial element in the gradual loss of status among Korean women that began in the seventeenth century. Without landed wealth, women could not properly carry out rites; by the same token, non-participation increased landlessness among women, and probably, as in Japan, non-participation in community policy-making as well. How slow the change was in some parts of Korea is illustrated by a document that shows a mother-in-law deeding property to a daughter-in-law on whom she "could rely to carry out the ancestor ceremonies," as late as 1694. A century later, however, women had apparently stopped bequeathing property to other women, and they no longer participated in ancestral rites (Peterson 1983: 44).

In Japan, like Korea, change in women's status was slow, but inexorable; here too it was closely tied to the loss of rights in local community organizations that held both religious and political authority. As Wakita points out, that exclusion was the logical result of the fact that, by the end of the fourteenth century, most women were no longer chief celebrants in local religious ceremonies, and they had become invisible (even if they actually held land) landholders on local registers. The fate of the *miko* seems to symbolize what happened to women in the countryside; once religious personages with no peer in folk tradition, *miko* were in fifteenth-century Japan "outside religious orthodoxy, and . . . well on the way to becoming outcastes" (Wakita 1984: 94-95).

Among the rising warrior aristocracy, the tendency had been, from the thirteenth century, to rule against divided inheritance, or, if an inheritance were granted to a woman, to limit it to her lifetime. By the fourteenth century, all inheritance rights for women were becoming a thing of the past for aristocratic women, and the standard marriage arrangement became virilocal—daughters out-marrying and living as new brides with husbands and their families.

Ultimately, as a result of constant war and the need to "guarantee" alliances among competitors, women were often made hostages in marriages that were designed to guarantee alliances between warrior families. Legal wives and potential male heirs were often confined as guarantors of a tenuous peace; if that peace was broken, wives and children were often killed, or died as residents of a castle under attack. Mary Berry describes an agreement by three important warrior families in 1554 that demonstrates how complicated these marriage alliances could become:

> To ensure the peace, the three families concluded a startling number of marriage alliances. Imagawa Yoshimoto's daughter married Takeda Shingen's son. Takeda Shingen's daughter married Hojo Ujiyasu's son. Hojo Ujiyasu's daughter married Imagawa Yoshimoto's son. Imagawa Yoshimoto himself was already married to Takeda Shingen's sister, and his sister was the wife of Hojo Ujiyasu. (Berry 1982: 36)

In the sixteenth century, it was not unusual for the head of a powerful warrior family to compel the divorce of one of his happily married sisters in order to offer her as a prospective bride to another warlord whose loyalty was in doubt.

Until very recently, the assumption of seriously declining status among aristocratic women in this period has not been challenged; however, there are now some historians of Japanese women who have raised the possibility that the legal wives in important warrior families may have been recognized as important managers of estates who were second in command only to their husbands. Wakita Haruko (1993) raises this possibility and makes the point that, in her view, gender was much less a barrier than we have been led to believe. In her words, "In medieval society, the difference between social classes was in fact far greater than differences due to gender" (p. 86). She believes that the change from Heian marriage institutions (in which husbands moved in with their wives' families [*mukotori*] or lived separately [*tsumadori*]) to the practice of wives moving in with husbands' families (*yometori*) in the medieval period should not be seen as resulting in lower status for women:

> The *ie* (house/extended-family/lineage) of the medieval period was managed by one husband and one wife. This couple formed a domestic organization of production and reproduction. All of the men and women within the *ie* were required to show subordination to this organization. Although the wife was second-in-command in the household, her authority was as strong as that of her husband, the patriarchal head of the household. . . . The responsibilities of the wife in a warrior's household . . . included not only overseeing the acquisition and preparation of food and clothing, but also managing the household budget, arranging the sale of tributary items, purchasing provisions, maintaining weapons and armor, and generally looking after other subordinate members of the household and ensuring that they remained loyal to their master. A typical example of a woman in this role is Hōjō Masako. Her husband's subordinates always obeyed her because she took very good care of them. Given her position, it is not surprising that she gained control of the shogunate after her husband's death. (Wakita 1993: 88–89)

Whether or not the status of women in powerful families was improved or diminished by medieval institutions (an important issue that has only begun to be addressed) it is very likely that merchant and artisan women were moving up in Japanese society. The growth of commerce and trade, which produced such independent merchant cities as Sakai on the east coast of Japan and supported merchant guilds or *za*, also brought women in merchant families a significant measure of power in the fourteenth and fifteenth centuries. Women were active in merchant guilds and often managed businesses, occasionally passing on monopoly rights to their daughters. Before 1550, landholding seems to have been possible for merchant women if it came as part of a commercial transaction.

Early Modern/Late Imperial Society, 1600–1800

In China and Japan, and to a lesser extent Korea, the seventeenth and eighteenth centuries were marked by growth that expanded earlier economic tendencies: commercialization, urbanization, and the growth of literacy and popular culture. Often, in spite of the best efforts governments made to control it, society was marked by greater geographic and social mobility, even though the gap between wealth and poverty was more striking than ever. Women played important roles in the far-reaching change that characterized this period, roles that recent scholarship has expanded and problematized. After 1600, for the first time Neo-Confucianism could be said to have a simultaneous, though not necessarily equal, impact on women's lives in all three societies.

NEO-CONFUCIANISM, LAW, AND SEXUALITY

Among the many reasons for the continuing growth of Neo-Confucianism in China we can include a desire to reform public morals, to separate Chinese from non-Chinese practices, and to provide the state with a vehicle for controlling unwanted social change. In Japan, Neo-Confucian adherents initially clustered around the Tokugawa family, whose patriarch, Ieyasu, was the founder of the Tokugawa shogunate (1600–1868); what Ieyasu and his successors saw in Neo-Confucianism was a system based on morality and the ascendancy of the patriline that could be used to stabilize Japanese society after centuries of constant warfare. Loyalty, filiality, and chastity in women were all virtues Ieyasu appreciated.

Korean Neo-Confucianism is often seen as the primary vehicle for the further sinification of Korean culture and society, but as we have already seen, there were strong elements of resistance to this in which women played a significant role. In fact, Korean women are often credited with the preservation of the native culture; while Korean men adopted Chinese lineage patterns and ancestral rituals that excluded women, Korean women continued to be active participants in traditional cultural rites that emphasized their roles as healers and entertainers in the shamanic tradition. *Kisang*—women originally employed by the state for their skills in music, dance, and medicine—

eventually were classified as entertainers whose existence conflicted with Confucian ethics, but whose roles were so critical to the functioning of Korean society no official dared abolish their class. They were defined by the state as the lowest social class, further subdivided into three grades: *kisang* at the highest level entertained at Court, while those in the lowest grade were simply considered prostitutes. Yet, according to Kim,

> The *kisaeng* [in the Neo-Confucian Yi Dynasty] had freedoms beyond any other group of women in traditional society. . . . They were the only women who had free access to public events. . . . While the ideal Confucian woman repressed her feelings, the *kisaeng* of the Yi dynasty expressed the essential character of the Korean woman. . . . We have the full variety of Korean women's traits in the character of *kisaeng*. There were wicked seducers as well as women of loyalty, justice and piety. We find women of keen wit and intelligence, and women with superior artistry and genius." (Kim 1976: 140–41)

We have already seen that in Ming (1368–1644) and Ch'ing (1644–1912), China saw the full development of the "cult of widow chastity" and various sumptuary regulations having to do with the purity of women. The issue of widow remarriage raised a number of demands that could be very contradictory; loyalty, filiality, and the preservation of female chastity could not always be honored simultaneously, but even in the Sung period (960–1279), the tendency was to honor chastity and fidelity as primary:

> Question: In principle it seems that one should not marry a widow. Is this the case?
> Answer: Yes it is. One marries to acquire a mate for oneself. If one seeks to acquire a mate for oneself by marrying someone who has lost the virtue proper to her, then this action has already lost the virtue proper to it. (For a wife is one who follows a single person until her death. For her to remarry is to lose the virtue that is proper to her.)
> Further question: If a widow is alone, impoverished, and with no one on whom she may depend, may she not remarry?
> Answer: This theory has arisen merely because in these latter days people are afraid of dying of hunger and cold. But dying of hunger is a trivial matter. Loss of the virtue that is proper to one is exceedingly serious. (Elvin 1984: 139)

In Japan, *samurai* women (see glossary; women from the aristocratic military, and later administrative and bureaucratic, class) were held to very strict codes of chastity; in the Neo-Confucian pattern, the sexes were separated at age six or seven, and from that time on, young girls and women were not expected to be in the company of males without careful supervision. What could happen to a *samurai* wife whose actions were perceived as detrimental to house and lineage is illustrated in a kabuki play entitled "The Drum of Horikawa." The playwright Chikamatsu wrote this play from his reading of contemporary newspaper accounts; the story involves the wife of a middle-ranking *samurai* often away from home for long periods, serving his lord in Edo (Tokyo). She is compromised by both her son's drum teacher and a local official to whom she was obligated to extend courtesies in the absence of other family members. Though it is not at all clear she was guilty of any wrongdoing, the official did attempt to rape her, and she was blackmailed by the drum teacher. For bringing a hint of scandal to the family doorstep, and her presumed failure to protect the patriline, she was required to kill herself.

In the Ch'ing period (1644–1912), Chinese women who died in defense of their sexual honor (and preservation of the patriline) were eulogized and honored by the state; women who survived rape were generally held responsible. Vivian Ng reports the introduction of stringent legal definitions of rape by the Manchus in 1646, and attributes it in part to a Manchu effort to "sponsor their own Confucian renewal, in order to convert conservative Chinese scholars to the side of the Ch'ing (non-Chinese) government" (Ng 1987: 59). The Manchu government added to earlier definitions of rape an emphasis on the woman's continued struggle. Any break in that struggle, or the survival of the woman, "would not be considered rape, but 'illicit intercourse by mutual consent.' Nothing, short of her death, or at the very least, serious physical injury, could convince judicial officials of the veracity of her rape charge" (Ng 1987: 61).

> Rape was a capital offense because it was a violation of a woman's virtue. The price of chastity was very high indeed. It was worth at least one life—that of the rapist. Sometimes, it exacted two lives—that of the victim as well. The rape law of 1646 compelled women to defend their chastity with their lives, and those who did precisely that were honored by the state. However, until 1803, such honor was bestowed only on those who were murdered because they refused to give in to the rapist, and those who committed suicide in order to escape being raped. Women who died after being subdued by the rapist were left off the honor roll. (Ng 1987: 65)

In both the Chinese and the Japanese cases, the nervousness the state exhibited about female sexuality seems closely tied to concerns about the disruptive powers of women not controlled by the family system. That in turn leads to the logical question: In this period of social and economic change, were significant numbers of women refusing to be controlled by Neo-Confucian ideas? Were they participants in what Neo-Confucians saw as a period of moral decline?

In this context, Bernhardt's research tying a decline in the legal status of women in Ming and Ch'ing is particularly significant, since it is so closely related to repeated legal initiatives designed to bring women increasingly under the control of the families into which they married.

> Overall, the transformation in the post-Song era brought about a decline in women's legal status. Specifically, a daughter could no longer inherit her father's property so long as there existed a suitable heir within the five grades of mourning [see glossary]; a widow could no longer take her original dowry with her upon remarriage; a wife had fewer grounds upon which to divorce her husband; a widow had to depend upon her marital family rather than her natal one to arrange a remarriage; and a betrothed daughter came to be treated as a wife in certain criminal matters and thus subject to the harsher punishments reserved for crimes committed by legal inferiors against their superiors. More generally, the post-Song changes removed much of the latitude the law had once provided a natal family to intervene on a daughter's behalf, and placed her more fully under the legal control of her marital family. (Bernhardt 1996: 56)

The intensifying interest of the Chinese state in enforcing compliance with definitions of female virtue connected with their roles in the family naturally makes one wonder what women were doing that prompted such action. Some of the answers may lie in popular culture, and the literature of the period.

WOMEN IN LITERATURE AND POPULAR CULTURE
The growth of literacy, combined with the continued development of other elements of popular culture in the cities, has left us plays, novels, and other forms of art that present interesting images of women in the seventeenth and eighteenth centuries. So far as we know, relatively little of the work produced was created by women, but women were significant players in the world of popular culture, and representations of women were everywhere in popular culture.

A consistent thread running from the Yuan (1279–1368) through Ch'ing (1644–1912) dynasties is the development of popular cultural forms that stood in stark contrast to the Confucian virtues in which the state was so heavily invested. Mark Elvin points out, for example, that the lower Yangtze valley was notable for "an unusually high number of cases of recorded female virtue" but "was also notorious for mothers who reared their daughters in the arts of seduction in order to sell them to the highest bidder" (Elvin 1984: 112). Susan Mann's description of Widow Quan makes the point as well:

> In every complex society, control over female chastity implies a recognition of the dangerous power of the seductive, lusty female. The widow who is not contained by the norms governing chastity may turn out to be, like Ancestor Widow Quan, aggressive, potent, domineering, with an insatiable appetite for sexual gratification and a charismatic power over men. Widow Quan herself, when not otherwise occupied in gambling dens, teahouses, or bed, was a spirit medium, a shamaness who prescribed medicine and charms to ward off illness and bad luck. The senior member of the dominant lineage in her village, she ran the entire community out of her home. (Mann 1987: 48–49)

In Tokugawa Japan, an early modern society unable to control a merchant class with money to spend on novels, teahouses, *geisha*, and *kabuki* theater, dangerous women were a favorite theme. Tokugawa officials banned women from the stage early in the seventeenth century. They were initially replaced by handsome young men who quickly became equally disruptive of Confucian mores; it took time for the refined *onnagata*, men who specialized in female roles, to develop a strong presence on the stage. (The banning of women from the stage was hardly unique to Japan, but it marked what may have been the beginning of the Japanese taste for homosocial theater still common in contemporary Japan.) In any case, *kabuki* theater was the creature of merchant money, and it remained virtually oblivious to Neo-Confucianism except as background to Chikamatsu's "domestic" plays emphasizing the conflict between *on* (obligation/duty) and desire. Even in this setting, however, it is not at all clear that obligations were seen in Neo-Confucian terms.

Saikaku (1642–1693), the prolific Tokugawa novelist, was from a merchant family and wrote almost exclusively about merchants. His perfunctory nod to Tokugawa censors interested in inappropriate sexual content was to include short passages at the beginning and end of his novels that fit Neo-Confucian formulae; as he said, censors rarely read anything but beginnings and ends of novels anyway. Saikaku's characters, men and women, are often humorous caricatures who depict the foibles of Tokugawa humanity but, interestingly, always pay for their indiscretions. Clerks fall in love with geisha and embezzle money to buy out their contracts; sons and daughters of merchants do not curb excesses and learn to take care of their obligations to the merchant household before they indulge themselves in the many pleasures of the age. All must find ways to pay back the social obligations they have incurred. On the stage and in literature, the primary conflict is duty versus desire, and in Saikaku's novels, duty always wins. Duty in this context is not necessarily Neo-Confucian; it is born of obligations to the *ie* (house) in all its forms.

In China, official censors staged unsuccessful running battles with an urban culture seemingly immune to the astringent virtues of Neo-Confucianism:

> Official denunciations of drama as an influence on public morals were belied by imperial enthusiasm and eager patronage even by members of the Hanlin Academy. Drama was not the sole form of Qing urban culture that came under censure. Gambling—in the form of dice, cards, and betting on cock, quail, and cricket fights—was commonplace among all social classes, despite repeated official assertions that it was associated with crime and violence. Less troublesome but still distressing to some, the sexuality of the opera stage was reflected in the real world as well. Prostitutes and actors, overlapping categories and both supposedly degraded statuses, behaved as social equals and bedfellows of the elite. Male and female prostitution were booming businesses. . . . There was a national traffic in beautiful concubines and elegant male servants, in "jade cocoons" (young girls) and "little hands" (young boys). The popularity of female impersonators in the Quianlong reign brought a new stylishness to homosexual relationships. (Naquin and Rawski 1987: 62–63)

It is likely to be a long time before we have a fuller reading of the elite culture, much less the popular culture, of the period from seventeenth through nineteenth centuries in China, Korea, and Japan. But what we already know indicates that, particularly for historians of women, the lives of women in all three societies suggest fascinating contradictions, significant differences, and untold stories that must be pursued if we are to understand the history of this important period.

THE MODERN PERIOD: WOMEN IN CHINA, JAPAN, AND KOREA SINCE 1800

The Nineteenth-Century Background

We still lack a sufficient number of good, general histories of Asian women in Western languages from 1800 to the present; and, of course, most general treatments of the "modern transformation" of Asia do not include women as important shapers of that history. Women in all three societies, however, played a number of significant roles in the modern period, where they often bore the brunt of imperialism, industrialization, revolution, and war. Some were community builders in times of social dislocation; some were workers whose labor earned the foreign exchange necessary to speed the process of industrialization; some were revolutionaries who died for political causes in which they believed. Most women, directly or indirectly, were caught up in the maelstrom of twentieth-century politics in Asia, where feminism, nationalism, and socialism were, at various times and to varying degrees, potential competitors for their loyalties.

The first half of the nineteenth century provides, in all three societies, an important backdrop against which to view the drama of the modern period. Traditional elements of dynastic decline were visible in China and Korea; in Japan as well, the seeming inability of the Tokugawa shogunate (1600–1868) to manage or protect a changed society prompted demands for reform or rebellion. But only in China, where male reformers often called for improved conditions for women, including an end to footbinding, were women central to an early nineteenth-century agenda for change. Why? Empathy for women among Confucian reformers was not, as we now know, a nineteenth-century phenomenon; throughout Chinese history, some Confucian scholars had argued for improved status for women. But, like Japanese reformers in the late nineteenth century, Ch'ing scholars were fully aware that changing Chinese society meant reforming the family and women's roles in it.

The nineteenth century, perhaps only because of its proximity, brings into sharper focus the regional and local diversity of Asia. Oral histories, so crucial to our understanding of women's lives in the modern period, have suggested how divergent women's experience was, dividing not only along class and ethnic lines, but regional ones as well. In some regions of China, for example, the economic importance of women was well-established, as were connections with religious traditions that sanctioned their resistance to marriage or non-compliance with footbinding. These characteristics were, interestingly enough, also common to the most visible groups of women participating in the cycle of rebellion that China experienced mid-century. Hakka women fought in the T'ai p'ing rebellion, approved the rebels' policy of unbinding the feet of women in areas they liberated, and later loudly expressed their disapproval of T'ai p'ing leaders lapsing back into the sexual double standard: concubines for men

and chastity for women. Ono Kazuko's description of Hakka women
is an interesting one:

> Although the Hakka people are Han Chinese, they originally were
> not native to this region of South China, but immigrants . . . [who]
> settled on remote hill land of such low productivity that they could
> not possibly support their families through agriculture alone. The
> men therefore found employment outside the villages, and the wom-
> en shouldered the burden of cultivating the land as well as of man-
> aging the household. In these virtually propertyless families, the
> men had no cause to dominate the women, and the women in turn
> had no reason to be dependent on the men. Hakka women also did
> not practice footbinding, the symbol of "the cultured woman." With
> their bare, natural feet, they spent their days in demanding physi-
> cal labor, sometimes in the company of men and sometimes in place
> of men who worked away from the villages. (Ono 1989: 2)

Cycles of rebellion and famine, endemic to nineteenth-century
China, meant an even more impoverished countryside where infanticide, focused primarily on female children, increased appreciably.
Mary Rankin reports the situation that resulted from the T'ai p'ing
rebellion:

> The many waterways of Zhejiang made drowning a convenient way
> for poor families to dispose of babies they could not afford to raise,
> and the floating corpses appalled both officials and members of the
> Zhejiangese elite. . . . Foundling homes accepted boys as well as
> girls, but they were primarily institutions for females. Many infants
> were weakened by exposure and malnutrition, dependent on a
> fluctuating supply of wet nurses and they died even in the best-run
> homes. Administrative abuses including the sale of older girls as
> prostitutes, were also common. (Rankin 1986: 95–96)

Other documents, written by members of the Chinese gentry who
established infant protection societies in their localities, make an interesting point about the economic importance of mothers in poor
families: "A day without work means a day without food. Whenever
the woman is in labor or cannot work, the family faces starvation. If
she can get a small subsidy, she will be able to rest a few days, the
infant can be saved, and the mother can also be nourished. This is
doing two good deeds at once" (translated in Ebrey 1981: 222–23).
Occasionally members of the gentry simply distributed cash to poor
families in hope of saving children and the family unit together.

Most scholars agree that, by the mid-nineteenth century, Chinese society was facing something more than cyclical dynastic decline. Whether or not one agrees with Judith Stacey's (1983) argument

that the Chinese family was at the front end of a major, irreversible crisis in this period, it is clear that the family, and by definition, women, became an even larger part of the state's agenda in the nineteenth century and beyond.

In early nineteenth-century Korea, the problems of famine, unrest, and ineffective government in the face of Western intrusion were characteristic as well. Interestingly enough, in a response that seems neither "conservative" (Confucian) nor Western, there was a renewed interest in the shamanic traditions women had so long preserved—indigenous traditions that perhaps reflect an early, nationalist response. But there seems little evidence in Western languages touching this question. What we do know is that Korean women, particularly in the countryside, where poverty and discontent were evident, participated in the Tonghak movement led by Ch'oe Cheu (1824–64); Tonghak beliefs combined elements from many "eastern religions" with traditional shamanism in an effort that was both anti-foreign and anti-dynastic. The Tonghak movement in Korea bears some resemblance to China's T'ai p'ing rebellion, and its followers did call for the right of widows to remarry, but the programs they advocated to improve women's status were very limited. Since Korean women influenced by an emerging Catholic missionary effort represented part of the menace of Western learning, many Korean women found themselves on opposite sides of these issues in the early nineteenth century, something that reflected their urban–rural differences as well (Kim 1976).

Though some regions of Japan in the nineteenth century were plagued by economic difficulty, Japan emerged from more than two centuries of relative isolation with advantages that accrue to an early modern society: the ability to finance an industrial revolution and make far-reaching social change in a relatively short time. There was, to be sure, "dynastic decline" in late Tokugawa Japan, but neither population growth nor infanticide were cause for alarm. Neither did the Japanese experience the devastating losses that would have come with revolution on a major scale. In contrast to China's devastating years of rebellion, Japan's old regime, faced by a Western threat that ultimately compromised Japan's sovereignty in an unequal treaty system, went rather quietly in 1868.

Even though primogeniture was the general practice in early nineteenth-century Japan, there were regional variations in, for example, the value attached to male children. In some areas, it was considered important that the first child be a daughter who could later take care of siblings while her parents worked together in the fields. Like sons, daughters from peasant villages were often sent to neighboring farms and villages as wage laborers. At home, females bore the brunt of the seasonal demands of sericulture; sleeping in shifts, women—grand-mothers, wives, and daughters—provided the highly intensive labor needed to produce crops of silk cocoons so important to the peasant, and later to the nation's, economy.

Whether it is because the labor of young women was appreciated in spite of the fact that they would marry out of the family, or simply that Japan's family system did not exalt lineage, there is no parallel in nineteenth-century Japan to China's overwhelming preference for male children. Still, Hanley and Yamamura report that sex ratios in regions they studied led them to conclude that Japanese families may have "tended to keep only males when they had reached a point where they felt they had had enough children" (Hanley and Yamamura 1977: 238-41).

IMPERIALISM, REFORM, AND REVOLUTION, 1850–1911

Imperialism presented special challenges to women; in all three soci-eties considered here, it changed the nature of the productive work they did and often immeasurably worsened the conditions under which they did that work. Western diplomats, traders, and mission-aries singled out Asian women as symbols of Asian backwardness and barbarity—and later often tried to take credit for the creation of feminist traditions in those countries. Mission schools offered intel-lectually challenging curricula to some young women living in cities; their foreign teachers—often complicated, unconventional, and rela-tively independent women—presented interesting contrasts, but they often demanded loyalty to a particular brand of Christianity as the price of admission.

Since so much reform was focused on the family, it is not surpris-ing that, as women struggled to define their own roles, they found themselves caught in a dialectic with men whose views of women were reformist and limited. At the same time, combining the goals of "women's liberation" (a term widely used in nineteenth-century Asia) with nationalism and revolution proved as difficult as it was promis-ing in some parts of Asia. Forging alliances with other women in the face of class differences, or facing the unrelenting pressure confront-ing all women who attempted to move beyond the narrow, socially approved confines of their particular circumstances, also provided sig-nificant barriers in this period.

JAPAN

There was little consensus among male reformers on the question of proper roles for women in the last three decades of the nineteenth century, and little concern about women among most members of a government oligarchy whose views tended to be stolidly Neo-Confucian, in keeping with their own *samurai* backgrounds. Aside from important decisions offering compulsory education to girls as well as boys, much of the early legislation produced by the new government after 1868 was designed primarily to placate and convince resident Westerners (who often claimed to be authorities on the relationship between respect for women and social progress) that Japan was indeed "civilized."

Outside of government, since many male critics equated the reform of the Japanese family system with Japan's survival and future success, women in the family became the centerpiece of a major debate in the 1870s. These thinkers (Fukuzawa Yukichi and Mori Arinori, among them) argued that, since mothers were going to bear much of the responsibility for teaching a new generation of young Japanese to be more independent and to think critically, women would have to be treated with more respect. That meant getting rid of the concubine system, but it also meant more power for women in the family, especially as educators of children (Blacker 1964). The second part of their argument—that women in elite families be given greater responsibility and authority, particularly over children—was, given Japan's recent past, a very radical proposal. It was also an idea many Japanese women welcomed, and embellished under the rubric "good wife, wise mother" even though they had to do so in competition with the government's version after the turn of the century (Sievers 1983).

The idea that women should play public, not simply private roles, came from small groups of women whose interest in playing a part in Japan's future sprang from both feminist and nationalist sentiment. Many early feminists had close relationships with strong mothers; many represented groups of strong-minded, relatively well-educated women in cities and countryside who probably never took Neo-Confucian prescriptions very seriously. Some were the daughters of low-ranking *samurai* who were critical of the recent past, particularly of government-imposed restrictions on their lives. Though these women eventually became conversant with the discourses of Western feminism, they did not think of their feminism as a core of new ideas borrowed from the West, but as a logical response to opportunities presented by rapid change in the late nineteenth century. Whether or not "feminism" is a Western cultural construct continues to be a focus of debate, but in the Japanese case at least, there is no doubt that many nineteenth-century women thought of themselves as creators of a Japanese feminism that owed little or nothing to the West:

"Kishida (Toshiko) [1863–1901] was convinced that social progress relative to women's issues was universally uneven, that no society could be called truly civilized since none had allowed women the place any rational examination showed they deserved" (Sievers 1981: 612). Perhaps, just as it is ethnocentric to assume that all the tools of modernization, including political modernization, had to be borrowed by Asia from the West, it is problematic to assume that feminism, or "women's liberation" was a borrowed set of ideas in the Japanese case.

From 1878 to 1888, a number of women joined in the turbulent political world of Meiji Japan; some spoke from lecture platforms on behalf of women and popular rights; a few participated in rebellions and other direct kinds of protest, and some were jailed for their political actions. Most of them had a very strong feminist consciousness. Kishida Toshiko astonished the public in the 1880s, not only because she made public speeches at a time when speech-making was something few people did; her intelligence and willingness to address basic questions about women's status, suggesting that women should be partners in the process of nation-building, shocked and sometimes delighted the crowds who heard her. Arguing for the kind of education that would challenge girls and prepare them for a kind of economic independence, she told her audiences that "daughters must be taught basic economics and the skills that will permit them to manage on their own. Even a woman who expects to be protected during her husband's lifetime must be able to manage on her own, armed with the necessary skills, if he should die" (Sievers 1983: 40). Her impact on like-minded women, among whom the most famous was Fukuda Hideko (1865-1927), was electric.

> Listening to her speech, delivered in that marvelous oratorical style, I was unable to suppress my resentment and indignation . . . and began immediately to organize women and their daughters . . . to take the initiative in explaining and advocating natural rights, liberty, and equality . . . summoning those of high purpose to the cause, so that somehow we might muster the passion to smash the corrupt customs of former days relating to women. (Sievers 1983: 36)

As her life was later to demonstrate, Fukuda, like the women whose debating style she admired, was convinced that economic and intellectual goals were equally important to women. Interestingly, none of these early spokeswomen was particularly impressed by Western feminism, or the effort to achieve suffrage for women, though they knew a great deal about it. They expressed admiration for the work that women in the United States and Europe were doing, but they would not have made suffrage a priority in the same ways, and they did not believe that women in the West had achieved very many of the goals they set for themselves. Their views of the West were colored by the experience of Western imperialism, but it seemed clear to them that, in terms of women's status, Western claims of superiority rang very hollow. To them, women in the West were no better off than were women in Asia, though their situations might have been different.

By the end of the century, there were few male reformers left in Japan who championed women's rights; the government had learned to deal very harshly with advocates of such fundamental social change. The state answered incipient feminist agendas in 1890 by denying women all rights of political participation, and by reinstating the most conservative and oppressive model of the family in the Civil Code that became law in 1898. The "new" Civil Code transformed all of society into a legal model of the *samurai* family—for women, perhaps the most oppressive model in their history. Primogeniture was reinstated, patrilocality was assured, and the patriarchy was delivered from the threat of social change by a backward-looking document that denied married women existence as juridical persons. After 1898, Japanese women were lumped together with mental incompetents and minors, unable to bring legal action in Japanese courts without a male representative or guarantor (Sievers 1983).

Shortly after the turn of the century, the Ministry of Education established a gender-specific curriculum and devised public school programs that segregated children by sex, in good Neo-Confucian fashion. Though the government clearly recognized the importance of educating women, its motives were now suspect; the state now made every effort to co-opt the content of the phrase "good wife, wise mother," molding it with seemingly traditional Confucian rhetoric, and stripping it of the power women had originally devised for it. "Good wife, wise mother" in the government's hands combined archaic Neo-Confucian prescriptions for women's acceptance of their gendered, limited roles in Japanese society, and added something new: mothering as the principal gendered role of women. As Niwa Akiko writes,

In the Edo (Tokugawa) period, mothers did not play the principal role in child rearing. The notion of child care as a maternal vocation, accepted as a matter of course today, is actually a construct that emerged from specific historical conditions. It was not until the Meiji period that mothers were thought to be the primary care-

takers and educators of children. The image of motherhood so
common today—of a mother who devotedly and lovingly raises children—is less than eighty years old, originating in Meiji ideology.
(Niwa 1993: 79–80)

If the original intent of "good wife, wise mother" had been to justify
increasing education for women, and by extension, greater public
engagement in political issues on the basis of their increased responsibility in the family, the state's version represented an effort to keep
women in their places, at home.

In summary, what Japanese women faced shortly after the turn
of the century was a powerful, centralized state that denied them all
political rights but demanded their allegiance to a nation that had
joined with Western imperialism in colonizing Asia. It was a state
that denied them legal standing and, in many ways, tied them to a
more oppressive family system than most of their mothers had faced;
but it was also a state that needed their labor in the textile mills, and
so developed a two-tiered, class-based approach to the "good wife,
wise mother" prescription. Women of good families stayed home.
Women in poor families, especially in the countryside, would be considered "good" if they left home to work in the mills, and, as "good
daughters," made their wages available to their mothers and fathers.
Good daughters simply reinforced the principles of the *ie*, or household, with their labor. Not until large numbers of working women
emerged in the cities, women who were part of an emerging middle
class, was the government's formula for women challenged in a fundamental way, on a large scale.

Cotton and silk workers in Japan were predominantly women
from poor farming areas who risked their health and many of their
future prospects in order to assist their own impoverished families.
This is not a new story in women's history, but what is remarkable
about the Japanese case is the fact that such a large percentage of Japan's early work force was female—about 60 percent—and that those
women have, until recently, been given so little credit for earning the
foreign exchange that made Japan's industrialization possible. It is an
open question whether individual workers were motivated primarily
by the needs of their families, or factory propaganda that stressed the
needs of the nation after 1900. But the fact that Japan was the world's
leading exporter of silk in 1910, and the importance of that fact to
Japan's economy, are incontrovertible (Tsurumi 1990).

Equally obvious is the fact that Japanese women continued the
struggle to redefine their roles and ease the most objectionable constraints in their lives in a number of ways after 1900. They founded

institutions of higher education for women; went on strike, something they did as early as the 1880s; petitioned for political rights, including suffrage; and found ways to raise the most fundamental sexual/political issues confronting them. Some of them, at great risk, became socialists and anarchists. Kanno Suga (1881–1911), hanged by the government in 1911 for her part in a plot to assassinate the emperor, resembles other radical women in Asia and the West who spent their lives in violent opposition to social institutions that oppressed women (Hane 1988; Sievers 1983).

What Kanno had in common with other literary women who were her contemporaries was a sense of outrage about the sexual double standard, social constraints on female sexuality generally, and the hypocrisy of the family system—something these women shared with many of the male writers of their day. When the Meiji period ended in 1912, it was clear that "the woman question" had not disappeared, in spite of government efforts to suppress any discussion of it and, after 1907, to censor any literature dealing with sexual issues or the family system.

CHINA

An attempted Confucian revival in the late nineteenth century brought Chinese male reformers like K'ang Yu-wei to conclusions about women that were very much like those of some Japanese intellectuals in the 1870s. In addition to an end to footbinding, K'ang wanted, within a revived and humane Confucian tradition, to educate women largely because they would be the mothers of future generations. But Chinese women who had access to education, whether in previously unpopular mission schools, or in newly founded gentry and state schools, emerged as opponents of Confucian reformism, because it was part of a system many of them did not think could, or should, be saved.

On the question of saving China, however, many women were quite clear. While, at the turn of the century, the Japanese government was exhorting and sometimes pressuring women to join the Patriotic Women's Society, young women in China channeled their anger at the family system and their desire for visible roles in China's future into the anti-Manchu republican movement. While in Japan mild-mannered women teaching in private schools struggled to impart a subversive definition of "good wife, wise mother" to their students, Chinese women's schools were becoming centers of the republican revolutionary movement.

The connections between feminism and nationalism in China developed naturally, perhaps because it was impossible to think about a new society in which women could play expanded roles without first rescuing the nation from imperialism and the futility of Manchu rule. Willing to give their lives to save China, they were at the same time saving themselves and other women from an old fate. One of the best examples of this tendency was Ch'iu Chin (1875–1907).

Brought up in a gentry family by a mother who allowed her to become strong and independent enough to defy convention, Ch'iu did not marry until relatively late, and ultimately left her husband and two children to join Chinese students in Japan in 1904. With the continuing support of her mother, Ch'iu continued on an ideological odyssey that led back to China and the republican movement. She was arrested as part of an armed anti-Manchu struggle in 1907, was tortured but refused to talk, and was executed by regional authorities July 15, 1907 (Rankin 1975).

After her death, Ch'iu was lionized as an anti-Manchu martyr, a model of the self-sacrificing heroes she so much admired in Chinese history. The mythic character of her life has much to do with her (for the time) unusual behavior. After returning from Japan, Ch'iu recruited students to the anti-Manchu cause, and behaved "with . . . deliberate iconoclasm. . . . A one-time student at the school remembers that she often wore a man's long gown and black leather shoes and combed her hair back into a queue. Even more scandalous, she rode horseback astride, and ordered girls to practice military drills" (Rankin 1975: 59). In Japan, Hattori Shigeko remembered seeing Ch'iu in Beijing:

> Was this person before me a man or a woman? A tall slender body bent slightly forward in Western male dress with a full head of trimmed black hair. A blue hunting cap sitting sideways on her head covered half her ears. A dark blue, secondhand business suit didn't fit her at all. The sleeves were too long and from her cuffs one could see just her white, delicate hands. She carried a slender walking stick. Beneath her baggy trousers, worn-out brown shoes peeped through. A green necktie hung loosely over her chest. (Ono 1989: 60)

When Hattori asked why she dressed like a man, Ch'iu Chin replied, "My aim is to dress like a man! As your husband well knows, in China men are strong, and women are oppressed because they are supposed to be weak" (Ono 1989: 60).

It has been important to later commentators to establish an ideological niche for Ch'iu: was she a nationalist or a feminist? But the salient fact of her life may have been that, unlike many contemporary women, Ch'iu' lived at a moment in time that allowed her to combine anti-imperialist, anti-Manchu, anti-Confucian, and feminist convictions in the same Byronesque stance. And, thanks to her mother, who gave her both economic and moral support, she never had to answer the question later put by the well-known writer Lu Hsun in his 1923 speech to Peking Normal Women's College: "What Happens After Nora Leaves Home?" (Yang 1973). Unlike Nora in Ibsen's play—who, as Lu Hsun pointed out, would eventually have to think of a way to buy a coat to ward off the cold—Ch'iu Chin did not have to think twice about money. She was free to think and to act in ways that she believed would bring a new life for China, and for the women of China: "I would now bind, ten thousand times ten thousand women . . . would rouse women's essence, spirit, to rise as birds in flight. . . . I desire that they be leaders, awakened lions; advance messengers of learning and intelligence; that they may serve as lamps in dark chambers" (Croll 1980: 67–68). In the first decade of the twentieth century, Chinese women, as Ch'iu saw it, could save themselves and China too.

Among many women who undertook dangerous assignments on behalf of the Republican revolution were Sophia Chang (who, as a student in Japan, borrowed the name "Sophia" from the celebrated Russian revolutionary Sophia Perovskaya) and Soumay Cheng (a member of the "Dare to Die" corps, who transported explosive devices in a suitcase and the lining of her coat). Countless other women organized themselves into battalions with names such as "The Women's Suicide Brigade," the "Women's National Army," and the "Zhejiang Women's Army" (Croll 1980).

KOREA

When Korea signed a treaty with Japan in 1876, ultimately opening its doors to Western imperialist nations as well as Japan, the split Korea had earlier experienced between "traditionalists" and "modernizers/Westernizers" became more acute. To some extent, the situation resembles the one Chinese women faced, even though the ruling Korean dynasty was not "foreign" as was the case with the Manchus. Like Chinese women in the late nineteenth century, Korean women were an important focus of a modernizing agenda put forward by male reformers, but they were also central to a developing nationalism. As Kim Yung-chang states,

> No other nation seems to have seen as intricate an intertwining of relations between the women's movement, society at large, and

historical circumstances as did Korea. . . . The first women's organization in Korea (formed 1898) was born during a time of intense conflict between the conservative government insisting on the preservation of tradition and the progressive sections pressing for enlightenment. Under such a political milieu, women in Korea participated in the movement for the nation's independence before launching a crusade for women's rights. (Kim 1986: 76)

Modernizing reformers such as Pak Yong-hyo, whose attempted coup failed in 1884, enunciated what were probably the first calls for reform focused on women: an end to the abuse of women, equal educational opportunities for boys and girls above the age of six, bans on child marriages, concubinage, and denial of widow remarriage—all seen to be remnants of Chinese Confucian influence in Korea. Pak wrote his recommendations from Japan, where he had been exiled for his role in the failed coup attempt (Chung 1986).

Protestant missionary schools opened in Korea after 1886 may have provided a more direct influence on women in the late nineteenth century, dedicated as they were to teaching equality between men and women, as well as the notion that educated women were critical to national success. As had been the case in Japan, mission schools for girls provided a challenging curriculum and the opportunity to move beyond Confucianism's prescribed roles for women. Most of the Western teachers in girls' mission schools were independent-minded American women, one of whom founded EWHA school, later to become Korea's prestigious EWHA Women's University.

As students began to return from a modernizing Japan and from Europe in the 1890s, Korea was facing an even greater crisis: Japan, China, and Russia all had significant interests in Korea, and after Japan's victory in the Sino-Japanese War (1894–95), the threat of colonization at the hands of Russia or Japan became more pronounced. In this situation, modernizers stepped up their calls for the participation of women; they pointed to the lack of education for women, and attacked Confucian restraints on their ability to participate in the affairs of the nation. These failings, they said, represented a major reason that Korea lagged behind Europe and Japan (Chung 1986).

After Japan defeated Russia in 1905, Korea was subject to increasing Japanese control, with the blessing of major powers in the area, including the United States. As Japan moved toward control of Korea, women joined a nationalist response that cut across many divisions typical of modern Korea, including class and religious affiliation. That fact was amply demonstrated by the ability of women to take the lead in a 1907 campaign to pay back Japanese loans that were thought to compromise Korea's independence. Women from elite families who rarely appeared in public joined with Christian women from mission schools in efforts to persuade Korea's women to give up grocery money or jewelry to "save the nation":

> Women number 10 million among our 20 million compatriots. . . . Once we repay our national debt, we will not only restore our national sovereignty but recapture equality with men by demonstrating our power. . . . We Korean women took it for granted not to speak about world affairs while residing in the inner quarters. Observing all the countries in the world, we know that women enjoy their rights in exactly the same manner as men even though there is a distinction between the sexes. (Choi 1997: 120–21)

The national debt repayment movement was ultimately shut down by the Japanese because of its anti-Japanese sentiment, but the idea that Korean women could unite effectively could not so easily be suppressed.

1911–1918

CHINA

In the transitional period after the revolution, women with revolutionary experience turned to women's suffrage and full participation in politics in an effort to capitalize on the creation of new provincial and national assemblies. This apparent move away from revolution toward a kind of "feminist reformism" by women like Sophia Chang and Tang Junying has often been criticized for its reformist focus and for its failure to address the needs of ordinary women in the countryside (Davin 1976; Croll 1980).

The Constitution of China's Suffragette Society did appeal primarily to educated urban women, but they had always been primary actors in the Republican revolution. It would have been unusual for Chinese feminists after 1912 to make serious efforts to connect with working or peasant women when no similar undertaking had been a part of the revolution itself. The question of a "feminist reformism" focused on the single issue of suffrage is more problematic, but even the most cursory look at their program reveals a very broad group of priorities. They demanded an end to footbinding and the concubine system throughout China, and an end to child marriage and prostitution; they also called for social services for working women. Suffrage does not seem to have been their only concern (Croll 1980: 96–101).

In any case, with the accession to power of the warlord Yuan Shikai in 1913, all reform-minded and revolutionary groups in China were harshly suppressed. Women in China now faced the same stringent prohibition of their political activities that Japanese women had experienced since 1890. The ministry of education ordered the dissolution of all suffragist unions in China, and women who still had weapons in their possession were routinely executed in the first year of the new regime.

JAPAN

On the eve of World War I, the prospect for any kind of social reform involving women was bleak in both Japan and Korea. Korea, annexed by Japan in 1910, now faced the harshest kind of censorship and control, and at home, the Japanese government made every effort to stifle critics and would-be reformers. Constitutional government in Japan prevented the excesses common to China's warlord government, but after the "Great Treason Incident" in which Kanno Suga was hanged in 1911, the socialist and anarchist movement in Japan was forced underground for nearly a decade. Even parliamentary socialists were a focus of scrutiny, and consequently, socialist efforts to champion the cause of women—an effort parliamentary socialists had taken on before 1911—gradually became the responsibility of various women's groups in Japan, including suffragist groups. They saw to it that bills calling for women's suffrage were introduced into each parliamentary session; the continuity of their effort is demonstrated by the fact that many pre-war Japanese suffragists were influential in seeing to it that women achieved suffrage during the U.S. Occupation after 1945.

In an era when "the woman question" and feminism were equally dangerous topics of conversation, and when the only acceptable politics for women was state-sponsored support for Japanese imperialism, a group of protected young women from well-to-do families emerged to claim their own creative powers and publish their own magazine. The Bluestockings (*Seitōsha*), who took the name of their magazine from an unconventional group of European women, innocently began in 1911 to publish their own work, without giving much thought to the storm of criticism such a simple act would bring. Hiratsuka Haruko (pen name, Raichō), who founded *Bluestocking* and published the first issue with money her mother provided, commented on the hostile reception of their journal: "That our literary activities would put us in direct opposition to the ideology of 'good wife, wise mother' was not unexpected. What we did not expect was to have to stand and fight immediately all the traditions of feudalism in the society" (Sievers 1983: 164–65). But, as we have already seen, many of the women of the *Seitōsha* were precisely those women from "good" families who were destined by the state to carry the banner of "good wife, wise mother"; their refusal to do so was symbolic of their refusal to acquiesce to "all the traditions of feudalism in the society."

In any case, women writers had been under attack for a decade by the time *Bluestocking* appeared in 1911. Yosano Akiko (1878–1942), who not only revived ancient poetic traditions in Japan, but who may have been one of the twentieth century's finest poets, was very severely criticized for the erotic content of her first published collection (*Tangled Hair*) in 1901, as well as for the famous anti-war poem she published in 1904. Tamura Toshiko (1884–1945), one of the few recognized women novelists of the period, had also been scolded by the press for autobiographical accounts of her own awakening to a sense of art and independence realized, in part, through a developing sensuality. Both Yosano and Tamura, focusing on their own sexual relationships to men and women, were among the first women in the modern period to raise issues of sexual politics, but *Bluestocking* and the group that supported the journal quickly became champions of the cause.

Tamura wrote of women who left their husbands because they found it impossible to express their art in relationships that allowed them no breathing room; of women who behaved self-destructively in relationships with men they no longer wanted; and of women who had to entertain men in order to survive economically when their own literary efforts failed to support them. The short story she contributed to the first issue of *Bluestocking* brought the full weight of government censorship down on the journal because it was an apparently autobiographical account of a one-night stand (Tanaka 1987).

The Bluestockings are often criticized for their lack of political consciousness, a characteristic usually attributed to their class origins. Raichō was certainly a radical individualist, but the battles she waged against the limitations of Japanese society were shared by many women Raichō could never personally have mobilized, but for whom, in a limited sense, she could speak. Delighted to be characterized as a "new woman" Raichō wrote that "the new woman . . . is not satisfied with the life of the kind of woman who is made ignorant, made a slave, made a piece of meat by male selfishness. The new woman seeks to destroy the old morality and laws created for male advantage" (Sievers 1983: 176).

Writing with courage at a time when the government carefully screened all public discussion of "the woman question," Raichō expressed contempt for Japan's inadequate educational institutions for women, and rejected all social conventions that were based on male privilege alone. Raichō made it clear she would not "submit to marriage" as it existed in Japanese society. Sexual fulfillment, she said, could only come through love, an emotion Japanese marriage often denied. She also expressed concern for women whose physical health had been ruined by successive pregnancies because they obeyed the convention requiring obedience to a husband's sexual demands, a situation made worse, in Raichō's view, by the fact that most Japanese women married without love in the first place (Sievers 1983: 179–80). Though she lived with a Western-style painter most of her life, she did not go through a marriage ceremony until very late, and then only to keep her eldest son from being drafted into the military.

The influence of women writers in Japan, and of *Bluestocking*, was felt long after the journal ceased publication in 1916. Important debates about abortion, prostitution, and special protections for women in the workplace were generated for a national audience on the pages of *Bluestocking*; so were anarchist and socialist discussions of the "woman question." All of these discussions continued long after the war was over in 1918, and perhaps represent a truer reading of women's concerns in Japan than suffrage, important as that was to women in the Taisho (1912–26) era.

WAR AND REVOLUTION, 1918–49

In the turbulent decades after World War I, economic crises dominated the countryside of both China and Japan. Women became increasingly important as workers, but the gap between urban and country women grew wider with the acceleration of social change in the cities. The ability of women to communicate across class lines became more difficult, and coalition around women's issues was complicated by competing claims for their loyalties. General social dislocation, war, and revolution meant that, for most women, priorities were focused on survival, but in China and Korea, nationalist movements provided a springboard for women's agendas.

CHINA

Anarchist intellectuals in the May Fourth generation, named for their protests on May 4, 1919, against the granting of German possessions in China to Japan after World War I (see glossary), made family revolution central to their politics. For them, free choice in marriage and divorce, and the replacement of the cult of chastity with a new morality of free love were requisites to the reform of Chinese society. Published anarchist writers, most of whom were men, made vows never to marry and experimented with communal living. As Judith Stacey points out, "family issues radicalized many of the future Communist leaders *before* their conversion to Marxism-Leninism" (Stacey 1983: 75). Mao left his own village after refusing a partner in marriage arranged by his parents. Stacey recalls Mao's early interest in family revolution:

> If we launch a campaign for the reform of the marriage system we must first destroy all superstitions, of which the most important is destruction of the belief in "predestined marriage." Once this belief is abolished, all support for the policy of parental arrangement will be undermined. The army of the family revolution will arise *en masse*, and a great wave of freedom of marriage and freedom of love will break all over China. (Stacey 1983: 75–76)

This anarchist emphasis on family revolution changed after the Chinese Communist Party (CCP) was founded in 1921, and after the Kuomintang (KMT) and CCP joined in a united front two years later. As many historians have pointed out, the CCP's initial handling of the "woman question" was very orthodox. Virtually ignoring women's rights groups—including those who made women workers their priority—the CCP seemed to view feminism as bourgeois and politically irrelevant. Why, for example, ignore women workers if the proletariat was key to a successful revolution? Emily Honig offers some possible answers to the apparent failure of Xiang Jingyu, director of the Women's Bureau, and others to organize women workers:

> Although Xiang, Wang and Yang all had reputations as spokespersons for women workers, and Xiang and Yang sometimes spoke before crowds of striking workers, it is not clear how much direct contact they had with female cotton mill workers. (One hindrance to developing contact was the Hunanese accent of Xiang and Wang.) And though it is possible to find references to other women who became leaders in the labor movement, they almost always turn out to be intellectuals like these. None of the active leaders at the time of the May Thirtieth Movement were women workers. . . . Union rosters are not available, but . . . we do know that women, 52 percent of the Shanghai work force on the eve of the 1927 coup, made up only a scanty 15 percent of total union membership. (Honig 1986: 209)

Gilmartin has explored this issue further and comments that

> Perhaps because of the importance attributed to the proletariat, Communist men did not allow much space for women to develop their own organizing niche within the Communist labor program. This

assertion of male power in this area of communist work definitely hampered the party's ability to develop strong links with women factory workers, especially as Communist male organizers were known for manifesting a condescending attitude toward women's work. This general disdain for women workers was evidenced in the "Resolution on the Labor Movement" passed at the fourth party congress in January 1925, which portrayed women workers as a hindrance to the development of the labor movement because they were "still trapped under a religious and traditional society." (Gilmartin 1995: 130)

The leadership of the party was overwhelmingly male, and "attachment to an important male communist not only served as an unstated requirement for a woman's attainment of a high-level political position but was required for the maintenance of that high status" (Gilmartin 1995). The classic example of party weakness in this area was, as Gilmartin points out, the removal of Xiang Jingyu from her position as director of the Women's Bureau in spite of her success in building a mass women's movement. Xiang's failing marriage to party leader Cai Hesen and interest in another man were clearly connected to her removal from office and banishment to Sun Yatsen University in Moscow, where she would have time to reflect on her bourgeois attitudes (Gilmartin 1995).

It is ironic, but instructive, that until recently most commentary on Xiang's performance as director of the CCP's Women's Department has been negative. She has been described as critical of feminism in China, and—in keeping with the party's urban strategy —exclusively interested in organizing women workers. Christina Gilmartin's recent work presents her in a very different light. Xiang's feminism is demonstrated in an article she wrote for *Women's Weekly* in 1924, criticizing the exclusion of women from a proposed national convention in that year:

> Can student unions, trade unions, or commercial organizations represent and raise such issues as the need to protect the rights of mothers, freedom in marriage and divorce, women's right to inherit property, professional equality, equal access to education, and the rights to pursue other social and political actions? . . . If women's organizations are not seated in the National Convention that is to be called to resolve national problems . . . no one would be there to wage the struggle. (Gilmartin 1995: 127)

The organizational skills and network-building successfully carried on by Xiang and other women made it possible for them to participate in the national response to the May Thirtieth movement (see glossary), protesting the killing of thirteen students and workers in the International Settlement in Shanghai in 1925:

> The May Thirtieth Incident electrified the organizational networks that Xiang Jingyu had established among different sectors of women during the preceding year or two. Major successes were registered among students, professional women, and workers. Indeed, the incident arguably produced more female student activists than any previous Chinese revolutionary upheaval of the twentieth century. (Gilmartin 1995: 132)

During the period of the KMT/CCP United Front, it was possible for women organizers to focus on nationalist issues that so readily brought together women of disparate class, ethnic, regional, and political backgrounds. In spite of obviously different long-term agendas, women from both CCP and KMT worked on many of the same problems in the twenties, and galvanized a larger debate over women's issues in the process.

The reorganized KMT had set up a Central Women's Department in 1924, headed by Ho Hsiang-ning, later joined by Teng Ying-ch'ao, who acted as secretary. The staff of the department were often at odds over priorities, and there seem to have been strong generational differences, but as a direct result of their work, the KMT reluctantly agreed to a number of demands—marriage reform among them—and the KMT passed major resolutions in 1924 and 1926 reflecting the department's work. In a series of resolutions, the KMT agreed

1. To enact laws regarding equality between the sexes.
2. To fix the right of women to inherit property.
3. To prohibit trade in persons.
4. To protect women who escape from marriage because of oppression.
5. To enact marriage laws based on the principles of free marriage and free divorce.
6. To enact labor laws for women based on the principle of the same pay for the same work, of protection of womanhood and of child labor. (Quoted in Croll 1980: 122)

The problem of turning such paper resolutions into something concrete was complicated, as the leadership of KMT-CCP women's groups realized. The decision they ultimately made was to train women to organize women's groups in the cities, but, for the first time, to move into the countryside as well. Part of the overall KMT strategy was to produce teams of women who would follow behind the armies of the Northern Expedition, doing political work that would be beneficial to both the KMT and to women who needed to learn about their new rights in a new age. They explained their work among peasant women to Anna Louise Strong.

> We explain first the difference between the northern troops and our revolutionary forces. We tell them we came to save them from oppression and to bring a new way of thinking. We explain that men and women are now equal. Even though you are a woman you are still a person. . . . We explain the new doctrine of free choice in marriage, that young folks have the right to select their own life partners. We also explain that the feet of young girls must not be bound. (Quoted in Croll 1980: 127–28)

Though from the beginning, many peasants were outraged by the appearance of young women with "big" (unbound) feet walking unaccompanied through their villages, others expected much more than "women's unions" could offer. The problem emerged early in Hailufeng where many men

> hated the women's unions because, as one participant stated, they defended the rights of women and took care of the divorce problem. The union investigated women's complaints about family maltreatment, trying to make sure the women received either better treatment or a divorce. The union thus became known as the "Bureau of Divorce and Remarriage." (Johnson 1983: 46)

Women's unions in various parts of China did occasionally act as judge and jury in cases of mistreatment, and sometimes held kangaroo courts, where offending husbands were forced to walk through town wearing dunce caps and shouting feminist slogans. Eventually women's groups in the cities and countryside confronted a combination of debilitating factors: inadequate resources, impossible needs, and a growing criticism within a CCP that did not want to risk losing the loyalty of men who were unhappy with the unions. Soong Chingling, head of the Hankow Women's Training Center, put it this way: "If we do not grant the appeals of women, they lose faith in the union and in the women's freedom we are teaching. But if we grant the divorces, then we have trouble with the peasant's union since it is very hard for a peasant to get a wife, and he has often paid much for his present unwilling one" (Johnson 1983: 46).

Though it is true that the women's unions in the countryside were able to attract the support of many younger women, their enthusiasm was not matched by an older generation of men and women who were experiencing what Judith Stacey calls a "realization crisis," in which peasant families faced "an alarming decline in their capacity to realize proper Confucian family life, or any family life at all" (Stacey 1983: 68). They not only wanted to reconstruct the family system they had lost; they wanted, as Margery Wolf tells us, to keep what little they had. "Rural women had worked out their own ways of coping . . . and the new freedom espoused by the students threatened not only their own sense of propriety, but their very survival" (Wolf 1985: 14).

It can be argued that the debate over this issue in the party was made irrelevant by the KMT attack on the CCP in 1927, but this early experience must have been formative. Women's groups and their organizers came increasingly under male control in late 1926, and those who wanted to continue an emphasis on women's issues were pointedly made aware of the importance of a unified peasant base. Mao Tse-tung suggested in 1927 that premature and precipitous actions were eroding the party's peasant base, and he reminded everyone that consolidating political power in the countryside was properly the first order of business. The clear implication was that agitation on behalf of women was dangerous because it compromised the ability of the party to build that base; and it was unnecessary, because the emancipation of women would flow from victory in larger economic and political struggles. After the violent end of the KMT-CCP alliance, the CCP in 1928 subordinated women's organizations to the development of peasant associations.

In the attacks that drove the CCP from the cities, left-wing KMT and CCP women were special targets. In the White Terror (right-wing KMT attacks that began in Hankow in 1927), women with bobbed hair were shot for their supposed radicalism; in Canton, young women thought to be members of the CCP were wrapped in gasoline-soaked blankets and burned alive; everywhere the White Terror prevailed, women were raped before they were finally killed by KMT agents and troops. A number of observers reported seeing mutilated female bodies with breasts cut off lying in the streets of Shanghai and other major cities (Croll 1980).

Nationalists and warlords throughout China justified the killing and execution of Communist organizers on the basis of supposed sexual immorality; all radical women were, by definition, promiscuous and disruptive of the social order. And as Gilmartin reports, when Xiang Jingyu, former director of the CCP's Women's Bureau, was publicly executed in 1928, "the official statement that appeared in Nationalist newspapers emphasized her sexual conduct and the break-up of her marriage, insinuating that the most important facet of her political career had been her sexual behavior" (Gilmartin 1995: 212). This issue is significant for a number of reasons, some of which are clear from the earlier history of China. But it was also no doubt simpler to rationalize to the Chinese public the idea that these women were killed because they were "bad" women, not because they were political women. If, as Gilmartin suggests, the twenties represented an enormous surge in women's political activities, activities often focused on the improvement of women's situation in China, violence was designed to bring them under control:

> Yet the appalling instances of violence against women would have been unthinkable without the previous large-scale mass mobilization of women. Female activism came to be viewed as a disturbing indicator of a world turned upside down. The White Terror inflicted on these women served to repress the women's mass movement and to vividly demonstrate the penalty for political participation. In so doing, it showed implicit recognition that a critical aspect of their power to challenge traditional gender arrangements resided in their ability to be active in the public sphere and to organize a women's movement. (Gilmartin 1995: 213)

After 1928, the KMT struck down what was left of women's organizations and began to redefine women's roles in the "New Life Movement." In fact, the KMT's program for women was very similar to its proposals for the nation. Ignoring the profound social, intellectual, and economic crisis China was experiencing, KMT philosophers offered a formula of legal reform—Confucian morality blended with Christian individualism—and a return to the virtues of the family. "Politics" was now, in the new Women's Commission as elsewhere, a code word for communist influence. Closing their eyes to the incredible barbarity of the White Terror, women in the KMT reflected on the future: "The meaning of the women's movement is not to annihilate masculine strength, men's valor, nor is it to put an end to the grace of women's nature or evade the function of motherhood. . . . The women's movement from now on must cut out, root and branch, this attitude of antagonism of the sexes" (quoted in Croll 1980: 155).

The KMT's most significant effort to legislate equality came in the 1930 Civil Code, a document that gave important legal rights to women in the family. Women under the new code were supposed to be able to choose their own husbands, apply for divorce, and inherit property; adultery was a punishable offense, not only for women but for men. New factory legislation protected women from work that might be physically harmful and theoretically paved the way for equal pay

for equal work. Male educators and members of the KMT now proclaimed Chinese women emancipated; there was now no need for
"politics" since, "unlike their American and European sisters," Chinese women no longer had to "battle against opposition from members of the opposite sex" (Croll 1980: 157).

For the CCP in the Kiangsi soviet period (1929–34; see glossary)
"politics" was the order of the day, but predictably, the rural areas the
CCP held were an inhospitable environment for social reform bene-
fiting women. Concerned with constant KMT attacks and the pressing need to build a political base, the relationship between party
leadership and the soviet's women assumed a classic form. Women
were to be mobilized against KMT encirclement, not by joining CCP
forces, but by encouraging husbands and sons to join. Once that succeeded, women—who, in this part of China, had a history of high
participation in outside work—would take over agricultural tasks in
the absence of men. Trade unions organized women workers to sew
for the army in their spare time, and women were organized into
rear-guard defense units. A few women, including K'ang K'e-ch'ing,
who later married the famous general Chu Teh, were members of the
Red Army in Kiangsi, but recruiting women for the army was not a
part of CCP strategy (Johnson 1983).

Like women elsewhere who have learned new skills and gained
confidence in their abilities in wartime, Chinese women were politicized by their experience; but radical reform, especially marriage reforms, foundered on the same rocky soil of peasant resistance that
had surfaced early in the twenties. Marriage regulations established
in the Kiangsi soviet challenged the most basic structures of the family; it made divorce available to either party in marriage and, once re-
quested, took effect immediately. More importantly, women retained
full property rights, their full land allotment, and half of any property
accrued in marriage. They were favored in decisions involving custody of young children, and poor women were entitled to economic
support from former husbands in the form of farm labor. It was, as
Kay Ann Johnson has said,

> the single most radical clause in the marriage regulations, going as
> far as any formal law could go in providing women with the legal
> basis to nullify the patriarchal power of exchanging women and to
> establish their own "rights in themselves" with regard to marriage.
> . . . Totally contrary to the customs of patriliny, the woman was
> favored in the custody of young children, which would be crucial to
> any Chinese woman with a vested interest in her uterine family.
> . . . Without the economic provision requiring the support of former

husbands, divorce would have been economically impossible for many women. (Johnson 1983: 54–55)

These regulations turned out to be as unenforceable as new legal rights under the KMT, but for very different reasons: cadres often refused to enforce them and punished, in various ways, women who dared to request divorce. Women who insisted on the validity of the divorce regulations were, as before, accused of being out of step and failing—for personal reasons—to see revolutionary priorities in their proper alignment. Finally, as the KMT moved in on the CCP's Kiangsi stronghold, the CCP issued revised marriage regulations in April 1934, sharply cutting back the divorce right of soldiers' wives, who made up the dominant segment of the soviet's young female population. They were required to get their husband's consent before applying for a divorce. This clause remained in all future documents regulating marriage, in spite of changes in both the need for military service and the CCP's strategic position after 1934 (Johnson 1983).

It has been convincingly argued that providing special consideration for military men was understandable in the midst of civil war; it is also true that the 1931 regulations covering divorce were very radical, and probably unenforceable anywhere in the world in that period. The importance of the change in divorce regulations in 1934, however, is that it was not an isolated or even an unusual policy change. It was one of many policy reversals that, taken together, seem to provide a barometer for gauging the CCP's priorities. An important question raised by research, including the work of Kay Ann Johnson (1983) and Judith Stacey (1983), is the extent to which the revolutionary goals of women were sacrificed to a "backward toward revolution" strategy, in which the CCP won peasant support by promising a retention of the "traditional" family in the countryside. The family crisis in the Chinese countryside has been well documented; it was this crisis to which Mao referred in a 1931 investigative report, linking the problem of poor peasants losing their wives to their inability to maintain the semblance of a proper family. Mao suggested that, over time, ending brideprice and the ruinous financial burden of marriage ceremonies would allow more peasants to get wives. But, as Johnson points out, for women the issue was not the ease with which men could "get wives." "Marriage reform . . . was not a means of redistributing females to the poor," but of changing the definition of marriage in ways that allowed women to 'get themselves' through self-determination in both entering and leaving a marriage" (Johnson 1983: 56).

The 1931 marriage regulations, especially the provisions for divorce, cut straight to the heart of patriarchal, patrilineal, patrilocal family structure. If they had been enforced, could there have been anything left of a family system already battered by demographic and economic pressures? Judith Stacey suggests that the party seriously considered whether the CCP could survive to create a successful People's War if cadres had made a more serious effort to enforce 1931 divorce regulations, and the party decided it could not. The Kiangsi soviet provides no definitive answers; it lasted only five years, and its goals and priorities were quickly overshadowed.

In 1934, the CCP left Kiangsi on the Long March, traveling through extremely difficult terrain to reach Yenan province in the Northwest, from which base they fought against and eventually overran the KMT in 1949. Here, in a countryside even more conservative than the one they had left, the pattern of compromising the effort to improve women's situation in favor of winning over the peasantry intensified. According to Kay Ann Johnson,

> Mao and other leaders hoped to be able to straddle the two sides . . . the intellectual's iconoclastic struggle against a decadent tradition and the poor peasant's struggle to hold on to some semblance of the old norms of decency and legitimacy. Yet, when there were sharp conflicts between advocates of women's rights and the poor male peasants, Mao, like most of the Party-Army leadership, empathized with the latter, who constituted their most crucial constituency. This pattern which tenuously and somewhat ambiguously emerged in Kiangsi, later became fully articulated, entrenched and dominant when the Party center moved to the more conservative environment of the Northwest. (Johnson 1983: 60–61)

In the Rectification Campaign (1942–44), the writer Ding Ling called for an attack on the sexist attitudes of cadres and comrades. Severely criticized for raising an issue (sexual equality) that, according to the party, had been successfully addressed, she was removed from all official duties for a period of two years, and in 1943 the Party formally chose to avoid future discussion of the social and political inequality of women (Feuerwerker 1982).

KOREA AND JAPAN

Japan's annexation of Korea in 1910 meant that Korean women would have to work out any significant change in their lives within a strongly nationalist framework. Korea was a colony of Japan from 1910 to 1945; in that long period when the permutations of Korean nationalism were many, Korean feminists often found it difficult to find a niche within which they could effectively operate. When, for example, the Japanese government initiated change or—as some governors-general did—attempted to rewrite Korean history, the natural response of Korean nationalists was a call to restore native traditions, many of which were demeaning to women. When nationalists became advocates of change themselves, many women joined them, but social reform that might have been beneficial to women was not a priority.

In the first decade of direct Japanese rule, Korean women organized nationalist activities through what became a secret society. Led by Hwang Ae-dok (1872–1971), the organization was highly disciplined and effective enough in organizing nationalist sentiment to have been instrumental in staging Korea's March First Movement in 1919. March First activities in Korea spread nationwide, demonstrating the power of anti-Japanese nationalism; women from all classes, including *kisang* entertainers (see glossary), joined the demonstrations. Many were wounded or imprisoned by Japanese authorities. Not until a group of women students sent a petition to the Paris Peace Conference, however, were women's issues raised directly by demonstrators; the letter sent to Paris appealed for justice and an end to the oppression of women, as well as Korean independence.

In the twenties, given the reality of harsh Japanese rule, Korean nationalism had to organize outside the country to be effective, but few women were able to participate directly in these overseas efforts. Some of them were still in prison in 1920, the result of their participation in the March First Movement; others like Maria Kim (1891–1945), who escaped jail in 1919, found it impossible to organize openly around nationalist or reformist goals in the face of increasing Japanese surveillance. After Kim was jailed in 1920, much of the promise of 1919 seemed lost; radical groups that could not function openly lost their constituencies, as Japanese colonial policy for Korea encouraged a benign, ladylike reformism focused on women's education and similar issues; it was colonial policy designed to make "good wives" and "wise mothers" of Korean women (Kim 1976).

In the thirties, Korea was increasingly captive to the Japanese military's continental ambitions, and, as a result, colonial policy focused once more on "traditional" virtues for women, at the same time it exploited them as workers. From roughly 1930 until the end of the war in 1945, Korea was a productive satellite of Japan, and Korean workers (men and women) were often "exported" to Japan to provide needed labor there. Though the historical relationship between Japanese and Koreans is extremely complex, it is clear that in the

colonial context, Koreans were considered inferior to their colonizers—for some Japanese, that inferiority had racial connotations. From
the Japanese point of view it was the function of colonized Koreans
to assist in the extension of Japanese power in Asia. While intially
that may have meant the exploitation of Korean resources and Korean labor, it also implicitly meant that colonizers reserved the right
to employ the "colonized sexuality" of Korean women in any way
they chose. In the Japanese hierarchy of race and power, a hierarchy
represented more clearly by the military than many other elements
of Japanese society, Koreans existed for Japanese use; if we add to
this mix the military's fiercely patriarchal values, the fact that Korean women were ultimately singled out for a special kind of violent
exploitation and abuse seems, if not predictable, unsurprising in a
wartime context. The notion of "comfort women" who would provide sexual services for the Japanese military was not a new one in
Japan's modern history; military planners had long been concerned
about the effects of venereal disease on the health of troops, and had
long championed use of 1) condoms, and 2) "approved" prostitutes
whose bodies could be inspected by military or civilian doctors and
certified "safe" for consumption by Japanese troops. Japanese wom-
en were recruited, often unknowingly or against their will, to work
throughout Asia as prostitutes earlier in the twentieth century; they
earned foreign exchange, helped to support families in Japan, and
provided sexual services for a military and civilian clientele. The story
of one of these women (referred to collectively as *karayuki-san*) is told
in a well-known Japanese film, *Sandakan No. 8*.

As Japan's Asian empire grew, and the army was stationed in
various colonial outposts for long periods of time, the military simply
extended policies developed earlier to provide sexual services for its
troops, and to "conscript" women into a system that would allow the
military to screen them for venereal disease. This system, it is clear,
required cooperation between "private" suppliers and "state" consumers to work; this cooperative system continued to operate in Korea
and other parts of Asia until the Pacific War dramatically changed the
terrain on which the system operated. No longer was the military
willing to rely solely on private recruiters and suppliers; instead they
undertook the creation of "comfort divisions"—women whose recruitment and posting now parallelled those of divisions of the Japanese
army. Though it is clear that Japanese women continued to be recruited to serve as "comfort women" throughout the war, usually
providing sexual service for "officers only" in a kind of reinforcement
of racial and military hierarchy, the military's decision to recruit "com-

fort divisions" meant that the brunt of the exploitation would fall on other women in Asia, particularly Korean women. Recent evidence suggests that the wholesale "recruitment" of non-Japanese "comfort women" to serve the Japanese military began in earnest in the late 1930s, when the Japanese army began to envision the possibility of continuing, large-scale conflict in Asia; some evidence also suggests that the Japanese military redoubled its efforts to provide "comfort women" for its troops after the brutality and sexual violence of Japanese soldiers in the infamous "Rape of Nanking" (December 1937) was reported in photographs and news stories throughout the world.

Before the Pacific War ended, women from all parts of Asia (including some women from European colonial regimes in Asia) were forced to provide sex for the Japanese military, but it is clear that Korean women bore the greatest burden of this inhuman treatment. An estimated 150,000 to 200,000 women from various parts of Asia were abducted by "hunters" or enticed by recruiters who deceived them; it is likely that 80 percent or more were women of Korean origin. They became the Japanese military's chattel, forced to provide sex for troops wherever they were sent; many died in attacks of sexual violence; others died of disease and starvation. Untold numbers of women were not accounted for after the war, and it is widely assumed that those women who might have survived would never return home because of the shame they felt.

In 1991 a few survivors, encouraged by women's groups, came forward to demand retribution and a public admission on the part of the Japanese government that Japan had engaged in such practices during the war. In 1993, the Japanese government admitted the truth of the evidence; it maintained, however, that these practices were not systemic in the Japanese military, and that no orders sanctioning such practices ever came from the top levels of the military or government. Some compensation for victims of these wartime atrocities has been paid, but the issue is likely to be around for a very long time. A law suit against the Japanese government has been filed by survivors, and women's groups in Korea and Japan will continue to demand a full accounting, as well as revision of Japanese history texts to reflect this wartime outrage.

In spite of the fact that some Korean women active in nationalist circles were resident in Japan in the twenties, Japanese women seem to have been largely unaware of their struggle. Japan emerged at the end of World War I as a creditor nation and the only industrialized country in Asia; that it was also an imperialist country with Asian colonies, and was a target of both Chinese and Korean nationalism, had significant implications for Japanese feminism that no one seemed prepared to recognize in the twenties. Only after 1945, when Japanese feminists began to identify their goals with those of other women in Asia, was the problem of Japan's imperialist history fully recognized as a major barrier.

There was a huge gap between city and countryside in the twenties, providing Japan's largely urban women's movement with a challenge few tried to meet. With the exception of women on the left who were organizers in the tenant union movement, the women's movement did not connect with dissatisfied women outside the cities, women who, in 1918, had initiated a series of violent attacks on rice merchants and their warehouses. At the end of these "rice riots" 500 villages and towns in Japan had experienced the wrath of wives and mothers who burned down and looted the warehouses of rice speculators, forcing the government to declare martial law.

In the wake of the Great Tokyo Earthquake in 1923, another kind of violence gripped the city, as police brutalized supposed leftists and anyone of Korean ancestry resident in Japan. Itō Noe, an anarchist and former editor of *Bluestocking*, was arrested and strangled in her jail cell, along with her well-known lover, the anarchist Ōsugi Sakae. Ōsugi's young nephew was also strangled by the same police officer that day.

Viewed against this backdrop, the goals of the Japanese women's movement in the twenties seem quietly reformist. The campaign to achieve all rights of political participation for women, including suffrage, continued. Suffragists made international connections with women's rights advocates; they won minor revisions of political restrictions in 1922, and debated the merits of legislation protecting women, especially mothers, in the workplace.

But with the Manchurian Incident in 1931 and Japan's subsequent annexation of the province of Manchuria (see glossary), Japanese women found themselves increasingly caught in the middle—not only of various factions in the women's movement, but of pointed government agendas as well. "[The] prewar liberal women's movement in Japan . . . in relation to women's issues—occupied a middle ground between the proletarian movement on the one hand, and government-sponsored or patriotic associations on the other," notes Nishikawa (p. 49). Japan's women's movement, according to Nishikawa, reached its zenith just prior to the outbreak of the Manchurian Incident in September 1931. This, she says, was partly the result of rising class consciousness stemming from financial and political crises beginning in 1927, and partly a result of a raised consciousness over women's political rights that came in the wake of Japan's first election under universal male suffrage held in 1928. Japanese women held All-Japan Women's Suffrage congresses from 1930 to 1937, most of which were designed to parallel sessions of the Japanese parliament. These congresses represented the closest approximation of a united front of autonomous women's organizations Japan had ever experienced. Congress resolutions underscore the opposition of women to war, and to the right-wing terror that gripped Japan in the early thirties, resulting in the assassinations of prominent Japanese politicians, business people, and bureaucrats. In 1932, the same year Prime Minister Inukai was assassinated, the women's congress passed a resolution voicing "our firm opposition to the forces of fascism which are gaining momentum at the present time" (Nishikawa 1997: 53).

Though support for Japan's expansionist policies on the continent was never precisely offered as the quid pro quo for achieving suffrage, the same pressure to provide support for national policy in return for the right to vote in Britain and the United States was common to the Japanese situation. Still, the issue of women's support for their country from 1931 to 1945 is a very difficult one, and raises a number of issues beyond the quest for suffrage.

> As Japan's movement toward war in the 1930's accelerated, it was not only soldiers but women, who at first had articulated their opposition to war . . . who had to stifle the doubts that surged in their hearts and articulate their affirmation. After conceding to the government's declaration of a state of emergency, they eventually came to be absorbed into the Greater Japan Women's Association, that vast organizational network that encompassed all Japanese women. Just as they had initially opposed the war from their standpoint as the bearers and nurturers of children, they now developed a woman's logic that supported it. But the process through which subjects persuade themselves to comply with the state can be more cruel than the experience of being broken by force. . . . Tragedy befell those who sought to think and act as autonomous, individual citizens. It is easy to point out today that the reasoning these women used to persuade themselves was constructed from an extemporaneous and even preposterous logic. Yet must not those of us who truly wish to learn from history and construct a logic of opposition to war take another look at that "flimsy" logic of the past, try to understand its appeal to subjects trapped, precisely as those in the war had been, in a situation from which there appeared to be virtually "no exit"? (Nishikawa 1997: 48–49)

As Japanese women increasingly became targets of a government mobilizing for conflict, birth control was made illegal as the country adopted a pro-natal policy. Courageous women, among them Ishi-moto Shidzue, formed the Women's Birth Control League of Japan in 1932, and opened a clinic in Tokyo in 1936; Ishimoto was arrested in 1937 and later released, but the birth control movement was forced to go underground and did not reappear until after the war (Ishimoto 1984: xix–xx). As was the case in Japanese-controlled Korea, "tradi-tional" virtues and dress were officially the order of the day for Japa-nese women, and political criticism of any kind was severely punished. When Japan fully mobilized for war, women were drafted as medical aides and nurses but they were not asked to assume non-traditional work roles until the war began to be felt more strongly in Japan itself, after 1942.

The women of Japan's Communist Party, and leftist women writ-ers who had suffered continuous government harassment from the twenties to the outbreak of the Manchurian Incident in 1931, found themselves in even greater difficulty as the nation moved closer to full-scale war. Some, like Miyamoto Yuriko, agreed to stop writing—both as a protest of the direction Japan was taking, and as security against the possibility that their work could somehow be used to make the state's case for its policies. But for some women—like Sata Ineko, who was severely criticized by the Left for her decision to continue writing—not writing meant not feeding her children (Tanaka 1987: 164). Life in prison for Japanese on the left meant physical torture, long separation from family, and sometimes death; in the face of this pressure, some leftists recanted their beliefs and were rewarded by release from prison. Others, like Miyamoto Yuriko, refused to give up her belief in communism and the coming liberation of women. Those who endured, like Miyamoto and her husband, were greeted as he-roes by many Japanese when they were released at war's end (Hane 1988).

Just two years after Pearl Harbor, women, children, and elderly men were left to try to find food for families as Japan's production waned and supply lines were cut. Young women were recruited for factory duty, and everyone in neighborhood associations participated in fire drills that were hopelessly inadequate to meet the fire storm they were to face in 1945. On March 10, 1945, U.S. planes flying virtually unopposed (so low people on the ground reported being able to see the pilots' faces) crisscrossed the city of Tokyo, dropping fire bombs. When the raid was over, more than 100,000 people had died, most of them women and children. Firebombing, a tactic that closed off avenues of escape and maximized the potential for secondary explosions inside urban fire lines, was designed to prove the efficacy of U.S. air power in bringing a civilian population to surrender. Japanese cities, where most buildings and homes were made of wood, were especially vulnerable.

Though the postwar focus in wartime Japan is quite properly the cities of Hiroshima and Nagasaki—and the effects of the atomic bombs that were dropped there August 6 and August 9, 1945—the recollections Japanese women have only recently begun to publish make it clear that, for them, the war at home had assumed a monstrous reality long before Hiroshima and Nagasaki. Moriyama Yoneko remembers one night of firebombing in the city of Tokyo in these words:

> I do not remember where we ran throughout the night, but by dawn we had reached Ueno Hill. We pushed our way through mountains of corpses. There was a mother with a baby strapped to her back; the infant was on fire. Wounded people called for help, but no one heeded. . . . Later, at the burned-out site where our house had stood, I met a friend named Yasuko. She was crying, and said that her mother was missing. We later learned that her mother had taken refuge in an air-raid shelter . . . [but when] the shelter was finally opened the following day, there were no survivors. Yasuko turned over one corpse after another, but none of them seemed to be her mother. I tried to encourage her by saying that her mother was bound to come back soon. My father even offered to take her in as his own daughter. But Yasuko only looked sadder and sadder. Then, a few days later, she vanished without saying good-bye. (Sokka Gakkai Women's Bureau 1987: 164–65)

WOMEN IN THE POSTWAR PERIOD, 1945–PRESENT
JAPAN

A U.S.-controlled Occupation (1947–52) took a number of legal steps that dramatically improved the ability of women to raise their status in Japanese society. Convinced that women were important to the health and growth of democracy in Japan, Occupation bureaucrats, in concert with women in the Occupation itself and Japanese women who had been a part of the prewar women's movement, wrote into Japanese law women's right to vote and stand for office. That change was followed by major revision of Japan's Civil Code and a new Constitution with language so liberal that it guaranteed equality to women in marriage, education, and work—legal protection U.S. women have never enjoyed (Borton 1955).

Shortly after the new Constitution took effect in 1947, the Japanese parliament approved the right to legal abortions in cases of economic necessity, believing that population control was crucial to Japan's economic development (Coleman 1983). Japan's 1908 Criminal Code had made abortion illegal, and as we have seen, the government pursued pro-natal policies in the 1930s, in preparation for war. Still, new legislation legalizing abortion in some cases should not be seen as a complete reversal of earlier policies by the Japanese government; it does stipulate that economic reasons, pregnancy resulting from rape, and threats to the mother's health provide legal grounds for abortion, but abortion in other circumstances is still punishable under the current Criminal Code. And current legislation requires the consent of the unborn child's father, violating what many Japanese women consider a basic right of privacy. Japan's population has grown very slowly in the postwar period, but in recent years politicians expressing fear of a combined falling birth rate and labor shortages have led a number of attempts to amend, or end, access to abortion under 1947 provisions. In any case, the denial of alternative methods of birth control, including birth control pills, to unmarried Japanese women meant that these policies promising greater autonomy and access to reproductive rights had little or no effect on the lives of most women. Denial of access to methods of birth control widely used outside Japan (birth control pills, unavailable to Japanese women, were exported by Japanese companies) meant that most Japanese women, especially young women, found themselves with little choice but acceptance of long-standing rigid social norms in matters related to women's sexuality. For most women there was no real or imagined "sexual revolution" engineered in part by new reproductive technologies; the sexuality of young women, unmarried or not, continued to be carefully controlled by peer pressure and social institutions. Contemporary Japan has seen the development of greater access to a wide variety of reproductive methods, but government control of this access, and government anxiety about falling birth rates, remains a potentially serious barrier.

The Constitution and new Civil Code promulgated in 1947 presented a radically different view of marriage. No longer was marriage to be seen as a vehicle for perpetuating the family line, a social institution in which the inferiority of women was assumed and perpetuated. Instead, postwar law described marriage as an institution

> . . . based on principles of family life grounded in respect for individual dignity and equality of both sexes. . . . Legal equality of wife and husband was recognized. The wife could now exercise individual legal rights based on her own free will. The right of a husband to manage and gain profit from his wife's assets was abolished; a

wife and husband could now separate their finances. Parental rights became operative in marriage, and after divorce either parent could seek custody. . . . Moreover, monogamy was made binding on the husband as well as the wife. Adultery on the part of either spouse was made legitimate grounds for divorce, and it was no longer to be considered a criminal offense. (Yoshizumi 1996: 188)

Half a century later, it is clear that making such legal changes in the face of long-held historical and cultural habits is not easy. Divorce rates in Japan are still among the lowest in the world, in part because women continue to be restricted by a relative lack of material resources, or access to them; by peer pressure stemming from disapproval of divorce, and by cultural demands that Japanese women "endure" as they have in the past. It is interesting, however, that the number of divorces among middle-aged and older women is increasing; most observers assume that this phenomenon is attributable to the fact that these women feel that many of their responsibilities as parents are over, and they now can take advantage of recent changes in divorce laws providing them with a share of their husband's retirement income and one-half of the wealth they have accumulated with their husbands. Japanese women have also moved in recent years to maintain separate surnames in marriage and to overcome legal barriers to single mothers' right to children, initiatives that underline a continuing demand for a recognized separate existence within marriage, as well as the choice not to marry (Yoshizumi 1996).

The revised Constitution has been beneficial to working women, primarily those with union financial backing who have been able to litigate inequities in the courts. Japanese justice has moved very slowly in this area, but an impressive number of court victories have been won by women over such issues as differentials in age of retirement mandated by large companies (Cook and Hayashi 1980). In recent years, hiring practices have been more difficult to reach, because, on the surface, equality has seemed to prevail. Japanese women and men were often hired at the same entry level, but large companies, favoring seniority as a measure of value and loyalty, encouraged Japanese women to drop out of the work force, marry, and raise children, then return—in effect, depriving them of most of the accrued privileges of the Japanese seniority system operating in large companies. Occasionally, large corporations announced that they would not interview women with four-year college degrees in a given year, sending a message to all upwardly mobile young women that they should not overprepare themselves for a challenging professional life. The Equal Employment Opportunity Law (EEOL) was supposed to ad-

dress some of these problems after its passage in 1985. Japanese wom-
en concede that the legislation was prompted by external pressures,
particularly Japan's position as a signatory to the International Convention on Elimination of All Forms of Discrimination Against Women
(Kawashima 1996). The EEOL was also designed to reverse what many
thought to be the overly protective regulations embodied in the 1947
Labor Standards Law—regulations that could be used by employers
to exclude women from overtime or night work, effectively denying
their opportunity to move up with male cohorts in the company, giv-
en the importance of the corporate habit of working late hours and
socializing with colleagues after work. Under EEOL, there are greater restrictions on menstrual leave, but maternity leave has been increased; there are still a few restrictions on overtime work, including
holidays and late-night hours, but generally, women who want to
move up in the company no longer face the kinds of restrictions based
on gender that were common under 1947 regulations.

One of the immediate results of EEOL was the decision on the
part of large companies to institute a two-track system: a managerial
track for those who aspired to upward mobility in the firm, and a
general track for those less interested in promotion, or a career with
the company.

> While all men are placed on the [managerial] track, women are
> given a choice between the two. . . . A small number of career-
> oriented women have opted for the [managerial track]. . . . It has
> opened to women some opportunities that had been closed to them
> in the past, especially to four-year university graduates—but many
> of those who venture into the male-dominated world quit their jobs,
> frustrated or worn out. The attrition rate among [managerial track]
> women is nearly 50 percent. . . . [Managerial track] women are
> expected to fit into a work place created by men, one that includes
> long working hours and transfer if necessary. Their heavy share of
> the responsibility at home, however, remains virtually unchanged.
> . . . Those who have chosen this option are faced with many hard-
> ships in surviving in a world that does not yet welcome women.
> Lacking role models and a support system, they find themselves
> isolated. They are also paying heavily in terms of their mental and
> physical health and family lives. (Kawashima 1996: 287–89)

The other single factor that seems to have had greatest effect on
working women in the wake of the passage of EEOL has been the
long economic recession. In its wake, women's participation in the
work force has not kept up with men's, and a number of discriminatory practices have again emerged:

For some time after the enactment of EEOL, there seemed to be a
growing equality between men and women—more new women
[four-year] graduates were getting jobs, and more new women
graduates were being promoted to important posts. We realize now
that at that time companies were simply short-handed due to the
so-called "bubble economy." With the current recession, the employment rates for new women graduates has dropped much lower
than it was ten years ago. . . . Among the complaints voiced by new
women graduates were: they were denied the opportunity to get
information—they failed to receive responses to their requests for
company brochures; they were not allowed to attend some meetings for new graduates; they were not allowed to take some employment examinations; and they were excluded by the imposition
of such discriminatory conditions as "we only accept students who
live with their parents," and "we only accept unmarried students."
(Nakano 1996: 69)

Even more importantly, the recession, coupled with the growing importance of the service sector to the Japanese economy, has fueled an
apparently successful effort to create a "flexible" work force—one that
can be expanded or cut back based on an individual company's needs.
This is particularly unsettling at a time when a very high percentage
of women entering the work force are already part time workers—
2.9 million of 4.6 million between 1985 and 1993. This "flexibility,"
reinforced by the Temporary Workers Law in 1985, means that increasing numbers of Japanese women will be working for very low
wages, in firms where there is no opportunity for promotion. And
like women part-time workers before them, they will also be working long hours. The legal definition of part-time work in contemporary Japan is any assignment under 35 hours a week; however, it has
long been the practice of many part-time women workers to spend
more than 40 hours at work, even though they do not receive any of
the benefits that come with recognition as a full-time employee.

There are endless debates in Japan about how much has changed
in women's status since the war, but the more difficult question is
determining what has generated the very substantial change that has
taken place. The women's movement began a third phase after the
war, building on the experiences of a first generation in mid-Meiji
(1868–1912) and a second in Taisho (1912–26) and Showa Japan,
from its inception in 1926 until the end of the war in 1945. The third,
postwar phase was created partly as a response to the experience of
women activists during the anti-Vietnam movement of the 1960s and
early 1970s, and partly as a result of women's work in the student
movement that shut down more than 100 universities in the same

period. Educated, middle-class daughters of Japan's upwardly mobile urban families initiated what many Japanese women describe as the "radical" or "revolutionary" phase of the women's movement from 1970 to 1977. In a succession of strategies, women's groups in this period analyzed the inadequacy of Marxist analysis for feminist revolution, demanded that birth control pills be made widely available, published critiques of the "myth of motherhood," and published radical essays in such journals as *Eros*. Though Japanese institutions, particularly the media, studiously ignored them except to report occasionally on what they considered the antics of the lunatic fringe, these "radical" actions, and the analysis of Japanese society they provided, seem to have had an impact on many women in Japan. However, there is general agreement that with International Women's Year in 1975, a more moderate group of women successfully began the effort to bring women's issues into the mainstream. Partly through cabinet-level committees promised in the first UN-sponsored International Women's Year in Mexico City, "laws that were disadvantageous to women were reevaluated, and the number of women who participated in policy making increased" (Ehara 1993: 51).

Women's Studies programs have made steady progress in Japan since 1978, when the First International Women's Studies Conference was held in Tokyo; in successive years, an increasing number of books on women were published by women's studies scholars working in and out of the academic world. By the 1980s, it had become commonplace for important research on women to be published by Japan's mainstream presses, including prestigious university presses (Fujieda and Fujimura-Fanselow 1995).

In Japan, as elsewhere, there has been continuing criticism of political and academic mainstreaming and the implied co-optation of the movement by conservative social institutions. These differences are clearest in ongoing discussions among Japanese women focused on the quality of women's lives at work as well as in the family; the connections between feminism and the environment, theory and practice, and the place of Japanese feminism in the world at large. The ambivalence Japanese feminists have felt vis-à-vis Western feminism continues, as does the effort to connect with Asian feminists. Within the feminist community in Japan, familiar arguments continue over the perceived differences between Japanese and North American feminists, and the idiosyncracies of Japanese culture and society in relation to feminist questions. The notion that North American women are, for example, primarily interested in power as opposed to basic change in the gendered roles of men and women remains, as does the sense that North American women cannot deal with difference simply by ignoring it. The subtext of much of this discussion is the continuing assumption of U.S. (including U.S. feminist) hegemony, a subject apparently too dangerous to discuss openly (Buckley 1997).

Dramatic change in postwar Japan's women's lives also came from an economy whose rapid growth changed the nature and structure of the Japanese family in both city and countryside, dramatically and irreversibly. The current generation of young families in Japan's major cities are not, with rare exceptions, productive units; for the first time in Japan's history, the typical pattern is the nuclear family, a consuming family in which the husband goes off to work and the wife stays home to care for young children. What was initially liberating for women was that mothers-in-law no longer lived with them; eventually they came to realize a power in their households few women in recent memory had enjoyed in their own right: they became the primary agents in the education of their children, and they were responsible for managing family finances. Only recently have women in increasing numbers come to realize that the price of this change, in the absence of other developments, has been very high.

> A typical middle-class Japanese white-collar husband spends most of his waking hours working, even on weekends and holidays when he has to socialize in bars and restaurants or on the golf course "for business"; often comes home after midnight, uttering only "supper," "bed," and "bath"; reads the newspaper, even when his wife is talking about the children or what she did that day; and avoids matters concerning the children by saying, "Wives are responsible for the education of the children." This typical Japanese husband in no way senses that he is neglecting his family. Rather, he believes that he is fulfilling the role of husband and father by earning wages to support his wife and children. In reality, however, he has very little time or emotional energy to give to his wife and children, and, as a result of this, his presence or position within the family has come to assume increasingly less importance. (Yoshizumi 1996: 185)

Mothers-in-law are not always available to provide child care, and children in urban nuclear families are no longer socialized by multiple adults and siblings—the pattern in the extended family. Generally, Japanese society does not provide adequate child care, but there is a clear social expectation that women will raise well behaved, successful children. In the family itself, there is the general expectation that wives will manage the budget efficiently. In practice that often means a wife will supplement her husband's income with part-time work, especially if is necessary to pay for private tutors that will make her children more likely to pass college entrance exams. Wives have an obligation to husband and family; if their children are not academically successful, it is expected that the wife will take responsibility for their failure. Iwao relates this process in her description of one mother:

> Ordinarily a very understanding and supportive husband who tried his best to make up for his long absences, Kazuo became emotional about their son's poor academic performance, blaming Akiko for not doing enough to prepare him for the entrance examination competition. He and Akiko had a bad fight when he made it sound as though their son's failure was solely her responsibility. She had been furious but was unable to counter Kazuo's charges of inadequate attention to their son's preparatory study because her mother had been hospitalized and a great deal of time had, in fact, been taken up with care of her father, who was helpless without his wife at home, and with visiting her mother at the hospital. Akiko does not want to go through a similar scene with her husband again, so she plans to send her daughter to an expensive but highly reputed preparatory school. (Iwao 1993: 55)

The Japanese press carries almost daily coverage of the "problems" of the Japanese family. It is clear that the Japanese family system is in transition, and that many of its former tasks—care for aging parents, for example—have not been assumed by any other agency and can no longer be assumed by an extended family structure. In this situation, most critics seem to be satisfied to lay most of the blame for the family's current failures at the feet of women in the nuclear family who have primary responsibilities as mothers and wives. "Education mothers," it is said, are producing neurotic children; "working mothers" are abandoning their primary social responsibilities. The result is, according to the press and intellectual critics, children who are out of control and families that do not live up to Japanese standards. A catalogue of the most dramatic problems attributed to the failure of the family system in contemporary Japan includes child suicide; family violence that spills over into the school system; unwillingness or inability to care for aging parents; and most recently, sons and mothers with neurotic sexual attachments to one another.

Young wives and mothers have been made the primary culprits in this scenario; mention is rarely made of structural change in the Japanese family, or of the fact that Japanese business practices assure the continuance of what is, in practice, a single-parent family in contemporary Japan. This pattern continues, even though it has been moderated by business initiatives designed to trim the length of the work week.

KOREA

Japan's defeat in September 1945 ended thirty-five years of colonial rule, but Korea now faced the reality of the Pacific War's devastation, coupled with the fact that Koreans now found themselves in the center of Cold War maneuvering in Northeast Asia. Before Koreans had even begun to celebrate the end of Japanese rule, they faced north-south divisions and the very substantial challenge of rebuilding a shattered economy. By the time the Korean War (1950–53) had ended, Korea faced seemingly permanent division, splitting families between north and south. Facing enemies in North Korea, China, and the Soviet Union, South Korea entered a period of what might be called permanent vigilance, if not emergency—a state of affairs that helped to justify dictatorial rule, revitalize a sense of nationalism, and tie Korea ever more closely to the United States and its military power. American troops now became a fixture on the Korean scene.

Accordingly, women in postwar Korea found themselves in what must have seemed a different, yet disturbingly familiar situation. Constant preparedness in the face of putative enemies meant renewed demands that women make support for nationalist causes a priority; it also meant that basic social reform would not be on the state's agenda. Instead, the South Korean state, in an increasingly defensive mode, continued to support Neo-Confucian views of women in the family, views intensified by Japanese colonial rule. As early as 1948, the government answered the liberalism of a new Constitution with a Civil Code that enunciated anachronistic, Neo-Confucian roles for Korean women in the family: women would continue to function in a patrilineal, patrilocal family structure in which primogeniture was firmly established. The staying power of Neo-Confucian institutions in the countryside was obvious to Clark Sorenson, who observed them in 1983:

> Women in general are confined to the domestic domain, running the household and taking care of the children; while men take care of most affairs in the public domain. Politics are in male hands: Positions of authority requiring direct interaction with the government bureaucracy and rural or urban elites are invariably occupied by men. . . . In the ancestral sacrifices, the most conspicuous rituals in which the relationship between households is expressed, only men make offerings; women must watch them from the sidelines. (Sorenson 1983: 63–64)

Beginning in the 1970s, Korean women worked to reform the Civil Code, making the obvious argument that it was, among other things, at odds with a Korean Constitution guaranteeing voting rights and equal treatment/opportunity for women. They were ultimately successful in 1989, but, as Moon tells us, even after the revised law went into effect in 1991,

> [the Civil Code] still prohibits marriage between persons with the same family name and ancestral seat and the formal succession of household headship. The marriage prohibition is an extreme manifestation of exogamy based on patrilineage. An assumption behind this legal taboo is that one's identity is determined by her/his father's blood, which is presumably identified by his surname and ancestral seat, or the putative place of his clan's origin. The formality of the succession . . . persists even after most mandatory rights and obligations between the [household head] and his family members are eliminated. Both of these elements strongly reflect the Neo-Confucian principle of patrilineage that reduced women to mere breeders to continue agnatic family lines. (Moon 1998: 53)

Korea's 1948 Constitution provides women the right to vote, and generally makes discrimination based on gender unlawful. However, women are heavily under-represented in national politics (as they are elsewhere in the world); in 1993, three cabinet ministers and five women in the National Assembly (out of 299) served as visible women in national politics (Gelb and Palley 1994: 278). Still, with the election of reformist president Kim Young Sam in 1992, women have become more optimistic about their political futures and the possibility of significant social change in Korea. Sohn Bong Scuk's comments are typical of this new optimism:

> The growth-oriented strategy in Korea has brought the people material prosperity. However, serious environmental degradation accompanied the economic development. The major issues confronting South Korea's politicians are such environmental problems as clean air, clean water, recycling, and the associated problems of community health and social welfare. Women are better informed on these community issues and usually more interested in solving these problems than men. As these community issues become more politicized, women may be able to participate in politics on a more equal footing with men. An increasing number of women will also find themselves fit to take leadership positions. The restoration of local self-government has opened new opportunities for women. Hence, women's position in the realm of politics is expected to improve in Korea. (Gelb and Palley 1994: 267)

Before the Korean "economic miracle" began in 1960, the presence of women in the work force remained relatively small (about 200,000); today, more than two million Korean women contribute to the economy as workers. They played a critical role in the "economic miracle" by providing low-wage labor for light industry that anchored Korea's development in the 1960s and '70s. According to Kim Seung-kyung, then-president Park was "a great admirer of Japan's modernization during the Meiji period, and held it up as a model for Korea. The incorporation of young women into a national struggle for modernization as low-paid factory labor is only one of many parallels between Park's regime and that of Meiji Japan" (Kim 1997: 11).

Early efforts on the part of women workers to protest working conditions and to establish unions in the textile industry were met with government brutality and occasionally sexual violence on the part of male workers. One unusual example is the so-called "nude demonstration" that was staged at the Tonghil Textile Company in 1976; women unionists occupied the factory in protest of management efforts to subvert the union. An observer describes what happened when government riot police arrived to evict them:

> They surrounded the workers and began forcibly arresting them. Then an astonishing thing happened: the women workers took off their work clothes to protest the arrests. In the hot summer heat . . . the workers were mostly wearing only bras under their work clothes; so when they removed these they were half-naked. In that state they sang as loudly as they could, thinking that not even the worst policeman would lay his hands on a naked woman's body. But the police brutally arrested them, beating them with clubs, and the helpless women ran and fell, screaming and bleeding . . . more than seventy were wounded, and fourteen had to be hospitalized. (Kim 1997: 26–27)

Violent scenes involving women factory workers were not unusual in the 1970s; in some cases, the Park regime sentenced women to prison terms for attempting to organize workers.

In the contemporary workplace, the problems Korean women face are familiar ones: women with four-year college degrees find it difficult to get jobs; many Korean women work in part-time, low-wage (though not necessarily unskilled) jobs; with every small sign of economic instability, women workers face a choice between losing a job, or working more for less pay. Largely as a result of women's efforts, Korea enacted an Equal Employment Act in 1987 (revised in 1989) that provides for equal pay for equal work, maternity protection, and the right to work after marriage and childbirth. Penalties are provided for employers who violate the law, but the legislation itself has not been effectively enforced. Korean women activists expect that it will take time and continuing effort to bring about change for working women, and they indicate that part of that change must come from women with a more fully developed consciousness of their rights and responsibilities in the workplace (Gelb and Palley 1994: 252–53).

Many Korean feminists have expressed the view that the weight of Korean nationalism continues to smother efforts Korean women have tried to make to improve their status since 1945. If, as Kim and Choi suggest, "Feminism and nationalism are the antinomic offspring of modernity" (Kim and Choi 1998: 7), the recent work of Korean women suggests they believe Korea may be one of the twentieth century's best examples of that fact. Nationalism in Korea has undergone many reformulations, but Moon Seungsook finds the nationalist rhetoric created after 1960, in a period of rapid economic growth, to be most telling. State nationalism, she tells us, is predicated on the assumption of the state as the major element of both industrialization and national defense. Its effectiveness

> depends on the collective memory of Japanese colonization and the Korean War, as well as on popular recognition of neo-colonial aspects of the American military and strategic dominance in Korea and Korea's dependence upon the United States and Japan. However, the state's attempt to conjure up the image of a timeless Korean nation through representations of its history and tradition is highly contradictory because this very discursive practice masks the marginalization of women and their exclusion from the putatively homogeneous and egalitarian community. (Moon 1998: 33–34)

Government pronouncements, textbooks, and representations of contemporary Korea are consistently androcentric and linked to the reformulation of Korea's history. From the mythology of Tan'gun, son of "heavenly man" and "bear woman" and founder of Korea, to stories of warriors who protected the state in the face of invasion, it is clear that the "order of the nation is firmly rooted in essential and hierarchical differences between woman and man" (Moon 1998: 57). The ideal Korean man is head of the patriline, and a warrior; the ideal Korean woman carries "a reproductive and domestic identity that preempts [her] full membership in the national community" (Moon 1998: 58).

Sexual violence has been a central part of the history of Korean women in the modern period, partly because of Korea's colonial history. In contemporary Korea, U.S. troops are serviced by "camptown prostitutes" who have, in the view of some government officials, sacrificed themselves for the good of the nation. Katharine H. S. Moon reports a government official's recounting of a conversation with camptown prostitutes whom he asked: "Why did Japan develop from nothing to greatness?" He answered for them by admonishing them to imitate the spirit of Japanese prostitutes who sold their bodies to the post-1945 U.S. occupation forces. "The Japanese prostitute, when she finished with the GI, did not get up to go get the next GI (for more money) but knelt before him and pleaded with him to help rebuild Japan. The spirit of the Japanese prostitute spread to the rest of the society to develop Japan" (Moon 1998: 154).

In a strange but perhaps predictable way, the "comfort women" issue often seems to have been co-opted by a Korean government interested primarily in its usefulness as a focus of nationalist sentiment, not what it says about the brutalization of Korean women. Hyunah Yang reports the following letter from a male reader of a Korean newspaper:

> "This [Military Comfort Women] issue will not end with the apology of the Japanese prime minister. Nor will the issue be settled by compensation only to the old women victims. The event amounts to an act in which the Japanese throw their dirty sperm bucket into our Korean people's face." (Quoted in Yang 1998: 130)

Yang wonders who "our Korean people" might be. She points out that

> The underlying assumption here is that since Korean women had been humiliated, so too have all Koreans. . . . When the male reader wrote "the Japanese" he clearly meant Japanese men. . . . The sperm bucket itself offers a clue through which we can trace why the humiliation of Korean women amounts to the humiliation of Korean men. . . . The reader's letter thus exemplifies how males become the only subjects involved in questions of nation and sexuality. . . . The nation becomes gendered, and women's sexuality becomes nationalized. Nation is equated with the male subject position, and women's sexuality is reified as property of the masculine status. (Yang 1998: 130)

Korea's continuing emphasis on an anachronistic model of the family in the contemporary period has, in the eyes of some Korean women, virtually guaranteed increasing domestic violence. Women's groups have organized to provide shelters and worked to raise public consciousness of domestic violence as a national problem, but it is clear from recent history that this awareness will be difficult to achieve.

CHINA

The 1950 Marriage Law was the first of many initiatives begun by the new government that improved women's situation in China after the revolution. It also reopened significant debate on family reform in China, and revealed that Marxist, nationalist, and May Fourth arguments about the family, and about women, were still contending. Marriage reformers, echoing many of the sentiments of May Fourth intellectuals, argued that women's status in the family must be addressed before anything else. Economic change alone would not produce such reform, they said, especially if it were left in the hands of self-interested local communities, where males dominated family policy.

The CCP set up an All China Women's Federation in 1949, recognizing women as an important revolutionary constituency, but occasionally demonstrating an unwillingness to recognize that the interests of women and those of the state might be opposed. It was part of a top-down strategy designed to inform women of state programs and to raise the political consciousness of women. In the process of carrying out its mandate, the Federation became an umbrella for many different women's constituencies and provided resources for grass roots organizations, especially among workers and peasant women. When, for example, implementation of the Marriage Law began, the Federation complained of abuses in the countryside, even though its arguments were largely ignored by the Party. In urban areas, implementation moved forward and was welcomed by many city women for whom the Marriage Law was symbolic of the Party's commitment to gender equality. In the countryside, as a familiar kind of peasant resistance presented itself, the Party chose to leave enforcement in the hands of local cadres who were mostly male, and sympathetic, as they had been before 1949, to the complaints of male peasants. As Elisabeth Croll reports,

> The Women's Federation noted in a report on the state of affairs in southern China that to get a divorce, there were three obstacles to overcome: the obstacle of the husband, of the mother-in-law and of the cadres. Apparently it was the latter which was often hardest to overcome. (Croll 1980: 235)

Kay Ann Johnson believes that this Party policy had an impact that went beyond simple postponement of significant structural change in the family and village; it meant women were unable to "translate the weakening of direct patriarchal economic control which developed with collectivization and the gradual expansion of women's roles into greater self-determination and influence in marriage and family" (Johnson 1983: 223).

It is difficult to underestimate the importance of the Party's decision to downplay gender, or "the woman question," in collectivization. Good arguments can be made to support that decision, arguments that parallel those made during the revolution: when you desperately need the peasantry and are already forcing great change on them, it is not a good idea to add women to the mix if it is not absolutely necessary. But once collectivization was declared complete in 1957, the Party and the Women's Federation dropped the struggle for gender equality and liberation, calling instead for mobilizing women in industry that would modernize the country (Zhang and Wu 1994: 9). In the Cultural Revolution (1966–77), "the woman question" was moot, since the Party pronounced men and women equally capable. The Women's Federation was disbanded, and there were no serious discussions or initiatives related to the "woman question" for a decade.

Why, in spite of mobilization, collectivization, and industrialization, did women's roles in the countryside of China change so little? For many scholars, the answer seems to be that the "traditional" Chinese family, or its most patriarchal character, was restored by the Chinese revolution. From this point of view, the place of women in the family is not simply a "feudal remnant" of an anti-feudal revolution: it is also central to the preservation of unreformed elements in the countryside whose support has been more important to the Party than has "the woman question."

Is there also an unremitting attachment to a kind of Marxist orthodoxy never able to deal successfully with the "woman question?" According to Heidi Hartmann's well-known turn of phrase, in Marxism, the "woman question" has never been the feminist question. In Kay Ann Johnson's view,

> Engels, who has been made the highest theoretical authority on such matters, effectively depoliticizes many of the culturally embedded issues of women's status and the family. . . . An understanding [of these issues] requires that central consideration be given to the role of kinship and of the familial-religious underpinnings of community in peasant society. . . . One would do far better to begin with theoretical issues such as those suggested by Lévi-Strauss and Rubin. (Johnson 1983: 220–21)

Judith Stacey, arguing that the Chinese revolution has demonstrated not simply the compatibility but the inevitability of patriarchy and socialism, is also strongly convinced that "socialist family practices cannot be theorized adequately within Marxism, and the contradictions cannot be resolved via socialist theory and practice alone" (Stacey 1983: 267).

Without significant representation during the Cultural Revolution, Chinese women did not fare well. As many Chinese and Western feminists observed in the late seventies and early eighties, the physical abuse of women accelerated as a result of birth control policies that, in the absence of basic change in the family system, made women who bore female children the victims of the "one child" policy. Female infanticide and forced marriages, those "feudal remnants" of family life, seemed alive and well, and prostitution and pornography were increasing. As a result of economic change,

> discrimination against women in employment in the state sector increased as enterprises gained more control over personnel and hiring. Rural girls dropped out of school to help with family planning as agriculture once again was organized by households rather than collectives. The number of women holding political positions declined as a result of direct election. Prostitution and pornography became more prominent in areas experiencing rapid development of a market economy. (Zhang and Wu 1994: 11)

The Women's Federation, reorganized after the Cultural Revolution, took the lead in campaigns in the early eighties to remedy some of these problems; one of its major accomplishments was state legislation aimed at protecting the rights and interests of women that went into effect in 1993. The Federation has so far failed to win departmental status in the government but has had a substantial impact through its network of committees, and it has been particularly successful in winning government resources for women in the countryside. In programs designed to make rural women more productive and efficient farmers, the government has provided loans and technical assistance through Federation efforts. By 1993, more than 120 million women had participated in these programs (Zhang and Wu 1994: 13). Nongovernmental organizations, particularly in China's major cities, have successfully supplemented the work of the federations, establishing hot lines and shelters for women.

The women's movement in contemporary China is a very interesting one; there are still significant differences between women in the countryside and those in the cities, where the women's movement is—as it was before 1949—strongest, but problems connecting urban and rural areas may be less severe than they were in that period. A critical question may be whether several different women's organizations, in and out of the government, can coexist and pursue overlapping but different agendas. It seems likely that, as the women's movement in contemporary China becomes more visible and articulate, it will define itself in ways that do not necessarily invite comparison with the West, or even other parts of Asia; but however the "character" of the Chinese women's movement is ultimately defined, it will certainly include the histories of women who have lived through difficult times. To those who remember the state's seeming ability to shut down the women's movement in China and who, for that reason, wonder whether the contemporary movement will be able to survive if and when its interests conflict in basic ways with the state, Chinese women point out that many of China's strongest and most influential feminists, women who are in large measure responsible for the contemporary movement, became feminists in the fifties, partly through the policies created by the state, and partly in opposition to the state.

SOURCES

A NOTE ON THE ROMANIZATION OF CHINESE TERMS

For the most part, this text uses the old Wade-Giles system of romanization, primarily because that is the system still currently used in most world history textbooks. However, Wade-Giles (Peking) is now very much out of date, and the *pinyin* (Beijing) system of romanization, one most Chinese scholars consider superior, is gradually replacing it. This transitional period produces some confusing combinations for readers who may find themselves reading a direct quote from an author using *pinyin* romanization, followed by text employing Wade-Giles.

NOTE ON BIBLIOGRAPHY

This bibliography is selective; it makes no attempt to cover the enormous and rapidly growing literature of the histories of women in China, Japan, and Korea. Since one of the primary functions of both text and bibliography is to provide accessible materials for teachers and students in a general framework, it is also limited to English-language sources.

Ahern, Emily. 1975. "The Power and Pollution of Chinese Women." In Witke and Wolf, *Women in Chinese Society*.

*AMPO, eds. 1996. *Voices from the Japanese Women's Movement*. Armonk, N.Y.: M. E. Sharpe.

Anagnost, Ann. 1989. "Transformation of Gender in Modern China." *Gender and Anthropology: Critical Reviews for Research and Teaching*. Washington, D.C.: American Anthropology Association.

Ariga, Kizaemon. 1956. "Introduction to the Family System in Japan, China, and Korea." *Transactions of the World Congress of Sociology* 3d, vol. 4: 199–208.

*Ariyoshi, Sawako. 1978. *The Doctor's Wife*. Tokyo: Kodansha.

*———. 1980. *The River Ki*. Tokyo: Kodansha.

*———. 1986. *The Twilight Years*. Tokyo: Kodansha.

Association of Korean Christian Scholars. 1978. *Korean Women in a Struggle for Humanization*. Memphis, Tenn.: Association of Korean Christian Scholars.

*Bacon, Alice M. 1892. *Japanese Girls and Women*. Boston: Houghton Mifflin.
*——. 1900. *A Japanese Interior*. Boston: Houghton Mifflin.
Bak, Sung-Yun. 1983. "Women's Speech in Korean and English." *Korean Studies* 7: 61–75.
Barlow, Tani. 1989. "Asian Perspectives." *Gender and History* 1, no. 3 (Autumn): 21–36.
——. 1990. "Theorizing Women: Funu, Guojia, Jiating." *Genders* (March).
——. 1993. *Gender Politics in Modern China*. Durham, N.C.: Duke University Press.
*Barlow, Tani, and Gary Bjorge, eds. 1989. *I Myself Am a Woman: Selected Writings of Ding Ling*. Boston: Beacon Press.
*Basu, Amrita, ed., with the assistance of C. Elizabeth McGrory. 1995. *The Challenge of Local Feminisms: Women's Movements in Global Perspective*. Boulder, Colo.: Westview Press.
Bernhardt, Kathryn. 1996. "A Ming-Qing Transition in Chinese Women's History?" In Hershatter, et al., eds., *Remapping China*.
*Bernstein, Gail Lee. 1983. *Haruko's World*. Stanford: Stanford University Press.
*——, ed. 1991. *Recreating Japanese Women, 1600–1945*. Berkeley and Los Angeles: University of California Press.
Berry, Mary E. 1982. *Hideyoshi*. Cambridge: Harvard University Press.
Birge, Bettina. 1989. "Chu Hsi and Women's Education." In DeBary and Chaffee, *Neo-Confucian Education*.
*Blacker, Carmen. 1964. *The Japanese Enlightenment*. Cambridge: Cambridge University Press.
*——. 1986. *The Catalpa Bow*. London: Allen and Unwin.
*Blake, C. Fred. 1994. "Footbinding in Neo-Confucian China and the Appropriation of Female Labor." *Signs* 19, no. 3: 676–712.
Borton, Hugh. 1955. *Japan's Modern Century*. New York: Ronald Press.
*Bowring, Richard. 1982. *Murasaki Shikibu: Her Diary and Poetic Memoirs*. Princeton: Princeton University Press.
*Brazell, Karen, trans. 1973. *The Confessions of Lady Nijo*. Stanford: Stanford University Press.
Bridenthal, Renate, Claudia Koonz, and Susan Stuard, eds. 1977. *Becoming Visible: Women in European History*. Boston: Houghton-Mifflin.
*Buckley, Sandra. 1997. *Broken Silence: Voices of Japanese Feminism*. Berkeley and Los Angeles: University of California Press.
Butler, Kenneth D. 1978. "Women of Power behind the Kamakura Bakufu." In Hyoe and Harper, *Great Historical Figures of Japan*.
Cahill, Suzanne. 1986. "Performers and Female Taoist Adepts: Hsi Wang Mu as the Patron Deity of Women in Medieval China." *Journal of the American Oriental Society* 106: 155–68.
*——. 1993. *Transcendence and Divine Passion: The Queen Mother of the West in Medieval China*. Stanford: Stanford University Press.
Carlitz, Katherine. 1991. "The Social Uses of Female Virtue in Late Ming Editions of Lienu Zhuan." *Late Imperial China* 12, no. 2 (December): 117–48.
*Cha, Theresa Hak Kyung. 1995. *Writing Self Writing Nation: A Collection of Essays on DictaEE*. Berkeley, Calif.: Third Woman Press.
Ch'en Tu-hsiu. 1964. "The Confucian Way and Modern Living." In DeBary, et al., *Sources*.
Cho Haejong. 1979. "Neither Dominance: A Study of a Female Diver's Village in Korea." *Korea Journal* 19, no. 6: 23–24.

————. 1983. "The Autonomous Women Divers on Cheju Island." In Kendall and Peterson, *Korean Women*.

Choe-Wall, Yang-hi, ed. 1985. *Memoirs of a Korean Queen*. London: KPI.

*Choi Chungmoo, ed. 1997. Special issue on "The Comfort Women." *positions east asia cultures critique* 5, no. 1 (Spring).

Chow, Rey. 1992. *Women and Chinese Modernity*. Minneapolis: University of Minnesota Press.

*Chung, Sei-wha, ed. 1986. *Challenges for Women: Women's Studies in Korea*. Seoul: EWHA Women's University Press.

Chung, Sue Fawn. 1979. "The Much-Maligned Empress Dowager: A Revisionist Study of the Empress Dowager Tz'u-hsi (1835–1908)." *Modern Asian Studies* 13, no. 2: 177–96.

Cohen, Myron Leon. 1976. *House United, House Divided: The Chinese Family in Taiwan*. New York: Columbia University Press.

Coleman, Samuel. 1983. *Family Planning in Japanese Society: Traditional Birth Control and Modern Urban Culture*. Princeton: Princeton University Press.

Contogenis, Constantine, trans. 1994. *Brief Songs of the Kisang: Courtesan Poetry of the Last Korean Dynasty*. Seattle: Broken Moon Press.

*Cook, Alice, and Hiroko Hayashi. 1980. *Working Women in Japan*. Ithaca, N.Y.: Cornell University, School of Labor and Industrial Relations.

*Croll, Elisabeth J. 1980. *Feminism and Socialism in China*. New York: Schocken Books.

————. 1983. *Chinese Women since Mao*. London: Zed Books.

————. 1995. *Changing Identities of Chinese Women: Rhetoric, Experience, and Self-Perception in Twentieth-Century China*. Hong Kong: Hong Kong University Press; Atlantic Highlands, N.J.: Zed Books.

*Croll, Elisabeth J., Delia Davin, and Penny Kane, eds. 1985. *China's One-Child Family Policy*. New York: St. Martin's Press.

*Davin, Delia. 1976. *Woman-Work: Women and the Party in Revolutionary China*. Oxford: Clarendon.

DeBary, William Theodore, and John Chaffee. 1989. *Neo-Confucian Education: The Formative Stage*. Berkeley and Los Angeles: University of California Press.

DeBary, William Theodore, Wing-tsit Chan, and Burton Watson, comps. 1960. *Sources of the Chinese Tradition*. New York: Columbia University Press.

Deuchler, Martina. 1980. "Neo-Confucianism: The Impulse for Action in Early Yi Korea." *Journal of Korean Studies* 2: 71–112.

————. 1983. Preface to Kendall and Peterson, *Korean Women*.

Dikotter, Frank. 1994. *Discourse of Race in Modern China*. Stanford: Stanford University Press.

*————. 1995. *Sex, Culture, and Society in Modern China*. Honolulu: University of Hawaii Press.

Dorson, R. 1963. *Studies in Japanese Folklore*. Bloomington: Indiana University Press.

Duberman, Martin, Martha Vicinus, and George Chauncey, Jr., eds. 1989. *Hidden from History: Reclaiming the Gay and Lesbian Past*. New York: Penguin Books.

Duke, Michael S., ed. 1989. *Modern Chinese Women Writers*. Armonk, N.Y.: M. E. Sharpe.

Ebrey, Patricia Buckley, ed. 1981. *Chinese Civilization and Society: A Sourcebook*. New York: The Free Press.

*———. 1993. *The Inner Quarters: Marriage and the Lives of Women in the Sung Period*. Berkeley and Los Angeles: University of California Press.

———, trans. 1991. *Chu Hsi's Family Rituals*. Princeton: Princeton University Press.

Ehara, Yumiko. 1993. "Japanese Feminism in the 1970s and 1980s." *U.S.-Japan Women's Journal* 4: 49–70. English Supplement.

Elvin, Mark. 1984. "Female Virtue and the State in China." *Past and Present* 104: 111–52.

*Enchi Fumiko. 1971. *The Waiting Years*. Tokyo: Kodansha.

Epstein, Israel. 1993. *Woman in World History: Soong Ching Ling*. Beijing: World Press.

Feuerwerker, Yi-Tsi Mei. 1982. *Ding Ling's Fiction: Ideology and Narrative in Modern Chinese Literature*. Cambridge: Harvard University Press.

*Field, Norma. 1989. *The Splendor of Longing in the Tale of Genji*. Princeton: Princeton University Press.

Freedman, Maurice. 1958. *Lineage Organization in Southeastern China*. London: University of London.

———. 1966. *Chinese Lineage and Society: Fukien and Kwantung*. New York: Humanities Press.

———. 1967. *Rites and Duties; Or, Chinese Marriage*. London: G. Bell and Sons.

———. 1979. *The Study of Chinese Society*. Stanford: Stanford University Press.

———, ed. 1970. *Family and Kinship in Chinese Society*. New Haven: Yale University Press.

Fujieda, Mioko and Fujimura-Fanselow, Kumiko. 1995. "Women's Studies: An Overview." In Fujimura-Fanselow and Kameda, *Japanese Women*.

*Fujimura-Fanselow, Kumiko, and Atsuko Kameda, eds. 1995. *Japanese Women: New Feminist Perspectives on the Past, Present, and Future*. New York: The Feminist Press at the City University of New York.

Fulton, Bruce and Ju-Chan, eds. and trans. 1997. *Wayfarer: New Fiction by Korean Women*. Seattle: Women in Translation.

Furth, Charlotte. 1987. "Concepts of Pregnancy, Childbirth, and Infancy in Ch'ing Dynasty China." *Journal of Asian Studies* 46, no. 1 (February): 7–36.

*Furuki, Yoshiko. 1991. *The White Plum: A Biography of Ume Tsuda, Pioneer in the Higher Education of Japanese Women*. New York: Weatherhill.

*Gelb, Joyce, and Marian Lief Palley, eds. 1994. *Women of Japan and Korea*. Philadelphia: Temple University Press.

Gilmartin, Christina. 1989. "Gender, Politics, and Patriarchy in China: The Experience of Early Women Communists." In Kruks, *Promissory Notes*.

*———. 1995. *Engendering the Chinese Revolution*. Berkeley and Los Angeles: University of California Press.

*Gilmartin, Christina, Gail Hershatter, Lisa Rofel, and Tyrene Whites, eds. 1994. *Engendering China: Women, Culture and the State*. Cambridge: Harvard University Press.

Goto, Hiromi. 1994. *Chorus of Mushrooms*. Edmonton, Canada: NeWest Press.

Guisso, Richard, and Stanley Johannesen, eds. 1981. *Women in China: Current Directions in Historical Scholarship*. New York: Philo Press.

Hamaguchi, Tan. 1904. "Some Striking Female Personalities in Japanese History." *Annual Meeting of the Japan Society*, London, May 13, 1903. London: The Japan Society.

Handlin, Johanna. 1975. "Lu K'un's New Audience: The Influence of Women's

Literacy on Sixteenth Century Thought." In Witke and Wolf, *Women in Chinese Society*.

Hane, Mikiso. 1982. *Peasants, Rebels and Outcastes: The Underside of Modern Japan*. New York: Pantheon Books.

*———, trans. and ed. 1988. *Reflections on the Way to the Gallows*. Berkeley: University of California Press, and New York: Pantheon Books.

Hanley, Susan B. and Kozo Yamamura. 1977. *Economic and Demographic Change in Preindustrial Japan, 1600–1800*. Princeton: Princeton University Press.

Harvey, Youngsook K. 1979. *Six Korean Women: The Socialization of Shamans*. American Ethnological Society Monograph No. 65. St. Paul: West Publishing Co.

———. 1983. "Minmyonuri: The Daughter-in-Law Who Comes of Age in Her Mother-in-Law's Household." In Kendall and Peterson, *Korean Women*.

Havens, Thomas R. H. 1975. "Women and War in Japan, 1937–1945." *American Historical Review* 80, no. 4: 913–34.

*Hershatter, Gail. 1986. *The Workers of Tianjin, 1900–1949*. Stanford: Stanford University Press.

———. 1992a. "Courtesans and Streetwalkers: The Changing Discourses on Shanghai Prostitution, 1890–1949." *Journal of the History of Sexuality* 3, no. 2 (October): 245–69.

———. 1992b. "Regulating Sex in Shanghai: The Reform of Prostitution in 1920 and 1951." In Wakeman and Yeh, *Urban Sojourners in Shanghai*.

*———. 1997. *Dangerous Pleasures: Prostitution and Modernity in Twentieth Century Shanghai*. Berkeley and Los Angeles: University of California Press.

*Hershatter, Gail, Emily Honig, Jonathan N. Lipman, and Randall Stross, eds. 1996. *Remapping China: Fissures in Historical Terrain*. Stanford: Stanford University Press.

*Hinton, William. 1986. *Fanshen*. New York: Vintage Books.

Holmgren, Jennifer. 1986. "Observations on Marriage and Inheritance Practices in Early Mongol and Yuan Society, with Particular Reference to the Levirate." *Journal of Asian History* 20, no. 2: 127–92.

*Honig, Emily. 1986. *Sisters and Strangers: Women in the Shanghai Cotton Mills*. Stanford: Stanford University Press.

———. 1992. "Christianity, Feminism, and Communism: The Life and Times of Deng Yuzhi (Cora Deng)." In Johnson-Odim and Strobel, *Expanding the Boundaries*.

———, ed. 1997. Special issue on history of women in China. *Journal of Women's History* 8, no. 4.

*Honig, Emily, and Gail Hershatter. 1988. *Personal Voices: Chinese Women in the 1980s*. Stanford: Stanford University Press.

Hopper, Helen. 1996. *A New Woman of Japan: A Political Biography of Kato Shidzue*. Boulder, Colo.: Westview Press.

Hori, Ichiro. 1968. *Folk Religion in Japan*. Chicago: University of Chicago Press.

Hyoe, Murakami, and Thomas J. Harper, eds. 1978. *Great Historical Figures of Japan*. Tokyo: Japan Culture Institute.

Imamura, Anne E. 1987. *Urban Japanese Housewives*. Honolulu: University of Hawaii Press.

*——, ed. 1996. *Re-Imaging Japanese Women*. Berkeley: University of California Press.

Ishimoto, Baroness Shidzue. 1984. *Facing Two Ways*. Introduction and Afterword, Barbara Maloney. Stanford: Stanford University Press.

Iwao, Sumiko. 1993. *The Japanese Woman*. New York: The Free Press.

*Johnson, Kay Ann. 1983. *Women, the Family and Peasant Revolution in China*. Chicago: University of Chicago Press.

*Johnson-Odim, Cheryl, and Margaret Strobel, eds. 1992. *Expanding the Boundaries of Women's History*. Bloomington: Indiana University Press.

Judd, Ellen. 1994. *Gender and Power in Rural North China*. Stanford: Stanford University Press.

Kahn, Harold. 1967. "The Politics of Filiality." *Journal of Asian Studies* 26, no. 2: 197–204.

*Kamens, Edward. 1990. *The Buddhist Poetry of the Great Kamo Priestess*. Ann Arbor: University of Michigan Center for Japanese Studies.

*Kang, Sok-kyung. 1989. *Words of Farewell*. Seattle: Seal Press.

Kawashima Yoko. 1995. "Female Workers: An Overview of Past and Current Trends." In Fujimura-Fanselow and Kameda, *Japanese Women*.

Keene, Donald. 1955. *Japanese Literature*. New York: Grove Press.

——. 1976. *World within Walls*. New York: Grove Press.

*Keirstead, Thomas. 1995. "The Gendering and Regendering of Medieval Japan." *U.S.-Japan Women's Journal* 9: 77–93. English Supplement.

Keller, Nora Okja. 1998. *Comfort Woman*. New York: Viking Penguin.

Kelly-Gadol, Joan. 1977. "Did Women Have a Renaissance?" In Bridenthal, Koonz, and Stuard, *Becoming Visible*.

*Kendall, Laurel. 1985. *Shamans, Housewives, and Other Restless Spirits*. Honolulu: University of Hawaii Press.

*——. 1995. *The Life and Hard Times of a Korean Shaman*. Honolulu: University of Hawaii Press.

*——. 1996. *Getting Married in Korea: Of Gender, Morality, and Modernity*. Berkeley and Los Angeles: University of California Press.

Kendall, Laurel, and E. Dix, eds. 1987. *Religion and Ritual in Korean Society*. Berkeley, Calif.: Institute of East Asian Studies.

Kendall, Laurel, and Mark Peterson, eds. 1983. *Korean Women: View from the Inner Room*. New Haven: East Rock Press.

Kidder, J. Edward. 1977. *Ancient Japan*. Oxford: Oxford University Press.

——. 1979. "Problems of Cremation in Early Japan: The Role of the Empress Jito." *Humanities, Christianity and Culture* 13 (March): 191–208.

Kim, Doo-hun. 1963. "Confucian Influences on Korean Society." *Korea Journal* 3, no. 9: 17–21.

*Kim, Elaine, and Norma Alarcon, eds. 1993. *Writing Self, Writing Nation: Essays on Theresa Hak Kyung Cha's DictaEE*. Berkeley, Calif.: Third Woman Press.

*Kim, Elaine, and Changmoo Choi, eds. 1998. *Dangerous Women: Gender and Korean Nationalism*. New York: Routledge.

Kim Seung-kyung. 1997. "Productivity, Militancy, and Femininity: Gendered Images of South Korean Women Factory Workers." *Asian Journal of Women's Studies* 3, no. 3: 8–44.

Kim Yung-Chung. 1986. "Women's Movement in Modern Korea." In Chung, *Challenges for Women*.

——, ed. and trans. 1976. *Women of Korea: A History from Ancient Times to 1945*. Seoul: EWHA Women's University Press.

*Kittridge, Cherry. 1987. *Womansword: What Japanese Words Say about Women*. New York: Kodansha International.

*Ko, Dorothy. 1994. *Teachers of the Inner Chambers: Women and Culture in China*. Stanford: Stanford University Press.

Koh, Hesung Chun. 1982. *Korean and Japanese Women: An Analytic Bibliographic Guide*. Westport, Conn.: Greenwood Press.

*Kondo, Dorinne. 1990. *Crafting Selves: Power, Gender, and Discourses of Identity in the Japanese Workplace*. Chicago: University of Chicago Press.

————. 1997. *About Face: Performing Race in Fashion and Theater*. New York: Routledge.

Kruks, Sonia, Rayna Rapp, and Marilyn Young, eds. 1989. *Promissory Notes: Women and the Transition to Socialism*. New York: Monthly Review Press.

Kuninobu, Junko Wada. 1984. "The Development of Feminism in Modern Japan." *Feminist Issues* 4, no. 2 (Fall): 3–23.

*Kurihara, Sadako. 1994. *Black Eggs*. Ann Arbor: University of Michigan Center for Japanese Studies.

Kwon, Yung-hee Kim. 1988. "The Female Entertainment Tradition in Medieval Japan: The Case of *Asobi*." *Theatre Journal* 40, no. 2: 205–16.

Lebra, Takie S. 1984. *Japanese Women: Constraint and Fulfillment*. Honolulu: University of Hawaii Press.

Lee, Mary Paik. 1990. *Quiet Odyssey: Pioneer Korean Woman in America*. Seattle: University of Washington Press.

Li, Ju-chen. 1965. *Flowers in the Mirror*. Berkeley and Los Angeles: University of California Press.

Li Xiaojiang and Li Hui. 1989. "Women's Studies in China." *NWSA Journal* 1, no. 3 (Spring): 458–60.

Li Xiaojiang and Zhang Xiaodan. 1994. "Creating a Space for Women: Women's Studies in China in the 1980s." *Signs* 20, no. 1: 137–51.

Lim-Hing, Sharon, ed. 1994. *The Very Inside: An Anthology of Writing by Asian and Pacific Islander Lesbian and Bisexual Women*. Toronto, Canada: Sister Vision Press.

Ling, Amy. 1990. *Between Worlds: Women Writers of Chinese Ancestry*. New York: Pergamon Press.

*Lippit, Noriko Mizuta, and Kyoko Iriye Selden, eds. and trans. 1991. *Japanese Women Writers: Twentieth Century Short Fiction*. Armonk, N.Y.: M. E. Sharpe.

Mackie, Vera. 1988. "Motherhood and Pacifism in Japan, 1900–1937." *Hecate* 14, no. 2 (Winter): 28–49.

*————. 1997. *Creating Socialist Women in Japan: Gender, Labour and Activism, 1900–1937*. Cambridge: Cambridge University Press.

Mann, Susan. 1987. "Widows in the Kinship, Class and Community Structures of Qing Dynasty China." *Journal of Asian Studies* 46, no. 1 (February): 37–56.

————. 1992. "'Fuxue' (Women's Learning) by Zhang Xuecheng (1738–1801): China's First History of Women's Culture." *Late Imperial China* 13, no. 1 (June): 40–62.

*Matsui, Machiko. 1990. "Evolution of the Feminist Movement in Japan." *NWSA Journal* 2, no. 3 (Summer): 435–49.

Matsui, Yayori. 1989. *Women's Asia*. London: Zed Books.

Mattielli, Sandra, ed. 1977. *Virtues in Conflict: Tradition and the Korean Woman Today*. Seoul: Royal Asiatic Society, Korea Branch.

*McCann, David, ed. 1977. *Black Crane: An Anthology of Korean Literature*. Ithaca, N.Y.: Cornell University East Asian Studies Series.

McCann, David, trans. 1993. *Selected Poems of Kim Namjo*. Ithaca, N.Y.: Cornell University East Asian Studies Series.

McCullough, William H. 1967. "Japanese Marriage Institutions in the Heian Period." *Harvard Journal of Asiatic Studies* 27, no. 1: 103–67.

*Mellen, Joan. 1976. *The Waves at Genji's Door: Japan through Its Cinema*. New York: Pantheon.

Minamoto Junko. 1993. "Buddhism and the Historical Construction of Sexuality in Japan." *U.S. Japan Women's Journal* no. 5: 87–115. English Supplement.

*Miwa, Kai, trans. 1984. *Diary of a Japanese Innkeeper's Daughter*. Ithaca, N.Y.: Cornell University East Asian Studies Series.

Miyamoto, Ken. 1975. "Itō Noe and the Bluestockings." *Japan Interpreter* 10, no. 2: 190–204.

Moon, Katharine H. S. 1998. "Prostitute Bodies and Gendered States in U.S.-Korea Relations." In Kim and Choi, *Dangerous Women*.

Moon, Seungsook. 1998. "Begetting the Nation: The Androcentric Discourse of National History and Tradition in South Korea." In Kim and Choi, *Dangerous Women*.

Mulhern, Chieko Irie, ed. 1991. *Heroic with Grace: Legendary Women of Japan*. Armonk, N.Y.: M. E. Sharpe.

*Murasaki Shikibu. 1960. *The Tale of Genji*. Translated by Arthur Waley. New York: Modern Library.

*———. 1976. *The Tale of Genji*. 2 vols. Translated by Edward G. Seidensticker. New York: Alfred E. Knopf.

Nakagawa, Zennosuke. 1963. "A Century of Marriage Law." *Japan Quarterly* 10, no. 2: 182–92.

Nakajima, Michiko. 1994. "Recent Legal Decisions on Gender-Based Wage Discrimination in Japan." *U.S.-Japan Women's Journal* no. 6: 27–44. English Supplement.

Nakamura Hirotsugu. 1996. "Women in Agricultural Labor in Japan: Current Conditions and Issues." *U.S.-Japan Women's Journal* 11: 61–81. English Supplement.

Nakano Mami. 1996. "Ten Years Under the Equal Employment Opportunity Law." In AMPO, eds., *Voices from the Japanese Women's Movement*.

Naquin, Susan, and Evelyn S. Rawski. 1987. *Chinese Society in the Eighteenth Century*. New Haven: Yale University Press.

*Nelson, Barbara J., and Najma Chowdhury, eds. 1994. *Women and Politics Worldwide*. New Haven: Yale University Press.

*Ng, Vivian. 1987. "Ideology and Sexuality: Rape Laws in Qing China." *Journal of Asian Studies* 46, no. 1: 57–70.

*———. 1989. "Homosexuality and the State in Late Imperial China." In Duberman et al., *Hidden from History*.

Nishikawa, Yuko. 1997. "Japan's Entry into War and the Support of Women." *U.S.-Japan Women's Journal* 12: 48–84. English Supplement.

Niwa, Akiko. 1993. "The Formation of the Myth of Motherhood in Japan." *U.S.-Japan Women's Journal* 4: 70–83. English Supplement.

Ogai, Tokuko. 1996. "The Stars of Democracy: The First Thirty-Nine Members of the Japanese Diet." *U.S.-Japan Women's Journal* 11: 81–117. English Supplement.

*Ogasawara, Yuko. 1998. *Office Ladies and Salaried Men*. Berkeley and Los Angeles: University of California Press.

O'Hara, Albert H. 1955. *The Biographies of Chinese Women*. Hong Kong: Orient Press.

Omachi, Tokuzo. 1963. "Ashiire-kon, Putting-One's-Feet-In-Marriage." In Dorson, *Studies in Japanese Folklore*.

*Ono, Kazuko. 1989. *Chinese Women in a Century of Revolution*. Stanford: Stanford University Press.

Ooms, Emily. 1993. *Women and Millenarian Protest in Meiji Japan: Deguchi Nao and Omotokyō*. Ithaca, N.Y.: Cornell University East Asian Studies Series.

Pan Ku. 1973. "Two Imperial Ladies of Han." Translated by Burton Watson. *Renditions: A Chinese-English Magazine*, no. 1: 7–15.

Parish, William, and Martin White. 1978. *Village and Family in Contemporary China*. Chicago: University of Chicago Press.

Paul, Diana Yoshikawa. 1985. *Women in Buddhism*. Berkeley and Los Angeles: University of California Press. Originally published 1979.

*Pekarik, Andrew, ed. 1985. *Ukifune: Love in the* Tale of Genji. New York: Columbia University Press.

Pelzel, John. 1970. "Japanese Kinship: A Comparison." In Freedman, *Family and Kinship in Chinese Society*.

Peterson, Mark. 1983. "Women without Sons: A Measure of Social Change in Yi Korea." In Kendall and Peterson, *Korean Women*.

Pharr, Susan. 1981. *Political Women in Japan*. Berkeley and Los Angeles: University of California Press.

*Plath, David. 1980. *Long Engagements: Maturity in Modern Japan*. Stanford: Stanford University Press.

Potter, Jack. 1974. "Cantonese Shamanism." In Wolf, *Religion and Ritual*.

*Pruitt, Ida, trans. 1945. *A Daughter of the Han*. Stanford: Stanford University Press.

*Raddeker, Helene Bowen. 1997. *Treacherous Women of Imperial Japan*. London and New York: Routledge.

Rankin, Mary Backus. 1975. "The Emergence of Women at the End of the Ch'ing." In Witke and Wolf, *Women and Chinese Society*.

———. 1986. *Elite Activism and Social Transformation in China*. Stanford: Stanford University Press.

Rhee, Ma-Ji. 1989. "Moral Education in Korea under Japanese Colonialism during 1910–1945." Ph.D. dissertation. Rutgers University.

*Robertson, Jennifer. 1998. *Takarazuka, Sexual Politics, and Popular Culture in Modern Japan*. Berkeley and Los Angeles: University of California Press.

Rodd, Laurel Rasplica. 1991. "Yosano Akiko and the Taishō Debate over the 'New Woman.'" In Bernstein, *Recreating Japanese Women*.

*Rose, Barbara. 1992. *Tsuda Umeko and Women's Education in Japan*. New Haven: Yale University Press.

Rowe, William. 1992. "Women and the Family in Mid-Qing Social Thought: The Case of Chen Hongmou." *Late Imperial China* 10, no. 2: 1–41.

Rutt, Richard. 1974. "Women in the Yi Dynasty through Classical Novels." *Korea Journal* 14, no. 1: 41–45.

Seager, Joni. 1997. *The State of Women in the World Atlas*. Revised. New York: Penguin. Originally published 1986.

*Seidensticker, Edward, trans. 1964. *The Gossamer Years*. Tokyo and Rutlant, Vt.: C. E. Tuttle and Co.

Shaffer, Edward H. 1973. *The Divine Woman: Dragon Ladies and Rain Maidens in T'ang Literature*. Berkeley and Los Angeles: University of California Press.

Shen, Yichin. 1992. "Womanhood and Sexual Relations in Contemporary Chinese Fiction by Male and Female Authors: A Comparative Analysis." *Feminist Issues* 12, no. 1 (Spring): 47–68.

Shimazu, Yoshiko. 1994. "Unmarried Mothers and Their Children in Japan." *U.S.-Japan Women's Journal* 6: 83–110. English Supplement.

Sievers, Sharon L. 1981. "Feminist Criticism in Japanese Politics in the 1880s: The Experience of Kishida Toshiko." *Signs* 6, no. 4: 602–16.

*———. 1983. *Flowers in Salt: The Beginnings of Feminist Consciousness in Modern Japan*. Stanford: Stanford University Press.

Siu, Helen. 1990. "Where Were the Women? Rethinking Marriage Resistance and Regional Culture in South China. *Late Imperial China* 11, no. 2: 32–62.

Skinner, William G., ed. 1979. *The Study of Chinese Society: Essays by Edward Freedman*. Stanford: Stanford University Press.

*Smith, Robert J., and Helen Lurie Wiswell. 1979. *The Women of Suye Mura*. Chicago: University of Chicago Press.

Snow, Helen Foster. 1970. *The Chinese Communists: Sketches and Autobiographies of the Old Guard*. Westport: Greenwood Press.

*———. 1984. *My China Years*. New York: William Morrow.

*Sokka Gakkai Women's Bureau, comp. 1987. *Women against War*. Tokyo: Kodansha.

Sorensen, Clark. 1983. "Women, Men, Outside: The Division of Labor in Rural Central Korea." In Kendall and Peterson, *Korean Women*.

Spence, Jonathan D. 1978. *Death of the Woman Wang*. New York: Penguin.

*Stacey, Judith. 1983. *Patriarchy and Socialist Revolution in China*. Berkeley and Los Angeles: University of California Press.

Steenstrup, Carl. 1979. *Hōjō Shigetoki (1198–1261) and His Role in the History of Political and Ethical Ideas in Japan*. London: Curzon Press.

*Stockard, Janice. 1988. *Daughters of the Canton Delta*. Stanford: Stanford University Press.

*Stranahan, Patricia. 1983. *Yan'an Women and the Communist Party*. Berkeley: University of California Institute of East Asian Studies.

Sugimoto, Etsu. 1927. *Daughter of the Samurai*. Garden City: Doubleday.

Sunoo, Harold Hakwon, and Dong Soo Kim, eds. 1978. *Korean Women in a Struggle for Humanization*. Memphis, Tenn.: Association of Korean Christian Scholars in America.

*Tanaka, Yukiko. 1987. *To Live and to Write*. Seattle: Seal Press.

*———. 1991. *Unmapped Territories: New Women's Fiction from Japan*. Seattle: Women in Translation.

*———. 1995. *Contemporary Portraits of Japanese Women*. Westport, Conn.: Praeger.

Tonomura, Hitomi. 1994. "Positioning Amaterasu: A Reading of the *Kōjiki*." *Japan Foundation Newsletter* 22, no. 2: 1–6.

Topley, Marjorie. 1975. "Marriage Resistance in Rural Kwantung." In Witke and Wolf, *Women in Chinese Society*.

Toshitani, Nobuyoshi. 1994. "The Reform of Japanese Family Law and

Changes in the Family System." *U.S.-Japan Women's Journal* 6: 66–83. English Supplement.

Tsai, Kathryn. 1981. "The Chinese Buddhist Monastic Order for Women: The First Two Centuries." In Guisso and Johannesen, *Women in China*.

Tsunoda, Ryusaku. 1951. *Japan in the Chinese Dynastic Histories*. Pasadena, Calif.: Houghton-Mifflin.

Tsurumi, Patricia. 1981. "Japan's Early Female Emperors." *Historical Reflections*, no. 8: 42–49.

*———. 1990. *Factory Girls: Women in the Thread Mills of Meiji Japan*. Princeton: Princeton University Press.

Uno, Kathleen. 1991. "Women and Change in the Household Division of Labor." In Bernstein, ed., *Recreating Japanese Women*.

*Vernon, Victoria. 1988. *Daughters of the Moon*. Berkeley: University of California Institute of Asian Studies.

Wakeman, Frederick, trans., and Wan-shin Yeh, eds. 1992. *Urban Sojourners in Shanghai*. Berkeley and Los Angeles: Institute of East Asian Studies.

Wakita Haruko. 1984. "Marriage and Property in Premodern Japan from the Perspective of Women's History." *Journal of Japanese Studies* 10, no. 1: 73–100.

———. 1993. "Women and the Creation of the *Ie* in Japan: An Overview from the Medieval Period to the Present." *U.S.-Japan Women's Journal* 4. English Supplement.

*Walthall, Anne. 1998. *The Weak Body of a Useless Woman*. Chicago: University of Chicago Press.

Waltner, Ann. 1996. "Recent Scholarship on Chinese Women." *Signs* 21, no. 21: 410–28.

Wang Zhang. 1996. "A Historic Turning Point for the Women's Movement in China." *Signs* 22, no. 1 (Autumn): 192–99.

Watson, Rubie, and Patricia Ebrey, eds. 1991. *Marriage and Inequality in Chinese Society*. Berkeley and Los Angeles: University of California Press.

*Weidner, Marsha. 1990. *Flowering in the Shadows: Women in the History of Chinese and Japanese Painting*. Honolulu: University of Hawaii Press.

Whitney, Clara. 1979. *Clara's Diary: An American Girl in Meiji Japan*. Tokyo: Kodansha.

Widmer, Ellen. 1992. "The Epistolary World of Female Talent in Seventeenth-Century China." *Late Imperial China* 10, no. 2: 1–43.

Wilson, Sandra. 1995. "Mobilizing Women in Inter-War Japan: The National Defence Women's Association and the Manchurian Crisis." *Gender and History* 7, no. 2 (August): 295–314.

*Witke, Roxanne, and Margery Wolf, eds. 1975. *Women in Chinese Society*. Stanford: Stanford University Press.

Wolf, Arthur P. 1974. "Gods, Ghosts, and Ancestors." In Wolf, *Religion and Ritual*.

———, ed. 1974. *Religion and Ritual*. Stanford: Stanford University Press.

Wolf, Margery. 1972. *Women and the Family in Rural Taiwan*. Stanford: Stanford University Press.

———. 1985. *Revolution Postponed: Women in Contemporary China*. Stanford: Stanford University Press.

———. 1992. *A Thrice-Told Tale: Feminism, Postmodernism, and Ethnographic Responsibility*. Stanford: Stanford University Press.

Yamazaki Tomoko. 1996. "On the History of Asian Women Exchanges." *Review of Japanese Culture and Society* 8 (December): 1–9.

Yang, Gladys, ed. and trans. 1973. *Silent China: Selected Writings of Lu Xun*. London: Oxford University Press.

Yang, Hyunah. 1998. "Remembering the Korean Military Comfort Women: Nationalism, Sexuality, and Silencing." In Kim and Choi, *Dangerous Women*.

Yen, Chih-t'ui. 1968. *Family Instructions for the Yen Clan*. Leiden: Brill.

Yoon Soon-young. 1976. "Magic, Science, and Religion on Cheju Island." *Korea Journal* 16, no. 3: 4–11.

———. 1979. "Women's Studies in Korea." *Signs* 4, no. 4 (Summer): 751–62.

Yoshioka, Mitsuko. 1996. "Reform of Japanese Divorce Law: An Assessment." *U.S.-Japan Women's Journal* 11: 47–61. English Supplement.

Yoshizumi Kyoko. 1995. "Marriage and Family: Past and Present." In Fujimura-Fanselow and Kameda, eds., *Japanese Women*.

Young, Marilyn. 1989. "Chicken Little in China: Women after the Cultural Revolution." In Kruks et al., *Promissory Notes*.

Yu, Eui-Yong, and Earl Phillips, eds. 1987. *Korean Women in Transition*. Wilmington, Del.: Scholarly Research.

Yue, Daiyun, and Carolyn Wakeman. 1987. *To the Storm: The Odyssey of a Revolutionary Chinese Woman*. Berkeley and Los Angeles: University of California Press.

Zhang, Naihua. 1995. "Discovering the Positive within the Negative: The Women's Movement in a Changing China." In Basu, *The Challenge of Local Feminisms*.

Zhang, Naihua, and Wu Xu. 1994. "Searching for Identity and Voice: An Emerging Women's Movement in Today's China." Unpublished conference report.

Zhange, Xinxin. 1986. *The Dreams of Our Generation and Selections from Beijing's People*. Ithaca, N.Y.: Cornell University East Asian Series.

Zito, Angela, and Tani Barlow, eds. 1994. *Body, Subject and Power in China*. Chicago: University of Chicago Press.

NOTES ON CONTRIBUTORS

Cheryl Johnson-Odim is professor of history and chairs the Department of History at Loyola University, Chicago. She co-authored *For Women and the Nation: Funmilayo Ransome-Kuti of Nigeria* and co-edited *Expanding the Boundaries of Women's History*. She has published many articles and chapters on African women's history and on feminist theory. She is a past member of the board of directors of the African Studies Association and the American Council of Learned Societies and serves on the editorial boards of the *Journal of Women's History* and *Chicago Women, 1770–1990: A Biographical Dictionary*.

Barbara N. Ramusack is professor of history and heads the Department of History at the University of Cincinnati, where she is a founding member of the Center for Women's Studies. Her research specializations are the princely states of India, the interaction between British and South Asian women, and maternal and infant welfare during the colonial period. She has published *The Princes of India in the Twilight of Empire* and several articles on British feminists and Indian women. She teaches courses on modern South Asian history and women in India and China.

Sharon Sievers is professor of modern Japanese history and department chair at California State University, Long Beach, where she has also served as director of the Women's Studies Program. Professor Sievers is best known for her prize-winning book on turn-of-the-century women in Japan, entitled *Flowers in Salt: The Beginning of Feminist Consciousness in Modern Japan*.

Margaret Strobel is professor of women's studies and history at the University of Illinois at Chicago. Her book *Muslim Women in Mombasa, 1890–1975* won the African Studies Association's Herskovits Award in 1980. She is author of *European Women and the Second British Empire* and co-editor of *Three Swahili Women, Life Histories from Mombasa, Kenya; Western Women and Imperialism: Complicity and Resistance;* and *Expanding the Boundaries of Women's History.* She serves on the editorial board of *Chicago Women, 1770–1990: A Biographical Dictionary,* and is working on a book about the Chicago Women's Liberation Union.

INDEX

Names in this index are alphabetized by the "family" name, which sometimes comes first and sometimes comes last when written in the text.

A country in parentheses following a proper name identifies the present-day area associated with that individual, organization, journal, etc.

258   Index

Begum Samru (India), 41
Bengal, India: reform, 44, 45, 48, 49;
    mentioned, 30–31, 42, 43, 52–62
    passim, 67, 68, 74–75
Bethune College (Calcutta, India), 51,
    61
Beveridge, Annette Ackroyd (Britain/
    India), 53
Bhadralok, 3, 45
Bhadramahila, 3, 52
Bhakti, xxvi, 3, 38–39
Bharati, Uma (India), 72–73
Bhiksuni Lakshmi (India), 33
Bhopal (India), 41
Bhutto, Benazir (Pakistan), 74
Bihar, India, 31, 70
Bilateral kinship, 83
Birth control, xxx, 58, 69, 223–24, 226,
    230, 240. *See also* Population control
Bluestockings, 207–209, 222
Bombay (Mumbai), India, 47, 50, 54,
    55, 63, 70
Brahman (India), 3, 18, 20, 21, 30. *See
    also* Caste
Brahmanical patriarchy, 23, 29, 44
Brahmo Samaj (India), 45, 49, 51,
    53–54, 56–57
Brideprice, xviii, xix, 217
Buddhism: sexuality in, xxvii, 33, 174;
    views of women, 21, 33, 172, 173–
    77; nuns, 21; Theravada, 21, 80–81;
    Tantric, 33; Mahayana, 83, 173–74;
    Pure Land, 174; mentioned, 20, 26,
    57, 77, 78, 80, 87, 88, 184
Bureaucratic roles, 180
Burma, 77, 80–82, 87
Businesswomen, 188
Butler, Josephine (Britain/India), 44

Calcutta, India, 51, 52, 53, 54, 61
Cambodia, 77, 79, 80, 84, 85, 88, 93–94
Canton, China, 214
Capitalism, xlvii, 90, 106
Carpenter, Mary (Britain/India), 44
Caste, 3, 18, 22, 79. See also *Brahman;
    Jati; Kshatryia;* Untouchables;
    Vaishya; Varna
Catt, Carrie Chapman (U.S.A./Indo-
    nesia), 100
Chandra, Baba Ram (India), 61
Chang, Sophia (China), 204, 206
Charitable activity, 21, 54, 56–57, 67,
    81, 82, 180
Chastity, xxvii, xxviii, 25, 26, 28, 29,
    31, 34, 89, 160, 181, 188, 189–90,
    192, 195, 209
Chattopadhayaya, Kamaladevi (India),
    63, 67

Chenai (Madras), India. *See* Madras
Cheng, Soumay (China), 204
Children: childbirth, xxii, xxv, 21,
    54–55, 56, 71, 228, 235; child
    custody, xxix, xxxii, 64, 89–90, 91,
    216, 227; boy preference, 84, 163,
    196–97; child rearing, 198; child
    care, 231–32
Ch'ing dynasty (China), 168, 169,
    189–94 passim
Chin, Ch'iu (China), 203–204
Chipko movement (India), 70
Choudhury, Suniti (India), 61
Christianity: missionaries, 41–42, 45,
    50, 51, 53, 54–55, 196, 197, 202,
    205, 206; mentioned, xxvi, l, 77, 89,
    91, 92, 215
Civil Code of 1898 (Japan), 200
Civil Code (1930, KMT), 215–16
Civil Code of 1948 (Korea), 233–34
Cochin-China, 85, 86
Code, Le (Vietnam), 94
Collective action, xxxix, 56–65 passim,
    207–16 passim. *See also* Associations
Colonial expansion, xxiii, li, 88–95,
    40–41, 218–23
Colonized women: legitimation of
    colonialism by status of, xxiv, 41;
    representations of, 42, 47, 48, 197
Colonizing women, 44–45, 92–93, 197
Comfort women, 145–46, 158, 220–21,
    237. *See also* Prostitution
Commission on the Status of Women
    (India), 68
Commodification, of women, 183–84,
    212. *See also* Prostitution
Communalism, 72
Communist Party, 61, 75, 98, 105,
    210–12, 214, 224
Concubinage, xx, xxviii–xxix, xxxiii, 85,
    90, 91, 92, 94–95, 98, 146, 180, 184,
    193, 194, 198, 205, 206. *See also*
    Slavery
Confucianism, xx, xxvi, xxx, 28, 79, 84,
    87, 88, 94, 158–60 passim, 163, 166,
    179, 191–92, 194, 202, 205, 215. *See
    also* Neoconfucianism
Constitution and Civil Code of 1947
    (Japan), 225, 226–27
Constitution of 1950 (India), 66
Constitution of 1972 (Bangladesh), 75
Courtesans, 21, 27, 192, 193. See also
    Geisha; Prostitution
Cousins, Margaret (Ireland/India), 44,
    57
Crafts, xxxiii, xxxv, xxxvi, 82, 99, 104,
    167, 201
Cross dressing, 37, 192, 203